THREE
CHORDS
AND THE
TRUTH

ALSO BY LAURENCE LEAMER

The Kennedy Women: The Saga of an American Family

King of the Night: The Life of Johnny Carson

As Time Goes By: The Life of Ingrid Bergman

Make Believe: The Story of Nancy and Ronald Reagan

Ascent: The Spiritual and Physical Quest of Willi Unsoeld

Assignment: A Novel

Playing for Keeps in Washington

*The Paper Revolutionaries: The Rise of the
Underground Press*

THREE CHORDS
AND THE
TRUTH

Hope, Heartbreak, and
Changing Fortunes in Nashville

Laurence Leamer

HarperCollins*Publishers*

FIRST EDITION

Library of Congress Cataloging-in-Publication Data

Leamer, Laurence.
    Three chords and the truth : hope, heartbreak, and changing fortunes
in Nashville / Laurence Leamer. — 1st ed.
      p.   cm.
    Includes bibliographical references and index.
    ISBN 0-06-017505-2
    1. Country music—Tennessee—History and criticism. 2. Fan Fair (Nashville,
Tenn. : 1996) I. Title.
    ML3524.L33 1997
    781.642'09768'55—dc21   97-5070

97 98 99 00 01 ❖/RRD 10 9 8 7 6 5 4 3

In Memory:
Pearl Payne Burkey
and
Maco Stewart

Contents

Photographs follow page 242.

Acknowledgments

When I decided to write a book about country music, I moved to Nashville. As an author I have never dealt with people who spoke with such honesty, depth, and passion about themselves and their profession. To whatever extent I have succeeded in this book, it is because people in Nashville opened their lives to me. To whatever extent *Three Chords and the Truth* falls short, it is entirely my fault.

This book is based largely on events that I have seen and interviews I conducted. I spent a month traveling through Europe with Emmylou Harris. Tony Brown was the first major figure in Nashville to talk with me, and I could not have begun with a more deeply respected figure in the country music community. My visit with Tony's mother, Agnes Brown, in Winston-Salem is one of my fondest memories of my research. Again and again Scott Hendricks took time out from his harried schedule to talk to me. His fellow Oklahoman, Tim DuBois, was equally candid. I met Linda Hargrove when she was playing at the Bluebird Café, and we became friends. I was on the road in the United States with James Bonamy and in the studio with Vince Gill and Mindy McCready. Mindy invited me several times to her home in Fort Myers, Florida. I knew Ron Wallace when he had a record deal. I was there the day he gave it up, and months later back in the studio with him doing some wonderful new songs. I started hanging out at Robert's Western World watching BR5-49 when it was just a few regulars. I met Garth Brooks backstage at the Grand Ole Opry when he performed, and Sandy Brooks backstage at the ACM Awards in Los Angeles. I talked to Belinda Rimes sitting in the empty theater of the Grand Ole Opry an hour before the 1996 CMA Awards show in which LeAnn Rimes was such a sensation. I was invited out to the Nashville Speedway to be with Kix Brooks and Ronnie Dunn when they were racing, sitting on their bus with them. Patty Loveless had me over to her town house in Nashville. Vince Gill dislikes doing interviews, but he sat down one evening backstage at the Ryman for a lengthy interview. Mandy Barnett held little back when we had our talks. I joined Reba McEntire's fan club, and I was standing there with all the other fans when Reba left Fan Fair '96 to the immense distress of many of her fans. I flew out to Maui to spend five days talking with Jimmy Bowen. Harlan Howard gave me my title, and the truths of his own life, and I am honored to say that I know him.

I received much valuable information through the reporting on country music in such publications as the *Nashville Tennessean,* the *Nashville Banner,* the *Nashville Scene, USA Today,* the *Washington Post,* the *New York Times,* the *Los Angeles Times,* the *Chicago Tribune, Country America, Rolling Stone, Country Weekly, Music City News, Billboard, Country Weekly, Country Music, Music Row, Radio and Records,* the *Toronto Star,* and the *Timmins Daily Press. Billboard, Cashbox,* and *Radio and Records* all have charts that are touted by Nashville record labels and publicists as proof of the success of their artists. To keep my narrative simple, I have exclusively used the *Billboard* charts. For anyone with a deep interest in country music, there is no better source than the *Journal of Country Music,* a nonprofit magazine that is little only in its circulation. The publication is available for eighteen dollars a year from the *Journal of Country Music,* Subscriptions, 4 Music Square East, Nashville, TN 37203.

I was extremely fortunate to have had a marvelous Nashville photographer, Eric England, taking photos during Fan Fair '96. I have photos from other fine photographers, including Nubar

Alexanian, whose recent book of musicians' photographs is called *Where Music Comes From;* and Bill Rouda, whose book of photographs of Lower Broadway will be coming out soon. I am especially indebted to Ronnie Pugh and Kent Henderson at the Country Music Foundation Library and Media Center. No matter how esoteric my question, they always had not only an answer but the answer. Mike Martinovich offered me not only his expertise but good old Montenegrin hospitality. And there was no one like Holly Gleason, always there with her telling insights into the music she loves so much and serves so well.

I owe a great apology to those I interviewed whose names and stories do not appear in the text of *Three Chords and the Truth.* Some of these people gave much of their time, and I am sorry that much material did not make it into the final book or appears only in a limited way.

What follows are the names of most of the people who contributed to this book. Those who have helped me include: Nubar Alexanian, Pat Alger, Thomas Baldrica, Mandy Barnett, Gary Bennett, Ed Benson, Jordan Berliant, John Berry, Ron Bledsoe, Amy Jane Bonamy, James Bonamy, Jimmy Bowen, Agnes Brown, Jerry Brown, Tony Brown, Trey Bruce, Rodd Buckle, Al Bunetta, Allen Butler, Toby Carr, Tom Carrico, Tom Carter, Douglas Casmus, Michael Ciminella, Jack Clement, Barry Coburn, Jewel Coburn, Steve Cox, Peter Cronin, Rodney Crowell, Karen Cushing, Green Daniel, George Dassinger, Ansel Davis, Bob DePiero, Paul Dickson, Bob Doyle, Janine Dunn, Ronnie Dunn, Laurie Parker Duren, Tim DuBois, Tabitha Eads, David Ezell, Steve Fishell, Larry Fitzgerald, Rhonda Forlaw, Joe Galante, Mac Gayden, Vince Gill, Tompall Glaser, Holly Gleason, Arthur Grace, Mary Grant, Jeff Green, John Greenebaum, Jack Grochmal, Glen D. Hardin, Linda Hargrove, Ivy Harper, Emmylou Harris, Lon Helton, Scott Hendricks, Don Herron, Monty Hitchcock, John Hobbs, Harlan Howard, Melanie Howard, John Hughie, John Huie, Eddie Jaffe, Mike Janas, John Jennings, Doug Johnson, Fred Johnson, Phil Kaufman, Ralph Keyes, Otto Kitsinger, Sandy Knox, Allen Kovac, Ken Kragen, Buzz Ledford, Albert Lee, Amy Leintz, Susan Levy, Luke Lewis, Pam Lewis, John Lomax III,

Dennis Lord, Charlie Louvin, Terry Lovelace, Patty Loveless, Mark Luna, Lorrie Lynch, Lorie Lytle, David Malloy, Jim Malloy, Joe Mansfield, Mary Martin, Mike Martinovich, Mindy McCready, Tim McCready, Bob McDill, Jay McDowell, David McGee, Chuck Mead, Stan Moress, Moon Mullins, Juli Musgrave, Reuben Musgrave, Paula Nash, Jozef Nuyens, Carey O'Donnell, Ray Pennington, Gretchen Peters, Aubrey Preston, E. J. Preston, Collin Raye, Allen Reynolds, Robert Reynolds, Joyce Rice, Belinda Rimes, Michael Roberts, Bob Romeo, Wayne Rosso, Rick Sanjek, Vinnie Santaro, Bob Saporiti, Bud Schaetzle, Rick Shipp, Evelyn Shriver, Inez Silverfield, John Simson, Roger Sovine, Steuart Smith, Clarence Spalding, Gary Spicer, Ken Stilts, Jerry Strobel, Marty Stuart, J. D. Sumner, Fred Tatashore, Martha Taylor, Liz Thiels, Chuck Thompson, Eddie Tichnor, Bob Titley, Michael Tomic, John Unger, Trisha Walker, Ron Wallace, Pete Wasner, Mike Weber, Renee White, Mandy Wilson, Norro Wilson, Shaw Wilson, Walt Wilson, Craig Wiseman, Paul Worley, Roy Wunsch.

I must especially thank Marty Gottlieb, an old friend of mine. We were talking one day about book ideas and he said, why don't you write a book on country music? Marty, then the managing editor of the *New York Daily News,* believes that the Deep South begins somewhere in New Jersey. I figured if even he was interested in the music, I better explore the idea. I had become a fan of the music back in 1971 when I was working for several months in a West Virginia coal mine.

Several friends of mine read the manuscript. Raleigh Robinson, Marianne Gilly, Lee Tomic, and Jim Morrissey made this a better book than it would have been without their comments. But this is my book and they are in no way responsible for its weaknesses. Diane Reverand, my editor, believed enough in me to allow me to take a vague concept and go down to Nashville to live and write the book I wanted to write. Joy Harris, my agent, was encouraging from beginning to end. Vesna Leamer, my wife, did the library research and was my profound emotional support. Don Spencer did his usual exemplary job transcribing my interviews. Pam Pfeifer and I talked about our mutual love for country music when she was the publicist of my previous book, *The Kennedy Women*, for another publisher; imagine my delight to learn that she had not only moved over to HarperCollins but would be working on *Three Chords and the Truth*.

Finally, I would like to thank the fans of country music I met in many places, from Nashville to Milan. Most of you didn't know my name, and I often didn't learn yours, but your ideas and insights are found in many places in *Three Chords and the Truth*. I am one of you, and proud of it.

FAN FAIR
1996

~

NASHVILLE, TENNESSEE

The Tennessee State Fairgrounds

Tuesday,
June 11, 1996

~

1

~

"Don't Get Above Your Raisin'"

As fans poured into the Tennessee State Fairgrounds, a man in a pickup truck parked his vehicle and sauntered slowly onto the grounds, talking to a relative who had accompanied him. He wore a cowboy hat and jeans. Fan Fair was full of people so devoted to *their* star that they tried to copy his or her dress. Scores of youths and men dressed in starched jeans, striped cowboy shirts, and boots, an outfit popularized by Garth Brooks. Teenagers wore teased hair and hip-hugging jeans with their navels proudly on view, all in honor of their idol, Shania Twain. Middle-aged men shambled along in dyed hair and black shirts, in deference to the original Man in Black, Johnny Cash.

The weeklong Nashville event was a pilgrimage of devotion. The twenty-four thousand fans did not push ahead elbowing their way a few feet forward. They stood and talked and laughed, holding on to their ninety-dollar tickets before they entered the gates.

They exchanged reminiscences of previous years. They passed out tips to those attending their first Fan Fair. They prepared themselves for an event that for many of them had all the physical rigors and spiritual highs of a great adventure.

Fan Fair began twenty-five years ago to thank the loyal country music audience and to help keep fans away from the annual Country Music DJ convention. With its haphazard array of shedlike buildings and cinder racetrack, Fan Fair had a humble, homespun aura almost gone from American public life. The four exhibit halls at the sold-out event could get so crowded that the air-conditioning seemed to be pumping steam into the building, and the press of bodies pushed a person along, regardless of intentions. The fans might have to wait two, three, five, even ten hours for an autograph and a moment with their favorite star. If they were hungry, they would probably be standing in line for an hour or so to get the free luncheon barbecues served by the Odessa Chuck Wagon Gang.

The fans knew that they would be sitting out in the grandstands or on the field at the Nashville Speedway attending the shows that each record label put on. The shows went on day and night, no matter the weather. It was already as hot as the Sahara. Over at the Curb Show thirteen-year-old LeAnn Rimes was making her Fan Fair debut before thousands of enthusiastic listeners enthralled by her throbbing, powerful voice. This heat was bad enough, but it almost always rained too, thunderous storms visited upon the fairgrounds, great sheaths of rain and wind that could not drive the fans away.

The man in the cowboy hat and gray T-shirt ambled along as hundreds of fans hurried past along the pathway, entering the main buildings laid out like a gigantic trade fair. All the stars had elaborate booths that sold T-shirts and other merchandise. The booths were as much shrines as stores. Brooks and Dunn's had a southwestern desert motif, including an immense fake longhorn skull. Alan Jackson's booth looked like a house, with a roof, his framed pictures on the wall, and a little gazebo. Vince Gill's booth had his name as the only decoration. Reba McEntire decorated her booth with a life-size photo of herself, looming down on the fans, reminding them of her eminence. In Shania Twain's booth, the diminutive Canadian singer who had brought a sultry sexuality to country music was already signing autographs. The line was hundreds long, running outside into the torpid heat.

Fan Fair was a feast of celebrity unlike anything else in American life. Movie stars sell access to the highest bidders, telling their tales in exchange for magazine cover stories and television coverage. Baseball players charge for their autographs. But country music is a moral universe of a far different standard. Almost all the stars of country music would be here this week signing autographs for hours and singing on that great stage for no reward except the love of their fans.

Fan Fair '96 would not just be the artists and others in 174 exhibit booths, and the 116 acts performing on the great stage. It would be fan club parties that most of the stars gave all over town, awards shows, other musical performances outside the fairgrounds and special events such as Wynonna's auction of her personal belongings for charity. There would be hundreds of journalists from all over the world interviewing the artists. Struggling artists would try to catch a flash of attention while songwriters and managers and hangers-on stood around backstage gossiping about Music City.

The man walking past the cattle sheds appeared just another Garth wanna-be, though not a particularly good one. He wore a gray felt cowboy hat that set down low on his face, and a gray Oklahoma State baseball T-shirt as if to advertise that he, like Garth, hailed from that western state. The man seemed nothing like the country stars who were being brought over to their booths either in golf carts or walking along surrounded by their entourages like boxers at a championship fight. They all had this aura of celebrity. This man walked with the modest, unassuming demeanor of someone who was not used to having a fuss made over him, a man who opened his own doors and made his own coffee.

As the man continued walking along, a fan turned and did a double take. It was unthinkable. Garth had announced that he wasn't coming to Fan Fair. His wife, Sandy, was pregnant and Garth was off on tour. He hadn't even been here since 1992, when he had created pandemonium, and he wasn't half as big then.

"My God! It's Garth!" a fan shouted. Others turned to look. As though a camera had suddenly come into focus, the fans realized that the biggest star in the history of country music was walking along the same pathway as everyone else. A dozen people formed around him, a hundred, and then two hundred, three hundred, four hundred, five hundred and more.

Garth could not move. He was trapped within this massive cocoon of fans. He was six feet one, but he could hardly see beyond the fans. Garth might have called in security to help him work his way to his own booth. That way the thirty-three-year-old singer would have had a table counter between him and the fans, and a little air-conditioned breeze, not the constant press of flesh and the sweltering heat out here. Garth only sidled over to an open livestock shed, where the crowd slowly sorted itself out into a long line down the length of the shed and beyond. Garth then began signing autographs and talking to his fans one by one.

Fan Fair '96 was just beginning, but already Garth's entrance was as dramatic a moment as any in the quarter century of the event. To these thousands of fans, some of them standing in line waiting for Garth, thousands more off at the racetrack hearing Tim McGraw and LeAnn Rimes, and others jamming the buildings getting autographs, country music was not just an occasional diversion but the song of their lives. They came largely from small towns and little cities across America. Their average age was older than the demographics of the hot young country music audience of the nineties.

The dramatic rise of country music has been one of the greatest changes in American popular culture in recent years. In 1990 country record sales stood at 9.6 percent of the record business. For years that had seemed roughly the natural audience for country music, 8 to 10 percent. Three years later sales had almost doubled, to 18.7 percent, taking the music to a whole new audience. The radio audience was even larger; country music was played on over 2,600 radio stations across America, by far the biggest musical format of all. Tens of millions more watched it on The Nashville Network (TNN) and Country Music Television (CMT).

The Country Music Association (CMA), the cosponsor of the event, was trying to sell a new upscale country music to advertisers, bragging about the supposedly affluent demographics of the country music consumer. The CMA trumpeted research purporting to show that 40 percent of those with incomes over $40,000 listened to country radio, with a third of those earning over $100,000 a year. Many of the fans had saved for months to make this pilgrimage, and they were unlikely customers for the advertisers the CMA was courting.

The fans talked of their favorite stars who would be here this week as if they were their intimate friends. They mused about Garth, the greatest-selling American artist of all time, and his pregnant wife, Sandy, and how amazing it was that he had shown up so unexpectedly at Fan Fair. They gossiped gently about Reba McEntire, whose great new building was rising on the skyline of Music Row near downtown Nashville. They shared reminiscences of seeing Vince Gill perform and shook their heads in dismay as to why Vince and Patty Loveless had never recorded a duet album. They wondered about Wynonna and if her new baby would be born this week. They shared stories about seeing Brooks and Dunn in concert, and the spectacular show they put on. They talked about Alan Jackson, and those who had tickets to his Fan Club show felt doubly blessed.

Most of these people were full of immense excitement at the prospect of seeing their favorites later this week. They loved *their* favorite stars with unqualified devotion. In return, no form of celebrity demanded more of those it raised to its pedestal. The stars were expected to be accessible to their fans after their performances. They were never supposed to get too full of themselves and forget that they came from the same common loam as their admirers. "Don't Get Above Your Raisin'," one classic country song admonished.

During Fan Fair, country music was confronted with its past, with the down-home friendliness and heartfelt emotion that were so much a part of country music culture. Waiting here and throughout the fairgrounds were many people in wheelchairs and with other disabilities to whom country music gave a solace beyond word or imagination. Even beyond that there was a deep poignancy to this moment. Fan Fair only had two more years left on its lease at the fairgrounds. After that, the event would probably move downtown to the sleek new arena and football stadium, and these years here with their folksy intimacy would only be memories.

Country music was becoming part of a sophisticated media economy. Nashville's music was no longer simply part of the South, no longer the mom-and-pop store of American popular culture. Country music had broadened its audience immensely in recent years into music played regularly in Minneapolis as well as in Memphis, and in Dublin and Tokyo too.

The music had seeped into the consciousness of Americans, many of whom didn't even realize they were listening to country music. It was used as background music in hundreds of television commercials, danced to in clubs from Portland to West Palm Beach, played in offices and stores, hummed by truckers and teenagers, farmers and attorneys.

As the music rose to astounding success, the Nashville record labels sought to create their own Garths. They dressed their new young male artists in starched jeans and cowboy hats, attempting to clone not only the singer's sound but his look. The top executives, almost to a person, admitted privately that they tuned out country radio, driven away by the mediocrity and the derivativeness of so much of the music that they themselves produced.

Nashville blamed radio and radio blamed Nashville, but the result was that the people out in the audience began to tune out as well. The devoted fans who came to the fairgrounds still listened to radio and bought albums. But country music was in danger of retreating from the beachhead it had made in places like New York City and Boston. New York City had lost its country radio station, WYNY-FM, which converted to a disco/dance format. In Chicago during the first half of 1996 record sales declined 18 percent. They were down 15 percent in Philadelphia. Overall they dropped almost 11 percent across America.

Now looking at the falling ratings and sales, Nashville was comforted knowing that sales still stood at 16.7 percent of the market, or more than $2 billion. Moreover, it was not just country music that was in trouble. The record industry as a whole was flat. The Nashville executives told each other that country music would bottom out at a far higher point than anything Music City had known until the nineties boom. They believed that the music would remain an integral part of people's lives all across America and continue to build new audiences across the world. There was, nonetheless, great fear in Nashville, and the shameful feeling that the industry had taken the kind of opportunity that is rarely given to a person, no less an industry, and mindlessly piddled it away.

The music itself was changing, moving away from the themes that for over a half a century had defined it, moving away from the people who had always given country music their allegiance. The people in the industry were changing too, trying for this week at least to appear what they once had been. They knew what they were gaining in the new Nashville: the ski chalets in Vail, the Mercedes convertibles, the Gulfstream jets, the bulging 401(k) retirement plans. This week they saw the world they were leaving behind, and some of them wondered if they were in danger of paying for their new lives with the very soul of the music these fans loved.

For the artists themselves, this week was one of the great litmus tests of their musical lives. Reba McEntire, Vince Gill, Patty Loveless, Alan Jackson, Brooks and Dunn and Shania Twain all would be here. Each of these stars had memories of his or her first Fan Fair, sitting in a booth hoping that someone would want their autograph, memories of the first time they sang before the enormous crowds at the racetrack. LeAnn Rimes, Mindy McCready, James Bonamy, and Mandy Barnett would be singing here for the first time, helping to define the new direction of country music. Unknown and once known singers would be playing downtown, or making demos. There would even be a few artists, including Emmylou Harris, Mary Chapin Carpenter, and BR5-49, not appearing this week, making their own strong statements about what mattered to them.

In these next four days everyone here from artists to managers, from songwriters to executives, and from producers to fans would experience the essence of country music. They would see its past, live its present, and help foresee its future. It would be an intense, passionate time, careers won and lost, lives confronted with their own truths. Garth had just walked into the fairgrounds, and on the great human stage of Fan Fair '96, the drama was beginning.

2

~

"The Dance"

Hour after hour, Garth stood in the heat and dust signing autographs and talking to the fans. Garth's whole life was in his eyes. He had a strange, messianic gaze that was like a sonar radar that, once it latched onto you, did not let up until it worked its will. He used it onstage in front of twenty thousand people. He used it on reporters. He used it negotiating a new record deal. And he used it on each person who came forward to talk to him here today at Fan Fair.

Garth treated each person as if this moment mattered as much to him as to the fan. He had no quota on the number of autographs he gave a person. He signed T-shirts, sweatshirts, baseballs, CDs, cassettes, photos, and scraps of paper. He had no strong-armed aides standing there ready to push people along. The thousand or so waiting fans could see that Garth was acting with goodness and fairness, and they responded with goodness and fairness of their own. He had no minions out there working the line, selling Garth Brooks merchandise either. If it was someone's birthday, then he

13

and the fans sang "Happy Birthday." If it was a young girl who began to cry, he calmed her down, and let her feel and see that he was nothing but a man. If it was a child in a wheelchair, he had words to whisper into her ear that she carried away like precious secret jewels.

This man standing here was the greatest-selling solo performer in the history not simply of country music but all American music. Garth had sold sixty million CDs and cassettes, more than any other artist except the Beatles. But just as country sales were declining, so were Garth's sales. No one was more aware of that than Garth. No one in country music had his ambition. No one wanted to go farther, to do more, to rise higher. It had only been seven years since his first self-named album had come out, seven years of incredible success, and now it seemed to be dimming.

Garth stood hour after hour, signing autographs and talking to fans with intensity, trying to recapture what once had been. He had this vision of making himself a troubadour of goodness, using his music and celebrity as an engine to propel people to live richer, deeper lives, but his life was not the same, not his vision, not the world around him, and not country music.

Garth and Pam Lewis were driving in the singer's pickup truck to a celebrity golf tournament outside Nashville. "What are you most scared about, Garth?" asked Pam, his new comanager.

Garth turned and looked with intense, questioning eyes at Pam. It was the beginning of 1989, and Garth's first album was about to come out. "You know, Pam, I'm kinda worried about this going on the road," Garth confided. "I'm afraid of other women."

All the time the two had spent together, and this was the first time the singer had confided about personal matters. Garth spoke with great urgency, a desperate tinge in his voice. It was like he was on a train pulling out of the station, looking down and realizing that if he did not jump now he was on this train forever.

"You know it's going to start getting really fast-paced," Pam said, looking into Garth's eyes. "I can recommend some people to talk to—to help you deal with success, because it's a lot to deal with. It's not just getting up there and singing."

"I'm really worried about going on the road," Garth said. "And I'm worried about other women."

Pam felt that there was some terrible darkness within Garth, and women were only part of it. The man appeared afraid that if he ever opened himself up, it would engulf him, swallow him up in endless night. As much as Pam tried to convince him, Garth wasn't about to talk to a therapist. Garth drove on and they rarely again discussed his inner life.

Pam felt Garth's power. She believed in Garth, in all that he might be and do. She was the least likely of people to be Garth's comanager. Pam was a graduate of Wells College, an urbane woman whose natural bailiwick was the West Side of Manhattan. Pam had made her name at MTV in the early eighties. RCA brought her down to Nashville from New York to head the public relations department of their country music label. Joe Galante, the willful, authoritarian, and eminently successful label president, found it difficult working with a willful, ambitious young woman full of new ideas and a brash style. Galante did what he often did with someone he found difficult. He fired her.

Pam had wanted to head back north, but as many résumés as she sent out, she could find nothing that would bring her back to New York in a decent position. So she stayed in Music City, scrounging up public relations jobs wherever she could, bartering her time for office space. She had been confident, even cocky, but Nashville had a way of making everyone pay his or her dues, and Pam felt beaten down by the place. When Bob Doyle approached her to work together on his new client, Garth Brooks, Pam jumped at it. Bob had been a publishing executive at ASCAP. He had given that up and mortgaged his house to start his own publishing company. He, in his way, was as hungry as Pam, and as much a believer in the potential of Garth Brooks.

Bob and Pam were feeling their way. They didn't have any money to hire subordinates to do all the mundane work. They did it themselves. Late at night in her bartered office, Pam faxed out her PR releases by the score to country radio stations. She dreamed about Garth at night. She fantasized about the dress she would wear when Garth won his first big award. Pam wrote the first promotional advertisements and laid them out, sometimes with Garth's help. As for Bob, when Garth went off on his first radio tour, Bob drove him around from city to city.

One night when Bob and Pam were working late, he turned to his partner. "You know it's like you and I are Mickey Rooney and Judy Garland," he said, so out of character for the usually undemonstrative executive. "It's like, let's do a play. Let's get our pennies together and do something."

The third crucial person around Garth was Allen Reynolds, his producer. Allen was a lean, bearded Arkansas native who thirty years ago had been one of the least likely bank managers in the history of Memphis, Tennessee. Allen had the passions of the sixties still smoldering in him. The songwriter/producer might seem a gentle soul, but he was full of righteous artistic anger. He did not like what he considered the crude Philistines of the Nashville establishment he had fought most of his professional life. The man was full of idealism, emotion, and wrath, all qualities that Garth too had in full measure.

The first time Garth and his associates went over to Jimmy Bowen's house to meet the new president of Capitol Nashville, things had not gone well. Bowen was the most powerful executive in Nashville. When he arrived from Los Angeles to head Asylum/Elektra in the late seventies, the industry was controlled by a small group of publishers and executives who treated the music as a lucrative cottage industry. They churned out cheap albums directed largely at a rural southern audience. At Asylum/Elektra, Bowen started spending fifty to a hundred thousand dollars producing albums, not the twenty thousand dollars spent before.

Bowen didn't like what he called "the honk factor" of country music, the distinctive tone that came from singing through the nose and was the vocal signature of country music. As Bowen saw it, the kids out there listening to rock 'n' roll on their car radios hated that cornpone hillbilly sound, and so did many of their parents. He didn't care about all the endless palaver about tradition that consumed Nashville, or that stripping that sound off Hank

Williams would have been like cutting his vocal cords. He wanted it out of there. He went right into the studio, and with his fancy new equipment cleaned that nasal tonality right out of the records he was producing. His critics—and they were legion—argued that he had destroyed country music to save it, turning the music largely into early-seventies rock 'n' roll.

As Bowen jumped from label to label, deal to deal, he not only made a princely sum as the top executive, but he ended up producing many top acts, adding more gold to his coffers. In his rakish graying goatee, Bowen looked like Nashville's version of Mephistopheles in baggy pants and golf shoes. A big, bulky man of formidable presence, he wore a Greek sailor's cap and dark aviator glasses, calculated trademarks that distinguished him from everyone else in Nashville. He rarely came into the office at all. Bowen preferred to have people come to his house when he wasn't cruising around town in his chauffeured sedan, moving from studio to studio, meeting to meeting. He played golf early in the morning, but he worked hours as long as anyone in Nashville. While he produced music, Bowen used marijuana the way others used a breath spray, taking a quick toke just before he went into a studio. He felt it helped him hear better.

When Bowen took over a label, he walked in that first day, cutting off heads high and low, from artists to receptionists. At Capitol Nashville, Bowen kept up his record, firing nineteen of the twenty-two employees, including Lynn Shults, who had first discovered Garth and pushed his signing. As part of his deal he brought with him the acts that had been part of Universal Records, an MCA subsidiary label. Bowen had just bought the company and sold it to his new label. Bowen renamed the enlarged label "Liberty" and later moved the entire operation to a new high-rise building away from Music Row.

"Sir, you didn't sign me," Garth told Bowen, who had originally passed on the singer. "And you let a lot of my friends go here at the label." Most young artists meeting with the new label president would have been concerned only with themselves.

"Yeah, well, that's just the way it is in business," Bowen said, dismissing Garth's concerns with a wave of the hand. Garth had no reason to like Bowen, and Bowen was not a man to fawn over artists, attempting to ingratiate himself. Bowen's thing was candor. "It was an inept operation and I'm going to make it great. Look at what I did at Warner Brothers and MCA. This will be the next one. And I'll take care of your music."

Garth's producer listened to Bowen with distrust. Allen was a lover of song, not of deals. Allen believed in Garth because Allen believed in the magic of song, and he believed that Garth could deliver great songs in a great way. When the two men first started talking, Garth told Allen, "I almost choke on the word 'love' in these songs like, you know, 'I love this woman, I love you so much, honey.'" Nashville was awash in meaningless romantic ditties. It impressed Allen that his young singer wasn't buying into the clichés, even if it meant a hit. He listened to Garth sing, and he loved the emotional quality of the man's voice. He loved his intelligence too.

In December of 1989 Allen set up a meeting with Bowen that the executive insisted take place in his car, moving between two other meetings. Garth's debut album had been out for eight months. Garth had gotten lost in all the hoopla over Clint Black, in part because Bowen's predecessor at Capitol Nashville had not supported him the way RCA was pushing their new artist. Clint's debut album, *Killing Time,* had opened with a number one single, "A Better Man." Clint's album was already on its way to becoming platinum, selling a million copies, and Garth wasn't even pushing gold or half a million. Garth was obsessed with Clint. Everywhere he looked he saw Clint's face and heard his music. Clint had every-thing. He was better looking. He had superb management. He wore a cowboy hat as if he had been born in it.

Allen knew that Garth had to set himself apart. "I think there's a song here that will distinguish Garth from the other hat acts," Allen told the executive as the sedan sped through the city. "I would like to ask you to listen to a song called 'The Dance.' It's the last song on the album. Garth's doing this song out there in his shows and you can hear a pin drop."

The producer cued up "The Dance" in the tape player. "Bowen, this is the career record for this kid. Please go see him in person so you know what I'm talking about."

Bowen listened intently as he sat there ensconced in the backseat. "The Dance," written by Tony Arata, was a perfect mesh of singer and song. Garth sang "The Dance" with the disciplined restraint that highlighted the message, not the man. It encapsulated Garth's philosophy that everyone should live their life fully. He sang, "I could have missed the pain, but I would have missed the dance." The song carried with it hope for what country music might do and say. There was a vein of fatalism running through the history of country music, a natural fatalism learned by poor people to whom life was something that was done to them. "The Dance" sent a message that life was something that each person had to reach out for and grasp with all his or her might. In such sentiments lay hope for a country music that flew above barriers of class or region or race, a country music that explored all the nuances of the human heart. The video for the song, with its clips of JFK, Martin Luther King, Jr., and the *Challenger* disaster was a daring piece of work for country music, resonating with the themes of "The Dance."

Bowen went to see twenty-six-year-old Garth, who was opening for the Statler Brothers. Bowen had gone to so many showcases and listened to so much hype that nothing could blow him away anymore. That night Bowen watched as Garth, his eyes as big as saucers, took the audience and held them, transporting them through his world. Bowen turned to Ginger, his fifth wife, and whispered, "My God, this is the biggest one ever." Backstage, he walked up to Bob and Pam. "You lucky sons of bitches," he said, shaking his head.

It was a time of as much danger as promise for Nashville. America was becoming a land of cultural diversity unprecedented in the world. The sounds of Michael Jackson's *Thriller* echoed down the most distant hollow in Kentucky from an eighty-dollar ghetto blaster, while out on a ranch in Oklahoma, families sat around the electronic hearth watching Madonna's erotic dancing on HBO beamed in by satellite dish.

Garth's own family was a perfect representation of this diversity. In the fifties, Colleen Carroll Brooks, Garth's mother, had been a country artist with a short-lived record deal on Cardinal and Camark Records. She was of the generation that showed up each week at the Grand Ole Opry in Nashville to hear performers they had known when they were young and that traveled out to Branson, Missouri, to see older country stars in concert. For most of these people, country music was a cultural identity that they now saw slowly slipping away.

Garth had been brought up listening to his parents' country records, but he had listened equally to the Beatles and Rolling Stones. As his songwriter models he took not Merle Haggard and Hank Williams but James Taylor and Dan Fogelberg. And it was a wild, flamboyant Kiss concert, not a Johnny Cash performance, that had shown him the direction he wanted his stage performance to take.

Like Garth, the younger audience had not grown up listening only to one kind of music. They were no more going to buy only a country album than to eat a grilled cheese sandwich down at the diner when there were McDonald's, Taco Bells, and Pizza Huts out along the pike. The key to this great new audience was to push your dish to the front of the table so invitingly prepared that it was almost impossible not to take at least a nibble. This was called marketing, and in Garth's career it was applied with a daring, vengeance, and muscle the likes of which had never been seen before in Nashville.

Joe Mansfield, the architect of the marketing plan, arrived at Liberty from Los Angeles soon after Garth's first album came out. On the West Coast, Joe had orchestrated the campaign for Bonnie Raitt that had made the seemingly over-the-hill artist a multiplatinum success. But that was pop and this was country. Nonetheless, in the spring of 1990, with Bowen's approval, Mansfield took almost his entire annual marketing budget for all artists of $756,000, and placed his pile of chips on Garth. Garth's sales began to rise dramatically, so Mansfield and Bowen kept raising the stakes, pouring more and more money into Garth. They bought special displays at the end of rows in major retailers such as Wal-Mart, K mart, and Target. They lined up premier ad space on CMT and TNT two years in advance, blocking out competition.

"I believe I can sell six million copies of *No Fences*," Mansfield told Garth, boasting that the singer's second album would be the biggest-selling album in country music history. This was a song Garth liked to hear, and Pam made a point of praising Mansfield in print as a visionary and making sure that he got quoted in articles about Garth's success.

In the spring of 1992, when Garth's album was well on its way to selling not six million but twice that, Mansfield came over to Bowen's house to negotiate a lucrative new employment contract. He believed that he deserved more than the coins that were falling his way, and wanted his salary to be tied to album sales. Bowen listened intently. The next day Mansfield was summarily fired, for reasons the executive never quite understood.

Mansfield's only failure was that he had succeeded too well, been praised too much, and walked too tall. For Garth there was a lesson here too. With fame and power and money came jealousy and pettiness and deceit. The train he was on was barreling across the American landscape, and anyone with him who fell or was thrown off now might suffer grievous wounds. Garth was a man who lusted after control, and despite his immense success his world was still full of uncertainties and conditions over which he could not gain sovereignty.

The one constant in Garth's life was his wife, the former Sandy Mahl. He had met Sandy back in Stillwater when they were both students at Oklahoma State University. Garth was making pocket money working as a bouncer at Tumbleweeds. He was one of the smaller bouncers, relegated primarily to keeping women from fighting. The country dance club had an unruly mix of blue-collar country music fans and college students out looking for friends in new places. Nineteen-year-old Sandy had tried unsuccessfully to punch out another woman who had accused her of trying to rustle her boyfriend. The mark of Sandy's failure was that she was standing in the women's room with her fist stuck through the wall.

Garth had a reputation as a womanizer. The man was always on the prowl for a new candidate, especially an attractive woman so unusual as to think fisticuffs a womanly sport. "Look, my roommate's gone for the weekend," Garth said as he escorted Sandy to her dormitory that evening. "Why don't you come on up, and I'll drive you home in the morning?"

"Drop dead, asshole," she answered.

The woman Garth let off at her dorm that evening was not some rowdy, half-drunken party animal. She was as similar to the college women who hung out at the club as Garth was similar to the men. The men in these country dance clubs often tried to be something they were not. Garth might wear cowboy boots and hat, but he had grown up in the small town of Yukon, Oklahoma, not on a ranch. He had grown up wary of horses and romanticized cowboys in part because he knew so little about them.

Sandy was a rodeo barrel rider and a horsewoman of the first order. She dressed in tight jeans and cowboy hats and had that swagger, spirit, and a sometimes aggressive sexuality that she could give full range in this country music world. She had been brought up with modern ideas of career and freedom. That was all intellectual, however, and when confronted with problems of love and marriage, her emotions took over and she became a "stand by your man" kind of woman.

That phrase had become an epithet disdainfully spat out to condemn women supposedly hopelessly in thrall to their man. The classic country song by Tammy Wynette and Billy Sherrill actually expressed the moral superiority of a woman who stands by her lover because "after all he's just a man." That was a basic tenet of country music culture expressed in a thousand songs: There was a moral difference between the sexes, and women were better and stronger. It may not be true; men and women may be equally mired in sin. Sandy lived as if it were true, and living it she made it so.

Sandy soon learned about Garth's complicated family. Although Garth waxed rhapsodic about his loving, traditional family, they too were part of this morally complex new world. His parents had grown up in a community and an era where a divorcée was a scarlet woman, to be spurned by good, God-fearing, church-going people. Yet both his parents had been divorced, bringing their own four children into this second marriage. Only Garth and his younger brother, Kelly, were born of this marriage. The Brookses were a family in which "stepparent" and "half brother" were fighting words. They were also a family far from those idyllic scenes shown in videos on TNN and CMT. There was emotional trouble in Garth's family kept hidden away. Only his sister, Betsy Smittle, talked to her friends about growing up in a family where her parents often fought. This story was kept hidden away as if it might destroy the image that Garth had so laboriously constructed. Garth was close to his siblings, however, and several of them became part of his close-knit group of associates, including Betsy, who played bass and sang backup in his band, and Kelly, the road manager.

Sandy stood by Garth through the years when life provided only thin gruel. Garth didn't even bring his Oklahoma girlfriend with him when he first came to Nashville in 1985 after graduating from Oklahoma State. He thought he was leaving her for good. He lasted only a day in Music City before he drove home to Oklahoma. Nashville had a way of doing that to outsiders, greeting them with a smile and a slap on the back, and then shutting the door so quickly that they were thrown back into the street. Sandy hadn't gone with Garth, but she was there when he returned home, there to solace him, to put salve on his wounded pride.

Back in Stillwater, Garth and Sandy married. Garth had an artist's ego, and he found nothing so appealing about Sandy as the fact that she adored him so completely. "I thought Sandy was so crazily in love with me and that God had brought us together," he reflected.

Garth became the lead singer in a regional band called Santa Fe, while Sandy helped support him. In 1987, Garth and Sandy joined the other band members to try to make it in Nashville. They discovered a Music City full of people pursuing goals they would never reach. You could see the broken dreams in the hundreds of guitars in the pawnshops. You could see the dreams born anew in the singers and pickers who bought the used guitars. You could see the broken dreams down at the Greyhound Station on the faces of passengers on buses pulling out. You could see the dreams born anew on the faces of passengers on buses pulling in.

Some of the most talented singers and songwriters arriving in

Nashville had the spoiled quality of natural beauties, thinking that anyone who could not see and appreciate them was blind. Talent was a given. But persistence was the name of the game—persistence, persistence, and more persistence. Garth was a man of immense, often dangerous pride. Without Sandy he probably would have packed it in, refusing to suck up to a world of such insensitivity. The rest of the band gave up. They left, and Garth was thinking of leaving too.

"Look, I was around when you came back the last time, and I'm not going through that again," Sandy told her husband. "I think you're good enough and you think you're good enough, so we're going to stay right here. We'll get jobs, work and live here, and you'll work on your music."

Garth got a job as manager of a boot store. Sandy worked there too, letting her husband sit in the back writing songs. At times, she had three jobs at once to keep them going. Garth didn't like his résumé. He was a small-town middle-class kid, not some horny-handed son of toil. His father was a drafter and engineer, not a cowboy. At Oklahoma State Garth had thrown the javelin, not Brahman bulls. He had studied advertising, not agriculture. He had to remake himself in the cowboy image, dressing himself now in a ten-gallon hat, jeans, and boots.

Garth made extra money singing demos. He also intended to make it as a songwriter. Nashville has the greatest community of songwriters in the world. It is a fraternity in which it doesn't matter where you went to school or if you went to school at all. It mattered if you could do the job. Bob Doyle helped set up sessions with several established songwriters.

Garth started writing with a struggling songwriter named Pat Alger. Pat was a literate, passionate man, and he and Garth hit it off. Pat was a small-town boy, from La Grange, Georgia. He grew up six houses from the mill where everyone in his family worked.

Garth was a small-town boy too, as were most of the people in Music City. This was the one part of American culture that was *theirs,* the universality of the music spreading outward from that life experience. Country music chronicled the emotional life of a people who were part of one of the great, unheralded American migrations. This was the journey of poor whites from the farms and mountains of the largely rural South to hundreds of mill towns and the growing cities of the region, on to Detroit and Chicago and places west. The journey began largely in the twenties and transformed the South as much as did the journey northward of black Americans.

Jimmie Rodgers, one of the greatest names in the history of country music, was a small-town boy, the son of a rail worker and himself a railroad worker, traveling the vast expanses of the South and West. Hank Williams, with whose name Rodgers is linked in greatness, was another rural small-town lad. His mother ran a boardinghouse, a symbol of the itinerant life on the journey off the land. There is a small town at the center of everyone's soul, a small intimate place to which we all seek to return, and the songs of country resonated with yearning and sentiment that almost everyone could feel.

Garth and Pat were part of that tradition. They went into Garth's publisher's office and sat in an office for two or three hours in the morning, fiddling with ideas, jiggling lyrics around, strumming tunes on a guitar. Pat fancied himself more of a folksinger than pure country. His songs had strong narratives, and he and Garth worked on various ideas, always packing it in around noon and going out for lunch.

Out of those sessions came several songs, including "The Thunder Rolls," a melodramatic ballad about a wife whose husband comes home during a storm smelling of "a strange new perfume." Along with Larry B. Bastian, Pat and Garth wrote "Unanswered Prayers," the story of a man who at a high school football game meets his old girlfriend, only to appreciate the wife he has, as he realizes that "some of God's greatest gifts are unanswered prayers."

Sandy saw her husband slipping away into this seductive new world of fame and adulation. The other women were the worst of it. She was a stand-by-your-man kind of woman, not a standby woman waiting passively while other women made passes at her husband.

With his chipmunk cheeks and baby fat, Garth was no Hollywood leading man, but he was a natural seducer, to twenty thousand or to one. He was a man who truly loved women and was more comfortable in their company than he was around men. Women were drawn to him and to his music. They were seduced by the two extremes, the sheer spirituality and the stained-sheets sexuality. That was the way he saw country music, as the music of emotional extremes.

"Sometimes it's very, very filthy in what it talks about," Garth told NBC's Jane Pauley. "Sometimes it's as pure as, you know, as a newborn baby in what it talks about." The audiences heard and responded to both Garths. They heard him sing that classic, spiritual affirmation of life, "If Tomorrow Never Comes." Then they heard him sing about a man stuck in an airport picking up a waitress "who pulled off the apron that she wore. . . . Every time it rains I can see that dress fall."

Sandy knew her husband. On one of his early shows a woman came onstage and started dancing with Garth as he sang. Sandy bolted onstage and threw the woman off. The woman had no idea that this had nothing to do with her. This was Sandy's message to her Garth.

Garth did not want to listen. Sandy did not tour with Garth, and he devoured the feast that was set before him. The greatest gift the women fans wanted to give him was themselves. They stood in line and asked him to sign an autograph, and sometimes offered nothing on which to write his name but their bodies. Sandy was a pert, cute, young woman, but she was not a stunning beauty like some of those young women who pressed up against him. Sandy loved Garth Brooks, but he was becoming "G.B." That's what he called himself when he went onstage, this gigantic figure that he had created. It was G.B. these women loved, and as G.B. he was a god as much offstage as on.

Garth was at an airport in Texas when he received an urgent phone call from Sandy. Someone had called her and told her about Garth's philandering. She wasn't going to wait until he got home to talk about it. "It ain't happenin', you've been fed a bunch of lies," Garth replied quickly. Then he got on the small prop plane that flew him and his band to the next gig in Cape Girardeau, Missouri. The wind whipped the plane like a twig in the flooding Mississippi.

Garth liked always to be in control, but he was not in control, not any longer. The lyrics of his own song "If Tomorrow Never Comes" played through his mind. The song told of a man who has had friends die before he has told them of his love. He is lying in bed wondering "if the love I gave her in the past, gonna be enough to last, if tomorrow never comes." His own words condemned him. He had become a man of such moral stupidity that he denied what he knew best and felt most and believed deepest. When the plane landed, Garth ran to a phone and told his wife that he had lied.

At the concert that night Garth began to sing "If Tomorrow Never Comes." When he came to "Sometimes late at night, I lie awake and watch her sleeping . . . ," he stopped and began to cry. Country lyrics were often about the small emotional truths of life, and this song was country at its best. The song had been right and true, more than he ever knew. "Man, sometimes the road is just pure hell on a marriage," Garth said, and started the song over again.

Garth was a man who could weigh the value of things. He weighed Sandy's value against the beauties of the road, the flattery, the long nights of betrayal. He weighed Sandy's love, her loyalty, her faith, her honesty, and the scale buckled under the weight. When he got back to Nashville, Sandy was there waiting for him with open anger. She was a country girl who wanted a country girl's life—kids and a little house, and a man who came home at night. She had none of that in a world that thought she had everything. Garth begged her forgiveness, and vowed that he would be different.

Garth was a man who wanted full value from things, be it his record label or his wife. He boasted that "the wife I got back after my infidelity was fifteen times the woman I had. Like 'I'm gonna show you that anytime you leave this house, you're losing something.'" As for Sandy she knew that women were still out there hitting on him—the beauties, the sophisticates, the buxom cowgirls, thinking, why Sandy, why not me? Her answer was a simple one: "Because I fell in love with a long-haired country boy long ago. I was there when it was like 'How many ways can we figure out to cook potatoes?'"

Sandy thought of going back to school to study elementary education. That way she could teach, make her own contribution to the world. But with Garth's schedule and all the pressures almost nobody understood, that never worked out. Garth promised he would spend more time with his wife, but the months that he said he would be with her always seemed to turn into weeks, and the weeks into days, and the day into hours. So she waited until those rare mornings when Garth would say, "Okay, there's nothing." Then he would spend the whole day with the woman without whose nurturing he would long since have given up his dream of country music.

By 1992 Garth had become Nashville's pied piper with his picture on the covers of *Forbes, Time,* and *Life,* celebrating the rise of country music into the national consciousness. Above it all stood Garth, whose 1991 album *Ropin' the Wind* became the first country album to sell so many copies so rapidly that it debuted as number one on both the country and pop charts.

Garth's and country music's sales benefited dramatically from a technological innovation, Soundscan, a computerized system that accurately tabulates the sales in music stores. Until then individual stores and chains could exaggerate sales on albums that weren't selling. They could fudge figures when a record label was paying for a special promotion. Or they could ignore music they thought did not matter. In May of 1991, when the new system became operational, Garth's nine-month-old album *In Pieces* jumped from number twenty-six to four on the pop charts of overall sales of music in America.

A gigantic party for Garth at the new CMA headquarters brought out almost every major player in Nashville to celebrate not only his success but the whole genre's newfound prominence, taking on pop and rock music on equal terms. Garth's unprecedented rise was pushed forward as much by the world outside Nashville as by the music. Rap was not only king of the ghetto but moving out into high schools and colleges across America. As for the rock music world, it had become to older listeners the self-conscious music of alienation, full of discordant sounds and lyrics that had to be deciphered, not simply heard. Megadecibel heavy metal banged away, driving the parents of teenagers into momentary despair. For anyone who cared about melody and sentiment, country radio beckoned. Moreover, it was the age of AIDS, a time of moral conservatism and the growth of conservative faith. Here too the lyrics of country music expressed feelings about love, family, and home that rang with bell-like truth and clarity to millions of Americans.

Nashville had music that could spread far beyond the borders of the old country music world, not simply Garth but Clint Black, Travis Tritt, Randy Travis, Reba McEntire, Vince Gill, Wynonna, John Anderson, Dwight Yoakam, Alan Jackson, George Strait, Patty Loveless, and many others. In the late eighties, Randy Travis had been the first major artist to tunnel out of Nashville into that larger world with authentic country music. Clint Black had seemed to be the new leader. But then came Garth, who leveled the mountain that separated country music from the rest of popular culture.

Garth helped carry country music to places it had not gone before, not simply in terms of sheer numbers of fans but of social acceptance. Faddish teenagers in the sprawling suburbs of America had long considered country the music of hickdom and hayseeds; they made "Friends in Low Places" a teen anthem, part of the rites of passage to adulthood. Matrons in Grosse Pointe and mothers in Scarsdale had been brought up to think country music unspeakable and unlistenable. But they heard "The Dance" or "The River" on their car radios and were touched enough to go to their local record store to buy their first country album. The songs played on country radio, but they were universal themes, exquisitely rendered.

In January of 1992, Garth appeared in a top-ten-rated television special on NBC. He was an enormous star by this time, yet he came across at the beginning like a country cousin in the big city for the first time. "Hi, I'm Garth Brooks," he introduced himself, peering straight into the camera. "I'm fortunate enough to play

country music for a living. I'm from the state of Oklahoma and—
wait." Garth put up his hands as if to stop viewers from turning off
at the dread sound of the phrase "country music."

"I know what you're thinking. Dull." The camera showed
Garth bashing his guitar into drum cymbals. "Old hat!" There he
was onstage spraying water into the air. "Kinda like watching paint
dry." Two guitars smashed together, like some musical demolition
derby. "Well," he said softly, like Perry Mason knowing he has won
his case, "all I got to say is, welcome to the nineties."

Garth took the emotions of country and wedded them to all
the pyrotechnics of rock, creating an American hybrid. Onstage he
climbed high on the light tower, jumped out of a ring of flame,
threw water on his band, and then stood by himself alone in the
spotlight singing the most tender of ballads. He compared his concerts to great sex, moments of frenzied passion culminating in tender bliss, rising again and again until one partner collapsed in
exhaustion.

As Garth saw it, this was a true partnership, the audience as
much a part of it as him, fifteen thousand of them standing and
cheering, one great organism in ecstasy. Garth told one of his associates that being up there on that great stage was not only like sex,
it was better than sex. It was better than sex, and Garth was on top.
He had these crowds beneath him, whimpering, crying out,
screaming.

In one of his early shows in Tucson, he looked out and he saw
people sticking their hands in the stage lights, as if they could feel
no pain, nothing could touch them or burn them but Garth's
music. He realized that one word, one word, and they would have
torn the building down. "My God, this thing could explode any
moment," he thought. He realized that part of him wanted it,
wanted the whole scene to erupt in smoke and fire and light. He
was playing with life, and in playing with life he was playing with
death. He had taken his act as far as he dared, putting his hand on
the knob of the black door from which there was no return, but he
had backed away.

It had never reached quite that point again, and the crowds
were not quite the same any longer. He could still get it up in front

of these great ecstatic crowds. When it was great it was good, but when it was only good it was terrible. On evenings like that he knew he could not envision himself one day hauling himself up there before half-empty stadiums and passive crowds, standing there exposing his spiritual and artistic impotence. When it reached that point, he was gone.

Garth had success beyond anything anyone in Nashville had dreamed possible, and still the man was as far from happiness as dusk is from dawn. Country music had a tradition of unhappy artists, Hank Williams on booze and uppers, Jimmie Rodgers singing with his last breath, dying of tuberculosis, and poor Patsy Cline full of loneliness and brokenhearted laments.

This was different. Garth didn't appear unhappy. The man had a self-deprecating charm that was close to irresistible. He had a sense of humor that he was willing to turn on himself as much as on others. Yet he had a temper that was like a violent squall. "At any moment I can fly off and go totally nuts," he admitted. He sought a perfection in himself and others that was not to be found on God's good earth. He was self-absorbed, consumed both with the minutiae of his career and with grandiose ideas that had a chance of fulfillment only in his imagination.

Garth was a musical philosopher imploring people to live each moment of their lives, but he had long been obsessed with darkness and death and decline. Two of his closest friends had died in accidents back in Oklahoma, and Garth felt the dark angel of death sitting on his shoulder. On the canvas of his life, he painted with great melodramatic strokes, in dark purple, and black, and bloodred. He wanted to star in a film, not as a singing cowboy but something dark "like a priest by day who, at night, turns into a psychopathic killer." He did not envision himself passing on in some humdrum gray moment, hooked up to tubes and monitors. No, he saw himself dying in a great operatic scene, watched by the world. He wanted to go out "making the last catch, hitting your head on the goalpost and dying in front of sixty-five thousand people."

Garth liked the way Roberto Clemente, the great Pittsburgh Pirates ballplayer, had died, going down in a plane full of supplies for suffering kids in Nicaragua. Or what if one evening as he climbed up on that great light tower on the stage, he suddenly fell off, his body falling through the light, smashing against the floor of the arena. "That ain't so bad," he told himself.

When he sang his signature song, "If Tomorrow Never Comes," in those great arenas, the audiences stood swaying gently, holding matches and lighters aloft, thousands soundlessly mouthing the words. Garth admonished his listeners to tell their own lover of their feeling, for they too must be prepared "if tomorrow never comes." Garth had written another song about death, "Twilight Flight," but he never recorded it, or any other song that openly danced with the darkest part of his obsession.

The singer's music swept from what he called dirty sexuality to pure spirituality. Out on the road, he and the band members protected one another from the sexuality. They watched out for one another, warning a band member when he lingered too long with a female fan. There was no protection from the spirituality. People out there lived his songs. They believed his songs. They told him that "If Tomorrow Never Comes" changed their lives, saved a marriage, renewed a faith in life.

They played "The Dance" at funerals, and it gave as much solace as a preacher's words. They came to Garth as they would to their minister or their best friend. When children were dying or terribly sick, they wanted to see Garth. And if you were as famous as Garth, you learned that children are always dying. He went often to hospitals. He went without cameras. He went with all his heart, and all his emotion. He could not succor every dying child. He could not always be there. And those he could not visit remembered his slight and said that Garth had changed, that he was not the man he said he was.

Garth tried to cut back on his outside obligations. He tried to get some measure of the joy that he thought should come with his immense success, but it did not come. Although *Forbes* estimated that Garth earned $44 million in 1991 and 1992, he was not greedy for the things of this world. He had this nightmare vision of himself ending out of touch "like the Beverly Hillbillies in these houses made of forty tons of marble." While his large house in the countryside outside Nashville was being remodeled, the thirteenth richest-earning entertainer in America and his pregnant wife lived in a large trailer nearby. Sandy did her own laundry and picked out the kind of Mickey Mouse motifs for the nursery that could be found at Wal-Mart. When the couple hired an interior decorator, they took him to a store that sold La-Z-Boy recliners to give him an idea of what they wanted their living room to look like.

When Garth wasn't onstage, he tried to be the same person he was the day he arrived from Oklahoma. For breakfast he often drove down by himself to the Pancake Pantry off Music Row and waited in line with everyone else. He remembered those who had been good to him before he was somebody, and he was loyal to most of them, a good, considerate friend. He refused to become part of the do-good charity apparatus of Nashville, having his name used to make money. That would have been an easy way to show that he cared, but he didn't like things he couldn't control, and he didn't like being used. Privately, however, he was a soft touch, giving thousands of dollars to causes nobody ever learned about.

Garth remembered all the slights of his early years too well and too deeply. When great corporations wanted to license his name, he turned them down, seemingly because they had not wanted him when he was nobody. He was full of a terrible anger that was in part a fury at the unfairness of life and human society. He didn't appear capable of understanding that at the level of power and fame in which he lived people used one another. It wasn't a matter of not being used; it was being used for the right things in the right way.

Garth was a religious man, and believed that God had given him this incredible bounty of fame and money for a reason. It was all kind of vague, what he could do with this incredible thing that had happened to him, but to him it wasn't just music and money. It was something else, though he couldn't articulate what or how.

In their own ways, both Bob and Pam found managing Garth frustrating. They were making millions of dollars. But they had a difficult time getting Garth to respond. Pam was almost embarrassed by how little she saw Garth and how difficult it was to get him to return her phone calls. She had the feeling that nobody had any idea what it was like trying to manage Garth.

"You can tell him but you can't tell him much." Bob shrugged.

"Right," Pam agreed. *"Ropin' the Wind*. What we should do is retitle the album *Managing the Wind."*

Garth was consumed with the idea that if he could get a new fair deal with his record label, he finally would be happy. "I'm just not as happy as I ought to be," he told one journalist. "Now I'm bringing a lot to the table, and I feel I'm due a lot in return."

Garth went into the label to talk to Bowen about his new contract. "I want a deal like Michael Jackson's." Jackson had what was supposed to be the biggest contract in history, and Garth thought that he deserved the same.

"But you aren't Michael Jackson," Bowen replied. "You're just not going to get a Michael Jackson deal."

If Bowen had spent a week crafting a reply guaranteed to raise Garth's ire to a place it had never been, he could not have done any better. For all Garth's immense savvy about Nashville's musical world, he was full of a dangerous mixture of arrogance and naïveté when it came to the world beyond country music. Garth was outraged at what he considered the unfairness of record deals. The artist paid the recording costs of an album out of royalties, but no matter how much the record earned, the company owned the copyright forever. It was a setup that Allen called "a racket." Garth wanted to become true partners with his record label, sharing the risks and sharing the profits.

Garth called his little group together and said that if this new deal didn't work out, he would take it as a sign that it was time to retire. Garth was consumed with control over his musical empire, reaching out for greater and greater power. In that respect the man was a mirror image of Bowen. The two camps had become like menacing armies vowing neither retreat nor compromise. Garth pushed and pushed and pushed, while Bowen arrogantly stiffed Garth and his demands.

Bowen had watched from a distance what this kind of success did to a person. The Beatles. The Rolling Stones. Elvis. They had ended on drugs. Garth was on a drug too. His drug was power. That was the big golden needle in his arm.

Garth flew down to New Orleans to attend the annual National

Association of Recording Merchandisers (NARM) convention, where he received three major awards. Afterwards while the pictures were being taken, Garth put his arm around Joe Smith, the president/CEO of Capitol-EMI Music. "Joe," Garth said in his best ingratiating manner, "I'm having trouble making a deal with Bowen."

"Well, try to work it out. But if you can't, give me a call."

When Garth returned to Nashville, he went in to tell Bowen about his little chat in New Orleans. For once, Bowen didn't have a quick reply. "That wasn't very smart, was it?" Garth said with a slight smile on his lips. "But Bowen, I don't want to talk to Joe. I've got to go to Jim Fifield. He's the only one who can give me the deal I want."

Garth flew out to Denver and drove on dangerous winter roads to Aspen to meet with Fifield, the president and CEO of EMI Music, the parent company. They made a tentative deal, and Garth insisted on following it through, detail by detail, point by point, sitting in on meetings with corporate lawyers in New York. These lawyers spent their lives putting as much space and caveats as they could between the word and the deed. This infuriated Garth. What they considered nuances, he called lies. He was a singer/songwriter, not some deal-making, deal-breaking attorney, and the reservoir of bitterness would not empty simply because he got his way.

At the end of 1992, after almost a year of negotiations, thirty-year-old Garth got the deal he wanted. It essentially made the label and Garth partners, sharing the profits, by some estimates tripling what he was making before on each album. When Pam saw the contract, she had the sickening feeling that Garth had outsmarted himself. He had scorched the earth, and on scorched earth nothing could grow.

Bowen had refused to negotiate seriously with Garth, and the contract was Garth's revenge. Although the parent company would continue to make major profits manufacturing and distributing Garth's albums, Liberty Nashville was left with only a few coins. Garth had ended the "racket" of his record deal, but had only made the careers of the other artists at the label infinitely more difficult. In his melodramatic way, Bowen read the destruction of Liberty Nashville written on those contract pages. If he called Garth an angel of destruction, then Bowen was the other dark angel. For Bowen had helped to bring Liberty Nashville down with his own incredibly rich contract, and the cost of all the artists the label had picked up as part of his deal.

Garth had a new daughter, Taylor Mayne Pearl Brooks, born in July of 1992. He should have been happy or happier, but the glasses had hardly been raised to toast the new five-year contract before his anger flared up again. The initial sales of his fifth album, *The Chase,* had been half those of his previous album, so disappointing as to seem like a dread omen. He blamed Bowen and his label. He insisted that Joe Mansfield be brought back in to market the album.

Garth thought of himself as a singer of songs of great messages. His new album contained two songs daring in their social agenda. In "Face to Face" by Tony Arata, a woman confronts the secret shame of date rape. That was scarcely the fantasy of romantic country songs. Garth had insisted that the first single be "We Shall Be Free." The song preached the gospel that we shall not be free until we do not notice the color of skin and "we're free to love anyone we choose." It was not a message commonly heard on country radio. The song rose to number twelve on *Billboard's* country chart only because Garth was the artist.

Garth was the one artist in Nashville who could have stood up to radio and its increasingly narrow format. He could have stood up to it for the scores of artists who were seeking to expand the themes of country music at a time when the commercial sensibilities were narrowing. Instead, he vowed to call radio stations and "basically apologize for sending them something that didn't work, I guess."

The money flowing into Garth's accounts was buying a new freedom, but not necessarily for Garth. Pam believed that Bob and Garth had offered her a cut of the publishing money. When that never happened, in 1993 she decided to start her own company, an ambitious operation that included not only a record label run by her fiancé, Andrew Frances, but plans to make movies and television programs. Pam thought that what she was doing was no different from Bob, but Garth thought otherwise. Major Bob Publishing worked in tandem with Garth's career, but Pam's multifaceted operations had nothing to do with him, except that his commissions allowed Pam to begin such a major enterprise, and Garth's name helped it succeed.

Pam had her own large ego and enjoyed cutting a wide swath across Nashville. She continued to put in long hours working for Garth, but she believed that Garth was acting differently toward her. She was the person who had sought to mediate with Bowen, and now she felt that Garth considered her doubly disloyal for starting her own company and for trafficking with the enemy at Liberty Nashville. Pam felt that Garth was upset that she knew too much. She had seen too deeply into his darkness. She was a witness he didn't like having around. She felt that Garth was so insecure, so paranoid, so afraid that one day someone would pull down the mighty facade he had constructed around himself and expose him as an impostor. He had created "G.B.," this great figure who walked out on the stage, and he feared that one day G.B. would go away, leaving only Garth Brooks.

Garth had visions and dreams that were as overwhelming as they were vague. There was a world out there of music, but that was not enough for Garth. He talked of this revolution, this "G.B. thing" that somehow was going to change the world. The more Bowen heard such talk, the more he thought that this man living within this cocoon of adoration had lost a sense of the world outside. Garth was so used to having his way that he could not stand to hear unpalatable truths.

Garth went on Barbara Walters's 1993 Academy Awards Night Special in good celebrity company with Sharon Stone and Denzel Washington. He admitted to his gently beseeching inquisitor that yes, his sister, Betsy, was gay, which was one reason he recorded "We Shall Be Free." "I'm sorry I just can't condemn somebody for being happy and loving somebody else." He had not told his sister that he was going to out her on national television. Those close to

Betsy feel that Garth's revelation had a devastating emotional effect on a woman who had a right to the truths of her own life. He also told Barbara that "I've got more money than my children's grandchildren can ever spend."

When Walters recorded the interview, Pam was so appalled at Garth's revelation about his sister that she went to the singer and asked him if she could go to the producers to try to have it edited out. Garth would hear nothing of it. The rest of the interview was bland, and here at least was something that would generate publicity.

Soon afterwards, Garth had another one of his confrontational meetings with Bowen over the disappointing sales of *The Chase*. Bowen thought of candor as a bludgeon to be used to beat his enemies into submission. So he flailed away at the biggest singing star in America. "Pal, it's several things," he began. "You had the ideal situation. Everybody in America loves you until you talk. When you outed your sister on national television and said that you could do what you wanted to because you had more money than your grandchildren could spend, and that you could say and act and do what you wanted to do, you know what happened. Rednecks sent us cassettes and CDs back with the nastiest letters you've ever seen in your life. 'He can go to hell. He lied to us. He fooled us.'"

Bowen was on a roll. "All I suggest is quit doing television talk shows," he continued, "because every time you go on, you're getting rid of some of the people who loved you. Second, for the last year and a half of your life, you've been busy negotiating new record contracts. You've been negotiating book deals, movie deals. And you know what, the music isn't as good. You may think it is. But I'm telling you it's not. And there's your two main problems. There's two reasons your music has fallen saleswise.

"And the third is, you know, when Owen Bradley was producing, he said it once, 'Sometimes Americans don't need a third piece of chocolate cake.' That's where the truth lays. If you want to fix it, go do it in the studio. Do it with your music."

Garth sought only to make friends out there in the world, but he was constantly being confronted by how difficult that had become.

When Sandy gave birth to their second daughter, August Anna, in May of 1994, the family received a note with the return address of the widow of a legendary country star. Garth was a man of courtly gestures, and it meant something to him that this woman would take the time to write. He opened the card to find it wasn't from the widow at all. It was a death threat against Sandy and the baby. On another occasion he performed in Memphis when a death threat seemed so serious that he was asked to wear a bulletproof vest, a request he refused. That was a measure of the madness alive out there in the world.

Garth's emotions swept from this immense insecurity to an equally immense arrogance. "I want you to set up this meeting with President Clinton," he told Pam one day, "with this press conference saying that we talked about world peace."

"It's half baked, Garth," Pam told him. "You're going to look foolish. It's very noble to want world peace, you know Jesus Christ did, Gandhi did. Mother Teresa wants it. None of these folks have been very successful. You'll come off looking foolish. I mean we do a press conference and they're not going to ask you how many records you sold, but hard questions."

Pam talked Garth out of the press conference but not his grand scheme. "I want to make 1996 the Year of Peace," he told *TV Guide* in April 1994. "In that year, during all my foreign concerts, we will try to reach the world's leaders to encourage them to establish peace on earth. . . . I want them to participate in something called the Peace Chain. For every day there is no war on Earth, we will add another link to the Peace Chain."

Bowen continued to fill his days with an endless series of recording sessions, and meetings, and phone calls, but he knew it was not the same. He realized that he wasn't enjoying it anymore, and when you don't enjoy producing, you don't produce very well. He didn't have to get those phone calls from New York to know that the label was in trouble. He just didn't care anymore. He blamed himself. This time he hadn't cut the artist roster down the way he always had before. He had not done so presumably because he had brought most of these artists with him from Universal as part of his initial contract. He felt he had gotten soft, tender, forgiving, weak. By early 1994 he could see that country music was heading down again, even if nobody else saw it, or if they did, he was the only one to say so publicly.

Bowen believed that Garth was out to get him. The only thing that kept him temporarily safe was that New York couldn't be seen to be dictated to by an artist, even if it was Garth Brooks. But he believed that it was only a matter of time before Charles Koppelman, the chairman/CEO of all EMI Music labels in North America, would fire him. He heard the rumors that Garth swore he would not record another album until Bowen left. The label executive had a five-year deal, with four years still running. Bowen told his wife that two more years and he would be out of there living in their Maui home playing eighteen holes of golf a day.

Then Bowen came down with thyroid cancer. He was an intense, mercurial man and he blamed the illness in part on the stress that Koppelman and Garth had put him under. He went out to the Mayo Clinic and tried to figure out what to do. The cancer wasn't life-threatening, and he figured he could live his normal life. He had made a lot of enemies, but he had not made many friends. He received few cards and goodwill wishes from the people of country music. Garth didn't call or write expressing his concern. When Bowen announced his retirement early in 1995, his career merited a major retrospective in the Nashville dailies and the trades, but almost nothing was written about the man who took the honk out of country.

Bowen was gone, simply gone. Out on Maui, Bowen played golf every day and found peace he had never known in Nashville, rarely thinking of all that had happened to him at the label he had called Liberty.

Bob and Pam had worked so well together not so long ago, but their partnership was ending with the bitterness and rancor of a marriage gone bad. Garth did not renew his contract with the duo, though he was still tied to Bob by his publishing contract. Pam hired an attorney and began plans to sue Bob for taking money that she believed was hers.

Garth was doubly free now. Pam was gone, with her harping and outside schemes. Bowen was gone, and Garth was the only king on the throne.

While the fans walked past the closed buildings of the fairgrounds heading for the evening MCA Nashville show, Garth was still standing there in a cattle shed signing autographs. He vowed to stay until he met everyone in the line. He left for a few minutes to go to the bathroom, but other than that he stood here, not eating, not resting, hour after hour. He greeted each fan with the same gentle good manners and graciousness he had when he stepped onto the fairgrounds in the morning.

For the hundreds of fairgoers in line, these hours with Garth had become the great epic adventure of their week in Nashville. One woman with a cellular phone ordered pizza for the group around her. The people talked and laughed and the time passed, on and on through the evening. And still Garth stood there. He stood there all night and into the next day. He did not leave until ten the next morning, after having signed autographs for twenty-three hours straight. And then he left as he had arrived, sauntering off to his pickup truck with his brother, Kelly.

3

~

"All the Way"

The couple stood in the shadow of the scaffolding of the great stage on the infield of the Nashville Speedway in passionate embrace. They kissed deep and long in a frozen moment, oblivious to the world around them. They were dressed alike in stylish tan linen shorts, as if they had decided to advertise their oneness. Suddenly, Tony Brown cocked his head and pulled back from Elise Loehr, the sumptuous twenty-nine-year-old German woman with whom he lived in his gated mansion in Belle Meade among the social elite of the city. Tony was a man with feral alertness. While still embracing Elise, he cast his gaze across the clutter of buses, trucks, and equipment and tents full of kibitzing industry types, journalists, radio executives, and others who had copped the desired backstage passes.

Tony slowly disengaged from Elise. Hand in hand the couple walked up the stairs to the onstage bleachers where the MCA Nashville show was about to begin. As the president of MCA Nashville, Tony was head of the most successful label in country music. He had been named by *Entertainment Weekly* as one of the hundred most powerful figures in the entertainment industry. Just two months ago in a cover article, the *Los Angeles Times Magazine* had dubbed him THE KING OF NASHVILLE.

The president of MCA Nashville had once made his living playing a killer piano for Elvis and Emmylou Harris. Even now Tony spent most of his days not in staff meetings, going over business plans, crunching numbers on a computer, or planning the latest downsizing, but in the studio, producing Vince Gill, George Strait, Wynonna, Reba McEntire, Marty Stuart, David Lee Murphy, Mark Chesnutt, and others. Singers wanted to be produced by Tony. Not only was he the most successful producer in Nashville, he was a music man who felt and understood their work.

Tony was a small man, not over five feet four inches tall, with feet so disproportionately large that it appeared that no wind of misfortune could keel him over. He looked a decade younger than his forty-nine years. He had an impeccably trimmed black goatee, straight hair brushed forward, a long narrow nose, and small piercing eyes that darted back and forth like a squirrel, sweeping the world in front of him.

Music City didn't have any truck with producers or executives who decked themselves out in fancy wardrobes as if they were better than anybody else; even some executives who earned seven-figure incomes dressed as if all they needed to complete their wardrobe was a bowling ball. Tony was one of the few exceptions, a man of compulsive neatness and exacting style. Whether in jeans or black tie, he managed to dress elegantly but without strutting his style and offending others.

This evening Tony looked nothing like a CEO about to have his fiftieth birthday who earned three or four million dollars a year and traveled in an elite world of private planes, ski vacations in a villa at Vail, and a chef at his Nashville estate. He led the most peripatetic of lives. On Saturday he had been with Ron Meyer, president of MCA, Doug Morris, chairman and CEO of MCA Music/Entertainment Group, and other top MCA executives. They had flown into Nashville to get a taste of country music.

Sunday he had taken them to the celebrity softball game out at Greer Stadium, and afterwards flown with them on a corporate jet to an executive meeting in Orlando with Seagram's, the Canadian liquor giant that had purchased MCA. Tony and the other executives had flown back this afternoon. After the show Tony and the other executives would be flying back to the meeting, with Tony returning tomorrow afternoon in time to attend another event in Nashville.

As Tony sat in the stands next to Elise, he kept stealing glances back at Meyer and Morris to try to figure what they were thinking. By all appearances, they were enjoying the evening, and Tony relaxed a bit. In a softening market, the more Morris and Meyer knew about Nashville and the more they liked the music, the more likely things would keep going well for Tony.

Tony grew restless sitting still on these hard benches. First as a musician and then as a producer, Tony had spent his life traveling from gig to gig. He worked with passionate intensity for a few hours or a few weeks, giving everything he had and then moving on. He almost never pondered past mistakes or fondly savored old triumphs. He knew that if he looked down or back too often, he would stumble over the obstacles that lay ahead. It had been that way since he was a little boy. If he had not thrust himself out of that world with all his wit and energy, he would have never left.

Suddenly, now, there was a new restlessness about the man. He had won all the accolades that Nashville passed out to producers. He was as ensconced in his position at MCA Nashville as an executive could be in the mercilessly competitive world of 1990's American multinational business. Yet several of the artists at MCA Nashville seethed with discontent, and a rising chorus of complaint was reaching his ears.

Tony was not putting in those workaholic days so often any longer. A few years back he never would have been making out with a woman within eyeshot of the MCA executives. He would have been working the room, schmoozing for all he was worth. At times, there was a strange distracted quality to him now. Friends had drawn back from him since he started living with Elise, and some felt that at his core Tony was lonely out there on his great estate.

Tony had begun to think about things he hadn't thought about for years. For a long while he hadn't paid too much attention to his family. His two grown-up children from his first marriage had moved back to Nashville, children he had rarely seen when they were growing up. His second marriage had ended in divorce too, his ex-wife still living in Nashville.

In recent days, Tony had thought more about his roots, questioning his mother about their history. He had tried to tear all those pages out of his book of life, but they were still there. He had traveled so very far from those days, yet they were coming back to him again, like a melody he thought he had forgotten. He could look at these thousands of eyes looking up on this stage gleaming with anticipation, hear a few words on a demo tape from some songwriter whose name he didn't even know, or sit there in the studio producing Vince, George, or Wynonna and hear a song or a remark, and suddenly be transported back to a little house outside Winston-Salem. He thought he had come so far, but sometimes he felt for all those miles that he had only been traveling in a circle, and if he were blessed his soul would end back where he began.

When the Chevrolet station wagon stopped at a traffic light in Winston-Salem during the summer of 1959, the pedestrians waiting to cross the road stopped in their tracks. The old Chevy looked as if it should have been mercifully executed and laid to rest in an auto graveyard up in the hills somewhere. The vehicle had a foot-high yellow "Jesus Saves" sign on the back, and on the sides hand-painted in still bigger letters the words "The Brown Family Gospel Singers" with a phone number underneath.

Floyd Brown sat behind the wheel, waiting for the light to change, a lean man in a flashy red suit and tie, dressed so spit-and-polish neat it could have been his wedding day. Next to him sat Agnes Brown, his wife, as neat as Floyd, in a red dress and wearing not even a smidgen of lipstick or rouge. Four children sat in the back: three boys—two of them, Henry and Jerry, teenagers—little Tony, and the youngest child, Nancy. The girl was as perfectly dressed as her mother, in a red blazer. The boys wore identical plaid pants and red jackets, and polished shoes, but Tony's shoes had just a little more gleam and his pants were as perfectly creased as those of a Marine on parade. In the car it was as hot as a tobacco barn, but the Browns kept their windows shut so Floyd and the boys wouldn't mess up their slicked-back hair.

The bypassers kept on staring away until Tony rolled down the window and the whole family started singing in perfect harmony. The Browns were making music so fine that the onlookers forgot about crossing the street and just stood there. The light finally changed, and the old Chevy slowly started moving ahead, the sounds of gospel music drifting out into the languid air until the little boy rolled the window back up.

Tony was twelve years old, though he was so tiny, so fine of feature, so fragile in health, that he appeared no more than seven or eight. Agnes loved all four of her children with endearing love. She fretted over Tony, though, and felt that he was special not only in his needs but in his sensitivities.

Agnes worried about poor Tony and how he was going to make out. She had such a spiritual kinship with her youngest son that she felt she knew what he was thinking. Tony had all kinds of foods that he couldn't eat or he'd start itching and have terrible rashes. She could have about cried when she'd see Tony at the candy counter down at the five-and-dime, just standing there shaking his little head, knowing that if he ate some of those jawbreakers or one of those Sugar Daddies he might end up in bed.

The Browns' little house outside Winston-Salem didn't have indoor plumbing. At Christmas the Goodwill truck delivered bikes without fenders and other gifts from a hand-me-down Santa Claus. The three boys shared one bedroom, while little Nancy and her parents slept in the second bedroom.

The Browns were poor white southerners, one of the most derided groups in American culture. Rednecks. Hillbillies. Lubbers. Crackers. Dirt eaters. Woolhats. River rats. Piney-wood tackies. Lintheads. The poor white southerner has been called as many names as there are epithets. In American literature they have often been portrayed as a violent indolent breed; they lived on Tobacco Road and bred like incestuous rats, these sly, sullen, slothful sons and daughters of the South.

These poor white southerners were people of such contradiction that it was no wonder they were so easily caricatured. They were legendary for their hospitality, yet they were equally people suspicious of anyone unlike themselves. They were people of humility, understanding a man's modest and transitory place in the world, and they were full of the most confounded pride. They were conservative, but it was not a clubby Republican conservatism but a radical don't-mess-with-me backwoods individualism. Theirs was a conservatism of the soul, a philosophy learned when a baby expired at birth, a crop perished in a drought, or credit died out at the store. They were usually fundamentalists when they went to church, breast-beating, hymn-singing, Scripture-quoting, God-fearing fundamentalists who felt the Lord not as some prissy abstract God force but as an awesome presence in their daily lives. And when they didn't go to church but hung out at the honky-tonks and the juke joints, they were fundamentalists too, interested in basic pleasure, and whether it was liquor or sex they didn't ask too many questions about the vintage.

The whole spectrum of life was broader here among these poor whites than it was in most of the rest of America. The beliefs were more deeply lived. Sins were larger. God was alive and so was the devil. When a man was happy he was about as happy as a man could be. And when he was sad he was so hangdog down that it was a sight not to behold. There was nothing new in this world, and there never would be. And their music was an endless mantra of love and loneliness, joy and sadness, courage and dismay, loyalty and betrayal. Country music was their gift to the world, and it was *their* world captured in a thousand country songs.

The roots of country music were about as diverse as the South itself, a rich amalgam of cultures and musical forms. Those southern hills were full of those of Anglo-Saxon and Scots-Irish heritage. One could not hear an Elizabethan folk tune without thinking of some classic country ballad, or listen to a Celtic bagpipe without hearing a country fiddle. There was black gospel music alive in country music too, and the blues. Others heard the harmonics of German immigrants, or minstrels' tunes, and they may have heard right too.

Country music was a relatively new addition to American popular culture. Its first commercial success began in 1923. That year Ralph Peer of Okeh Records went down to Atlanta to record Fiddlin' John Carson singing "The Little Old Log Cabin in the Lane" and "The Old Hen Cackled and the Rooster's Going to Crow." Peer was so appalled at the amateurish wailing that he refused even to give the "horrible" record a number in the Okeh catalog. Those southerners who had moved to Atlanta and the other new cities and towns of the South heard in the music the nostalgic sounds of their childhood memories. They helped to make the record the genre's first authentic hit.

Two years later on November 28, 1925, the Grand Ole Opry broadcast its first program from WSM in Nashville. The National Life and Accident Insurance Company started the musical evening to sell life insurance to listeners across the South. The program became so popular that amateur singers and pickers turned professional, performing everywhere the WSM signal reached across America. It was not until after World War II, however, that Nashville became the major recording center for country music.

To many of these musicians religion was a profound, emotive experience that led to a promised land that was more real than the veil of tears on earth. As country music developed, the music was full of this spiritual quality, both in explicit lyrics about God and faith but more so in music washed in the spirit. So were morbid, tragic ballads. The music was full of nostalgia for family and home. That too became part of this music—poor lonely humans stuck on this road halfway between the blessed sanctuary of childhood home and heaven far beyond. There were songs too about the romance of the road, sung memorably by country music's first big star, Jimmie Rodgers. The singing brakeman sang often of journeys on singing rails. He was that wailing train whistle in the middle of the night, carrying its passengers on a journey that had no end. That too became one of the great themes of country music.

Its critics condemned the music as sentimental, but the road that leads from sentiment to sentimentality has no markings. Some believe they have crossed the line into sentimentality miles before others feel that they reached it. This was "hillbilly music," treated with the same disdain as the poor white southerners who loved it. "The 'hillbilly' is a North Carolina or Tennessee and adjacent mountaineer type of illiterate white whose creed and allegiance are to the Bible, the chautauqua, and the phonograph," *Variety* authoritatively described the audience in 1926. "Illiterate and ignorant, with the intelligence of morons, the sing-song, nasal-twanging vocalizing . . . intrigues their interest."

Floyd Brown was a fine country guitar player and a man of righteous self-esteem. Floyd spent World War II playing in a hillbilly band on a navy ship in the South Pacific. After the war, Floyd had been doing just fine working at Farmer's Dairy making ice cream. Then he came down with a disease that ate away one of his lungs and part of the second. At the VA hospital they told him a man couldn't breathe long on half a lung. The family doctor heard what the specialists said, but he had seen healing powers unrecorded in the medical textbooks. "If Floyd will take care of hisself," the doctor told the Browns, "he may can live a long time on that little piece of lung he's got."

Floyd knew that if he lived it was because the good Lord wanted him to live. He vowed to spend what days he had left bringing the unsaved to Jesus' sweet embrace. His father had been a drinking man, and all Floyd could remember of the man was a casket sitting in the living room. No liquor would touch his lips or those of his wife or children, and he would bring them up nurtured in the admonition of the Lord.

Floyd could have made extra money playing hillbilly music, but he vowed to play only gospel songs. Agnes came from a musical family, and she accepted Floyd's word and turned her song to gospel. The children were blessed with perfect pitch and resonant voices, and they too turned their gifts to the service of the Lord.

So the Brown family headed out, night after night, from church to church, town to town. They traveled throughout North Carolina and to South Carolina and Virginia. They sang for Baptists. They sang for Methodists. They sang for Pentecostals.

They sang in a Winston-Salem rest home. They sang in great churches. They sang in revival tents. They sang for the Salvation Army on the street corners.

Between songs, Floyd got up there to lead them into the fold and wash them in the blood of the lamb. He had felt the cold hand of death touch his face, and when he spoke of eternal damnation you could feel the fire and fumes of hell. When he spoke of heaven, he lifted you up by his very words. He took out his handkerchief, and in a sweeping gesture wiped the sweat off his forehead. Then he asked for those ready to be saved and give their lives to Jesus to come forward. "You know I'm not trying to scare you," Floyd said in a voice that sounded like a shiver, "but you could be killed going home tonight and go to hell. I'm not trying to scare you but you could be killed. Why, I knew a young man who was sitting in that same pew where you're sitting tonight and . . ."

Whenever Floyd got full into his preaching, rocking back and forth on his feet, his finger pointing out on the saved and the unsaved alike, his lips would turn blue, and Agnes feared that one day he would keel over right there by the pulpit and die before their very eyes. Tony had heard his father preach a thousand times, but Floyd's words never failed to send a shudder through him. He had come forward and been saved a half a dozen times or more, but he wasn't sure that it was enough, done right enough, deep enough, true enough. He was born again, but sometimes his religion filled him with shameful guilt, sometimes with embarrassment. When he stood on a street corner singing with his family and one of his friends drove by, he wished he could have disappeared into the night. In school, too, he was doubly different, shorter than most of the boys and girls in his class, and carrying a big black Bible wherever he went. The girls his own age looked down on him, and it drove him near batty having these teeny-weeny ten-year-olds chasing him around the school yard.

Floyd didn't allow a television set in his house, or the radio to play anything but gospel music. He didn't let his children go to football games or to dances or to movies. When his older brothers came home from their music lessons, little Tony sat down on the stool and started plunking away on the keys as if he had been the one studying music, not Jerry and Henry. Tony learned one gospel song, "All the Way." The next time the Brown family performed, Tony played a solo. The folks in the pews went wild, clapping their hands that this little boy had such magic in his fingers. Tony loved the attention. He learned a second song and a third, and there wasn't a night when he didn't drive the folks half crazy.

For the summer of Tony's thirteenth year, Floyd decided to send Tony down to Dallas for six weeks to the Stamps Quartet School to study gospel music. Tony had never been without his family for very long before, but he got on the Greyhound bus and settled in for the long ride as if he were a traveling man. As good a piano player as Tony was, his greatest gift was not for music but for observation and mimicry. He noticed what people said and did, all the subtle nuances of character. He had lived in a tiny, constrained world, and when he stepped outside, the universe beyond was doubly bright and rich, and there was little that he missed. That gift of observation and mimicry served him well as a musician too, and at the music school he listened close and well, picking up a multitude of new techniques.

The woman who taught Tony piano was a member of the Robinson Family, a well-known gospel group in Louisiana. Mrs. Robinson was so impressed by Tony that a few weeks later she called Agnes. "We'd like to have Tony come live with us," Mrs. Robinson said. "We're a good Christian family and he can play piano with us and I'll give him lessons."

Agnes didn't like sending her son off to Louisiana, but she knew that God had given him this gift of music. To make his way in the world, he had to learn to play as well as he could. "Now, Tony, you've got this talent and you can use that talent to make a living," Agnes told her son. "It's up to you." Tony went down to Louisiana to live with the Robinsons.

The next year another family invited him to stay and sing with them in Durham, North Carolina. Tony had thought the Robinsons well off, and so they were when compared to the Browns, but they were nothing compared to this new family. The father was an executive at a glass plant.

Best of all, they had a spanking-new Delta '88 Oldsmobile that they let Tony drive back to Winston-Salem to visit his folks. Tony came cruising down the road and pulled up ever so slowly in front of his parents' little house. The neighbors' jaws dropped as if they were witnessing the Second Coming. For days, all anyone talked about was how little Tony had got himself a Delta '88 Oldsmobile, up living with the rich folks.

Tony was a shy young man of quiet, subtle charm. He stayed in Durham for two years until he graduated from high school. Tony, unlike his big brothers, wasn't about to head off to Bob Jones University to study to become a minister. He played piano for the opening act when J. D. Sumner and his famous Stamps Quartet arrived in town to play their brand of gospel. For the most part, the Stamps played in churches. Tony thought they were the coolest bit of show business he had ever seen. They dressed in green and blue and pink suits so bright that the devil would have to shield his eyes to take one look at them. And when they sang they got in the spirit so that it was a wonder to behold. Tony subtly ingratiated himself with J.D., the leader and proud owner of the deepest bass voice in Christendom. One day the call came that the Stamps piano player had quit, and would nineteen-year-old Tony fly up to Boston to take his place?

Tony traveled the circuit with the Stamps Quartet, and then with other groups. He eventually joined Voice, who had been hired to play exclusively at the whim and will of Elvis Presley. Tony had not grown up listening to rock music. To him Elvis was not the king of rock 'n' roll but the king of celebrity, the king of Hollywood, the king of wealth and privilege. He didn't say a word when the group was ushered into Elvis's presence to sing the black gospel music that Elvis liked. These were the songs of Elvis's lost childhood. He had them sing them a dozen times or more, Elvis's voice blending in with the others. Then they would be ushered out.

Voice traveled wherever Elvis happened to be, from Palm Springs to Memphis to Beverly Hills. Sometimes the phone would ring and the group would be told to stand by at two in the morning. Then another call would come telling them that Elvis had decided he was too tired. Other times the group would be told to be at the airport and they would fly to Fort Worth and back, never singing a word, never knowing where they were going or why. Elvis could have anything he wanted, from cars to drugs to women to live gospel music, all of which he could turn on and off with no more effort than twisting the spigot on a water faucet. He had everything, and having everything at times he seemed to value nothing. It was while playing piano for Voice in December of 1969 that Tony married Janie Breeding, a young woman of strong religious sentiment. They had two children, Brandi and Brennan, and Tony spent much of the time away from his wife.

Elvis had some hangers-on whose primary activity was calling everyone else a hanger-on, trying to push others away from the goodies that fell to those nearest to Elvis. It was duly noted that Voice did far more sitting than singing. Their penance would be to open for Elvis's opening act, the Sweet Inspirations, an artistic purgatory if there ever was one. Even so, Tony was happy to be back to the life of music, especially since it gave him a chance to get to know some of the famous, richly paid musicians who played backup for Elvis. He just sat there and listened to James Burton and Glen D. Hardin and the others tell their tales of playing with everybody from Neil Diamond to the Grateful Dead, wishing he could get some of those big-money gigs. Tony worked his way up to being the piano player for the Sweet Inspirations.

Elvis had become a bloated, drugged-up caricature of his youthful self, stumbling through his set. Elvis's musicians were the best-paid backup band in America; they were stellar players, but this wasn't about music anymore but mechanically re-creating semblances of Elvis's greatest hits. Glen D. had been with Elvis long enough to know that there was little left but echoes and shadows. The piano player walked away one day in 1975—walked away never telling Elvis that he was gone for good.

Tony could smell the rich scent of opportunity, so he put in for the gig and got the job. Up on that stage Tony knew that he was the new man, and he wasn't as good a musician as some of the others. He thought to himself: "Nobody cares. It's just about keeping the gig and keeping your mouth shut." When Tony had been with Voice, Elvis had drawn him close a few times and talked to him. Now Elvis was as walled off from Tony and the other band members as he was by the audience out there in the dark reaches of the stadiums and theaters.

At first, Tony had felt as if he hardly belonged, but as the months went by he became as much a part of the band as anyone. In his flowing locks and white jumpsuit, he looked more like Elvis's little brother than a preacher's son. The money was good and the times were good, and Tony figured the gig could go on forever. Tony was in Nashville on August 16, 1977, waiting for the band plane from Los Angeles to take the musicians to Portland, Maine, for a concert. It had been a sunny summer day, but suddenly it turned cloudy and cold and began to storm. And then the musicians were told that Elvis was dead.

Tony had no job. He had no marriage either. He was thirty-one and he had nothing. His wife had had enough of life with a musician, the endless gigs, the late nights, the road trips. She took their son and daughter with her to Colorado, as if they too had to be shepherded from what she considered his wanton ways. He was still the son of an evangelist, and he was laid low with guilt. He took it all as God's sign that he had strayed too far from the path of righteousness, strayed away from gospel music.

Tony was a man of frenetic energy, and he didn't do well sitting around musing about all the might-have-beens. About a month passed by when Tony learned that Glen D. had decided to leave Emmylou Harris's Hot Band. Tony had sat down at Glen D.'s vacant piano stool once before. With his Elvis credentials, Tony signed on to play piano with the best backup band in country music.

Emmylou was the hottest new woman artist in country music, a beautiful, statuesque woman with an angel's voice and a reverence and respect for the roots of country music. Here was Tony, a true poor son of the South, scion of the people who created country music, and he didn't know George Jones from Grandpa Jones. And here was Emmylou, with her fancy background, and she was teaching *him* about country music. On the tour bus and in the cars, that's about all she let anybody play or listen to on the radio. He started living within country music, appreciating the form.

Emmylou brought to the music a rock 'n' roll edge, and passion and devotion, elevating the music by her concerns. Tony saw what the music could be. He listened closely and heard the strains of gospel music somewhere there in the background. He knew that in celebrating country music he was celebrating his own roots as well.

Emmylou's Hot Band contained nothing but stellar musicians, including Rodney Crowell, Ricky Skaggs, Emory Gordy Jr., and Hank DeVito. In such company, Tony felt like the poor relative who fears that if he opens his mouth, he'll be shown up as a know-nothing. Tony just sat there quietly while Rodney and Hank and Emory held forth. He was an observer not out of calculation but because of his insecurity. He might have seemed like just another musician who looked on life as little but an endless series of gigs, an intimate part of the boozing, coke-snorting world of music, but sitting there on the bus and backstage, he was like a novelist, taking mental notes, gathering insights and observations not to write a story of the past but to create his own musical future.

Tony had been this country boy looking wide-eyed and awestruck at the big-city folk and their world. During those three years with the Hot Band, he learned to be comfortable around all kinds of people, including musicians and others he might once have dismissed as hippies or freaks or the bizarre flotsam of LA or New York. Emmylou taught him that country music could be hip and youthful and daring, and that music was what mattered, not celebrity, not wealth.

Through Emmylou and the Hot Band he met other musicians, including Vince Gill, Rosanne Cash, Guy Clark, and others, an amorphous group that one day would create their own country renaissance, revitalizing Nashville's music. Tony felt blessed to walk in their company, but he was not one of them. As much as his friends wanted stardom, most of these artists thought that obscurity was a sign of virtue, a mark of not compromising their music. Tony valued popular success more than they did, and he had to answer the same questions about music that they did, even if he answered them differently. To compromise without compromising one's art. To sell well without selling out. For people who cared deeply about music, these were terribly difficult choices.

★ ★ ★

When Emmy became pregnant and came off the road in 1978, Tony needed a new gig. He ended up in the artists and repertory (A&R) department at Free Flight Records, a pop subsidiary of RCA Records in Los Angeles. An A&R person lives by his ear and his instincts, listening to thousands of artists, traveling showcase to showcase, club to club, tape to tape, trying to find the bands and the singers worth signing to the label. Tony had a natural ear, and when the label folded, he moved to Nashville to fill a similar position at RCA.

Nashville did not look kindly on outsiders who thought they could run from pop to country, flying into town with an LA sensibility. The town had its own way of dealing with outsiders. Tony thought that he might get some work as a session musician, but he never was called. He thought that he might produce an album, but he was not on anybody's list.

Defeat has more lessons to teach than victory, and Tony left Music City with a new degree in his musical education. Back in LA, he joined the Cherry Bombs, the backup band for Rosanne Cash and her husband, Rodney Crowell. There was no one in the band whose work he admired more than that of Vince Gill, a lanky Oklahoman who played a brilliant guitar and sang in a rich, poignant tenor. Tony identified with Vince and Rodney and Rosanne and Ricky and Hank and Emory. He believed that these people, not the establishment in Music City, represented the creative edge of country music. Tony had seen in Nashville how tradition had often become a code name for a prison of form and ritual that celebrated the mediocre and the predictable, but he knew that Nashville *was* country music. If he and his friends hoped to succeed, the road led back to central Tennessee.

Tony returned to Nashville to work in A&R at RCA. The Music City of the mid-eighties was a very different place than when he had left, full of a very uncountry existential angst and uncertainty. In 1980 the hit movie *Urban Cowboy* and its unlikely roustabout hero, the Hollywood sex symbol John Travolta, had brought new listeners by the millions into the fold. The movie portrayed the world of Gilley's, an enormous Pasadena, Texas, country nightclub, where oil workers, secretaries, accountants, students, and clerks came each evening in boots, jeans, and cowboy hats to dance to country music. Country was a style that these honky-tonk cowboys put on and took off with the whim of fashion.

Instead of trying to create a larger audience for real country music, Nashville had displayed its insecurities by trying to cloak its music in a garish pop wardrobe. As much as this desire to move into the pop world was one of the great temptations of Nashville's musical life, it was also considered the ultimate betrayal. It was moving into a better neighborhood and getting rid of your hillbilly friends. It was a better section in the record stores, a classier place on the dial. It was the same journey that thousands had made who had grown up with country music and, as they became affluent, had discarded it like dirty overalls and work boots.

By the middle of the decade, the industry had dropped precipitously, the number of gold records certified in 1984 the smallest number in a decade. In the end country pop artists such as Crystal Gayle, Anne Murray, Mickey Gilley, Barbara Mandrell, and Kenny Rogers found their crossover appeal dying. They left in their wake a residue of denatured country music that pleased neither the new fans who had mainly departed bored with the genre nor the old-time fans who had stayed on.

The industry had fallen so dramatically that the *New York Times* carried a front-page article in 1985 saying that "audiences are dwindling, sales of country records are plummeting and the fabled Nashville Sound . . . may soon sound as dated as the ukulele." Out at the Grand Ole Opry, the audiences were as aged as the performers. There were none of the energy and anticipation of those years when Hank Williams and Patsy Cline had performed. The old rural South was emptying out, packing up and moving to the suburbs, or the suburbs were moving out, spreading onto old cornfields and pastures. A modern South was rising, great cities like Atlanta and Memphis, world's fairs in New Orleans and Knoxville.

That left the creators of country music, the poor white southerners, like a shantytown that had to be torn down to make way for high-rises. They were the only ethnic group in politically correct America that could still be openly caricatured. They were the hillbillies, the rednecks, laughed at and laughable. Country singers played into these stereotypes to get national exposure. Loretta Lynn had been presented on the *Tonight Show* as a bizarre specimen lured out of the Kentucky hills. Dolly Parton played her part as a living breathing Daisy Mae, straight out of the cartoon pages of *Li'l Abner*, then writing and singing some of the greatest country songs of her time.

Young southerners had their Walkmen tuned in to Bruce Springsteen singing "Born in the USA," not Dolly Parton or Loretta Lynn. Their parents may have tuned in WSM Saturday evenings and listened to country on the radio, but many of these young people thought of Nashville's music as a badge of shame, the atavistic, embarrassing sound of the Old South.

Tony's new boss at RCA was Joe Galante, an Italian American whom the parent label had sent down from New York in the seventies for some seasoning in the minor leagues before moving back to the rock 'n' roll world. Galante rose to become president of RCA Nashville, slowly turning it into the most powerful label of the eighties. Galante kept hearing the complaint that this new generation wanted its own music. Joe saw that the older acts on his label weren't selling. Dolly Parton. Charley Pride. Waylon Jennings. They were three of the greatest names in country music and they were all on RCA. But it was about business, not sentiment. He cut them from the label.

Joe wanted dynamic, youthful acts. Tony got his old band mate, Vince Gill, to come back to Nashville and signed him to the label. That was the kind of power he dreamed of having, helping artist friends he admired. Tony was still reveling in that moment when he got a call from Jimmy Bowen, the new president of MCA Nashville, offering him a position as vice president of A&R.

When Tony accepted, his first and hardest job was to tell Vince. Tony knew how isolated an artist's life could be, how performers hung to the people they knew, the ballast to help hold them steady. He felt as if he were betraying poor Vince, even though it was not Tony but another Hot Band alumnus, Emory Gordy Jr., who was producing him. "Vince, man, I'm sorry," Tony said. "I got this chance. But, man, you'll be okay 'cause you know you're really good and you still did the right thing by coming here, but I've got this opportunity."

Vince understood the ways of the music industry almost as well as Tony. "Man, hey, I'm with you," Vince replied immediately. "I hate to see you go, but go for it. Do it."

Tony was going to work for the man who was chief architect and instigator of this new country music, the most controversial executive in the whole history of country music. Bowen took exquisite pleasure in rubbing the face of Music City into what he considered its contradictions, fallacies, and warped traditions.

At MCA as well as RCA, Tony was part of an inbred Nashville world of six labels (CBS, RCA, MCA, Warner Bros., Capitol/EMI, and Polygram), who divided up the business like feudal lords. The producers often had their own publishing deals and studios, choosing their songs and their studio often to the detriment of everything except the producer's pocket. Bowen believed in the salutary virtue of purging, cutting his list of artists in half, from fifty-two to twenty-six, firing practically every employee. Thus, he had plenty of room on his staff at MCA Nashville, including a prominent place for Tony Brown.

The cupboards were bare at MCA Nashville, and Tony had an enviable freedom to go out and seek new artists. Wherever he went, people pitched songs and artists to him. Nashville was full of singers and songwriters whose dreams had turned desperate. One of those artists was Steve Earle. The singer was at the head of that line of desperation. Working on his third divorce, he had a taste for drugs and for wives. He had gotten some cuts as a songwriter, but he knew that he couldn't churn out the neat ditties that Nashville seemed to want. If Tony didn't sign him, then probably it was all over.

"I was born in the land of plenty," Steve sang to Tony, "now there ain't enough." Steve's small town was a place to get away from. "I got me a '67 Chevy, she's low and sleek and black, Someday I'll put her on that interstate and never look back." He wasn't cruising up the four-lane interstate either, but "traveling down that Hillbilly Highway." When he sang of "My Old Friend the Blues," he wasn't splashing around in sweet romantic unhappiness but admitting to an existential depression that he tolerated only by accepting, his little trick on despair. And when he sang his truck-driver song to Tony, it wasn't the romance of big rigs and tough men. It was about some poor bastard standing there at a phone booth in a truck stop "somewhere on the Arkansas line" calling home and telling his "Little Rock 'n' Roller" that "your daddy won't be home for a while."

Steve's voice had a slurring quality that made him sound as if he pulled himself out of a drugged miasma to sing one last time. As Tony listened to Steve's songs, he sensed that he had heard the possibility of greatness. The line that led from Hank Williams and Johnny Cash and Merle Haggard straight through to Steve was not an artistic emulation but an emotional inheritance. They had torn the labor camps down but the lost highway traveled on, past strip malls, Denny's, and Motel 6, past kids sitting in day-care centers when Mommy and Daddy worked, past television sets glowing in the night, and crack dealers hanging out in small towns.

That was the world of which Steve sang. At its greatest that was the clarion call of country music—not nostalgia, not emotional excess, but the courage to look at the intimacies of life and death, love and loneliness, straight on.

Tony also listened to a cassette of Steve's Texas friend, Lyle Lovett. Lovett was a very different singer from Steve, choosing the rapier of irony over the bludgeon of emotions. His songs were full of wry cultural references and musical affinities with everything from Bob Wills's western swing to urban folk. What the two singer/songwriters shared was a compulsion to construct their music out of the real things of their lives, their pasts, their emotions, their experiences. That was not being done much in the publishing companies along Music Row, where writers sat in their little offices with their briefcases and rhyming thesauruses attempting to prune away at their ideas until they could cut and paste them into the formulas of the Nashville Sound.

Lyle was as unable to do that as Steve. Lyle had grown up in Klein, a tiny Texas community outside Houston that had been engulfed by the great waves of suburbanization. In one song on the cassette, "This Old Porch" (cowritten with Robert Earl Keen), Lovett sang of the onslaught of the new, an essay in song. When he sang of a "Cowboy Man," it was about a Texan who wasn't a cowboy at all.

Tony knew that his whole career would rise and fall on the success of *his* artists. Moreover, he had a direct, immediate incentive to sign singers whose albums would move out of those bins by the millions; he would receive a producer's cut of the royalties. By starting at MCA Nashville with Steve and Lyle, he was signaling to Nashville that he stood full square with the most daring music the community produced.

First, however, he had to get Steve past Bowen. The new MCA Nashville president had no interest in positioning the label out there on the fringes of the marketplace. He found Steve's music unlistenable. But he was willing to sign Steve if Tony could at least play one song that he liked. Tony went into the studio with Emory Gordy Jr., the coproducer, and worked primarily on "Good Ol' Boy (Gettin' Tough)," one of the songs on what would become his first album, *Guitar Town,* getting Steve to pronounce each word. Bowen listened to the song. Then looking as if he were standing downwind from the city dump, Bowen said: "Well, that sounds OK."

There are no schools to teach producing. If there were, they would teach philosophy as much as technique. At one extreme is the Phil Spector Wall of Sound rock 'n' roll approach, in which the producer is the artist, plugging in largely interchangeable performers. Nashville had no producer with the ambition and overweening control of a Phil Spector. Music City did have several producers, notably Owen Bradley and Chet Atkins, who had produced most of Nashville's music using the same musicians, and gauging their success by how closely they captured that mainstream Nashville sound. At the other extreme were producers who left their artists almost completely alone, artistic coupon clippers who sometimes weren't even in the studio when much of the record was being cut. Tony stood somewhere in the middle, a man who believed that less was more, but he was always there subtly touching the music, a gentle hint here, a suggestion there.

Tony wasn't going to produce anybody whose music he didn't

respect. That made life simple. Thus, he saw his job as helping *his* artists produce *their* vision. Tony wasn't going to clean up Steve's musical act. Tony was a musician, and he respected the artist's condition as only one who had been there could. He and Emory took Steve's demos, and either largely copied them in the studio or made small changes. Although *Guitar Town* was not a major commercial success, it was one of the seminal albums of the 1980s and had a great impact on the musical world of country music. Nashville, after all, was a small musical community of listeners. Hearing the album signaled that in Nashville one might once again expect the unexpected.

That message was reinforced by everything Tony was doing. Lyle Lovett's first album (*Lyle Lovett*) was full of wit and rancor, love and loss, most of it miles outside the Nashville mainstream. Tony signed another Texan, Nanci Griffith. She had a voice of exquisite vulnerability that seemed better fitted for the coffeehouses of the college world than the honky-tonks and arenas and fairgrounds of country music. Tony signed her anyway. He gently insinuated enough country tenor into her album, *Lone Star State of Mind,* that it took the music to another place it had not gone before.

Lyle and Nanci did not sell particularly well, nor fit comfortably within the confines of country radio. Nonetheless, they added immeasurably to the cache of what were truly new Nashville sounds, and to Tony's status as the premier progressive producer in Music City. Tony had a reputation as just another party-loving, good-time musician, but he was discovering that he was full of ambition. That ambition would not be realized, however, until Tony produced popular acts, not just cutting-edge, prestigious boutique artists who hardly sold.

Lyle, Nanci, and Steve were all part of an emerging country music that looked equally at the past and the future, respecting and appreciating the traditions of country, while evoking the music for a new generation. Texan George Strait and Oklahoman Reba McEntire both sang songs that would never cross over to pop. Out in California Dwight Yoakam was creating a daring existential country that sounded as if it had been born in Bakersfield, traveled through honky-tonks from Kentucky to west Texas, visited with

Emmylou and Bob Dylan, before settling on the outskirts of LA.

Another of the artists who were considered part of this movement of New Traditionalism was Ricky Skaggs, who like Yoakam considered Emmylou one of his musical mentors. Skaggs was a brilliant fiddle and guitar player, who as a member of Emmylou's Hot Band had helped shape her classic bluegrass album, *Roses in the Snow*. Skaggs took country music back to its Appalachian roots in his bluegrass and country songs. In 1985 Skaggs won the prestigious CMA Entertainer of the Year Award, signaling Nashville's belief in a resurgent traditional country music.

As much as anyone, Randy Travis was the singer who defined this new epoch in Nashville. From his 1986 album *Storms of Life* through the rest of the decade, Travis became the most popular Nashville artist of his time, selling records in larger numbers than any hard-core country artist had ever sold. He was a new kind of crossover artist, for he was recording uncompromising country music; it was the pop audiences that were crossing over to the Nashville side of the street, and Randy was hardly nudging a foot to greet them. In his late twenties, he was helping to draw a new young audience to country music.

When Tony looked back at his early years at MCA, he tried to forget the pain and humiliation. He tried to pretend that every lash, every slur, had been part of a learning experience. Those who had been there remember it otherwise. They watched in appalled fascination as Bowen did everything to embarrass his vice president of A&R but kick his chair out from under him and pull his beard. They watched as Tony simply took it, with that little upturn to his lips, a grimace that pretended to be a smile.

Bowen had good reason to be rankled at Tony. He could hardly pick up a trade paper without reading another gloriously fawning article about wonderful Tony, looking so hip in his little beard, making inspiring little statements about Steve, Lyle, Nanci, and the others. And these *artistes* weren't selling any records. Bowen, as he saw it, was merely imparting to Tony the realities of business life at a record label. Nonetheless, there were those at MCA who believed that Bowen was jealous of Tony.

It rankled Tony's supporters at the label that the man never stood up to Bowen. He took it. He took it. And he took it some more. Then late in 1988 Bowen left MCA Nashville to run Universal Records, a new label backed by MCA, leaving Bruce Hinton, the newly elevated president, and Tony to run MCA Nashville. At Bruce Hinton's house at the staff Christmas party, Tony practically jumped up and down shouting, "Hinton, we are free."

Less than a year later Bowen announced that he wanted to meld Universal back into MCA Nashville, and to return as the president of the enlarged company. Tony thought that he saw the shadow of his professional death at MCA pass before him. He knew that he and Bowen saw country music so differently and their ways of dealing with people were so opposed that if his former boss returned, Bowen would fire him.

Tony steered around the wrecks in the highway of his life, glancing to the side only a moment before speeding onward. This time he believed that if he wanted to stay at MCA Nashville, he had no choice but to make a stand. He flew to Los Angeles to meet with Al Teller, the president of MCA Records, and told the executive that he had to choose between the two men. Bowen had made enough enemies at MCA that Tony's message was heard sympathetically. In the end, the label head chose his largely unproven producer.

Tony did not know that Bowen had no intention of ever coming back to MCA Nashville. He was merely using the threat as a ploy in his negotiations to buy the Universal label. He knew how Tony and Bruce would react. Tony had played Bowen's game one last time. When Bowen left, he cleaned off the shelves, taking with him most of the older artists to his new label, Capitol Nashville. Reba and George were the two major-selling artists who remained, and they were foundation stones on which Tony built the new label.

Tony had made his name as producer of a few great young artists—Lyle Lovett, Steve Earle, Nanci Griffith—who were going to change the nature of country music. By the time Tony and Bruce took over, these artists were gone or going to make their ways in the pop or rock worlds. Tony might have fought for them to stay as Nashville artists, but that was not his nature.

Tony was nonetheless a brilliant producer with an artist's sensitivity. He wooed that fickle goddess success with art and guile. He baited his albums with songs that he felt would be almost irresistible to radio and to the great audience out there. He heralded the artist's way with big promotion budgets, stroking journalists to court their reviews and attention.

Tony evolved into not simply the most respected but by some measures the most successful producer in Nashville. He produced quality albums that sold in the millions, helping to bring not simply a new mass audience to country music but a new respect. In 1993 he renegotiated his contract and was named president of MCA Nashville, with Bruce becoming chairman. Tony neither had nor wanted the power that went with his title. Bruce may have been gray and faceless in image but he wielded power with a subtle, imaginative, and at times bloodless grasp, allowing Tony to spend his time producing.

Tony had constructed that wonderful public image of himself as the hip progressive king of Nashville, as creative an act as any of the albums he produced. As that image reached heights beyond even his imagination, Tony knew the truth was set in a different frame. He knew, moreover, that several artists with whom he had built his career were declining and likely finished with him.

He had produced one platinum (one million) and four double platinum (two million) albums for Reba McEntire, the longtime queen of country. She had grown away from her country roots, and as she had done so, had grown angry with him and restive. He knew it was unlikely that he would ever produce her again. He had produced one triple platinum album and one platinum album for Wynonna. Wynonna had perhaps the greatest voice in country music, but that didn't matter. She had become so surly and demanding that it was almost unthinkable that he would ever work with her on another album. He still had George Strait, for whom Tony had produced one triple platinum album, one platinum album, and one gold album. George was pure country, moseying down that same old trail, and he was pure pleasure to produce. So was Vince for whom Tony had produced one triple platinum album and three platinum albums.

Tony didn't like much of what he saw happening in Nashville. He knew that he wouldn't be part of the new Nashville world if it meant churning out bubble gum country. He wouldn't sign such acts. He didn't much like the country music he heard on radio. He wasn't about to stand up and say something. He wasn't about to take big chances at MCA Nashville. He didn't have any room on the label anyway. And he wasn't hungry any longer, out haunting the clubs and bars, looking for the next good thing.

One afternoon Linda Hargrove came in to see him. In the seventies she had been known as the "Blue Jean Country Queen." That had been a long, long time ago. Linda was in her mid-forties, and looked every one of her years. Tony knew that Linda was looking for a record deal, and he saw her largely out of courtesy and deference to a talented artist. Linda played some of her new songs for Tony, and then told him of her dream. "I want a deal, Tony," she said beseechingly. "I'm writing great. I'm singing the best I ever have. I've come back from the dead, Tony. I got a story to tell."

Tony had heard it all a thousand times. "You don't understand, Linda, what it's become," he sighed, gently letting her know that she would find no deal at MCA Nashville. "You don't want it. We're looking for kids. Don't you get it? We take these kids. Never sung anywhere, never paid their dues. Run 'em through media training. Turn 'em into something they're not. Throw 'em out on the road. And a couple years later they're through, outta here. We destroy them, their marriages, their lives. You don't want it. Believe me."

At Fan Fair, Tony saw that Vince Gill was about to take the stage. Vince was the final act, and Tony knew that the long evening was ending. He turned attentively toward the stage. No artist meant more to Tony. No relationship went back so far. No respect went so deep. Tony knew that probably never again in his life would he experience anything like what he had with Vince. They could say that Tony had lucked into Reba and George at MCA Nashville, but they couldn't say that about Vince. They couldn't take away the awards Tony had won working with Vince, the good times, the music they had made together. Nobody could do that.

Tony turned back a final time to look at the MCA executives and saw that they were still eagerly attentive. He glanced over to the side of the stage where Vince stood kibitzing with his band, looking as casual as if he were coming off the eighteenth tee. And he knew that for now all was right with his Nashville world.

4

~

"When I Call
Your Name"

Vince Gill lumbered onstage with the manner of a man embarrassed that he could be the focus of such a fuss. As he looked out on the audience with what he considered a goofy smile, the fans stood clapping, stomping their feet, and whistling. Vince didn't wear the regulation uniform of a country sex symbol: starched, faded jeans as tight on his body as a coat of paint. Nor had a costume consultant set a cowboy hat on his brown hair. He didn't thrust his hips suggestively, or bounce around the stage with frenetic energy, or leer down with eyes full of sexual menace at the young women who had worked their way up to the front of the stage.

Vince was wearing exactly what he had on today signing autographs for eight hours in his booth: an extralarge green flowered Hawaiian shirt that looked as if it could be not only worn but planted, loose hanging tan shorts, and work boots. It was hardly anybody's idea of sexy. That was the way Vince wanted it. He was as close to an anticelebrity as anyone in American public life. As host of the annual CMA Awards show, he had been full of merciless wit that he turned mainly on himself, refusing to be typecast as some distant superstar. Vince would gladly have played for this Fan Fair audience half the night. He wanted them here for his music, not because of an image.

Vince thought of himself as an ordinary man who played music in an extraordinary way. He hated giving interviews because he didn't think he had anything to say, and when he wasn't onstage, he hated being treated like a star. Ultimately, the man believed in those thousands of people out there in the dark looking up. He believed that somehow they would get his music and let him continue.

In refusing to don the glittery toga of image at a time when the country market was shrinking, Vince was taking a daring step. He was thirty-nine years old and his six-foot-four athlete's body was slowly turning to bulk. His own label had tried to get him to dress like a star, but he would hear none of it. He was becoming even bolder in his refusal to merchandise himself and his life. Just a few months ago, he had shaved his head and grown a goatee so that he was scarcely recognizable. He had looked like an overgrown version of Andre Agassi. Rejecting the tennis star's advertising motto ("Image is everything"), Vince was attempting to say that "image is nothing."

Vince told his friends that he had cut his hair because of his fifteen-year-old daughter, Jennifer. Jenny was his only child, and he fretted and worried over her. Jenny had reached that self-conscious age when teenagers snubbed those who did not cut the momentary fashion. He did not want her to become prisoner of her image as Vince's daughter, and he was trying to show her what mattered.

Jenny had come to him just a few days ago to complain about her father being away so much of the year. "Boy, Dad, I sure wish you were around here more," she told her father.

Vince was always trying to do the right thing. Sometimes his wife, Janis Oliver Gill, and his daughter didn't get as big a share of his life as they wanted and needed.

"Well, I do too," Vince said. "But you know why I work so hard."

"No, I don't," Jenny said, having inherited her mother's boldness.

"For you. It's my job. It's to provide for you and hopefully make life better for you than it was for me. In some ways. You see how we live. You don't see me with a house in Florida or the Bahamas, a big yacht, a ski boat. I don't need that. You don't see me out grandstanding how much money I've made. I'm just working my head off for you."

Vince lived in a pleasant house on a golf course outside Nashville, but it wasn't a tenth of what he could have had. It wasn't what Tony or Reba or Garth or any of them had. He didn't want that, not for himself, and not for his daughter either. He was proud that he was working not only for Janis and Jenny but for the band and the drivers and the stage crew and their families. Most of all, however, he was working because he loved living a musician's life.

Vince thought of himself as a musician, not a star, and he did everything he could to lead a sideman's life. Any other superstar would have had a private jet flying him back and forth from Nashville while the band and crew traveled behind on buses. Not Vince. Any other star would have had his own bus separate from the band. Not Vince. Even a singer starting out with only one bus for himself and the band would have slept in the stateroom in the back. Not Vince. He slept in a bunk like everybody else.

Backing up Vince this evening was arguably the best road band in country music, and unquestionably the happiest. He had chosen each member for his musicianship. He paid them fine salaries and profit-sharing. And best of all they were a band of friends out there on the road, traveling together from gig to gig. Vince's anger was about the only minus. One time or another they had all been the brunt of Vince's foul temper. He could lash out with a voice that was like being smashed in the face with a closed fist. Those outbursts were almost always about music. They rarely happened, or never lasted very long.

Of all the members of the band, Peter Wasner went back the furthest with Vince. Pete was a Minnesota boy who in the seventies had made his way to Los Angeles. Those years Pete rarely thought about anything more than his next gig. He was happy just making a living earning fifty dollars a night playing in a bluegrass band. Vince was far more successful, a member of a popular country rock band, Pure Prairie League. Vince liked to sit in with Pete's group at their regular Monday-night gigs, taking his turn singing songs. When Vince moved to Nashville in 1984, he kept nagging his piano-playing buddy to join him in Tennessee. Pete finally agreed, and for the past five years had been a member of Vince's band while writing songs and doing some session work as well.

Pete didn't like these enormous stages any better than Vince did. He could hardly see John Hughey, the pedal steel player, on the other end of the stage. But whatever the conditions, the band hung together. Pete dressed in a Hawaiian shirt covering his pudgy frame and wore a hat to hide his balding forty-four-year-old pate. He had a life now that had never entered his fondest aspirations: a lucrative career, the respect of his peers and community, a lovely young wife, twin babies, a studio out in the country, and a fine house. He knew that he owed most of it to Vince, though it was not the kind of thing that Vince liked hearing. Not only did Pete play in the band and on albums but Vince cowrote songs with him. That had put hundreds of thousands of dollars into Pete's bank account. Pete knew that Vince didn't need him. Vince was talented enough to write his own songs. It was just another way of sharing.

Pete was shy, hardly the image of the swinging musician. For years Vince and the other musicians on the bus made fun of their old bachelor buddy. After one show in Dayton, Vince had invited a group of young women onto the bus.

"Pete has some property over there in Tennessee," Vince said, in his best incestuous moonshiner *Deliverance* accent. "And we're tryin' to marry the poor boy off."

Pete laughed nervously, the only alternative to shrinking back into his bunk. Vince invited the group the next evening for a show hundreds of miles away, promising the women tickets and backstage passes. Three years later Pete married Sandy, one of the women, out in the woods near a creek on the land that became his studio.

Far on the other end of the stage stood John Hughey. At sixty-three, John was not simply the oldest member of Vince's band, he was the oldest musician in any leading backup band in Nashville. Onstage in his sport coat or dress shirt and slacks, he looked like a grandfather who had won a charity raffle to play one night with Vince Gill.

The pedal steel is the most modern instrument in country music, not even invented until the 1950s. Yet, along with the fiddle, it provides much of the distinctive instrumental sound of the more traditional country music. In the late 1940s, John had been a kid in Helena, Arkansas, when his dad had taken him into the radio station to hear the Arkansas Cotton Choppers. John had wanted a guitar, but when he heard the sound the lap steel player got out of his funny little instrument, he knew he had found his thing. His daddy thought his son should play electric guitar, but he couldn't stop John from ordering a lap steel and an amplifier from Montgomery Ward.

When he was nineteen, John auditioned for a band in Memphis. He got the gig. He played with a local band for nineteen years. Then it had bothered him that many people didn't like his chosen instrument. They took one look at a pedal steel and thought the group was nothing but another fool hillbilly band. The instrument was like a small desk with the strings running across the top, manipulated by the fingers and the foot pedals. To disguise his instrument John fixed a piece of cloth around the front. That way anyone sitting out front couldn't see him working the pedals with his feet and plucking the strings. They could tell when he played, coaxing sounds that were like some strange animal calling out into the lonely black night, a moaning, groaning, whining, mysterious sound that wrapped pure emotion around the music. After hearing John play, a reporter for the *Indianapolis Star* wrote, "If tears made a noise, this is what they would sound like." A minister friend with whom John sometimes recorded gospel music told him once that his hands were anointed, and so perhaps they were.

When John's old friend Conway Twitty started recording country songs, he called on John to add his distinctive flavor to his road band. That had gone on for two decades, and as good as it had been when it started out, it was that bad when it finished. Conway was the kind of star who never introduced his band, didn't believe in raises, and every night played the same set of songs in the same way. A musician in his fifties with a mortgage to pay didn't give up a regular gig that easily, but finally John walked away.

That's why it was all the more amazing that John was not only working now but had the best gig of his life. He was still married to the same woman, and he was making the best living he ever made playing the music he loved to play. Vince was the son John never had. He loved him. He loved his band mates. He loved the crew. And best of all he loved what he was doing. He had been at it long enough to know how rare it was to come across an artist capable of such acts of generosity and grace.

John would take to his grave the memory of that night in June of 1993 when Vince won the Instrumentalist of the Year Award at the Music City News Awards Show. It was Vince's night, but the singer insisted that old John come up and share the honor with him. John knew that most of the vast audience out there that night didn't know who John Hughey was. Onstage every evening, Vince didn't just introduce John with a couple of words. He celebrated him and his music, giving him solos. He pushed John and his band mates out there into the spotlight as long as he could without losing part of the audience.

"We're glad to be here at Fan Fair," Vince said, looking out into that torpid Nashville night and a panorama of fans enveloped in the darkness. In front of the stage ran a wide track, filled with a straggling army of amateur photographers five or six persons deep and a quarter mile long, moving endlessly, flashbulbs popping. "Hope that you all are having a great time. Hey, I know you are. I think I saw most of you today. I was out there eight hours. I know you're tired. My new album just came out, and I'd like to do some songs from it. *High Lonesome Sound.*"

> Whenever my soul is lonely
> Whenever I'm feeling blue
> I start thinkin' bout my blue-eyed darlin'
> And my heart starts pinin' for you.

Vince recorded the title track of his new album and two other songs on the first of December. In the morning Vince showed up in the massive control room in the high-tech Masterfonics Studio hidden behind Shoney's off Music Row. He came rumbling in, driving his restored 1967 Cadillac. He wore an ancient plaid work shirt, unlaced brown boots, and several days' growth of beard. He looked like a cross between a model in a Ralph Lauren ad and a worthy companion for the derelict who stood along Demonbreun Street hitting motorists up for change. Out of his battered old black leather bag, he pulled several songs, on foolscap paper.

"The cleaning lady threw away some of my songs that were lying around," Vince said. No one in the room would have blamed her.

After an assistant made copies of the songs, Vince and the band members headed off into separate small rooms in the large studio and put on headphones to hear the other players. This way there would be separate tracks of each musician, and later Tony could mix the best versions of half a dozen takes or more. From the control room, Tony could see the various musicians through various windows, but it was hearing them, not seeing them, that mattered.

Tony and Vince had put together a superb band. They were paid double scale, or about $600 for each three-hour session. For what they gave, it was penny-ante. Pete and John played on this album as they played on all Vince's albums. Two of Los Angeles's top musicians had flown in, Carlos Vega on drums and Leland Sklar, a legendary bass player. With his long gray beard, Sklar looked like he belonged on a box of Smith Brothers Cough Drops. Steuart Smith, a frenetic perfectionist and a top session guitar player, had come from his home in Washington. Billy Joe Walker Jr., a Nashville guitar player, added to the mix as did Steve Nathan, on piano and synthesizer.

Sklar considered it a treat to come to Nashville. In Los Angeles, most producers had their songs worked out in advance the way Alfred Hitchcock blocked out movies. For those sessions all the bass player had to do was play what was put before him, and play it well. Here in Nashville the premier musicians practically produced their own parts, bringing all their creativity into play. That was what Tony tried to get out of musicians, and not let them fall into well-worn patterns.

In their hands the musicians held a song they were seeing for the first time. Tony sat before the immense console as the band cut its first take of "High Lonesome Sound." He took a Zen Buddhist approach to producing. He sat silently, immersed in the music. He rarely said anything, and then usually it was a gentle suggestion, nudging the session or a specific musician into a different direction.

> I wanna hear that high lonesome sound
> 'Cause my sweet baby ain't around
> When my life's got me down
> I wanna hear that high lonesome sound.

By the second take, Vince and the band were smoking. Each player was contributing his little riffs or flourishes, playing off one another. "This is just too cool," Tony said. "We got everybody out there playing everything. Let's do it again, guys."

The musicians had been together all week, but today was different. John had arrived with no idea what they would be playing today, but he knew how rare it was for a band to play together so seamlessly. This is what it was about: music, his life, Vince, all of it. Pete sensed that it was one of those rare, transcendent moments that happen as infrequently onstage as in the studio. He would have loved to have played "High Lonesome Sound" all day long. As for Tony, he had produced hundreds of albums, but he rarely had such a day as this one. Much of the time he was in the studio alone patching away, trying to create the illusion of a sound as perfect as these guys were playing today.

"Are we a little closer to the parking lot of the ballpark?" Steuart yelled.

"You're hitting pretty hard, John," Vince said, gently insinuating his suggestion.

"OK, I'll let up," John said.

"Did you hear about the Siamese twins?" Vince interjected,

always lightening things up. "They went to England so the other one could drive."

They played it again, and this time it was even better.

"You guys sounded great!" Tony exclaimed in that staccato rhythm of his, a southern Walter Winchell.

"This isn't one of those stinking bluegrass bands," Steuart shouted. "This is a smoking bluegrass band."

"This is cooler than you know what!" Tony said, slapping his open hand on his jeans.

"We sure don't have any fun, do we?" Vince asked rhetorically.

"Perfect," Steuart shouted.

"I love you guys," Vince said.

A few minutes later, Bob DiPiero walked into the studio, the soundproof door shutting silently behind him. The scruffy songwriter wore a wrinkled T-shirt, green khaki pants, and running shoes. Bob nodded greetings and sat on the sofa to watch and listen to Vince and the band working on a song.

Bob could hardly believe he was here, listening to musicians who earlier in the week recorded *his* song. He had known Vince for years but it had only been two weeks ago that he had written with Vince for the first time. Vince had come cruising into Bob's publishing company, a two-story frame house on Music Row at ten-thirty in the morning. They had gone upstairs to Bob's office, in a row of rooms that were as unkempt as a college dorm during exam week.

Bob appreciated what it meant to write with Vince. Bob was the Italian American son of a Youngstown podiatrist, not some Oklahoma farm boy. He had grown up loving the Beatles, not Johnny Cash. He had arrived in Nashville from Ohio in the late seventies with hopes of breaking in as a songwriter. He had ended up teaching kids guitar at five dollars a lesson. He wrote songs every day, but nobody recorded them. His wife said to him, "Bob, what if this doesn't work out?" And he said, "I can't think that way. It's working. We just don't know it's working."

Looking back on it, Bob could see that he had been irrational, obsessive. It was no wonder that his marriage ended. But he had been right. It had been working. He started getting cuts. After five years he quit his teaching job. He married Pam Tillis, a rising star and daughter of Mel Tillis, part of the aristocracy of country music. And just two months ago he and Tom Shapiro, his cowriter on "Wink," had won the BMI Song of the Year Award for the most-performed country song.

The morning he and Vince sat down to write together for the first time, Bob had no great song ideas floating out there in the forefront of his brain. "Listen to this, Bob," Vince said, strumming a chord progression, humming a little tune. Bob looked around the room as if he had stashed some killer lyrics somewhere, if only he could remember where. He focused on the door, the windows, then spied a magazine open to a clothing advertisement, the models sitting on coiled rope. "Rope," Bob said. "What about something about rope?" Two hours later the two men bounced merrily down the steps, holding the music and lyrics to "The End of My Rope Coming up Short Again."

Bob knew it wasn't a great song, but it was a worthy day's work. Over lunch they sat in a bar having hamburgers and fries, two middle-aged men talking about the everyday things of life. Vince and Bob both knew that when you took off the cloak of stardom, there was just another vulnerable human being standing there. They started talking about teenagers and their difficulties. Sam, Bob's stepson, was causing him and Pam no end of trouble, and the songwriter laid it all out there for his buddy. The kid had been sent off to school, and Pam felt endlessly guilty. Vince could understand, and he offered Bob the best advice he could. Then Vince talked a little about his knee troubles and getting back in shape after his recent operation. There was always something to deal with in life.

After lunch, the two men drove back to Bob's office to listen to the song they had recorded into a tape recorder. "Well, man, should we quit while we're ahead?" Bob asked. Vince shrugged, and Bob figured he should throw out another idea. "I got this title, 'Worlds Apart.' I'm not sure what it's about."

"'Worlds Apart'?" Vince mused. "You know how Don Henley can write a song and it seems mundane, but by the time he gets to the payoff it's universal and meaningful."

Bob strummed some chord changes on his guitar, and the two men started writing a song. It happened so rarely like this, the words seemingly plucked out of the air and fitted together. Vince took the song with him that day, and now two weeks later it was already recorded, going on the new album. Things just didn't happen that way, not in the real world.

Vince walked into the control room. The singer hugged Bob and patted him on the back. "Man, you're in the midst of cutting something," Bob said apologetically. "I'll come back."

"No, just hang out," Vince insisted.

"I don't know, Tony," Bob said, turning to the producer for confirmation.

"It's a fucking smash. Stay, man."

A few minutes later Vince motioned to Bob to follow him out of the studio. They walked over to Vince's Cadillac and plunked themselves in the front seat. Vince turned the engine on, pushed a tape of "Worlds Apart" into the tape deck, and sat back to listen.

> You were my best companion
> Now we lie silent in the dark.
> Why do we have to be worlds apart?

The tape was not of the highest quality, but Bob could hear the gentle cushion of sound that the band provided for Vince's pure tenor voice. The song floated out of the tinny radio speakers like an exhortation to life. Sitting there, Bob knew that it didn't get much better.

> Love is still the answer
> It's the only place to start.
> Why do you and me have to be worlds apart?

Back in the studio the musicians had begun to work on a new cut. "OK, you've passed your bebop exam!" Steuart yelled. "You've done your advanced jazz theory. And your funk exam and your bluegrass exam. But you can't get your degree unless you play a Vince Gill ballad without rushing."

That evening when the session was finally over, Vince asked the band members if they would like to hear the entire album they had recorded that week. That was an unusual gesture, and they quickly said yes. The band members sprawled out on the two sofas set against the back of the control room, and in several straight-back chairs. Vince sat up front in an executive chair next to Tony. As the engineer played the ten songs, the musicians tapped their feet, swayed back and forth in their chairs, and listened with passionate intensity. On the country rock numbers, Vince played an imaginary guitar.

High Lonesome Sound was Vince's most eclectic album in years, everything from bluegrass to blues to rock, the only common denominator the sheer musicianship of Vince and the band. When the last cut had been played, there was only silence.

"Killer album," Tony said finally.

"Thank you," Vince said, dragging out the words so he seemed to be half joking. "Thank you. . . . Thank you. . . . Thank you. . . . Thank you. . . ." Vince swiveled his chair around, gesturing to each member of the band. Vince often leavened his sentiment with humor, but everyone felt the sentiments of this moment. The ultimate metaphor for the Nashville musical life was a song, three minutes of emotion, deeply felt and then gone. That was the way these musicians lived their lives. They had come together this week. They had bonded together as men and as musicians. They had experienced moments of emotion, and now it was all over, and they might never come together again.

Vince was better at hellos than he was at good-byes. Once he had muttered his final thank-you, he picked up his old leather bag and headed out alone into the cold December night.

Most of the evening at Fan Fair, Vince had been singing one up-tempo number after another, practically flailing the great crowd to keep it alive and up on its feet. Now at the end of this long evening, he stood alone in the spotlight and sang a ballad, "I Still Believe in You." It was one of his signature songs, for which he had won two Grammy Awards and an Academy of Country Music Award as "Song of the Year." Those spectators in the infield remained standing quietly. Back in the grandstands other fans lit matches, specks of illumination shining in the night.

"You folks can sing along," Vince said, and so they did, swaying gently in time with the music.

> I still believe in you
> With a love that will always be
> Standing so strong and true
> Baby I still believe in you and me.

Vince had written the history of his marriage in his songs, and the history of his marriage was the history of most of his love and much of his pain. He remembered how he had left Janis in a foul mood the day he and John Barlow Jarvis had written "I Still Believe in You." It was a valentine in song, not the first and not the last.

Janis was a cool, elegant woman who dressed with a designer flourish that intimidated many of the casually dressed women of Nashville. There were those in Nashville who could not understand how this marriage of opposites could last, but last it had, far longer than many Nashville marriages. Despite Vince and Janis's decade and a half together, Music City gossiped about them and their troubles, but the townspeople saw only shadows in a window, and knew little about their joys and pain. In 1993 when he won the Music City News Song of the Year Award for "I Still Believe in You," Vince called Janis forward to share the award, and the two of them had cried there onstage.

Vince had met Janis almost two decades before, in 1977 when she and her sister, Kristine Oliver, calling themselves The Sweethearts of the Rodeo, had opened for Vince's group in a club in Redondo Beach. She was twenty-two and he a mere nineteen, at an age when each year seemed like a decade. She was a sultry, sophisticated Southern Californian who loved clothes. He was a self-styled "Oklahoma hillbilly," the son of a banjo-picking lawyer and judge. She was a woman of compulsive neatness. He was a slob. She enjoyed classical music. His idea of classical music was Bill Monroe playing bluegrass.

Vince asked Janis out, but she had a boyfriend and wasn't into dating teenagers. Vince kept trying, and finally, three years later, they went out on their first date, marrying a short time afterwards. Things were going fine for Vince. Not only was he married to the woman he had chased for three years, but he was the lead singer and major songwriter for Pure Prairie League working out of Los Angeles. It was then that he had the chance to move over to Rodney Crowell and Rosanne Cash's band, the Cherry Bombs, as a musician. The move made no sense careerwise, but he jumped. At the first rehearsal he walked in toting his guitar like a hired gun. When the group started to play, he felt as if he had been slammed back against the wall. "Man alive," he thought to himself. "You better just get on your toes because you're going to get left real quick."

Vince wasn't left behind. In three years with the band, he matured immeasurably as an artist, playing with Tony, Emory Gordy Jr., and the rest of the band. Tony was the first to make the journey eastward to Nashville, as an A&R man for RCA Nashville. "Man, you oughta come to Nashville," Tony implored him.

"Naw, I might be pissin' in the wind, but I think I want a pop deal."

"See, there!" Tony exclaimed. "That's a country expression!"

Vince moved to Tennessee, signed a country deal with RCA Nashville, and went out to promote his first album. As the lead singer for Pure Prairie League, he had been someone. As Vince Gill, he was just another guy out there struggling to get some attention. His first albums sat in the record bins like damaged goods. He and his band drove down to Bakersfield to play a grungy bowling alley. When the bus pulled into the parking lot, Vince looked up and saw his name misspelled on the marquee—VINC GIL—in letters smaller than those for the house band.

Vince and Janis had a little child at home, and they were rarely home together. Vince's failures were so richly poignant in part because his wife and her sister's duo, The Sweethearts of the Rodeo, had become one of the top groups in country music. Vince and Janis had become buses passing in the night. Vince was a man who had learned to channel his joys and his pain into song. He wrote "Everybody's Sweetheart," a gently mocking ballad about a woman who was "Everybody's Sweetheart but Mine." He and Reed Nielsen wrote a melancholy song called "The Radio" with the lines: "I haven't seen you in weeks, but I hear you on the radio, singing soft and low."

Vince wrote what he felt in his songs and he said what he thought in his words. He was an honest man, full of what Nashville considered lethal candor. "You just look at Nashville Network, and it's clear that most people in Nashville haven't caught on," he told one journalist, Liam Lacey. "So Nashville will go on having its six to eight percent of the market—unless it changes." He didn't like the bland middle-of-the road sound of acts such as T. G. Sheppard and Lee Greenwood. "I never listen to the stuff."

Vince sometimes flared up in frustration. He was a fine golfer, and he took his temper out on the golf course, throwing tantrums, and golf clubs, and invective. Sometimes he carried that temper home with him or over to RCA. An employee there remembers the day Vince kicked in Janis's car door in the label's parking lot, an event that neither he nor Janis recalls. He does remember the day someone on the label made a comment about his daughter, and Vince showed his disapproval by kicking in several doors.

Vince was not a man of emotional pettiness, but his pride at his wife's success was perhaps laced with bits of envy. He applauded her achievements, but he wanted some of it for himself as well. He was proud that his talents were appreciated in Nashville and that other people asked him to play on their albums. He felt rightfully that all across Music City—at the other labels, in the publishing companies, among the songwriters—people were pulling for him, hoping that one day he would succeed.

The one man who had seen what Vince had gone through was in an operating room at Vanderbilt Hospital. Any other year Larry Fitzgerald would have been out at Fan Fair sitting on the stage behind his client and friend. Alas, the problems with his degenerating disk had become so painful that he had to have an operation. It gave Vince's manager plenty of time to think.

He contemplated the ironies of his present life. Here he was,

Larry Fitzgerald, former jazz amateur and college dropout, former mail room boy at the William Morris talent agency, former hotshot manager of Chicago, Toto, and Three Dog Night. Here he was, seemingly the very epitome of those slick, name-dropping Southern Californians, the sweet smell of freshly minted dollars guiding them eastward. He recalled almost painfully how when he arrived from the coast in the mid-eighties, he hadn't been exactly greeted by laurels of welcome. He had to admit that he had sometimes acted with that I've-been-there-and-I've-seen-it-all arrogance that drove the Tennesseans half batty. He had toned down his ways. He had learned a great deal, and he had become accepted. He had a new wife and a new baby.

Nashville was his home now, and he didn't like what he saw happening. He was beginning to see the same kind of low talent acts in Nashville that he had seen in Los Angeles a decade before. If a fellow looked good in a hat and jeans, it didn't seem to matter if he could sing well; that could be taken care of in the studio. It didn't matter if a new baby act had ever performed much; get her a radio hit and a video that showed her navel and she could be propelled out there onstage surrounded by smoke and mirrors. Here he was more upset about what was happening in Music City than most of those who had lived there all their lives, but he had been there in Los Angeles. He had seen it. And he feared that the country music community was slowly turning into a Tennessee version of the self-serving California pop music world that he had been so delighted to leave.

Larry loved Vince in part because he was about as far from this new Nashville world as he could be. Here Vince was competing against performers like Garth, who swung around stage on a rope, and Brooks and Dunn, who had a stage set straight out of *Star Wars*. All Vince would do was stand onstage, half the time in tennis shoes with his shirt sticking out, and attempt to hold eight or twelve thousand people for two or three hours by the simple expedient of singing to them and playing his guitar.

For years Larry had tried to get Vince to dress up and spiff up his act with some spectacular staging, but Vince would have none of it. When Vince had shaved his head, he hadn't even told Larry, but of course Larry knew about it right away. It had gotten so much publicity that Larry was half tempted to give an interview saying "shaving Vince's head was part of my marketing strategy to reinvent my client at this point in his career." It would have been a marvelous little joke. The only problem was that it was just the kind of thing that was being done, and many people would have missed the humor.

Larry cared for Vince like a young brother or son. He had no written contract with the singer, and he knew that one day Vince might walk in and tell him good-bye. That was one of the little subtleties that made a manager's life in Nashville a difficult one. You could work for years for an artist, spending your own money and time, and once he hit the big time, it was bye-bye. It had happened to Barry Coburn, who had been fired by Alan Jackson. It had happened to Bill Ham, who had been fired by Clint Black. And despite everything, Larry knew that it could happen to him.

Larry knew that the greatest thing he ever did for Vince was to help him get out of his RCA contract and over to Tony at MCA Nashville. Nowadays a singer whose three albums had done as poorly as Vince's would have been booted off the label. RCA had been willing to give him yet another chance. This time, on Vince's fourth album, RCA insisted that he record other people's songs. Larry didn't pretend to have a great musical sense, but he knew that the man was his songs. So he went to Joe Galante, the president of RCA Nashville, and talked him into letting Vince go. It wasn't easy, and he offered up some points on Vince's first albums at his new label, but he got his way. Then he went to dinner with Tony Brown. They ate a lot of pasta, and they drank a lot of wine, and when the evening was over Vince was the newest artist at MCA Nashville and Tony was his producer.

The first two singles on Vince's first MCA album did not do as well as the label had hoped. Everyone knew that if the third single failed, then the album would fail and with it Vince's career at his new label. "If this doesn't work, man, I'm sorry!" Tony told his former band mate early in 1990. "I give up."

The song chosen as the next single, "When I Call Your Name," written by Vince and Tim DuBois, was the most country cut on the entire album. The mournful ballad seemed to have the restless wind of the Appalachian highlands sounding through its choruses, but that was Patty Loveless, a fellow MCA Nashville artist, singing harmony.

Radio was the game, not all radio but the approximately two hundred stations that reported to the trade magazines, *Billboard* and *Radio & Records* most notably, that put out weekly singles charts. MCA Nashville had promotion people working the single, pumping up the program directors around the country, trying to get Vince's single played on all the reporting stations in heavy rotation.

It was getting so competitive in Nashville that one reporting station not playing a single could prevent it from ever being a number one hit. Tim DuBois, the cowriter of the song and the head of the new Arista Nashville label, called the Seattle radio station that had not been playing the song and got it to add "When I Call Your Name," pushing it toward the top of the charts.

Vince discovered that fame was a magic wand that could turn laughter to tears and tears to laughter. In the summer of 1990, he was playing an amusement park in West Virginia. "When I Call Your Name" was a top single. And when he sang the song, people moved toward the stage, singing the words and crying over this tale of a man who goes home and finds "a note on the table that told me good-bye." People came up to him with the most anguished stories of how his songs had affected them. He could pass that wand over charity events and fund-raisers, and his presence raised tens of thousands of dollars. And no one in Nashville showed up at more charity events, no one visited more hospitals, no one used his fame to do more kinds of good.

> Somewhere along the way, I guess I just lost track
> Only thinkin' of myself never lookin' back.
> For all the times I've hurt you, I apologize.
> I'm sorry it took so long to finally realize.

As competitive as he was, Vince kept some distance between himself and his success. It was as if he feared if he fell in love with his public image, then one day that was all he would be. In October of 1991, he opened for Reba McEntire at the Greek Theater in Los Angeles. When Reba came to the side of the stage at the end of his set, she was startled to see that Vince's onstage monitor was a television set tuned to the World Series. Vince was scheduled to sing the National Anthem before the fifth game, and he was rooting for anything but a four-game sweep.

Vince knew that a career was not the same thing as a life, and he relished any opportunity to get away from the pressures of stardom. He got away for the first time in many months in January of 1991 to play some basketball and golf in the Bahamas. He and his three Nashville friends were playing on the Divi Beach golf course when two masked men jumped out of the bushes, pointed sawed-off shotguns, and demanded their wallets. Long afterwards he dreamed of those masked men on that sunny day, only in his nightmares the men shot him and left him lying there.

Vince's father had raised his sons with a rigid sense of right and wrong. There was an Old Testament sternness to the man, though it was not the Bible that Stan Gill used to raise his sons, but abstract ideals of justice and honor. Stan Gill was a judge at home years before he was one in the courtroom. He meted out stiff justice to Vince as well as to Bob, Vince's half-brother by his mother's first marriage. His parents' ideals of what a man should be were a heavy load, but Vince lifted them up and carried them out in the world. He tried to be a good man. He did not drink. He did not smoke. He did not do drugs. He tried never to get too full of himself.

Vince's older brother went out in that same world, and that same burden buckled his legs and brought him to his knees. He was twenty-two years old and drunk that night he was driving a hundred miles an hour and ran into a tractor-trailer. Bob stayed in a coma for months, and when he finally opened his eyes, it was on a world that never seemed the same. He disappeared for months at a time, wandering only God knew where.

Bob was Vince's half-brother, and he loved him with all the fullness of emotion. It was a love that no matter what happens in life is still there, a song whose melody is never forgotten. Vince took a lesson from Bob. His brother had nothing, and he complained less than those who had everything.

In March of 1993 Bob died of a heart attack. Vince was a man who lived by his emotions. He had been writing a song about Keith Whitley, the country star who had died of acute alcohol poisoning in 1989. Now he finished the song about his brother and called it "Go Rest High on That Mountain." As beautiful and poignant a song as he had ever written, it gave solace and peace to many, not least of whom his own family. It was as much Bob's gift to the world as it was Vince's.

One day Vince received a letter from a woman who said that she was dying. Her final wish was to have "Go Rest High on That Mountain" played at her funeral, only the lyrics of the song referred to a man not a woman. Vince was forever being asked to help the sick and dying. At his concerts, the promoters often brought back those in wheelchairs or distress. He could not see all of them, but sometimes it seemed that he tried. Vince cried when he read the letter. He went into the studio and recorded a special version of the song, and mailed it to the dying woman.

One problem with the magic wand of fame is that you can never put it down. Wherever he went, people thought he was different. People wanted to touch him, to take his autograph, or some part of him. People coveted his fame and coveted him, even other artists. He was always ready to sing on other artists' albums, but his beneficence sometimes turned on him and his own career.

Last year Dolly Parton had called Vince and asked him, "Would you come and sing with me on 'I Will Always Love You' for my new album?" At the age of forty-nine Dolly was part of the generation of older stars who did not get radio play. She was not ready to accept the purgatory of the old-timers, playing in places such as Branson, Missouri, selling her old hits with an 800 number late at night on cable television. Dolly knew that if Vince sang with her, she was sure to get radio play. For its part, MCA Nashville was justifiably protective of its artist. The label agreed that Vince could record the song as long as it was not released as a single to compete with Vince's own album.

When Vince's album was about to come out, Dolly called again. "This is great that you did this, Vince, but it sure would be nice for it to be a single."

"Well, let me go see what I can do," Vince replied, always trying to make others happy. "Maybe we can make it all work."

Vince knew that he couldn't end up competing with himself. Nonetheless, he pushed MCA Nashville to allow the duet to come out as a single once Vince's album had run its course. That was a generous gesture, but when Dolly's album was released, the radio stations started playing "I Will Always Love You." Vince's own single, "Go Rest High on That Mountain" had just come out. It was exactly the scenario that the executives at MCA Nashville feared when Vince first insisted on singing with Dolly.

Legally, MCA could have forced Columbia to withdraw the single, but once again Vince insisted on playing the good guy. "Let's just ask everybody to live in a perfect world for three months and see if both records can be hits," he said philosophically. He even agreed to sing the song with Dolly on the CMA Awards show.

In the end the duet rose to number five on the *Billboard* chart, whereas "Go Rest High on That Mountain" reached no higher than fifteen. Vince shrugged the matter off, but he knew that if not for Dolly, his song, his brother's song, might have entered even more deeply into the consciousness of country music lovers. The other reason the song did not reach higher on the charts was that some radio consultants refused to play "Go Rest High on That Mountain" because it was about death, a subject they believed did not go over well with their listeners.

Vince was a star who refused to act like a star. He was a star nonetheless, and that stardom had changed him and his marriage and the world around him. Once, he had been a man of surpassing candor. He had learned to harbor his honesty, holding it close like a gambler holding his face cards tight against his vest, almost never showing it around outsiders and journalists. As for his marriage, Janis's days as a top artist were all over. Although she and her sister continued to record on an independent label, to much of the world Janis had become Mrs. Vince Gill. He understood the cost of living in the shadows, the spotlight rarely shining her way.

Vince could not stand to have others think ill of him, whether it was Dolly, or his daughter, or his fans. He was devastated to get an angry letter from a fan, criticizing him for some supposed minor infraction of the unwritten code of a country artist. He had learned in the most painful and lengthy of processes that he couldn't please everyone, but he kept on trying.

"I just, you know, I'm not going to change," he reflected. "I'm always going to try to do the right thing or do what I think is the right thing regardless sometimes of the consequences. I'll get up and start the day as I always have. The phone is going to ring and I'm going to answer it. I'll react to this life as it comes before me. You know, at the end of the day when I go lay down, I gotta answer to me. Bottom line, I know what I've done and feel good about. That's all I need to know."

> I still believe in you
> With a love that will always be
> Standing so strong and true.
> Baby I still believe in you and me.

Vince had signed autographs for eight hours and performed before eighteen thousand fans. His face was streaked with fatigue, his shoulders slumped as he left the stage. As tired as he was, he was expected at an MCA party in the backstage area, to play the charming witty Vince Gill for an hour or so more. As he was led toward the MCA tent, hundreds of fans stood cordoned off to the side. "Vince! Vince!" they yelled, calling out for autographs. He had noticed in the last few years how the fans had changed. They could be almost merciless, so insistent in their demands. As he looked into their eyes, he thought they were saying, "I pay your salary. I'm the one that buys your records. I'm the one that puts your buses on the road. I do all that. You owe me."

Vince knew that there weren't even supposed to be fans back here. Even if he hadn't been so dog tired, he had no responsibility to sign even one autograph. No other performer was doing it. All he had to do was to keep his eyes forward, follow the security people, and walk ahead into the MCA party. He turned back toward the fans, and walked along that line, signing autographs, shaking hands, saying hello to every person who wanted to greet him.

Wednesday,
June 12, 1996

5

~

"Together Again"

Emmylou Harris lived in a fine old house in Green Hills, a few minutes from Music Row. For two decades, no artist had brought more passion and creativity to country music, but Emmylou was gone from Nashville this Fan Fair week. Country radio did not play her anymore, and her songs did not sound out across the land.

Emmylou could have been at Fan Fair. She could have sung one evening, and signed autographs from a booth. As much as she loved country music, she managed to create an excuse not to attend. This year she was off playing in Europe, where she believed they appreciated her music the way they did not any longer in the United States.

Emmylou had always had her loyal audience, but she had not sold anywhere near the numbers of albums that others imagined. Nor had she played much in the great amphitheaters and arenas where the headliners were paid a king's ransom for an hour's worth of song. She had spent her money on the finest musicians, on guitars and studio time and all sorts of artistic amenities. She was hardly well enough off to sit back and become the grande dame of country music, playing only occasionally for her devoted fans.

At the age of forty-nine, her career had lasted longer than that of any major woman artist in country music other than Dolly Parton. Emmylou, unlike Dolly, had amassed no great fortune and still had to work, and as her popularity declined, she had to work harder. That was the brutal economics of it. She couldn't just go off for occasional weekends. She had to take her band out for weeks on end if she wanted to take something home with her when it was all over.

At times Emmylou was tired beyond tired. Music gave her life vitality and exuberance and passion, and music took her life away, stripping her of energy and desire. She had been tired even before she had gone on her great European tour. Emmylou had agreed to go on the thirteen-country tour largely because it had been the twentieth anniversary of her original backup group. The Hot Band was perhaps the most legendary backup band in country music history.

In 1990 she had disbanded the electric Hot Band in part because it was hurting her aging voice to sing over loud music. Now she had disbanded her new acoustic group, the Nash Ramblers. Her records weren't selling that well any longer. She thought that from now on she might have to go off on tour with only a couple of musicians. For all she knew, this European reunion tour could well be the last time she ever had her own band.

Two other performers would be going off to perform with her, Trisha Yearwood and Marty Stuart, but Emmylou and her Hot Band were the great draw. This tour would be her musical life told from Paris to Madrid, Stockholm to Glasgow. It would be a story told whenever she sang her songs, songs that carried the weight of not only the music's history but her own past. Music was her muse, her autobiography written with blood and brain, heart and soul, written for anyone to read.

Emmylou flew into Dublin the evening before her first performance and met the Hot Band in the private bar at the Burlington Hotel, where they were staying. They were musical gypsies. They came together in moments of artistic passion and comradeship, traveled together for weeks on end, and then went their various ways, sometimes not even seeing each other for a year or more, or sometimes never again.

Emmylou didn't have to see most of these men to be bonded to them in ways that were so deep and mysterious that she could not even talk about it. It was as if each event, each woeful pain, each dark disappointment, each wonderful night, each glorious song had been laminated together, creating bonds so close and strong and solid that they seemed of a single piece.

Of all of them, Glen D. Hardin, the piano player, and Phil Kaufman, the road manager, had gone back the furthest, but even they had not been there at the beginning of Emmylou's career. She had grown up the daughter of a career Marine officer. As a teenager she had a tall girl's gawkiness, retreating into her own solitude, off in her room strumming her guitar and singing folk songs. She was the valedictorian of her high school class in Quantico, Virginia.

Emmylou was a studious, proper young woman whose shyness the young men in her class assumed was an arrogant lack of interest in their entreaties. Wanting to be an actress so she could cloak herself in the lives of others, she headed off to the University of North Carolina at Greensboro to study drama. She ended up playing in a folk music duo at a campus dive, The Red Door.

In the 1960s, Emmylou and her contemporaries were looking for new spiritual homelands. Some dropped out into the cultural radicalism of the hippie movement. Others moved leftward into political movements identifying with the poor and the downtrodden. A few like Emmylou sought much the same through music. Emmylou found in music not only a worthy substitute for her acting ambitions but a place to make moral and spiritual statements of high order. She left school and headed to Greenwich Village with dreams of becoming a folksinger.

Many people Emmylou met in New York despised country music as right-wing, redneck, hippie stomping music. They quoted the most important country song of the day, Merle Haggard's "Okie from Muskogee," a tale of small-town folks who didn't smoke marijuana and take LSD, didn't burn their draft cards, and down on Main Street "like[d] living right and being free."

The Bohemians and intellectuals in Greenwich Village feared that the song would help rev the yahoos into trying to kick the flag-burning, antiwar activists right out of the good old USA. They didn't see that Haggard's song was a brilliant evocation of the legitimate fears of millions of Americans whose values were dismissed in the secular urban society. They could not see that for all its commercial compromises, country music came closer to most Americans than did the songs sung by the folk bards of Greenwich Village. And neither could Emmylou.

Emmylou was a woman of fearsome intensity who looked upon her musical career as life itself. She could only share that life, or bits and pieces of it, with a man who was a musician. In New York City she met Tom Slocum, a singer/songwriter whom she married. She signed a record contract with a small company, Jubilee, that in 1969 put out her first folk-oriented album, *Gliding Bird*. The album was a commercial and critical failure. She gave birth to their daughter, Hallie, and the couple moved to Nashville.

Nashville had no special place for a twenty-three-year-old singer who looked like a hippie goddess and had no particular liking for most of the music the city produced. When Emmylou's husband left her, she took a job as a waitress at the High Hat Lounge, a bar across from the Greyhound Station whose only pretension was its name. She didn't earn much. Supplementing her income with food stamps, she stood in line at the Food Liner and tore off the stamps while customers made their own judgments about a beautiful young lady living off the government. Until now, she had been one of these liberals who sympathized with the poor while standing safely behind a cordon line of class. She had crossed that line now, and she felt and saw things that most of her contemporaries only intellectualized.

Emmylou's life resonated with the theme of a thousand country songs, but she remained a gentle Bohemian with disdain for much of country music. After a few months alone in Nashville, she returned to her family home in suburban Washington to live with her mother and father. Emmylou felt tired, worn-out, used up, eking out her life, counting the days in the small change of everyday life. Music was all that she had truly cared for, and most of the time her song was silenced. Emmylou met a bass player, Tom Guidera. They moved in together along with her daughter, Hallie, into a little house.

Washington had a vibrant indigenous music scene, but it was not the kind of place to make a national career. Emmylou sang sometimes in the back room at Clyde's in Georgetown, an upscale saloon with a dress code. The back room was a desolate spot, serving primarily as a temporary respite for those who had been humiliated in the singles games going on up front.

Clyde's was down the street from the Cellar Door, the premier club in Georgetown. On occasion, out-of-town musicians strolled into Clyde's after their evening gig. One evening Rick Roberts and Kenny Wertz, two members of the Flying Burrito Brothers, chanced into the back room. Emmylou was singing "It Wasn't God Who Made Honky Tonk Angels," the classic country song that in 1952 made Kitty Wells the first major woman country star. Emmylou had no great interest in country music and often sang country songs with her tongue placed squarely against her cheek. This evening, however, she sang it straight, going down into the emotional truths of the music.

The two musicians told their colleague, Chris Hillman, about the amazing chick singer they had heard at Clyde's, and the three musicians returned the next evening. They invited Emmylou to sit in with them the rest of their weeklong gig at the Cellar Door, and so she did. They talked vaguely of Emmylou singing with them somewhere someway. Then they left as musicians always left, full of fond farewells and promises of reunions, all fervently avowed and usually soon forgotten.

In this instance, a few months later Emmylou received a call from Gram Parsons, the leader of the Burritos. The group was giving a concert in Baltimore, and he wanted to meet Emmylou. "I'm in Baltimore. Could you come pick me up?"

A quarter century later, Emmylou could still hear that voice, so sure of itself, intruding itself on her solitude. And she could feel the way she had felt, the fatigue, the self-protective resignation. "No, that's fifty miles away." It was more than fifty miles away, it was a thousand miles, ten thousand miles away from her life now. "Oh, is it that far?" Yes, it was far to travel on a dark, rain-swept evening in her sad old Pinto, far to travel when that evening she had to perform for ten people at Clyde's for ten dollars, far to return alone over empty roads of broken promises. "Why don't you take the train down?"

Emmylou knew almost nothing about Gram Parsons. This scion of a family that had once owned a third of the orange groves in Florida, Gram was a child of despair. His family were members of that dissolute, drunken, self-indulgent breed who make the phrase "family fortune" seem God's little joke on the wealthy. His father killed himself when Gram was thirteen. He ran away from private school and headed north to Greenwich Village. Later he entered Harvard University and lasted a semester, spending most of his time in the clubs on Harvard Square.

Gram loved rock and country equally. In his quest to create what he called "cosmic American music," Gram was an alchemist taking country and rock, creating music that at its best combined the pulsating rhythms and energy of rock with the emotions and grit of country. It was this inspired mix that became the basis for much of modern country music, making Gram one of the most influential figures in the whole history of the music.

Gram was better at hanging out than speaking out, but he had a strange force of personality, influencing those who might have dismissed him as a heroin-shooting wanna-be. Gram was vain, self-centered, unreliable, dissolute, disruptive. He was an easy rider, out there on the great American highway looking for a past that never existed, moving willfully toward the embrace of the dark mistress of death.

Gram took the train to Washington and joined Emmylou at Clyde's that rainy Monday evening. A bartender put a card in the rain-swept window: APPEARING TONIGHT, GRAM PARSONS. There were only three people in the audience. Gram had long straight hippie hair, a scruffy mustache, and dark killer eyes. Emmylou had almost never sung harmony before, and she had never imagined that it was something she wanted to do. That night, she wound her voice around Gram's tenor, embracing each note, creating a sound that was far larger than the sum of their two voices.

The next day Gram was gone, and Emmylou returned to her life of ten-dollar gigs. Emmylou had learned to live like a long-term prisoner doing time, trying never to get too excited, burying the days in gray moods. A year later, Gram called and invited Emmylou to fly to Los Angeles to sing with him on his first solo album. She had tried to pretend that her dreams of a glorious musical life were over, but Gram's voice on the phone was enough to send her flying westward.

In Los Angeles, Emmylou was the only woman musician in a world of men. When she sat around with Gram and his band, she nestled quietly into a corner and knitted sweaters and outfits for her daughter, Hallie. Only when she sang with Gram did she seem to glow with life, touching places in her musical soul where she had never gone before. Each time she sang with him, she was learning to care for country music with an abiding love.

When she talked of Gram and what he gave her those months, her images were those often used to describe sexual ecstasy. To her "it was like day and night, the time before and after I'd spent with Gram. . . . It was incredibly wonderful too. I had no idea, it just brought me to life, since I had never done anything like that before . . . he brought out whatever music was in me. He was the one who drew it out."

Some of those who heard her speak and saw her love for Gram assumed that they were sexual partners. Theirs, however, was a marriage of souls and musical identities, their voices intertwined with perfect intimacy.

Emmylou called Glen D. Hardin "the heart and soul of the Hot Band." She wouldn't have thought of making this trip to Europe without inviting good old Glen D. He had an impish, cherubic face that looked out on the world as if each day were little more than an occasion to pick up a new story or two and have a few drinks. When he had those drinks in him as he did this evening, he was a raconteur *nonpareil,* telling tales of Elvis or Gram, of gigs from Australia to Miami. Emmylou laughed as loud as anyone, but she knew that music came first to Glen D.

Emmylou remembered how she had met Glen D. when she arrived in Los Angeles. She and Gram had gone over to Glen D.'s house to work on some songs for the new album. Gram had hired the piano player not simply because Glen was a marvelous musician, but because he was Elvis's piano player, and Gram was hoping some of that stardust might blow his way.

Glen D. struck the keys as if they were molten steel, his fingers jumping back off, creating a shimmering sound. Those who heard Glen D. perform assumed that he was playing with crazed abandon, but it was just the opposite. Glen D. practiced until he got each number exactly the way he wanted it. Then he played it the same way, hitting the keys with infinite precision. Glen D. was a man of meticulousness. He had been a Morse code operator in the navy, and his house in Nashville was full of clocks. On one of Emmylou's tours, he had been stopped going through customs. Half a dozen agents minutely examined his suitcase. They were not sniffing for drugs or contraband, but were in awe at the way Glen D. had packed, wrapping each perfectly folded shirt and pants in tissue paper.

The musicians had taken over a corner of the bar. There, hovering over Emmylou, stood a beer-bellied, foul-speaking, walrus-mustached, cheaply tattooed biker from hell. The man looked as if he would as soon pull out his handy stiletto or butcher knife or whatever instrument of horror he surely was carrying and slice the intruder from stem to stern as to bother asking him to move on.

Phil Kaufman had worked as Emmylou's road manager for nearly two decades. In his way Phil was as much a member of the Hot Band as Glen D. In the sixties, Phil made his living smuggling marijuana in the United States, Spain, and Sweden, where he spent eight months in prison. After being extradited to the United States, he was incarcerated for more years, including time at Terminal Island, where he met Charlie Manson. After his release, he hung out with Charlie, sleeping with Charlie's girls, talking music with Charlie, dropping acid with Charlie. In that surreal LA world, a bum was one deal away from becoming a millionaire, a druggie one bad connection away from death. Phil moved from Charlie to the Rolling Stones, working for a hundred dollars a week as their "executive nanny," shepherding them around the city.

That was how Phil met Gram and signed on as his road manager. Phil had found his calling and the name by which he would become known: "Road Mangler." For all the Mangler's public menace and often self-conscious vulgarity, there was a gentle core to the man. He liked to take care of musicians. He guided them through airports and hotel lobbies, managed the minutiae of their touring lives, eternally alert to dangers and threats.

Phil was with the group when Gram and Emmylou and his new band, the Fallen Angels, left Los Angeles in a bus on their first tour. They had tried to rehearse in LA, but there had been more drugs and booze than music, and she had spent much of the time off by herself in a corner knitting. Gram had put on fifty pounds since the early days, and he looked like a bloated ship, wallowing on the stage.

As the bus traveled eastward, Emmylou kept to her seat, constantly knitting. Phil loved Gram, and loving him meant protecting Gram from himself. The road manager played hide-and-seek with the singer's drugs, ferreting them out from his shoe or taped under a sink and flushing them away. He had to bail Gram out of jail in Blytheville, Arkansas, when Gram tried to punch a cop. And always offstage Emmylou kept knitting.

Emmylou had not had to scan the darkening sky looking for omens. They were everywhere. For the new album they sang Gram's signature song, "Hickory Wind." The exquisite ballad was about his yearning for the "feel of hickory wind" that he knew as a boy in South Carolina when he would climb the great old oak tree that rose above a field of pines.

Emmylou was at her family home in the Maryland countryside when the call came. On September 18, 1973, Gram had died in a room at the Joshua Tree Inn in the California desert, died far from hickory wind. He had been with several friends. The coroner's report said that he had died of "drug toxicity, days, due to multiple drug use, weeks."

Although Gram's stepfather had never been close to Gram, he now wanted his body brought back for burial in Louisiana. Only two months before at the funeral of one of their friends, Gram and Phil had vowed that whoever went first, the other one would take his body out to Joshua Tree National Monument, in the vast emptiness of the desert, and burn his remains.

Phil borrowed an old hearse, and he and another friend drove out to Los Angeles International Airport, where they pretended they were funeral home representatives, authorized to pick up the casket. They drove into the night with a case of Mickey's and a quart of Jack Daniel's as their companions. In the desert near Cap Rock, they poured five gallons of gasoline on the casket and lit a match, and for a few minutes the sky was ablaze.

There are spiritual pains that cannot be cleansed with tears. Emmylou hadn't cried when she heard the news of Gram's death. All she had wanted was to sing harmony with Gram, and now she was alone. All she had wanted was to wrap her voice intimately around his on stage after stage, record after record. And now she was alone again.

Reprise Records signed Emmylou to a contract. On the album cover of *Pieces of the Sky* twenty-eight-year-old Emmylou looked like a Renaissance princess in silent prayer. There appeared to be streaks of light shining in her dark brown tresses, but they were the first of her silver hairs. Although Emmylou's album had none of Gram's songs on it and his name appeared nowhere, *Pieces of the Sky* was a magnificent tribute to the man's spirit and gifts. He had wanted to make "cosmic American music," and now that music sang out.

It was country music surely, but it was country music that they could play in a jukebox in an east Texas honky-tonk and in a dorm room at Harvard, dance to in Haight-Ashbury and Austin, New York and Memphis. She had flung open many doors in this temple of music.

Many songs were laced with sweet melancholy, but one song was so dark that it was as if one had stumbled in on a confession only for the ears of God. "Boulder to Birmingham" was written by Emmylou and a Washington musician, Bill Danoff. Although his name was never mentioned, it had become a song about Gram

Parsons. It was about an emptiness that time would never fill, promises that would never be kept, dreams that would never come again, love that would never be fulfilled.

> I would rock my soul in the bosom of Abraham
> I would hold my heart in his saving grace
> I would walk all the way from Boulder to Birmingham
> If I thought I could see your face.

Emmylou had been half a million dollars in debt to Warner Brothers, working it off album after album. Most of that time she had kept on that straight country road, staying off the big pop highways where there were always secret tolls. To the young generation of singers, she was the most admired woman in country music.

Over the years she traveled far down that country road, in 1980 recording a bluegrass album, *Roses in the Snow,* that had a major impact in the resurgent popularity of that music. Five years later she recorded *The Ballad of Sally Rose.* The concept album told the story of Sally Rose, the pseudonym that Emmylou sometimes used on the road. Sally Rose meets The Singer, who teaches her all there is to know about music, but before she can pledge her love, The Singer dies in a car accident, and she spends the rest of her days spreading the message of his song ("I stepped into the light you left behind").

Emmylou married twice more, each time to her producer. Her second husband was Brian Ahern, father of her second daughter, Meghann, and her third husband, Paul Kennerley, a British songwriter/producer and her cowriter on *The Ballad of Sally Rose.* Emmylou continued to record strong, original albums that deserved hearing on their own full merit. In 1980 she won the CMA Award for Female Vocalist of the Year and *Roses in the Snow* for best country album. She won three Grammy Awards for Best Country Vocal Performance, Female and four others. That was the past, and Emmylou knew that she was aged as Nashville counted time. She had let her hair turn silver, and she was an outcast in this hot new young country world.

★ ★ ★

Rodney Crowell sat next to Emmylou at the bar, joining in the spirited conversation. Rodney had a rock 'n' roll presence in his jeans and black leather jacket, and the feline alertness of an alley cat. The man was exhausted. He hadn't slept for nights, on a manic jag.

Rodney was the first musician Emmylou hired for the Hot Band. Emmylou remembered the day she had been listening to tapes, looking for songs for *Pieces of the Sky*. She had listened to tape after tape, song after song, all neatly calibrated to fit the formula of the Nashville sound. Then she heard Rodney's tape, and it was as if she had stumbled onto a treasure chest full of jewels of such brilliance that they shone out even in the darkness. They were, however, jewels that were ill set. The songs had lyrics not fully worked out, and melodies that somehow didn't fit the lyrics, but there was magnificent promise, and that was what Emmylou heard. Listening to him singing, she was sure that Rodney would be the star, not her.

Love is a flower with many blossoms. For twenty years Emmylou's love for Rodney was a constant thing. She loved his art, his craft, his wit, his creative daring, his gentle concern for her. The son of a construction worker, Rodney was brought up on the bad side of Houston, in a house with a leaky roof alongside the ship channel. His father had wanted a musical career but had given it up to make a living and raise a family. Rodney wanted to be a songwriter. He set out to Nashville and ended up sleeping in his car and on people's floors. He washed dishes and sang for tips, and found in his life there not poverty, but a wealth of experience.

In those early years of her career, Rodney performed hundreds of times with Emmylou in the Hot Band. Then Rodney had a crush on Emmylou, but so did half the world, or so it seemed: The cowboys in the honky-tonks. The hippies at Armadillo World Headquarters in Austin. The truck drivers in Baltimore. Emmylou had seemed to Rodney like a deer, so lithe, and gentle, and sensitive, with that nervous alertness, like a fawn hearing a footfall in a forest glen. All that he wanted, all that he cared for was to make her voice sound true and pure, rising above the discord of life. Emmylou had sung harmony for Gram, and that had been all she wanted, and now he sang for her, and for a while that was all he cared for.

After writing several classic songs for Emmylou, Rodney eventually left the Hot Band to pursue a solo career. His albums were well reviewed but sold poorly, and he made his living primarily as a songwriter. He married Johnny Cash's daughter, Rosanne, a singer/songwriter of notable talent. With Rodney producing, Rosanne achieved a stardom that she could hardly abide and that her husband desired with a desperate passion. Among the things they had in common was a drug problem. Rodney was a man who reeked of unhappiness, of a despair that rarely lifted, and out of that came song after song after song, and after thirteen years and three children, a divorce.

Rodney had his time of stardom in 1988 with his album *Diamonds and Dirt* and its unprecedented five number one hits. Stardom was not an honor, a degree on the wall. It was a condition that had to be nurtured daily. Rodney was no good at the endless routines of success. Since then his albums had been one commercial disappointment after another, until now at the age of forty-five, he had about played out all the chances the major labels gave an artist.

For the original Hot Band, Emmylou hired two members of Elvis's band, Glen D. on piano and James Burton on guitar. When Burton left the Hot Band, he was replaced by one of the few guitarists in the world who was his equal: Albert Lee. Albert had come along on this reunion tour, and shared his reminiscences with the others in the Burlington bar. One of the three or four greatest country guitarists in the world, Albert was British.

With his wiry body, mop of gray hair curled like wood shavings, Albert looked like one of Fagin's cohorts in *Oliver Twist*. The son of a construction worker, he had heard the exotic sounds of Nashville played occasionally on the BBC and had taught himself the guitar. At the age of fifty-one, he relished this chance to play once more with Emmylou.

The pedal steel provided the vibrating twang that helped to define country music. For this instrument Emmylou called Steve Fishell. Steve had not joined the band until 1980, but he had kept with it for almost a decade. No band in country music had ever had so many of its musicians go on to become prominent performers, session musicians, producers, and executives as had the Hot Band. Since leaving the band, Steve had become a producer, doing albums with performers such as Pam Tillis, Radney Foster, and Rosie Flores.

Emmylou's former band members formed a natural aristocracy of country musicians. Since some of her associates simply could not get away to join the tour, for the final two members of the band, Emmylou hired two new players who had worked with Rodney. It was costing the bass player Michael Rhodes several thousand dollars in lost income from session work to join Emmylou's band for a month. Michael understood the honor of playing with Emmylou. Michael was well over six feet tall. He had once been as hefty as a Notre Dame tackle, but he had dieted until now at the age of forty-one he was impossibly lean, looking like a physical manifestation of his long black bass guitar. He had shaved his head and wore a ring in his ear. Onstage he looked like a villain in a James Bond movie.

Vince Santoro, the drummer, could have been his sidekick in the film. He played an evil set of drums, but he did not have all the session work that Michael had. Vince had a new baby at home, and a bank account that was leaner than the other band members'. It was a mark of his respect for Emmylou that he had given up so much to come along.

Emmylou was one of the first country singers to perform extensively in Europe. She had always had a special love for playing the Irish capital. Set on a crossroads of the world, Dublin was like an ancient trading city, not of goods, its warehouses full of spices, damask cloth, and jewels, but of ideas and culture. The Irish had embraced country music, as had no other people outside the United States. For the most part, they had taken what was best and ignored what was mediocre. They played country music on the radio. They bought it on CD. And they danced to it.

On a clear spring evening, the Irish filled the Point on the outskirts of Dublin. As she always did before a performance,

Emmylou sat by herself in her dressing room. Waiting was always the worst part, waiting and then having to come bursting out on-stage ready to rip. It was bad enough on any tour, but this time it would be even worse with three major acts. In a corner stood her black guitar with its rose, looking as much a work of art as a musical instrument. Around the room hung Emmylou's stage outfits—stunning sequined skirts, embroidered cowboy shirts, richly patterned jackets. Her metamorphosis was only for her moments in the spotlight. Then she removed her skin of cowgirl glamour, leaving the theater or arena dressed in black shirt and pants.

The Irish audience had already listened to close to an hour of Marty's hillbilly rock and an equal quantity of Trisha's country pop ballads. Emmylou could tell as she walked onstage that it was as if the audience were sitting there overfed, realizing they had ordered a bit too much for dinner. They applauded vigorously, but it was not going to be one of those transcendent evenings, not this first evening of the tour.

Emmylou could tell that several members of the Hot Band were nervous. They played so loud that as high as her microphones were turned up, she had to strain sometimes. She chose the set list each evening, varying the songs. Usually the numbers worked together, the ballads and the country rockers playing into each other. That night, however, the songs seemed disjointed, fighting each other, and she left the stage disturbed at her performance. "I'm such a perfectionist," she said as she rode the band bus back to the Burlington. "This evening I saved the tree, but I cut down the forest."

Emmylou feared that she had stripped her voice. She was coming down with a cold, too, and the beginnings of a rasping cough. Over the years she had canceled a concert or two, but this time the consequences were unimaginable. Eight days from now she was supposed to record a live album and video in London at Royal Albert Hall. Everything was in place, but how could she do that with half a voice? And what if she couldn't continue at all? It would bring the tour to a halt, hurt the livelihoods of scores of people, not just Trisha and Marty and the band members but the road crews, the caterers, the promoters, everybody. It was unthinkable, but if she couldn't sing it would be over.

The group flew out of Dublin to Brussels. There, Emmylou and the Hot Band picked up the British bus that would carry them across much of Europe. By then, everyone knew that Emmylou was half sick, and the tour in jeopardy. Emmylou managed to get through the concert in Brussels, but it was Paris that mattered. All her career Emmylou had followed the same pattern on the long bus journeys, burrowing into her bunk, shrouded by a curtain, rarely rising until she was at her destination. It was her mini sickroom now, and she didn't look up until the bus arrived at Hôtel du Nord and she hurried inside to her room.

That evening Emmylou arrived by taxi at the venue, La Mutualité, as hundreds of Parisians stood waiting to enter. Inside in her dressing room, her exquisitely crafted guitar was there. Her beaded black tops and shimmering costume jewelry were there. Her hand-carved leather boots were there. Everything was there except her voice.

Emmylou's warm-up exercises didn't seem to work. Rodney joined her and sang along with her. She sounded flat. She knew it. Soon, everyone would know it. She decided that she would have to consider getting a cortisone shot. Maybe that would help her through, but that wouldn't do any good this evening.

As Emmylou talked in a barely audible voice, Trisha Yearwood's singing sounded from the stage through the walls of the dressing room. Trisha had an enormous voice. She treated it like a teenager with her first car, running it up and down, seeing how fast and hard and loud it would play. No matter how strongly Trisha sang, she would never have the shimmering sound of Emmy. Still, it was like the clarion call of youth sounding through to Emmylou's soul. When Trisha finished her set, she came up the hall. Emmylou opened her door, applauded, then covered her cough with her hand and retreated into her dressing room.

La Mutualité was less a theater than a large ballroom. There were no chairs, and the eighteen hundred auditors crowded the floor. The French are a race of connoisseurs. If it was not the largest crowd Emmylou had ever played to in Paris, it was a great and a learned one. They loved the joyous country rock, but most of all they loved the sad ballads. They were an ironic people, but it was this American culture of relentless optimism that had spawned this music of the darkest sadness. They enjoyed Marty and Trisha, but it was Emmylou they had come to hear.

"This is the twentieth anniversary of the Hot Band," Emmylou told the crowd. "And I thought we'd come over here where people still appreciate us." And so they did. A blind man in the back of the room beat out the rhythms with his cane, looking up toward the sound. On the sad ballads Emmylou's sound seemed to well up from some reservoir of pain, as deep as life itself. The French swayed back and forth to the songs, lost in the recesses of the melodies. Albert played his sparkling riffs, and Vince was stunning. The band played with great force and power almost to overwhelm her. But Emmylou knew only one way to perform, and that was to give everything and then some. She forgot her voice troubles and sang out with rich vitality and strength. She sang on and on and on, and anyone who left that evening feeling he had been cheated did not know how to count the common currency of life.

On the trip to the Hague, Glen D. got the band together in the back of the bus. Emmylou did not call him the heart and soul of the Hot Band as an honorific. He knew that something had to be done. Up in front, hidden away in her bunk, Emmylou was in trouble. Her voice was pretty much gone. She was living on tea and prayers. Glen D. was not a man for speeches great or little, but he said what had to be said.

"We're playing too hard and too loud, guys," Glen D. told the band. "We're not playing with Emmy. We're messing her up."

The band shared their responsibility for her ravaged voice. They were not some punk rock band out to win the world and show off their talents to rows of pretty women. There was a hard moral center to the musicians' world, and every man there knew that Glen D. was right. He would not have to speak out again.

That afternoon at the Hague, Emmylou took a cortisone shot. At the sound check, she told Rodney: "How would you like to do the show tonight?"

That evening Emmylou added some extra solos for Rodney

and chose songs that didn't require so much of her voice. It began as a strangely subdued performance for a strangely subdued audience, as if on some unconscious level, the Dutch understood what was going on. Emmylou sipped on a glass of water during Rodney's solos. When she sang, she sounded like an old 78 record, her upper register gone. To the side of the stage stood Trisha, realizing the magnitude of the problem, helping the sound technician get the right blend of microphones. The band itself played with exquisite restraint, as if they were trying to create a sound that would lift Emmylou above her troubles, but the voice was just not there.

"Take a song there, Rodney," Emmylou said, her voice sounding scalded.

"Bear with me a moment there, Emmylou," Rodney said, stepping to the microphone. "Emmylou has far too much integrity and class to say this, so I'm going to say it for her. Emmylou is suffering from very swollen vocal cords. It's hard work tonight and I want you to give her a big hand for puttin' out the effort to be here. It ain't easy."

"I'm a professional," Emmylou said, her voice barely audible.

When they came running off the stage at the end, the band members felt an immense sense of relief. It was not simply that Emmylou had soldiered through the evening but that the band had played with her. "I think we found ourselves," Rodney said to no one in particular.

Emmylou stood in the dark passageway leading to the stage at Royal Albert Hall. Since the tortured concert at the Hague, the band had traveled by bus twenty hours to Glasgow for a concert, and from there to Birmingham for another performance, and then on to London. All four days Emmylou had been nursing her voice for this evening. She knew that behind the theater sat a sound truck to record the concert for a live album. Up the stairs and into the glare of the spotlight stood not simply a full theater but a series of video cameras. She had chosen an elegant chanteuse look for this concert, a black strapless dress, a six-inch-wide silver belt, and a leopard-spotted mini-shawl. Her hair and makeup were done to perfection, and she looked like a gorgeous queen of music. The only question was, would her voice betray her?

Emmylou walked onstage to an ovation. The Royal Albert Hall is one of the legendary theaters of the world, a tiered golden circle where many of the world's great artists have appeared. "We played here I guess in '77 or '78," Emmylou said, her gaze sweeping the thirty-three-hundred-seat hall. "Does anyone remember? I know this place sounds better and we look better. Everything improves with age."

Emmylou sang the old songs, upbeat country rock and sad country ballads, and after a while the video cameras didn't even seem there any longer. Up on the stage, Rodney, Steve, and Glen D. all had the same thought. They might never be up here again, and they better enjoy the moment. After a while, all that existed was Emmylou's music. On some numbers her voice was not all there, but it was close to a miracle that she could sing as she did. Her song list worked perfectly, a subtle meshing of mood.

The British audience loved the up-tempo songs, but it was the sad ballads that resonated the most through the great theater. Even when she was young and her beauty shone brighter than the rhinestones on her cowgirl suits, Emmylou was happiest singing sad songs. She would sing upbeat country rock, but it was the sad ballads she owned and the sad ballads that owned her.

Over the years she had entered deeper and deeper into the dark sad songs. It was as if she had been dancing in the entrance of a cave, then darting back to the light, venturing deeper and deeper, and running out again, until she could no longer see a way out, and the world that lay ahead appeared as black as the world behind.

"I lied about only doing old American music," she said when she was most of the way through her set. "I'm going to do one from my fast becoming old last album."

"Prayer in Open D" was one of the few songs Emmylou had written. It was the kind of theme that was almost never heard in American popular culture. Emmylou lived in a society of blame. There was always someone else responsible for your own unhappiness or failure. There was always someone who for the price of switching a television channel, buying a book, or reading a magazine would tell you it's not your fault. Most thrice-divorced women of her age had a litany of excuses to pass out for their aloneness. They blamed their state on everything from the abysmal condition of the male species to parental abuse, on everything but themselves.

In Nashville, Emmylou lived with her widowed mother and two daughters, twenty-four-year-old Hallie and fifteen-year-old Meghann. When Emmylou was not out on the road, she often walked Meghann to high school. She did so not because the teenager required supervision but as a renewed assertion of a mother's love. She knew that she had been an inattentive mother, especially to her oldest daughter. All those years Emmylou had been off on tours for weeks on end, mothering an occasional duty fitted between engagements. Hallie had grown up troubled and Emmylou blamed herself.

Emmylou was no worse than many working mothers, no more culpable than other mothers and fathers consumed with careers and pleasures and not their children's lives. She was a woman of exquisite sensitivity, her emotions laid bare. She felt her failures, felt them as deeply as her successes. Emmylou looked back on her life, and all the pain and loss and hurt and saw only herself.

> There's a valley of sorrow in my soul
> Where every night I hear the thunder roll
> Like the sound of a distant gun
> Over all the damage I have done.

Three small spotlights, diamond bright, punctuated the darkness with streams of light. Emmylou's voice sounded ripped, as if it had been torn on the jagged corners of life. The song was full of searing sadness, great cascading torrents of tears, the words wrenched from her, drawn from some deep place of pain and loneliness. The video cameras stopped moving along their tracks. Backstage Phil stood frozen. One of the technicians shuddered and looked stageward, as if he had been jolted into some desperate revelation. Stagehands, hearing the song for the first time, dropped their tools and turned their ear to the song. Even the guards left off kibitzing and began to listen.

And the shadows filling up this land
Are the ones I built with my own hand.
There is no comfort from the cold
Of this valley of sorrow in my soul.

As Emmylou and the Hot Band left London two days later, they felt an incalculable burden lift from them. Emmylou's voice had held up, and the pressure of the live album was over. They were loose and together as they traveled across Europe to give concerts in Stockholm, Copenhagen, Hamburg, Frankfurt, Zurich, and Milan, city after city, country after country, gig after gig, this merry band of brothers and sister.

Then, finally, it was ending. In Madrid, they had a free day before their concert in the Spanish capital, and a celebratory dinner together. Emmylou liked Trisha enough to invite her to come along, and the group trudged down from the Melia Madrid Hotel along Princess Street to a paradilla restaurant, specializing in roasts. The owner had prepared a long table in the cellar room. The musicians began drinking Spanish red as if it were a medicinal tonic guaranteed to ward off all the ills of life. Emmylou almost never drank, but tonight she emptied her glass each time almost as soon as the waiter filled it.

"More wine and bring on the dancing girls," Emmylou said, in as close to a shout as she permitted herself.

"This evening is right out of *Clockwork Orange*," Rodney declared, gazing up and down at his sodden companions.

"All right, you can't have more red until you finish your white wine," Emmylou said, shaking her head authoritatively. Then she turned to Trisha, who sat at the far end of the table, slightly apart from the group. "What kind of material are you looking for, songs?"

"I'm not looking for things that are going to be number one," Trisha asserted. "I'm not going to do that."

It was almost a sacrilege for a singer with Trisha's possibilities to speak this way. For a moment the musicians sobered up and listened. They all knew the story of how Trisha had become a star with her first big single, "She's in Love with the Boy." It had become practically an anthem for teenage girls.

"I remember when we played the second album for the people at MCA," Trisha continued. "And everybody is sitting in the control room and Scott [Scott Borchetta, senior vice president of national promotion] says, 'Well, I'm the one to stand out here and say, I'm sorry but I don't hear another 'She's in Love with the Boy.' And I said, 'You're damn right you don't. We did that already.'"

"Been there. Done that," Emmylou said, toasting Trisha and nodding her head in agreement.

"That song was such a mainstream country single that everybody thought I was going to be the new Reba McEntire," Trisha continued, fully warmed up to her task of trashing the narrowly commercial sensibilities of Nashville. "They thought I was going to be cranking that out all the time."

"I had the head of Warner country tell me I was going to destroy my career with *Roses in the Snow*," Emmylou interjected, telling one of her favorite music business tales. "I believed him when he said it would be a commercial disaster. What happened was that it was my biggest success. Even if it had been a commercial disaster, it would have been worth it down the line."

That was enough to write an end to melancholy tales of Nashville for the evening. Emmylou was listing to port, propping her head up with her hand. Phil knew how rare it was to see Emmylou like this. He could only remember twice, once holding her on Sunset Boulevard, and another time in New Orleans. The lady couldn't drink, and this evening she was proving it.

The wine had opened Emmylou's vault of memories, and she was suddenly back at high school in Virginia. "I was the valedictorian," she gently boasted. "I had a 4.0 average five years straight."

"And never had a date!" Phil shouted.

"And I would have given it up for one fucking date." Emmylou hardly ever swore, and she spoke the word as if she had just discovered profanity and found it a new delight.

"She did play the saxophone," Phil said, as if that made up for her lack of social life.

"I had no practical knowledge of anything," Emmylou said morosely. "I didn't learn a goddamn thing."

After the lengthy dinner, the group piled into several taxicabs and drove through a series of twisting, tiny streets to a country music bar. They were like missionaries arriving in some remote region the first time and stumbling into a group of believers who somehow had learned about the true faith. When they walked in, Rodney's song "Leaving Louisiana in the Broad Daylight" was playing on the stereo.

"They've got Emmylou's picture on the women's room door," Phil said after having cased the bar. "You know you've arrived when your picture is on the shithouse door."

From the bar Emmylou called a former band member, Jon Randall, at a radio station in Seattle, where he was promoting his first album. It had not gone well. "I hate those radio officials," Emmylou exclaimed as she drank the cheap champagne the bar owner brought the group. "They can't create anything that isn't rigid."

"They hate us and we hate them," Rodney said, turning away from pitching coins with Trisha, after having taken away most of her change.

In the background, Emmylou's album, *Live at the Ryman,* was playing. "Please play somebody except for me," Emmylou said despondently.

Emmylou took a puff on her Sweet Afton cigarette and turned back to her drink. "Everybody thinks I have so much money." Her eyes swept the room as if the culprits included even these anonymous Spaniards. "I wanted this guy to play for my birthday. See. This singer. And he wanted two thousand dollars. Two thousand dollars. So we played a record. Just as good."

Emmylou looked down at her drink and leaned across the table. "I'm at the bottom of the heap."

"Everybody admires you," Trisha said softly. "Everybody. You're the queen. Everybody thinks you're it."

"I'm a hard woman. A hard woman. And I'm at the fucking bottom of the heap."

★ ★ ★

Emmylou had a killer hangover. So did everyone in the band. Glen D. had an added souvenir of the long evening: a mysteriously swollen toe. He presumed that he had stubbed it somewhere during that extravagant night, the wine sufficient to deaden any feeling. Now he had a limp and a throbbing pain and had spent the day in bed, staring halfheartedly at Spanish television.

Phil, in one of his frequent bursts of excessive solicitousness, had agreed to let the band members check out of the hotel and go ahead to the theater. He would bring their luggage himself. The moment Phil saw the tiny bus that the promoter had hired to take Emmylou and the Hot Band out to the venue, he realized he had made a mistake. By the time the porters had jammed the luggage on the bus, there was hardly room for any passengers, much less Emmylou nursing a hangover, her mood as black as her dress.

Emmylou had hoped to relax before the performance, but the driver had no idea where the venue was located. The bus wandered from street to street, the ancient mariner of transports, crisscrossing the ravaged regions of the city. After several miles of seemingly aimless meandering, he stopped a police officer and asked directions. The bus started up again, moving through impoverished areas of Madrid, past gypsy caravans lining the roadway, fires in trash bins illuminating the dusk.

The old bus heaved its way up one hill laboriously, painfully, wheezing upward, finally reaching the summit. There far below, the driver pointed to a strange edifice that did not look so much like a building as the pathetic leavings of half a dozen architectural mistakes hauled here and set down in the gray dirt. There were multicolored tubes rising to the darkening sky, rooms jutting off to right and left, and immense steamy windows, all surrounded by hundreds of cars.

The driver pulled the bus around to the back of the building known as the "Aqualung." Emmylou hurried into the building, wending her way among garbage cans and immense trunks and boxes, finding her way to her dressing room. The dank cement basement room looked less like a dressing room than a cell where criminals were locked up to die of pneumonia or tuberculosis long before their terms were up.

Emmylou needed time to prepare her voice and her mind, but this evening she had to dress hurriedly in the chill room and walk up to the stage. She had appeared in some strange venues, but had rarely performed in a setting as weird as this one. There in the midst of the discotheque floor and on risers stood over a thousand rowdy Spaniards, some of them wearing cowboy hats and western garb. Dampness permeated the air from the indoor swimming pool.

"We had a night off last night, and so we're ready for you!" Emmylou shouted. There was no video crew here tonight, no recording being made, nothing but country music in a crazy homemade Spanish honky-tonk. All the doubts of the night before, all the mournful melancholy, all the regret, were gone now, as her voice sounded out pure and true. Trisha's musicians could have left, but they stood on a side balcony, listening with awe and admiration, applauding as loud and as hard as any of the Spaniards. They had heard these songs scores of times before, and they knew that they had never heard them played so well, so free. Even in the saddest of the ballads, there was the happiness of songs sung right and good, and in the country rock there was pure exhilaration.

This evening singing here Emmylou didn't care that there didn't seem any room on radio left for the dark sad songs that she loved to sing. Emmylou knew that the miracle was that deep true songs were still sung and recorded, and if one didn't make a dollar singing them, then one made a dime. If someone heard them and was moved, that was not only enough, that was everything. Emmylou was not leaving this sweet old world, this world full of the wondrous and the inexplicable, not least of which was a crazy Spanish honky-tonk on the outskirts of Madrid.

As Emmylou sang this night she knew that she might never again travel with Rodney and Glen D. and Phil and Albert and Steve and Vince and Michael. She might never again go out on the road with a full band. And on and on she sang, on into the Spanish night. The audience called her back again and again, and they would have called her back until the first light of dawn. Encores could not go on forever, and so finally she stood there on that stage

in the Spanish night and sang a Buck Owens song that back in 1976
was her first number one hit:

> Together again my tears have stopped falling
> The long lonely nights are now at an end.
> The key to my heart you hold in your hand
> And nothing else matters 'cause we're together again.

At Fan Fair, the Tower Record Store had many of Emmylou's
albums for sale, but most of the buyers were more interested in
the stars of the hot young country music of the nineties than a
singer whose first album was released two decades ago. There was
no booth for her fan club, no homage to her name, but the great
tribute was the lives of most of the women artists of country music,
and many of the men. She had proven that a woman could stand
alone in the spotlight, singing what she wanted to sing, how she
wanted to sing it, and there was no young female singer on that
great stage at Fan Fair who was not in her debt. She had proven
that country music could be hip and young while remaining true to
its deepest roots, a lesson that in all the clang of commerce often
went unheard. She loved country music as life itself, and that too
was a challenge to those who had come to Nashville attracted more
by the scent of opportunity than the sound of the music.

Emmylou felt sometimes that country music had left her. But
every time a woman artist sang a heartfelt song, her music was still
alive. And every time country music played the old songs not with
calculated sentimentality but spirited new interpretations, her
musical philosophy was still alive. As the fans wandered the fairgrounds seeking autographs and attending the label shows, few of
them thought of Emmylou Harris, but as long as the music stayed
true to its roots, she was still here.

6

~

"Fresh Horses"

Scott Hendricks sat on the railing at the back of the stage during the Capitol Nashville show. Scott was six feet, two inches tall, a lanky sort wearing faded jeans, a white short-sleeve shirt, and a close-cropped beard. He was the most unassuming of men. He looked not like the president of a record label but a struggling songwriter or would-be manager who had used all his clout to get an onstage pass. Although many other music industry people whispered animatedly, ignoring the performances onstage, Scott sat quietly, often looking at the floorboards. The president of Capitol Nashville had a strangely disengaged, quizzical manner as if things were happening around him that nothing prepared him for in life or nature.

Scott was a small-town Oklahoma boy. He had been brought up to take a person at his word, to stand tall and firm against the winds that blew across the plains of life, and to speak the truth. Those were virtues in Clinton, Oklahoma (population 8,000) in the sixties, but they weren't always virtues in Nashville in 1996.

Scott had been president of the company for a little more than a year, during which he had received one dispiriting lesson after another about human beings and their ways. The thirty-eight-year-old executive had thought he knew what he was getting into, but Jimmy Bowen, his predecessor, had left Scott with a sad muddle. One of Scott's first acts was to change the name that Bowen had given the label, Liberty, back to Capitol Nashville. That did not change one iota the realities at the label. It was as if the day Scott closed on his dream house, he discovered termites, rotting beams, and the foundation about to fall into the cellar.

Not the least of the problems was Garth's enormous contract, which made it difficult for the label to show a profit. Beyond that, it was often not easy working day-to-day with the greatest-selling country artist of all time. Instead, Garth had cast a pall upon the label. Even this week at Fan Fair, Garth's people had caused some more embarrassment for Capitol Nashville. Garth was so alienated from the label that his staff hadn't even bothered calling to alert them that the singer was showing up at the fairgrounds; thus, Scott's publicity department had appeared pathetically out of the loop.

The problems at Capitol Nashville would have been enough to try any man, but that was nothing compared to his other loss. When Scott had taken over as the new label head, he had been engaged to the country star Faith Hill. Faith was a small-town girl from Star, Mississippi, with a voice that sounded as pure as her all-American country girl image. Faith appeared a throwback to a time when the virtue of women was undisputed, and they stood on a pedestal far above the sordid pursuits of men. It did not matter that she was a divorced woman of twenty-seven; she seemed virginal and innocent. Faith was her name, and faith she looked to be. She sang her share of mindless ditties but still projected this image of a woman of immense spiritual qualities and virtues.

Scott was one of the most successful producers in Nashville, but to head Capitol Nashville he had given up producing artists on other labels, including Brooks and Dunn and John Michael Montgomery. Faith was the only outside artist he insisted that he be allowed to keep producing. That was the least of the signs of his devotion to her. Anyone who saw the couple together realized that Scott loved Faith with schoolboy devotion, relishing her every word and gesture, seeing in her the embodiment of everything he ever wanted in a woman. He had left his wife and marriage to start anew, and his new life was with Faith.

Scott had produced no one who was more of a perfectionist than Faith. If he hadn't been so in love with her, he might have kept another outside artist to produce while at Capital Nashville. He had been hurt last year by all the rumors about Faith and Troy Aikman, the Dallas Cowboys' quarterback. Aikman had even telephoned Scott when he was in the studio producing Brooks and Dunn, and told him it wasn't true. Scott believed in Faith. He trusted her. Thus, he accepted the two tickets to the Super Bowl game between the Cowboys and the Buffalo Bills that Aikman offered him, and forgot the whole business.

Early in 1996 Faith had gone off on tour with Tim McGraw, one of the hottest acts of young country. Scott knew that was an artist's life, and he had no qualms. First began the whispered rumors about Faith's affair with Tim. Then came the knowing guffaws from the gossipmongers along Music Row. Finally, the story made the papers. Faith was wearing Scott's engagement ring, and learning about the betrayal was a blow sufficient to have doubled him up in pain. But that was not what so devastated him, nor that he was being joked about behind his back. No, it was the manner in which he felt he had been betrayed, as if all his love and devotion had meant nothing. It seemed Faith's love for him had been just an illusion, an endless stage show. If he had been a different man in a different place, he might have packed his bags and moved a thousand miles away, where he would not be so haunted by her memory, but Nashville was his life.

Nashville trafficked in emotions. People led with their feelings. Men cried the way only women did in other places, tearing up over a song or a story or a sad memory. Scott made a living in part listening to love songs and producing them so that millions could hear them. He could not turn on CMT without seeing her there so beautiful, seemingly exuding every virtue. He could not listen to country radio without hearing her latest single he had produced. In

April when he went out to the Academy of Country Music (ACM) Awards show in Los Angeles, he could not help being there when she performed.

Faith was gone. And there was a merciless quality to the way she publicly exploited her new love, kissing McGraw onstage as if she had no respect or even memory of Scott's love. Still there was part of Scott that could not give up. For months he was obsessed with her, with the idea that somehow she might come back, somehow they might work it out. They had had such good times.

In November, Faith and Scott had flown to Dallas with Reba McEntire and Narvel Blackstock, her husband and manager. Reba had sung the National Anthem at sold-out Texas Stadium before the Dallas Cowboys–San Francisco 49ers football game. Over the years, Scott had been with many great Nashville stars, but he had never seen anyone get the kind of reception Reba received. It was as if everyone thought of her as their friend and wanted a hello or a handshake or a glimpse of that famous smile.

Flying back to Music City, Reba had been in one of her talking moods. She remembered the bad old days with her first husband, Charlie Battles, and how he and his sons had put her down, dismissing her as nothing but a woman.

"I had sung the National Anthem that day too, at this rodeo where Charlie had won some prize money and the boys had roped too," Reba said, settling into her story. "We were comin' home and now the boys say, 'Mom, what did you do? We roped and Dad, he was ridin', and Mom, you did nothin'.' I told 'em, 'I sang the National Anthem.' And they said, 'Why, you didn't get nothin' for that.' I told 'em they were wrong, 'I made a hundred dollars for that.' That made the boys' heads spin. The boys started singin' 'Oh, say can you see.'"

Scott saw how far Reba had come from those days. She had her own jet planes, a loving husband, and the biggest career of any woman in country music. It was just possible that you could have it all, just possible, Reba and Narvel, Faith and Scott.

Scott had been flying a lot recently. As his plane soared thirty-seven thousand feet high above Oklahoma, Scott looked down. There lay the wheatfield that he had plowed straight and true as a teenager while sitting on a big tractor listening to country music on the cassette deck. And there outlined in the field of wheat were the words "FRESH HORSES" and "GARTH" so big that he could just make them out way up here. The 350-acre field was in the flight path from Nashville to Los Angeles. Scott wanted the pilots of the great commercial jets pointing out the title of Garth's new album spelled out there in hundred-yard-long letters, pointing it out just the way they did the Mississippi River and other great monuments. It was a terrific idea, or so he had thought, but there was a drought down below, and Scott could hardly make out the lettering. He made a mental note that when he got back to Nashville he would have to call about that. Maybe they could color the wheat, or cut out the lines, do something.

Anyone would have figured that Scott and Garth would have gotten along famously. They were both Oklahomans, and Oklahomans watched out for one another. They didn't have that often strutting pride of their Texas neighbors, but they had their own belief in themselves and their state. The heat and the wind were enough to blow a lot of people right out of the state. Those who stayed, survived, and succeeded thought of themselves as a special breed.

The two men had grown up only fifty miles from each other, though Scott was six and a half years older. Their two high schools had played against each other in football. Scott's father was an Oklahoma highway patrolman, his mother an assistant to the school principal, a middle-class background not that much different from Garth's. Scott's mother was the great lover of country music in the family, as was Garth's mother. Both men grew up loving music, not simply country but rock, seeing no reason why a person couldn't appreciate both. And both men attended Oklahoma State University in Stillwater.

Scott was a consummate commercial producer, and Garth was the biggest-selling solo artist of all time. There was something else that made it seem that they would make a natural alliance. Garth had just ended a tortured relationship with the former label president; to the singer almost anyone had to be better than Jimmy

Bowen. As for Scott, he had extraordinary instincts for what the people out there beyond Nashville liked; and he knew that beyond everything else they liked Garth. He was mindful that Garth represented about 90 percent of the label's sales. To succeed at Capitol Nashville, he would have to maintain Garth at a high level.

Just as he was taking over, Scott was startled to read an interview with Garth in the *Hollywood Reporter.* "I wanted Joe Mansfield to run the company but they chose Scott Hendricks and Walt Wilson instead," Garth said. "I'll just have to put my faith in the fact that Charles Koppelman [chairman and CEO of EMI Records Group North America] and Jim Fifield [EMI Music Worldwide head] made the right choice."

Garth had pushed for his old friend. When Scott was named president/CEO, he had met with Mansfield to discuss the marketing executive coming aboard as executive vice president/general manager. But the new label president believed that Joe wanted too much money. Instead, Scott decided to go with Walt Wilson, who had been part of Tony Brown and Bruce Hinton's team at MCA Nashville. That was all decided now, and Scott couldn't understand why Garth would say such a thing. Garth was a man who was never more calculating than when he seemed the most spontaneous. And Scott interpreted his quotation as probably Garth's idea of a greeting.

The first time Garth came in to meet the new team at Capitol Nashville, Scott had every reason to make the singer feel at home. Scott greeted the biggest-selling American recording artist pleasantly, but not as if he was trying to ingratiate himself with the singer. Scott was not a flatterer in a business where flattery was the common language. One reason Scott had taken this position was that he was tired of some artists' egos. He understood all that performers went through, but he was fed up with the few prima donnas of country. He was a man grounded in modesty, and it rankled him to have to kowtow to other human beings.

Ego. Ego. Ego. Scott was no psychologist. For years he had puzzled over just what the word meant. He went to the library and looked up the word in books. None of them made sense to him. He went to bookstores and walked up and down the aisles looking for a tome that would help him understand. None of the definitions did it either. Then one day he was attending a seminar and the speaker said, "The definition of ego is real simple. It's the anesthetic that dulls the pain of stupidity." Scott shook his head and thought to himself, "That's it."

"We will bust our butts for you, Garth," Scott said earnestly. "I'm the kind of person that calls a spade a spade. And if there's a problem, I would rather have it up on top of the table than kick each other in the knees under the table."

Scott wanted to make sure Garth understood. "You know, Garth, if your shit stinks, I'm gonna tell you," Scott said, believing that candor was the highest respect he could show the singer.

Garth was a man of a country civility. Nobody spoke to him this way. Scott was not looking for difficulties with Garth, but Garth sensed that this man's nose was already sniffing at a foul odor. No artist had more of a sense of occasion than Garth. From Scott he expected if not deference, then at least the clear signs of respect. He did not hear that from Scott, not loud enough anyway, and as he puzzled over his words, he found nuances that Scott had not put there.

"I don't believe in you guys," Garth told the new leadership team in Scott's office. "And from what I understand, you guys are not very good."

Garth was only repeating to Scott's face what he was saying behind his back. It was a moment crying out for Scott to praise Garth profusely, to stroke that ego that Scott thought was "the anesthetic that dulls the pain of stupidity." But that was not Scott. He was not about to curry Garth's favor. Instead, Scott talked about the entire company and the other artists and their role in the company.

This lesson in philosophical modesty did not sit well with Garth and his associates. He was the franchise at Capitol. It sounded to them as if the label was trying to back away from the man who had brought them almost all their success. Walt sat in on the meeting as well. As the new number two executive listened to Garth, Walt felt that he was watching a brilliantly calculated performance. Garth was positioning himself as the eight-hundred-pound gorilla who got whatever he wanted to eat whenever he wanted to eat it. That was the message he was sending out to Scott and Walt.

Scott had been in his new office for only a month when he flew out to Los Angeles to take part in a ceremony giving Garth his own star on the celebrated Walk of Fame. His greatest-hits album had already sold six million copies, but there were still about four million sitting around, and the sales had slowed. Garth used the occasion to bury the master of THE HITS, though the label had other tapes of all the songs. Making a limited edition out of ten million copies of an album was just the sort of hokey idea that Garth would probably once have disdained, but he happily dug a hole and watched the following week as the sales doubled, pushing the album back to the number one spot on Billboard's country album chart.

Scott knew that it would take months and months to get up a new roster of acts. The success of his first year would rest almost entirely on Garth's new album, scheduled to be released late in 1995. Scott didn't pretend he had any great taste for the edgier, more daring sides of country music. He did have great instincts for hits. He thought that he might have something to contribute to Garth. At least he figured his new A&R staff could shoot possible songs over to Allen Reynolds, Garth's producer, at his studio, Jack's Tracks. Scott soon learned that Garth wanted no help from Capitol Nashville, and told them nothing about his new album.

Garth was not the only problem Scott was having with artists. Up onstage the tenor John Berry was performing. Scott had gone over to greet Berry when he came onstage, but all the hugs and smiles aside, there was a certain mistrust there.

When Scott took over, Berry had the best potential of any of the other acts already on the label. The tenor was no longer a bright new young act, but not a superstar, no-man's-land in the new Nashville. Scott loved Berry's voice. As he sat there, he mouthed the words to a cut from Faces, his new album.

Just before Berry went into the studio to cut the album, Scott had been talking to the singer. "John, would you consider cutting a couple of songs in a lower key?" Scott asked. "You know, some of the comments that we have gotten back from radio and research is that at times when you get up in the stratosphere, it's not as appealing as it could be."

John nodded his assent, but soon afterwards Scott learned that the singer was writhing in anger at the suggestion that his singing was not masculine. Performers often masked their insecurities by trying to sing high, and Berry did sound on occasion like a *castrato*. When the story of the tenor's anger was told along Music Row, some argued that if Scott had tempered his remarks with a modicum of subtlety and shrewdness, Berry might not have been upset at all. Others believed that Berry was a man of such obtuseness that Scott had to bludgeon him with his words to make him understand. The result, however, was that on this new album the singer did not attempt to challenge Pavarotti.

Scott was trying to put together a new team at Capitol Nashville. As his model, the new Capitol Nashville president looked to Arista/Nashville, the label run by another Oklahoman, Tim DuBois. Scott loved Tim like a big brother. He envisioned the day that he and Tim would sit on the porch in their rockers and talk about the good old days in Nashville.

The two men had met back at Oklahoma State. On the very day he arrived at college, Scott had gotten a part-time job in the recording studio at the audiovisual center. Scott was supposed to be recording professors' lectures, but he talked his boss into letting him record music after hours. Scott was a good enough guitar player in high school to have been twice named the All State Guitar Player for stage bands. At college, when he heard the playing of another would-be professional guitarist, Greg Jennings, Scott hit what he called "the reality wall." He had the sense to realize that his abilities lay elsewhere.

Scott was introduced to a young accounting professor, Tim DuBois, who fancied himself a songwriter as well. The two men started cutting demo tapes at the studio. Both men had good ears for a song, and Scott had a magical way with the soundboard, mixing the sounds on the modest equipment. Tim made the decision to move to Music City and try his luck as a songwriter first. Scott followed, with his bachelor's degree in engineering and architecture in hand. In Nashville he made a living as an engineer, slowly building his reputation as one of the best in town.

Some producers in Nashville are no more than glorified engineers, sitting in the studio tweaking up a song or two, walking out with their percentage. Some engineers are full of such creative concern that they rightfully should be called coproducer and given a cut of the royalties. Scott was a brilliant engineer, with a superb sense of the subtlety of sound. He was a musical nerd, at his best sitting there by himself after the artist had gone, working the soundboard, making it into a musical instrument, his fingers moving lightninglike up and down the switches.

Scott was so good at what he did that it was almost inevitable that he would move up to producing. He got his first chance when Tim was putting together a harmony-driven country rock band, Restless Heart. Scott figured the group was good, since it included the same Greg Jennings whose stunning guitar playing had ended part of Scott's musical dreams. Tim and Scott shared coproducing credits, but Scott was in the studio every day doing the nitty-gritty work. Restless Heart's gold albums convinced Scott he could produce. Tim had such belief in his Oklahoma friend that when he became head of Arista/Nashville, he brought Scott in to coproduce the label's first artist, Alan Jackson. In 1990, Scott introduced Ronnie Dunn, the winner of the Marlboro Talent Contest, to Tim. The record executive put Ronnie Dunn with another singer/songwriter, Kix Brooks, and a record-shattering duo was born. Scott went on to coproduce the phenomenally successful albums of Brooks and Dunn. By the time he took over the reins of Capitol Nashville, Scott had for four years running made *Billboard*'s listing of the five most successful country producers.

When Scott met with the top EMI executives at the Vanderbilt Plaza Hotel to discuss the presidency of their Nashville label, he said he didn't want the job. He had been wooed before by other labels, and he told the New York executives the obvious truth. He had no experience running a record company. Scott had such a glorious commercial track record as a producer that the top executives thought it didn't matter. The timing was right, and they made him such a sweet deal that he signed on.

At the label, Scott was painfully realizing how different this job was from everything he had known. When he walked out of the studio as a producer, he knew what he had accomplished. Here it was all paperwork, personnel, words, and spin. He wasn't a person who would flatter others when he didn't mean it. He wasn't a person who would lie to get ahead. He wasn't good at greasing his way out of difficult situations, sidling away from people and situations he found difficult.

Scott was what some would call a man of honor and others derided as a person of painful, pitiful naïveté. This was *his* label now, but the staff were either old Bowen people, new hires brought in mainly by others, or most crucially five executives that Walt had brought with him and put in top positions.

Scott was finding it wrenching trying to bring together the old team with the new, getting everybody to work together. Bowen had a grandiose operation going. Scott had to downsize. He hated calling in these employees and telling them the bad news, but he saw that as part of his responsibility. Some of them cried. And sometimes he cried too. And that was only part of his sad duties.

Under Bowen the label was top-heavy with artists too. That was part of Scott's predecessor's approach, to push up the label's market share by the sheer force of product, while keeping a whole second tier of artists waiting with hopes of having their albums go out into the marketplace. It came to Scott to tell the artists that they were losing their deals. Twenty-three times he met with artists, telling them that they were no longer on the label. He looked them in the eyes and told them the news, knowing that most of them would never get another major label deal. Nothing was harder than that, and sometimes he let the artist sit in his outer office until he couldn't put off the meeting any longer.

Scott was trying to put together a real team at Capitol Nashville, a boutique operation similar to what Tim had done at Arista. Even the key new people were not Scott's people. They were Walt's people. Scott wanted people to be happy comrades working together, but he sensed that people were afraid to be frank with him. They treated him as if they feared to speak straight with him. He was trying to change that, but it was a slow business.

Scott was still out there producing several of his new label's artists, often working until two in the morning. He was coproducing

Suzy Bogguss. Suzy was at a point in her career that if her album didn't make it, she might be over. Scott understood that and took that responsibility with the height of seriousness. Scott was also working with Trace Adkins, his first newly signed act. Both artists meant enormously to Scott. He would leave the studio after working on their albums, and instead of feeling satisfaction at work well done, he was already thinking about another new problem back at the office.

Garth was an enormous presence, dominating everything at the label. His new album might sell ten million copies or more, and the whole company had to be ready to roll like an army. There had to be time to press millions of CDs. It would require an enormous marketing campaign, planned out to the last detail. First, however, there had to be an album. Week after week, in the summer of 1995, Scott kept hearing different things. The album was coming. The album wasn't coming. Much of what he was hearing was secondhand. Garth hardly had anything to do with the label. Scott would have liked to pick up the phone and talk to Garth's managers, but nobody had replaced his previous management. The biggest-selling singer in the world was operating with less of a team than many new acts.

Garth was full of paranoia, fearing with a certain justification that everyone wanted something from him, and his job in life was to prevent them from getting anything but what he wanted to give. He knew that he needed new managers, but never again would he find people who cared about him the way Bob and Pam had cared. Bob had mortgaged his house and Pam had mortgaged her life. "So what do I do?" he mused. "My problem is that with anybody I go to now, I'm never going to go to bed at night convinced that they're not here because the money's good."

The anticipation for the album was enormous, not only at the label but in the entire industry. Country sales were slowly declining, and the man who had started the cycle upward was the man who could get things moving in the right direction again. Garth believed that "if in the next five years things go south for country music, I'll probably get the blame for it. Which is cool. You gotta take the good with the bad."

Garth had not had an album of new music for two years. The audience might be waiting with pent-up desire for Garth's newest songs, or they might have grown tired of him. Garth had merciless pressure on him to come through commercially and artistically. Everything Garth did had to be bigger than anyone else. Garth said that he listened to the incredible total of 4,700 songs on demo tapes.

Garth went out to Pat Alger's house to write. They sat out on Pat's porch and tried to write a good song. Those previous hits had been so enormous that Pat had earned about a million dollars in royalties on each one. A million dollars. They sat on the swing and talked. A million dollars. Back before, it had all just come to them, and then they had gone out to lunch. A million dollars. They talked and threw out ideas, but nothing sounded any good. A million dollars. Garth got up and left in his pickup truck, and Pat sat there wondering what it would take to bring back the innocence, or if it would ever come back at all.

By the middle of the summer, Garth had found only two or three songs he considered worthy to put on his album. It seemed impossible that his album would come out in 1995. Then suddenly, he was the recipient of what he told the media was a "miracle." He began to write, and in the end cowrote an unprecedented eight of the ten songs on the album. He discarded all but one song by Nashville's songwriters. In doing so, he was telling Nashville that *his* songs were better than the best that Music City's most talented writers could create.

When it got down to the deadline for the album, Scott called Garth's producer. "What's the story, Allen?" Scott asked, always cutting to the chase.

"Well, we're one song short," Allen replied in his languid Arkansas manner. "We've cut the song but he's still polishing the lyrics."

"Well, it's like two or three days away is our absolute outside window," Scott countered. "And I told Garth this."

"Well, he left here today, and I told Garth that I thought this song is important enough and good enough to warrant holding back this album deadline if it's not right."

"Oh, Allen, we can't be late," Scott replied urgently. "There's a full-page ad in *USA Today* setting the release date. Have you seen it?"

Allen saw the matter as a struggle between art and commerce. Garth liked to send signals out to Capitol that he was in control. He, however, was not an artist living in a garret working on a painting that would sell at his leisure. He was a singer who had won the most lucrative contract in the history of country music because of his unprecedented commercial success. Whether he liked it or not, he was part of a giant machine that could not work properly unless Garth turned in his album.

For weeks the executives had been meeting with Garth's people to discuss the marketing plan. Garth had brought in Joe Mansfield to add his expertise to the mix. Joe was the General Patton of marketing executives, believing that you should bombard the marketplace with your message, overwhelming it, creating an excitement that fed on itself. That was extremely expensive, and the sides spiritedly discussed how much money would be spent.

Garth's new contract didn't give the label much incentive to throw dollars around. Moreover, the more Walt looked at the terms of Garth's contract, the more Walt realized that it would be extraordinarily difficult to make a profit at the label. They needed this album to work enormously well. The two sides agreed to a budget of four and a half million dollars to be spent in the album's first four months, leading up to the beginning of Garth's monumental, record-breaking three-year American and international tour.

When Garth finally delivered the ten songs of *Fresh Horses* to Capitol Nashville, Scott and Walt listened to the music for the first time. Garth had insisted on releasing the album on November 21. That was the same date the Beatles' enormously anticipated double album was being released by Garth's parent label. The British group had sold more albums than anyone else in American music history. While Garth was rapidly catching up with them, what could be sweeter than besting the Beatles, especially on the same release date. If Garth succeeded in proving himself bigger than the Beatles, he would merit a new place in the annals of popular music. If he did not, it would seem either a daring failure or foolhardy arrogance.

The first week *Fresh Horses* was in the stores, Garth's album sold almost half a million copies. That was enough to make it the number one country album, but the Beatles' double album sold nearly twice that number.

In the next few weeks Garth's second single, "The Fever," a remake of an old Aerosmith rock number, met a resistance at country radio unlike anything Garth had ever experienced. Nashville had expanded the definition of country music beyond the borders of recognition. Still, there were limits, and some radio people felt that Garth had crossed them. In retrospect, it was a silly, arrogant gesture for Garth to thumb his nose at the greatest community of songwriters in the world, and then to dust off a discarded rock hit and attempt to foist it on country radio. The radio programmers had their moment of revenge. Instead of zooming up the singles chart, "Fever" moved up a notch or two at a time.

As for the vaunted marketing plan, everything seemed a little bit off. The articles in the trade press proudly announcing that the label was spending over four million dollars on marketing shifted attention to the promotion rather than the music. The crop art in Oklahoma never did get media attention, and the planes flew above, oblivious to Garth and his album. The television ads were cheap-looking gags, not even focusing on the music. Garth was supposed to appear on CMT and TNN for a number of weeks, but backed out. Garth did a television special on NBC ("Garth Brooks: Trying to Rope the World"). The program was less a celebration of his music and what it meant than a self-indulgent home movie about Garth and his European tour, with scenes of crowds screaming his name.

Fresh Horses received some of the worst reviews of Garth's career. Garth was consumed with the fear of decline and failure. The opening song on *Fresh Horses* was about the early years of Garth's career "back when the old stuff was new . . . [and] . . . It was one big party." Although Garth said that he was trying for a "garage-country" sound, there was an overwrought, frenetic pace to the album, as if he was so unsure of himself that he had to scream for attention. No one dared to speak the obvious truth:

Garth hadn't delivered the album that he had to deliver if he intended to sell what he once had sold.

Joe stood on the sidelines watching the tortured course of "Fever" on the charts, following the Soundscan sales figures with dismay. The marketing executive called Garth at home. "If you don't turn this thing around for the Christmas selling season, Garth," Joe told the singer, "you're not going to have a record in January." Garth was watching those figures and the reviews as closely as Joe, and the call played into his own fears and paranoia.

Joe found Walt at the Peninsula Hotel in Los Angeles, a favorite spot for record executives. "Garth is extremely concerned," Joe told Walt. "The bottom has fallen out of the record." The marketing executive believed that something dramatic had to be done, millions of dollars poured into the breach.

Walt felt the problem was Garth's single. As he saw it, radio was spitting the album right back at Garth, telling him the single didn't cut it. Garth's people saw it just the opposite. They felt that Walt and Scott were caving in to radio and not going out there, slugging it out, and making the songs work.

In the end, Walt and Scott agreed to take all the marketing money they had left and spend it now, bombarding television and radio and print with ads. If the marketing money did what Garth's people said it would, everyone would be happy. If the album did not do the extraordinary numbers that Joe predicted, then Garth would have to pay back part of the marketing money.

"Fever" only reached twenty-three on the *Billboard* country singles chart. Seven weeks after making its debut as the number one country album, *Fresh Horses* fell to number three. By March all the marketing money was gone, and so were the great hopes for the album. Garth was in the painful position of having to pay the label back a fortune.

The album sold by Fan Fair '96 over three million, but that was a dismal failure to Garth's gigantic expectations. At times Garth sounded like the rich boy who owns the one baseball on the block and will only play if his team wins. "I'm hoping the tour will make a difference, but if it doesn't, we'll have to take a serious look at where we are in our career," Brooks told Robert Hilburn of the *Los Angeles Times* in March of 1996. "If the record and ticket sales don't tell me that I'm stirring things up or changing people's lives, then I think it's time for me to hang it up. . . . You want to be remembered at your best. . . . If someone says I'm only saying that because of ego, I'm not sure they're wrong. I'm not sure why I feel this way. . . . But when you stop connecting with people, maybe you are in the wrong field. Maybe that's what God's trying to tell you."

Garth had said such things before, but for Scott and Capitol Nashville it was another layer of anxiety that they had to face each morning. As for the future, Scott knew that if Garth was going to come back as he wanted to come back, there would be only one way. "If we had an incredible record comparable to what he started with, we might be able to kick it back up there again," Scott mused as he stood looking out the window at downtown Nashville. "It's hard to say."

As Trace Adkins walked onstage to sing, Scott was suddenly even more alert. At the moment, Trace was Scott's one best shot at a new act. Over at Arista/Nashville, Tim had hit it big with his first act, Alan Jackson. To Scott this big guy out there was the new Alan Jackson. At six feet six, Trace was taller even than Alan. Trace was a good-looking fellow with a deep voice. Scott had taken Trace with him to visit radio across America. He had given out the word at Capitol Nashville that everything was to be done to make Trace happen. That meant pushing journalists to cover the baritone vocalist.

As sales declined and the labels stumbled over one another, there was a nasty tremor to the competitiveness. Scott knew that Trace had his troubles in the past, but he believed that that was no reason for others spreading rumors about a shooting incident between Trace and his ex-wife. Trace had told Capitol Nashville that his ex-wife had shot him. There were those at the label who argued that Trace should talk openly about the incident, and put it behind him before he became a big star. The matter was kept quiet, and rumors spread about what had really happened.

To try to stop one new band from even considering Capitol Nashville, another label told the musicians that if they talked to

Scott they would lose their possible deal. That's the kind of thing that wouldn't have happened in Nashville even two years before. Scott was trying to turn Emilio, an enormous Tejano artist, into a full-blown country music star, but his staff learned that other labels were making comments about the Mexican American artist to radio that Walt called "outright racist."

Scott was sickened by the brutality of so much that he saw happening, a world of such duplicity and betrayal that he never imagined existed. Scott's relationship with Garth was so distant that he had to learn about the singer's activities by reading the latest issue of *The Believer,* the magazine sent out to Garth's fans. Scott tried time and again to start some kind of dialogue with the singer, and time and again he felt rebuffed. Everywhere there were rumors that Garth was out to get him fired, just as had happened with Bowen before.

"Man, I just want to tell you the rumor's not true." Scott's old friend, the producer James Stroud, was calling from his vacation home in Colorado.

"What rumor?" Scott asked, genuinely startled.

"Well, that I'm coming over there to take your place."

That one Scott hadn't heard, but he knew that along Music Row they were doing everything but taking bets on what day he would get the ax. Nothing seemed to be happening for the label. And the man was in such pain over the loss of Faith that he seemed almost dazed to deal with such mundane business as his career.

"Scott, this is absurd," Susan Levy, his vice president of artist development, told him one day as she spoke frankly of her concerns. "Why do you put up with it? Garth, everything. The rumors. You're going through hell, Scott. Give it up. You don't have to put up with it."

"You don't understand, Susan," Scott said, shaking his head. "You people, you're the only family I have now."

Scott may have believed that, but he was not yet close to having *his* team the way Tony did at MCA Nashville or Tim at Arista/Nashville. Despite everything, though, Scott still had his own values rooted in his Oklahoma past. Sometimes when Scott had a few hours, he went out to his land in the country outside Nashville. There he got up on his big tractor the way he had done as a boy in the wheatfields of Oklahoma. As he drove, he listened to demo tapes, throwing the songs he liked in a box on the right-hand side, the songs he rejected into a box on the left-hand side. He wasn't going to quit, and knew that if the bosses in New York did fire him, he would hold his head up.

He thought often about his father's funeral. His father hadn't had much money, and he never had any fame, but there were so many people at his funeral, people Scott had never seen, people there to pay respects. Mourner after mourner came up to him that day and said that his father was a man of his word, a man of integrity. That's what mattered to Scott, not the money, not the awards, but that when he died, men and women would stand over his grave and say he, too, had been a man of honor.

Scott got the good news that despite the disappointment of *Fresh Horses,* Garth's total album sales had reached sixty million. The whole label was excited about the prospect of something positive happening between Garth and Capitol Nashville. If ever Nashville had an occasion to celebrate an artist's success, it was this one. Garth had sold more than Billy Joel, more than Michael Jackson, more than Madonna, more than Elvis, more than anyone but the Beatles, and he had done it in only seven years.

It was a sixty-million party, so why not a sixties costume party? Capitol Nashville took over the Sunset Studios soundstage and created their own stage setting. Garth controlled the guest list that his staff called "large but exclusive." Garth's invitation list included the governor of Tennessee, the mayor of Nashville, the executive director of the CMA, and the top executives of almost all of the major record labels. The guests were warned not to bring cameras or recorders, and told to come in appropriate sixties costumes.

On an evening in March, the guests arrived, dressed in tie-dyed shirts, bell-bottom pants, peace medallions, enormous Afros, garish tuxes with enormous lapels, long hippie hair, psychedelic glasses, and other sixties outfits. They left their autos with the valet parkers and entered through an exotically carved door, along a dark tunnel, past a Volkswagen Beetle, and into the cavernous studio. While the Chiffons sang "He's So Fine," two go-go dancers in miniskirts and white vinyl boots gyrated in a cage above a bar that served no liquor. On the far walls, newsreels and movie clips played on giant screens, while a Marilyn Monroe look-alike in the white dress from *The Seven-Year Itch* stood there exuding pouting sexuality.

Garth had invited over a thousand people to his party. The guests stood around in small groups, bemoaning the fact that there was nothing alcoholic to drink, exchanging industry chitchat, or complimenting one another on their exotic garb. No one was dancing, and the industry people were no more into this evening than into any other of the obligatory parties of their workweek. The governor had not been able to attend. Nor had the mayor. Nor was the executive director of the CMA here this evening. They all had their excuses. The most devastating of all the absences were other label heads.

Garth remained the most deferential of human beings, addressing any adult much over forty with a "Yes sir," "No sir," "Yes ma'am," "No ma'am." To him manners were the formal way that people honored the value of one another. The idea that these record company executives had not bothered to come was a devastating rebuke. They were busy men, and Garth was just another competitor, who cast his shadow across the bright aspirations of others. Most of these other executives had no feelings of great warmth or appreciation for Garth. They just didn't want to be there, to squander an evening celebrating Garth's triumph when they could be fostering their own.

Garth had shown his own sense of respect by choosing Jim Foglesong, the former president of Capitol Nashville, as master of ceremonies. Foglesong had originally signed Garth to the label. The retired executive was at an age when a person considered it an honor merely to have been invited, much less chosen for a central role. Foglesong led a champagne toast to Garth, the only liquor of the evening.

Garth stood on the makeshift stage wearing a St. Louis Browns baseball suit, next to Sandy, his very pregnant wife. Notable after notable came forward to bestow a gift on the singer, like some ancient tribute. Garth was used to this. On his concert tour each evening fans presented flowers, stuffed animals, and paintings, a myriad of offerings. This evening there were plates, plaques, paintings, and a Kawasaki Mule, but the best gift of all was a Ford New Holland front-loader tractor, a vehicle for which Garth had a ready use. As Garth stood watching, Scott drove the tractor onto the main floor. This tractor was for Scott what a plane or a Ford Mustang was for others, a symbol of freedom, of his mastery of his destiny. If it was possible to drive with panache the few feet into the center of the room, Scott did so.

Garth looked down on the tractor as if this was a gift he might keep. Then it was his turn to speak. "I've prepared no speech whatsoever," Garth said, choking up. Garth cried easily, not believing that manhood was lost in a few tears. There were those out there who cared for what he was saying, but most of the audience listened as if being quiet for a few minutes was the price of admission. Garth went through a litany of acknowledgments, missing almost no one who had lent him a hand across the many bridges of life. "My mom and dad are here and my sister is here."

Garth said each name not as if he were checking off some obligatory list but as if to forget one name was to miss some vital link in his life. "To Bob Doyle and Pam Lewis," Garth said, "here's to all the innocent fun things we had when it started."

Bob stood in the center of the room looking up at Garth. Bob was a cautious, self-conscious man who had not dressed up in sixties garb. Although Garth's other former manager had been invited, Pam had not even considered showing up. She bitterly dismissed the invitation as just another of Garth's endless public relations stunts. There had been innocent fun when Bob and Pam had first started managing Garth, but that was all over now. Pam was suing Bob over publishing money and other revenue she believed had been stolen from her (claims that she later dropped), and there was a sense of betrayal of both Garth and Bob that no sweet words or a party invitation could assuage.

"And hats off to you, Mr. Foglesong, thanks for signing me, and to Mr. Bowen and his family, hats off to you. Our hottest time was under your roof." This public acknowledgment of Bowen's contribution was the first time Garth had said anything positive about Bowen in years. Bowen had been invited too, but he had retired to Hawaii, full of bottomless disdain for Garth, who had bested him at the merciless games of power, blessing the day he had stopped having to deal with him.

"And to Scott and to the new people," Garth continued, turning toward the new president of Capitol Nashville. Scott was hopelessly inept at such basic games of power as pretending what he didn't feel. He was distant from Garth, and he stood there awkwardly unable to affect the backslapping camaraderie of the moment. "Anytime something old gets new, there are going to be fights. And if there is a new milestone, I hope it is with you guys and I hope you feel the same way about me."

When Garth's speech was over and the photos were taken, most of the audience quickly departed. Despite all the money, energy, and time spent on the party, it had been a strangely spiritless event, as much a dismissal of all that Garth had meant and done as a celebration. For all that Garth had dreamed of when he first arrived in Nashville, he could not have envisioned that so few would share his great night of triumph.

The press release that Garth put out concerning the twenty-three hours he spent at Fan Fair talked about breaking "an all-time autographing Guinness record." As so often happened with Garth, he and his people had taken what was a spiritual statement and turned it into yet another competition. Garth was terribly isolated, not simply from Scott and Capitol Nashville, but from the whole Nashville community. He seemed full of rage at the world that had given him everything and to whom he had given so much. He was happy to be out there in front of those arenas full of fans. "Pal, I'm glad you're out there in contact with your fans," Allen Reynolds told him. "That's what's real and that's what counts and this town has its head as far up its ass as it's ever had it. And it wouldn't be fun to be around here anyway."

★ ★ ★

As Scott stood on that great stage at Fan Fair, there was a glimmer of possibility for the man. He had not been fired, and in recent weeks the rumors had abated. He felt that good things were starting to happen at the label. He even noticed a few signs of respect on Music Row for the way he had soldiered through his first year. He finally could talk about Faith without wanting to hold his head in despair. He kept trying to connect with Garth, even eventually spending a day with him riding four-wheel vehicles out in the country, but there was still that terrible distance. He had taken part of his bonus for his first year in office and divided it up among his staff, all the people who had hung in there. Scott didn't want any publicity about this and was embarrassed when it was mentioned. He didn't believe he deserved all that money, and thought his staff did.

7

~

"Is There Life Out There?"

T he other stars either walked to their booths or rode electric carts, but the woman who was often called the Queen of Country Music arrived in a chauffeur-driven sedan. The auto moved slowly through the crowds, the security people walking beside her as if she were the president of the United States. The sedan stopped at a back entrance to Building No. 3 at shortly before three o'clock.

Reba McEntire got out of the sedan, shook her mane of red hair for a moment, gave a wave to the hundreds of fans, and walked into the building within a cocoon of guards and aides. Inside, along the corridor, other stars sat in their booths on the same level ground as the fans for their autograph sessions. Reba was helped onto a raised platform. There the forty-two-year-old singer perched on a pink director's chair with the name "REBA" embossed on the back and looked down on the milling scene beneath.

Only then was the first fan in line allowed to go to the foot of

Reba's temporary throne. Fred Johnson, like almost everyone else in the line, was not just some vague fan of country music, flipping on the radio in his car and liking what he heard. He was a Reba fan. He had joined her fan club and had gotten a backstage pass last year when she played in Tampa. Unfortunately, Reba didn't sign autographs after her shows any longer, and that's what he had come to Fan Fair to get.

Fred knew all of Reba's songs. At the Winn-Dixie supermarket in Tampa where Fred managed the produce department, his ears instantly picked up any Reba song coming over the sound system. "A moment of silence!" Fred shouted to the other fellows in produce. "It's Reba!" "It's Reba!" they shouted, making fun of his obsession. "It's Reba!" Fred didn't mind the way they joked. "You'll see, you'll see," he countered. "One day I'm gonna get up to her and I'm gonna tell her what I think and she'll leave her husband. Old Narvel doesn't have a chance. You wait and see."

Fred had flown up to Nashville Sunday night, rented a car, and drove out to look at Reba's farm and house from a distance. Then the night before he showed up at the fairgrounds at 11:15 to begin his vigil.

Fred was wearing his favorite black Reba T-shirt and cowboy hat so nobody could mistake him for anything but a Reba fan. Throughout the night he stood there, as thunder rumbled across a sky illuminated by bolts of lightning and rain struck his face. In the middle of the night the guards let him walk to the bathroom inside the gate. Afterwards, he stood for a few minutes watching Garth signing autographs when a gust of wind tore Fred's hat off his head and sent it sailing to Garth's feet. Garth smiled, picked it up, and handed it back. Fred could have asked Garth for an autograph, but he knew that wasn't fair to the other fans who had been waiting for hours.

At first only a few Reba fans stood waiting with Fred, but by dawn a hundred or more huddled at the gate, and hundreds more as the 9:30 A.M. opening approached. When the gates opened Fred ran as fast as his thirty-one-year-old legs would carry him, and plunked himself at the head of the line at the door to Building No. 3. His feet hurt. His shoes were wet. He had blisters. To make it even worse, it started raining again. But he didn't budge. He wasn't going to lose his place for anything.

Reba was ready. A security man nodded that Fred could go ahead into the building. He had bragged to the fellows in produce about what he would say to Reba, but he discovered that it wasn't like talking to a nice customer about the merits of the spring tomatoes. When he finally stood looking up at the great lady, he was dumbfounded. All he could manage to mumble was, "I met you in Tampa." He handed Reba a copy of her autobiography for her to sign, stood there a moment while another fan took a picture with Fred's camera, and then it was all over. As he walked away, Fred made a number one sign, his hand shaking and sweaty. By then Reba was signing other things for other people and Fred Johnson's moment was over.

Outside the door hundreds of fans waited in a long, ragged line. They pushed forward for their moment with Reba. This was the first time she had signed at Fan Fair in six years, and most of these fans had been here since the fairgrounds opened.

In the twenty years of her career, Reba had created a legion of fans. They wore her T-shirts. They bought her CDs. They paid to join her fan club. They dialed her 900 number. They attended her concerts. They watched her videos on CMT and TNN. They read her autobiography. They bought the Fritos Texas Grill corn chips in sizzlin' fajita and honey barbecue flavors that she advertised on television. These fans had made what they thought was a fair exchange with Reba, giving her loyalty, love, and dollars in return not simply for her music but for sharing the illusion of her life. Reba had created these fans, nourished them with her music and her moments of intimacy, and the special messages on the 900 number.

The fans loved Reba, but they talked about her like a lover whom they suspected of cheating on them. Some of them had been here at Fan Fair in the late seventies when Reba had first started showing up. Then she had been this mousy little thing wearing a name tag and hoping to be asked for an autograph. This gray little moth had crystallized into this extravagant butterfly soaring high above the world.

The fans had always been there for Reba, and they were sorely disappointed that she was divvying out only three hours of her time this afternoon. They whispered that Reba was only at Fan Fair because the CMA had told her that if she did not sign at Fan Fair this year, she would have to pay a half million dollars for her booth. That was not true, but the rumor passed up the line.

They talked about the ticket prices for Reba's shows, as high as seventy-seven dollars, more than four times what Garth charged. They discussed the merits of her show, which had become a Las Vegas extravaganza, carried from arena to arena in thirteen trucks, five buses, and her private plane, an entourage worthy of a small circus. They argued snappishly whether Reba had gotten so big that she had the right to stop signing autographs after her shows, when years ago nobody had signed more autographs than her. They talked about her new album, *Starting Over*, a collection of covers of pop songs, and wondered whether Reba had strayed too far from her country roots.

The women fans often had a passionate, personal feeling about Reba unlike any other performer. She was their musical angel. She had flown on the wings of songs to places they would never go, singing songs that resonated with their lives and their fantasies. She was not some distant ethereal creature, but like a sister who had dared to leave home, returning occasionally in dresses that they would never wear, telling tales of places they would never go.

During Fan Fair, most of the artists had parties for their fan clubs when their most loyal followers could spend more intimate time with them. Bryan White had his first fan club party for 450 members over at the Melrose Lanes Bowling Alley. Alan Jackson gave a show and signed autographs at the Ryman for the 2,000 of his 150,000 fan club members who won the random drawing. Yesterday, Reba had her party at the austere, concrete Municipal Auditorium in downtown Nashville. It was a venue better suited to auto shows and professional wrestling than to music. Some of Reba's fans had shown up at eight in the morning under the misguided notion that she was giving a brunch, but it was an afternoon show instead. Many fans were disappointed even before Reba appeared onstage. Reba, unlike every other performer at Fan Fair, was not signing autographs for her fan club.

Most artists performed intimate acoustical sets for their fan club members. Reba put on an hourlong extravaganza, a mini history of her career, changing clothes for each set, wearing the outfit she wore at that point in her two-decades-long career. Although there were about four thousand people seated on the concrete bleachers in the Municipal Auditorium, she had specifically excluded the media, limiting this occasion to her fan club members, not allowing any photos that might show up in the fan magazines.

Reba appeared suddenly on the massive, raised stage in front of her band singing her first hit, "(You Lift Me) Up to Heaven." The song dated from her 1980 third album. As her fans listened to the song, they resonated not simply with the song but with the story of Reba's own life. Most of these fans knew her life story as well as they knew her songs, how she had risen from poverty to become the biggest-selling female country artist in history. Dolly Parton. Loretta Lynn. Patsy Cline. None of them had topped her twenty million sales. Among women artists, only Barbra Streisand and Linda Ronstadt had sold more records.

Reba was the most chronicled of all country artists, her life written about not simply in her own best-selling autobiography but in *Good Housekeeping, Redbook, McCall's,* the *Saturday Evening Post,* and dozens of other magazines. Her face was almost as much a feature of the newsstand as Jackie's or Arnold's or Liz's, or Michael's, any of the other megacelebrities of our time. Reba's life story differed in that it was portrayed not as tabloid fodder but as if it had been cut and shaped to fit neatly into an hour on *Oprah.*

When Reba became a star, Burt Reynolds had joked to her about celebrities "outpooring" each other. This was a favorite sport in America, especially among country artists. It involved balancing exquisitely painful details about an impoverished past with an equal number of anecdotes about how purifying and enriching it had been, meeting so many fine folk, their faces etched not with poverty but with nobility.

Reba didn't have to outpoor anyone. The most authentic thing about her was her past. She talked of her early years with compelling candor and the tiny details that are usually the markers of truth. She was not one of these ersatz cowboys and cowgirls of Music Row, duded up for the cameras. She was brought up on a ranch outside Limestone Gap, Oklahoma. She had grown up poor, but this was not the world of the Great Depression any longer, the great swirling dust clouds, homeless Okies moving west. This was nineteen-fifties and early-sixties America, when affluence was so widespread that some crumbs fell to the floor of all but the most deprived. Reba might take her school-night bath in the same murky tepid water of the galvanized steel tub that her siblings had recently vacated, but afterwards she rushed into the little living room to watch the nineteen-inch color television.

Reba's father was a champion rodeo cowboy. Reba was her father's daughter. She could brand a steer, castrate a calf, rope a steer, vaccinate a cow, and maneuver a horse through the intricacies of a rodeo barrel race. If she had been a man, the image makers of Nashville would have kept her in jeans and dusty boots, merchandised as an authentic piece of the Old West.

Reba was her mother's daughter too. Her mother was an elementary school teacher and school secretary who as a young woman had her own dreams of a career as a country singer. In high school Reba sang in the Kiowa High School Cowboy Band and competed in rodeos across the plains. Upon graduation, she headed off to college, taking her horse with her to Southeastern Oklahoma State University in Durant where she studied elementary education.

"This was my first top ten record," Reba told the fans when they had finally quieted down. "Boyyyyy, that took me back awhile. Thank you for coming out for my party. The rain might be a little aggravatin' but thank God it's sure lots cooler than it was last year."

Reba had an exquisite sensitivity to her audience, realizing that these people would happily sit here like relatives looking through scrapbooks of yellowed pictures. "I'm gonna take you back a while," she continued. "This is some surefire nostalgia here. This is my very first show outfit right here. Mommy found and ordered the material. I dug it out of one of them trunks of mine out there at home."

The outfit was the frilly, vaguely cowgirl type that years ago Patsy Montana or Dale Evans might have worn. The idea that Reba might go up under the eaves to look for her old outfit seemed perfectly plausible to her fans. "So back in 1979 when I first heard that song, I was lookin' for a number one record so bad that I didn't think a top ten was enough. I was a cocky Oklahoman and I was cookin' a blackberry cobbler. I was really worried about bein' burned, so don't do that, folks."

The audience sat as if they were being let in on the secret inner life of their favorite star. "So Jerry Kennedy called me from Mercury Nashville and said, 'I got this song that's gonna be a monster hit.' Now in rural Oklahoma you don't have the best phone lines in the world and it was really chatty on the party line and I was listening and worried about my cobbler and I said, 'Jerry, will you call me back?' And he said, 'Okay, but why?' And I said, 'I have this cobbler in the oven and I don't want to burn it.' So after the pie got done I went and called him back and listened to the song and sure enough it went to number eight. And shortly after that Jerry and I went back to the studio. I was still lookin' to going a little higher on the charts and we found this next one."

Reba had lived through those long years before the elevation of country music into a truly national music. The first six years of her career she made not a cent of royalties beyond the modest advances her label gave her. When she performed onstage, she was "Nashville recording artist Reba McEntire," but when she went home she was Mrs. Charlie Battles living in a ramshackle house without running water.

Reba met her first husband on the rodeo circuit. Charlie had thrice been the world steer-wrestling champion, a star in a world that was as full of illusions as the music industry. He was a decade older than his bride, wrestling steers in a rodeo ring where a man was no better than his body, and a body didn't last much past thirty.

Charlie was a man like Reba's father, not some Saturday night cowboy, but a working cattle man, quick of temper and crude of speech, spitting the dark spittle of his chewing tobacco in a cup as he drove his three-quarter-ton pickup truck down the blacktop roads outside Stringtown, Oklahoma. Charlie had contributed a strange dowry to the marriage, forty thousand dollars in debts. Only Reba's family's help and her singing allowed the couple to move out of their sad little house and lease a two-hundred-and-twenty-five-acre ranch.

Reba sang of a woman's pains and joys, and she sang about them out of all the darkness of experience. At home she accepted her husband's emotional disdain as a woman's natural lot. After all, in many respects, Charlie wasn't acting that differently from many of the men of Reba's world. Underneath the swaggering bravado and the sly sexual asides, many of these cowboys treated women as if they were a different breed of cattle. They prodded them along as if women were dumb and docile, part of the background landscape in a man's true world. Charlie didn't hit Reba, but then there are beatings and there are beatings.

Only once did Reba fear that he was going to strike her, rearing up with a toilet kit in his hand that she had given him for Christmas years before. Reba remembered how her husband had cared so little for her gift that he had let his sons rip the bright-colored Christmas wrapping off the shaving kit. Reba found it so painful being saddled with these two stepsons that she vowed never to have a child of her own. "One of the main reasons I'll never have children is that kids nowadays have no respect for their elders," she said at the time, finding the visits of her nieces and nephews an added reason to avoid motherhood. "After they're gone, I go in the bathroom and eat a whole package of birth control pills."

Each time Reba finished a mini-set, she introduced one of the acts that her company, Starstruck Entertainment, managed. That gave them some publicity and her a chance to change outfits. After 4Runner sang its number, Reba returned to sing more of her hits, including "Whoever's in New England."

"Do you recognize this outfit?" she asked rhetorically, then waited for the applause to die down. "Yeah, it's my outfit on the *Whoever's in New England* cover. This is another one I pulled out of the trunk. We did part of the video out at the Belle Meade Mansion. If you want to see where we shot that, you can go right out there."

"Whoever's in New England" was not only a number one hit in 1986 but a seminal song in Reba's career. The theme was an updated, upscale version of "Stand by Your Man." In Reba's version of the theme, a business executive is having an affair in Boston. His wife is standing by her man, singing that her husband will "always have a place to come back to."

Reba had not set out to be part of any musical movement. Nonetheless, the gritty realism of her songs and the passion of her voice stood out on a country radio that in the early and mid-eighties often sounded like elevator music for the soul. The producer who allowed Reba the freedom to make her own music her own way was Jimmy Bowen. As the new president of MCA Nashville, Bowen purged his label of unwanted artists. For most of those artists who remained, including George Strait and Reba, he allowed them to fulfill their own artistic vision.

Bowen had a way with women artists, and for a while the musical and human sides of Reba developed in tandem. "Everything had been in her husband's name," Bowen reflected. "No matter who generated it, it went into his name. When she left him to get a divorce, she didn't have a bank account. She didn't have anything of her own."

Reba had been beaten down, by her husband and by the patriarchal system of Nashville. When Bowen went to hear Reba perform, he heard her do these jazzlike trills, bending the notes, playing with them. "Let me ask you something, Reba," the executive asked her afterwards. "You were doing all these trills and curls and stuff. But you don't do them on your records."

"Oh, no." Reba shrugged. "They tell me never to do that on a country record."

"They never sold any damn records!" Bowen fumed. "Why don't you be who you are?"

Reba went back into the studio and took Bowen at his word. Her great weakness both as a singer and as a human being was exaggeration, pumping up her music and her personality far beyond the human realm. Reba added these jazzy touches with a vengeance, much of which Bowen scrubbed off the music, leaving a few subtle touches.

Bowen set Reba up with a new producer and watched as she went into the studio to record her new album. Always before, she had come to Nashville, gone into the studio to record her tracks, and left everything else to her producer. This time, following Bowen's dictum, she got into the process of making an album. She helped add touches of fiddle and steel, sweetening the sound.

Soon afterwards, a steaming Reba came stomping in to see Bowen. "I can't believe what he did!" Reba shouted. "Bowen, he went and took all my stuff off and put his stuff on. And I don't like it. It's not my stuff!"

"Well, it's real simple," Bowen said slowly. "Fire him. He works for you."

Bowen went into the studio with Reba this time to produce her album. "Listen," he told her, "it's hard enough for a man to know what a man should say to reach a consumer. It's really hard for a man to know what a woman should say. So, woman, you've got to know. You've got to do it. And if you don't know what a woman can say that other women will want to buy, you ain't gonna make it."

"I know," Reba replied. "I can do it."

Reba was a country girl singing country songs. Across America, millions of women identified with the songs Reba chose and her life, seeing little distinction between the two. Although Reba did not write her own songs, her lyrics had a remarkable consistency. The best of her songs were about the secret inner emotional life of women. They were songs firmly in the tradition of country music lyrics. There was an implicit idea in these songs that women were morally superior. Women felt more, and thus they hurt more. Women were the center of life. Women were the hearth, the light, the warmth, but without a man they were a hearth that was an empty shelter, a light that shone on itself, and a warmth that heated no one.

At its best, this was adult music that looked the world face-on, music that was not about a world of easy choices. In her second number one single at MCA Nashville, Reba sang a song written by Harlan Howard and Chick Rains about a woman in a marriage in which "Somebody should leave, but which one should it be, You need the kids and they need me." The couple lay alone in bed together, the woman crying soundlessly with "those babies down the hall." In another number one single, Reba portrayed a woman realizing "the world isn't going to stop for my broken heart."

Women still stood by their men, but in the new world of country, the bright lights of freedom could be seen from the kitchen window and from a seat in the typing pool as well as in a women's studies class at college. Reba sang of a woman who has raised her kids and now looks out on the world wondering "Is There Life Out There?"

Reba's mother's generation had been taught to accept whatever their parents gave them as good enough. In her most poignant song, Reba sang of "The Greatest Man I Never Knew," the father who was almost never there. Love was out there for a woman, and freedom, and terrible dangers like AIDS. In "She Thinks His Name Was John," Reba sang of a woman who spent a night with a man she did not know and as a consequence "won't know love, have a marriage or sing lullabies."

Reba was part of what became known as the neotraditionalist movement of the mid- and late eighties. There were other acts whose sound cut through the mediocrity—Ricky Skaggs, Emmylou Harris, George Strait, Randy Travis, the Judds, Dwight Yoakam—and for a while they sounded like voices singing in the wilderness. Reba and the others helped to revitalize country music, to begin a march that with Garth's inestimable cheerleading brought millions of people back into the country music bins and to stop as they cruised along the radio dial.

Reba returned in an extravagant gown. "Oh, yeah, look at this outfit!" Reba enthused. "Do you remember this? How could you forget it? 1984. I was out in Los Angeles and I met this lovely lady and she had designed beautiful clothes for everybody in the world. She just forgot to tell me how much it was gonna cost. I about had a heart attack when I got the bill. But anyway, I wore the hounds out of it. I got it out of the trunk. My mommy calls me a pack rat. Now this next song was when I was going up to do this show in Nashville and I heard this tape, and I said you gotta hear this, it's a monster. And you thought so too. 'Rumor Has It.'"

I overheard a conversation
Oh rumor has it, she has you
Rumor has it you love her too
Oh talk is cheap but the price is high.

In the eighties Reba was spending most of her life on the road, and the road was a floating island with its own laws and codes. At the head of her team stood Narvel Blackstock, her road manager. The industry has several prominent people whose careers began in such mundane, earthbound, un-show-business-like pursuits as banking or accounting.

Narvel had been a Prudential insurance agent. A would-be musician, he had caught the country music fever to such an extent that he was willing to leave his wife and three children at home for the itinerant life on the road. He was a man who liked a party as much as anyone on the bus, but he brought the discipline of an insurance agent and the ambition of a man who knew that he could do far more than he was doing. Narvel spent more time alone with Reba in her bus stateroom than anyone else, where, in Reba's words, they "formed a little club." Like most stars, Reba found nothing so appealing as a man who loved her and her career with equal passion.

Reba divorced Charlie in a bitter court battle in which she ended up having to pay him off with $580,000 of what she considered *her* money. She moved to Nashville and in June of 1989 married her former road manager. Narvel had a vision as great as Reba's. He took over as her manager, with a single-minded devotion to her career. In February of 1990, she gave birth to Shelby Steven McEntire Blackstock, the child she thought she would never have, part of a life in which the professional and personal seemed a seamless bond.

In March of 1991, seven members of her band, her tour manager, and the pilot and copilot died in a plane crash in the mountains outside San Diego. The road always took its human toll, and the history of country music is full of tragic accidents.

Immediately afterwards, Reba gave an exclusive cover-story interview to *People,* a piece that many in Nashville considered a shameless bit of self-promotion. Her critics thought much the same of her appearance at the Academy Awards nine days after the accident. They were even more appalled when she fired six members of her band at the end of the year three weeks before Christmas.

Reba and Narvel were full of restless energy and endless ambition, and together they built Reba's legend. They did not want her to stand on the same even ground as other country acts. She refused to cooperate in ventures that made her appear no more than an equal. In 1993, Reba was the only major woman artist not to take part in the CBS documentary special "The Women of Country." In spite of all the publicity and money she made with her hit single "She Thinks His Name Was John," she did not take part in the AIDS awareness album, *Red, Hot and Country*. She was a country girl, but you never saw Reba singing at Farm Aid, raising money for beleaguered farm families.

Reba had a sense for the theatrical and the melodramatic that infused everything she did in public, from the notes she sang to every aspect of her business life. Nothing characterized this more than the massive twenty-five-thousand-square-foot headquarters that her Starstruck Construction Company was building on Music Row. The gigantic structure was bigger than the building that housed her record label, MCA Nashville. Taj MaReba, as the Music Row wags had dubbed it, looked like the world's largest Wurlitzer jukebox. The building was fronted by lifelike, full-size bronze sculptures of horses and a waterfall, a bucolic reverie in the midst of Seventeenth Avenue South. Reba's massive office sat at the top of the building and was glass enclosed, as were the offices of her subordinates.

Reba could watch what everyone else was doing and with a touch of a button turn her glass smoky. Then she could sit there in royal solitude or walk out on her private balcony waving at the humble folk far below. She had wanted her own helicopter pad on the roof so she could come flying in and out without ever touching earth, but that request had rankled others on Music Row and the city had twice turned it down. It hadn't seemed to have occurred to Reba that the helicopter noise might interrupt recording in the studios on Music Row.

Reba had once sung her songs in a straight and simple way. Now her gift for the theatrical continued down to the quietest note that she sang. "She approaches a lyric the way a turkey vulture dive-bombs a field mouse," wrote Mitch Potter of the *Toronto Star.* "She doesn't so much interpret the words as rips away at their flesh tearing them asunder." Reba had never met a syllable she didn't love, a note she didn't throttle, an emotion she didn't exude.

"In our show last year I would come up in this elevator and one night the elevator stopped working halfway up," Reba began as she stood in yet another spectacular gown. "Here I was halfway out in this beautiful dress. My dresser was underneath trying to boost me and I thought no way in thunder was anyone boosting me out, so I just climbed out like I was in blue jeans. This year we have a brand-new show."

Reba was the Siegfried and Roy of country. She and Narvel had created a stage show that was as extravagant and spectacular as anything in show business. Garth had his rings of fire and steam, but in the end it was a man standing there onstage singing his songs. With Reba it was New Year's in Las Vegas every night of the year, one awe-inspiring stage set and routine after the next.

Reba created an expectation in her audiences that each year the show would be bigger and bolder and brassier than the year before. In the 1996 version, her band arrived onstage in a yellow cab, while she appeared at the other end of the great arenas in a "jet" bearing the logo of Starstruck Entertainment. And that wasn't even the opening number. The greatness of country had been in simplicity, and when Reba sang some of her songs from the early eighties, there remained glimmers of that simplicity, but they were lost in the pyrotechnics, the movable stage, and the next costume change.

Everything in Reba's professional life sold something else. As her opening acts, she hired artists managed by her and Narvel's own company, Starstruck Entertainment. Frito-Lay sponsored her concerts and television specials and offered discount coupons for her autobiography on ten million bags of Fritos corn chips. Her book had the same cover photo as her album and contained a picture of her album and sold her concerts and her television specials.

Her concerts sold her book and her T-shirts and her albums and millions of extra Frito-Lay snacks. Her CDs and tapes contained a promotional photo of her book, though no sample of Frito-Lay. It all came together when the fan sat in her fifty-dollar seat nibbling on Frito-Lay tortilla chips, wearing her Reba T-shirt, clutching her Reba autobiography and her Reba CD, most of which she had paid for on her Reba Visa or MasterCard.

Despite everything, she was still Reba Anybody, the common woman writ big. She kept perfectly in focus and on role. She insisted that the word "however" be taken out of her autobiography wherever her collaborator, Tom Carter, had placed it. She didn't speak that way. None of that highfalutin nonsense for Reba, however much sense it might make.

Reba was on a seemingly endless roll. In the spring of 1995 she became the first woman to be named the Academy of Country Music (ACM) Entertainer of the Year since Barbara Mandrell in 1980. To Reba this award was the highest honor of them all. After all, to her God was not simply Jehovah, Heavenly Father, Almighty, Creator, and Lord. No God was, as she called him, her "Entertainer of the Year every year."

That same year Reba had been nominated for the CMA's Entertainer of the Year Award as well, an even higher honor. Everything was primed for her to make a clean sweep. In the week before the awards show in October 1995, buses rolled through the center of Nashville that had been repainted with the word "Reba" showing her jacket photo from her about-to-be-released album, *Starting Over*, next to the words "One Name Says It All."

On the weekend before the awards, Reba took over the downtown TPAC auditorium for a free show to introduce the industry audience to her new album. The event was considered so important that Al Teller, the chairman of MCA's music entertainment group, had flown in from Los Angeles to attend. It had been her idea to do an album of cover songs from the world of pop music. Tony Brown, her producer, had gone along with her, though Tony realized that it was almost impossible for a country artist to reinvent herself without losing her original audience.

Reba already had her doubts about the man considered the premier producer in Nashville. On her 1993 *Greatest Hits Vol. II* album, Reba insisted on using her road band for the two new cuts. Tony had not been happy with that. Tony had nothing against Reba's musicians, but the best musicians simply did not go out on the road. They didn't go out because they could make more money and have an easier life living in Nashville. Moreover, even the best of the road musicians didn't mesh together like the premier session players Tony had on call.

Reba arrived that evening at the TPAC auditorium in one of the Nashville buses with her name on the sides. Reba's show had brilliant sets and stunning costumes, everything but the kind of music she once had sung. That journey into pop looked so easy, so inviting, a little tuck in the lyrics here, a little push in the percussion over there, nothing to it, but country artists almost always ended lost out there in a scarred field of musical debris. Some of those in the audience cringed in embarrassment as Reba hammed her way through such numbers as Linda Ronstadt's "You're No Good," sentiments with which many concurred.

In many ways, Reba had become the very kind of country pop performer she had stood against artistically a decade ago. Reba had such a loyal audience that her album sold double platinum, but it received by far the worst critical reviews of her career. "If karaoke means ill-advisedly singing your favorite tunes in front of a crowd, then call this countryoke," opined *People* in a typical review.

Reba sat in a prime seat at the CMA Awards show out at the Opry House. She was still sitting when Alan Jackson was named the 1995 CMA Entertainer of the Year. Although Reba continued to sell out many of her arena shows, there was an ominous sense that like her massive mausoleum on Music Row, she had reached too far and built not with grace but with grandiosity, and it might one day all fall down.

"Before we go into the title song of my album I'd like to tell you about the brand-new album we're working on," Reba said, perfectly aware that these fans would be out there to get their copy.

"I haven't talked too much about it. It's not just that I'm superstitious. I've been working on it all this week and last week. We work every night on the road. We blend. We jell. I've loved working with the studio musicians, but I wanted to see what these guys could do. And you know what? They didn't even sweat. It's going to be out about October. We're just finishing up."

Reba had no use for Tony Brown any longer. She wanted to be her own producer now. She was producing *her* album *herself* with the help of John Guess, her longtime engineer. The only thing she did not have was her own record label. Although many in Nashville thought that she and Narvel would soon change that oversight, she in the end signed again with MCA Nashville.

Reba and Narvel had built an immense jerry-built structure reaching up to the very clouds. Sitting there Reba could find no way to work her way down without falling fatally to earth. She had to keep trying to climb even higher. She and Narvel had a management company, a construction company, a publishing company, an aviation company, a horse farm, and other enterprises.

Reba's new headquarters was more than a million dollars over budget, and she had no one to rail against except her own husband. She had weekly expenses that would have made a billionaire blanch. More than a hundred nights a year she flew out of Nashville in her private jet to give a concert in a great arena somewhere, returning late at night netting usually about $150,000 for her efforts. And still she kept on trying to climb higher. Associates felt that she had aged terribly, that all the pressure had begun to exact its inevitable toll.

Just yesterday she had agreed to appear at the third annual Country Radio Music Awards show where she was to receive an award as Entertainer of the Year and Loretta Lynn was to receive a special Legend Award. When Loretta's husband became so ill that she had to cancel, Reba refused to appear. It was a tiny insignificant act, but life was a mosaic of tiny insignificant acts, and those she had stood up shook their heads and said that after all, that was Reba, that was what Reba had become.

★ ★ ★

As Reba signed autographs inside Building No. 3, the line outside hardly seemed to move, and the crowd grew more sullen and surly. On previous days, these fans had waited in other lines where the staff of other stars had come out to cut off the lines so that everyone waiting would get a chance. Sometimes they asked the last person in line to carry a sign, handed out numbered cards, or directed the fans to grasp onto a rope so that no one could possibly push into the line. No one from Reba's entourage had bothered doing that here.

In the morning a man who said that he worked security for Reba had come out and talked to people in the line. "You know Reba, folks, she'll stay until they kick her out," he told the anxious fans.

"Garth stayed twenty-three hours and they didn't kick him out," countered Pam Olive, a licensed nurse whose husband was a union steelworker. Pam had been a Reba fan since the beginning. She remembered seeing Reba in Kansas City in the late seventies when the singer had worn a full skirt and a gold and silver belt buckle and looked like a hometown girl, not the glamour queen she had become.

"I've worked for Reba and Wynonna and Billy Ray," the security man said. "And I'm tellin' you Reba'll stay less'n she's crampin' or havin' a bad-hair day."

Another assistant made a count of the line, telling the first three hundred that they definitely would get to meet Reba. Other members of her staff worked the crowd of about a thousand selling $275 bomber jackets, $25 T-shirts, and $5 photos, taking the money, then hurrying back into the air-conditioned building, leaving the fans to stew in their own sweat.

For many of those in line, especially those who had been here waiting all day, their time with Reba would be the transcendent moment of their entire week. Some of them had saved all year to be here. Clarinda Hockett was one. She loved Reba because she believed Reba felt her pain. Whatever she had gone through in her life, she felt that Reba had been there. When she had gotten her divorce, she had played "For My Broken Heart," and the song had helped to heal her. When her father had died, she had played "The Greatest Man I Never Knew." Whatever happened to Clarinda,

Reba had a song that spoke to her heart. Clarinda didn't have much money. She worked on the line in a printing factory, but no matter how little money she had, she always had money to buy Reba's latest album and to attend her concert whenever her heroine came to Indianapolis.

Another of the fans waiting in line, Greg Bond, traveled from his West Virginia home to attend Reba concerts all over the eastern United States, from Indiana to Maryland to Pennsylvania. He had come to Fan Fair just to see Reba. Eighteen-year-old Heather Serena was one of the newer Reba fans, but the first-year college student from Tipp City, Ohio, stood behind no one in her devotion to the star.

As these fans stood waiting, they realized that so many people were butting into line that they were hardly moving ahead. When Fan Fair began a quarter century ago, it would have been almost unthinkable for a country music fan to push ahead in line or to use some petty subterfuge to get an advantage. That was not so true any longer. Nobody seemed to care, not the Fan Fair officials, not Reba's security people, nobody.

The fans had been promised autographs, and they knew that Reba would not leave them. It was almost six o'clock, but time meant nothing to Reba, not when she had hundreds of her most devoted fans out here waiting for her. Some fans had been at the fairgrounds for eighteen or twenty hours. They had made their covenant with Reba, and she would not deny them their moment of her time.

At five minutes to six, two security men shut the door into Building No. 3, and the crowd pushed forward in a moment of panic. The fans were streaked with sweat, their clothes damp and wrinkled by the rain and humidity. They were exhausted. They were hungry. They were thirsty. They pressed ahead, holding aloft their Reba pictures, and T-shirts, and bomber jackets, and CDs, and autobiographies. They yelled out seeking a denial, not believing that all their hours were coming to naught, that their belief in Reba would die there on a torpid afternoon in Nashville.

Other security men appeared, forming a phalanx around Reba's sedan. Then, suddenly, Reba appeared out of a side door, with that famous smile locked in a grimace, waving her hand to the crowd. As she stood there, her eyes caught a glimpse of her most loyal fans yelling "Reba" as if her name had become a curse, tearing up her pictures and throwing her image back at her.

As the car pulled away, the fans stood there in stunned dismay. Some of them hurried back into the building to try to return their Reba merchandise, but scores of them stood talking among themselves. Heather couldn't stop crying. This wasn't just her belief in Reba she had lost here today. This was something else, something she could barely understand. Clarinda vowed that she would never again spend money she did not have to go to see Reba. Greg told his new friends that he would no longer waste his free time traveling around to Reba concerts.

These fans didn't hate Reba. They simply didn't love her any longer. They saw her as just another human being. They saw her music as music. And for whatever innocence and faith they lost today, they gained even more. They regained pieces of themselves. They hugged and said good-bye and joined the milling crowds heading for the RCA/BNA show at the racetrack. All that remained outside Building No. 3 were scraps of Reba's photos in the dirt, trampled into nothing by thousands of pairs of restless, heedless feet.

8

~

"Any Man of Mine"

At six o'clock the guards guided the last of the fans out of the main buildings. There was an eerie solitude like a football stadium the day after the championship game, or a Broadway theater after a long-running play has closed. At six-thirty, however, fans in wheelchairs and on crutches began entering the buildings for what was called the special handicapped hour. The fans raced up and down the aisles in their wheelchairs hunting out stars or wandered from booth to booth taking pictures, looking at a scene that during the day would have been blocked from their view.

Country music has always succored those sick or in distress, and there were hundreds of these fans, from little children to the elderly, most of them in wheelchairs. There was even an impostor or two, having decided that it was far easier to get an autograph pushed along in a wheelchair than to stand in line for hours.

There were no reporters or photographers to witness this event, and the only reason to be here was because one cared about these folks. Of the few artists who were in their booths this evening, none of them was as bright in the firmament as thirty-year-old Shania Twain.

Fan Fair was a time of extraordinary memories for Shania. It was here in 1993 that she met her husband, Robert John "Mutt" Lange. And it was here just last year that she created such a sensation singing her three-song set from her new album. Now, a year later, she was the biggest-selling woman artist in country music. *Any Man of Mine* was the biggest-selling album ever by a female country artist, surpassing even Patsy Cline's.

Shania was working Fan Fair with immense energy and savvy, doing interviews, going to the awards shows, making her presence felt everywhere this week. She was in her booth for two to four hours every day. Shania's people, unlike Reba's, counted the fans, making sure that everyone in line got an autograph. Some fans complained that Shania wasn't warm. She seemed calculating, like a mechanical doll, flashing a smile for their cameras, and then looking to the next person in line.

This evening, however, Shania had a rapport with these fans. She listened and talked to each of them. She came out from behind her booth and had time and emotion to spend with those who came to meet her. It was as if after months of hype and sales and image making, she was confronted with a moment that touched her honestly and deeply. She talked to these fans as if something else was going on here today than creating an image that would sell seven million more CDs, and add even more wattage for her name to shine even more brilliantly above the Nashville skyline.

Shania talked to these disabled fans as if despite all her beauty and health and fame and wealth, she had some commonality with their lives, some touchstone with what they felt and saw.

Many of the fans already owned Shania's record-breaking album. In the past, Nashville's producers tried to capture an artist singing spontaneously in a moment of true passion. Shania's album was just the opposite of that. Her husband was one of the most successful rock producers in the world. British-born Mutt Lange brought all the techniques he used producing Def Leppard and

Bryan Adams to his wife's album. He spent more than half a million dollars producing the album, five times what many Nashville albums cost. He spent months in the studio reconstructing Shania. He layered her vocals, stacking the renditions on top of each other, creating the illusion of strength and power. He took tiny moments of Shania's singing, polished its surface, fitting it onto the digital tape, adding minute bits of guitar or drums, putting another layer on top, creating an artifact that existed nowhere but on that CD.

Shania's life story, like her album, was a brilliant reconstruction of such compelling power that it overwhelmed the facts of her life. Shania was born in Windsor, Ontario, and brought up in Timmins, 422 miles north of Toronto, and 1,111 miles from Nashville. As far as it was from Tennessee, in the geography of the soul Canada lies just across the border from Nashville. Whether it is in the great plains of Saskatchewan or the villages of Nova Scotia, Canada is close to nature and family and home, and country music is not some foreign import but a part of the Canadian esprit. The commonwealth not only has its own thriving country music, but Hank Snow, the octogenarian Nova Scotian, still performs on the Grand Ole Opry, and other Canadian singers on American country labels include Lisa Brokop, Paul Brandt, Terri Clark, Michelle Wright, and Charlie Major.

Many Americans have a vaguely patronizing attitude toward Canada, considering the country largely a few border towns with major league baseball teams, dropping off rapidly into impassable forests and tundra, igloos and dog teams. That ignorance was exemplified and exploited in the creation of the mythic Shania. *USA Today* said that Shania "grew up in a Native American community 'eating moose meat and beaver and partridge.'" In its portrait, *Esquire* wrote that Shania "grew up in the tiny Ojibwa Indian community of Timmins, Ontario." *People* said that "she grew up near the Temagami Reserve near Timmins," while the *Chicago Tribune* stated authoritatively that she was "reared in the wilderness around Timmins."

The town of Timmins where Shania was brought up is a thriving regional center of forty-seven thousand, its economy based primarily on mining, including the Kidd Creek mine, considered the biggest producer of silver and zinc in the world. Timmins has running water, electricity, a daily newspaper, a weekly paper, TV and radio stations, more bars than churches, and the creature comforts of any American town of the same size.

The American journalists who wrote so inaccurately about Timmins did not invent their garish misinformation. They learned it either from Shania or her publicists. Even if Shania was not the creator of this mythical rustic backwater village of Timmins, she clearly did not consider it one of her media duties to create an accurate image of her hometown. The mythic Timmins provided a perfect dark backdrop for the most poignant tales of poverty by a country star since the Great Depression.

Shania told interviewers that her father was a full-blooded Ojibwa Indian. She had a vaguely mysterious cast to her features, though the tiny singer hardly looked half Indian. Shania was born Eileen Regina Edwards in August of 1965. Her biological father, whom Shania never managed to talk about, was Clarence Edwards, of French-Irish descent, a common mix of heritages in Canada. Her mother, Sharon, came from Irish stock. Her father was a railroad engineer, a profession that resonated with some of the great themes of country music. Shania had little opportunity to hear her father's stories, for her parents were divorced when Shania was only two. Two years later her mother married Jerry Twain, who was indeed a Native American. Jerry was the man who brought Shania up and whom she learned to consider her father, and he was the reason she claimed to have Indian blood.

Shania was the second oldest of the five children in the family. Although the Twains lived in town, Shania said that "my father taught us to kill our own food, and my job was to set the rabbit snares." The snares must often have come up empty, for Shania said that in school she and her siblings often had no lunch at all or mustard sandwiches. "I'd judge other kids' wealth by their lunches," Shania remembered. "If a kid had baked goods, that was like, oh, they must be rich." Even at night, there was not enough to eat. "We would go for days with just bread and milk and sugar, and heat it up in a pot," Shania reflected. On other occasions dinner was a few potatoes. "In my house it was so wrong to take more than your share," she recalled. "If you decided to take an extra potato, someone didn't get a potato at all." The milk that was so readily available to be eaten with bread mysteriously disappeared when it was potato time. Shania came to believe that only fancy folks had their potatoes with milk poured over them. "To us, eating like that was only on TV."

In *Dallas,* a hit program when Shania was growing up, the multimillionaire Ewings rarely sat down to dinners of potatoes and milk. The rich much prefer caviar and foie gras, considering the humble tuber only a side dish. Shania may have as faulty a memory about her own poverty as she did about the eating habits of the rich on television. Canadians have built their social safety net further off the floor than their neighbors immediately to the south, and few working families exist on diets primarily of potatoes and bread.

Timmins was largely a working-class community. A man could earn a good living in the mines or in the forest if he didn't drink it away on the weekends. Most people knew what it was like to be poor and did not disdain those who had less than they did. Shania came from a poor family, but so did many children in school. Shania didn't have as much as some of her classmates. Her pants might have been mended, and her shoes resoled, but Shania and her siblings were sent to school clean, and that cleanliness and neatness was a moral statement of a high order. Her mother and stepfather cared about their children, and on what mattered in life their children were as good as anyone else.

Poverty, however, is a matter of perception. It may well be that this little girl *felt* her poverty the way few others did in school. There was at times a subtle prejudice against Native Americans that a highly sensitive little girl might have felt while others less aware believed it didn't even exist. Shania probably even imagined that she was being treated differently because of her background, when most of her classmates didn't even notice. Although others did not see her as especially poor, Shania had the hunger in the pit of the stomach that never leaves no matter how full the stomach.

That attitude of being true to your roots is at the moral core of country music. Country performers made a covenant with their fans, and that covenant is supposed to be the truth. Country music admonished its listeners not to get those "Stuck Up Blues" and to be as truthful to the past as to the present. During most of the history of country music, America and Canada were countries where most children did better than their parents, the rising tide of affluence bringing families even further up in the world. Many people liked to forget the modest origins of their parents or even themselves, leaving behind whatever could tie them to their past, from friends to music to accents. Others exaggerated their humble origins, believing it made their own successes seem even greater, while in fact it diminished the struggles of their forebears, and slandered those who had helped them.

Shania, like almost everyone else of her generation, grew up listening to all kinds of music from the BeeGees to Stevie Wonder to classical music. She also liked the soothing, syrupy ballads of Karen Carpenter, a singer to whom her own sound had many affinities. To her mother and stepfather, country music was the only music that mattered. They played it and listened to it on the radio, and got Shania to sing the latest hits.

In first grade during show-and-tell, Shania got up and sang "Take Me Home, Country Roads," then a big country pop hit by John Denver. There is no cruelty quite like the innocent cruelty of children, thinking they honor their parents by affirming their worse prejudices. Shania learned that day, as she recalled years later, that "country music wasn't really the thing to sing." It was the music of the poor and the unlettered. She recalled painfully how the students made fun of their classmate, taunting her with the name "Twang."

Despite her rebuke in first grade, Shania loved to sing. Her mother felt that through her daughter, she could achieve recognition and honor that she could not on her own. Her mother decked her daughter out as a little cowgirl in buckskin and denim skirts and vests and took her with her to the Mattagami Hotel. Her mother worked in the kitchen, but with a daughter who could sing she was not just another kitchen worker, she was somebody.

Shania couldn't sing until 1:00 A.M. when the sale of liquor ended. Then she was awakened and brought forth to sing to a room full of drunken loggers and miners in the dregs of the early morning hours. Little Shania stood there, grasping on to a guitar that appeared almost as big as she was, singing out her country songs in these smoke-filled halls, the smell of booze in the air. This was as tough a group of workingmen as there was in North America, and as tough an audience too. Shania was paying her dues, the way few country singers of the nineties pay them any longer, and she was only eight years old. She was paying them so her mother could have bragging rights.

In northern Ontario, the short brilliant summers are followed by months of darkness, days that seem to end almost as soon as they begin. Shania returned to her home after school on those dark winter afternoons to be greeted by a mother who was often as dark and depressed as the winter days. Sharon was too poor to be able to lie there wallowing in her depression, but had to go out and scrounge money working in a kitchen or helping Jerry out in the woods. Her husband had started his own little business doing reforestation projects. When Shania was sixteen, she was already working for him, leading a crew primarily of native workers. Such a job may have been seasonal, but it paid well. Jerry was a small entrepreneur with his own business now, hardly the classical image of poverty.

When she wasn't out in the woods, Shania was back in Timmins paying those same dues over and over again. In high school she was considered a reserved, distant young woman, with goals and ambitions far beyond those of the average student. She was celebrated for what was considered her unique powerful singing, the source of most of her identity. She signed *The Quill*, the 1982 class yearbook of Timmins High and Vocational School, of her friend Olaf Karl: "I don't have a funny rhyme to write so I'll be serious. You're the most serious friend I've got, HAH! Remember me when I'm famous and I'll remember you."

As a Canadian country singer, Shania was considered inferior goods by many of her compatriots. Just the way many Americans believe that the best classical musicians are European, so many Canadians believe that the best country singers come from the United States. In country music shows, the Canadian singers went on first, before the "real" performers from the United States.

While she was still in high school, Shania performed at country shows in Ontario. One evening in Sudbury as she was singing Hank Williams's classic "I'm So Lonesome I Could Cry," Mary Bailey, a well-known Canadian country singer, stood on the side of the stage waiting her turn. Mary had released two singles on RCA and produced records on her own label, but she was still relegated to opening for the Americans. She loved music, but she was about to pack it in and retire as a performer.

Mary had heard the Hank Williams song scores of times, but as this tiny teenager belted it out, she stood crying, stunned by the emotional power of Shania's voice. Shortly after Shania graduated from high school, her mother called Mary and asked if she would like to manage her daughter. By then, Mary had given up on her own career. She believed in Shania's talent. Although she had no experience managing, Mary decided to go ahead. Shania had already been down in Nashville, her way paid by another would-be manager. Mary bought that contract out, took the teenager back to Nashville, and tried to get her a deal. Mary felt that Shania was too young, more interested in rock and pop than country, and like so many things in life, the agreement simply petered out.

Shania was still a small-town girl, and she stayed in Timmins, just another would-be singer living from gig to gig, club to club. In 1987 when Shania was twenty-one, her mother and stepfather were driving to a reforestation project far out in the bush. A logging truck bore down on them from the opposite direction, smashing head-on into their car, killing both of them. For Shania, it was a tragedy of unimaginable proportions, and a defining moment of her own life. She learned the terrible fragility of life in a way few learned it so young. She became the surrogate mother now to her two half-brothers, fourteen-year-old Mark and thirteen-year-old Darryl, both of whom were still living at home.

It was a tiny, gaunt Shania who was faced with all the burdens of life without parents and with children. She told *People* that "she rented a tiny house for her family and did the laundry in a stream when the well went dry." Those who knew her well back then have no idea what house she is talking about. Even if she was exaggerating her difficulties, Shania had to settle the estate, learn about taxes and other obligations, and shepherd the two teenagers through their grieving.

In her desperation, she called Mary Bailey and asked for help. "You have great talent," Mary told her, reassuring Shania that her dream had not died with her parents. Mary had a son but no daughter, and she reached out to the young woman, doing everything she could to help her. She arranged for her to get an audition to perform at the famous old Deerhurst Resort, 150 miles north of Toronto. She won a full-time position singing at the resort. With her regular income, Shania bought a house and a truck, and had a regularity to her life. Eileen Twain took on the stage name "Shania," an Ojibwa Indian name meaning "I'm on my way."

For the next three years Shania performed at the resort. She was a lounge singer, as well as a singer in a Las Vegas–type review. She covered everything from pop to show tunes to country. For some creative performers it would have been a dispiriting kind of gig, playing for people who had not come to see you, and for whom you would probably never play again. It was a merciless training ground, however, learning how to hold these audiences, keeping them turned away from their conversations at least half the time, pushing away the drunks that hit on performers, pushing away all the promises of good times. When she stepped off that stage, she had things to think about that most women her age didn't have to consider, showing up at parents' meetings at the school, dropping off Mark and Darryl at the teen dances, and picking them up before they got in trouble. Three years later, the two boys were finally both out of high school, out on their own, and she said that she "felt like a forty-five-year-old woman whose kids had gone away to college."

With the boys gone, Shania called Mary and told her that she was ready now to pursue a new career in country music and she wanted her friend to manage her. Mary believed in Shania the way only one other person in the world did, and that person was Shania herself. Mary saw her young protégée as a woman of limitless talent, whose only limitations were the boundaries of her own aspirations. Mary loved Shania. She was not only the daughter Mary never had; she was the career Mary never had. Now when Shania stepped out on a stage, it was Mary stepping out there too, it was Mary who was ready to pursue a new career in country music.

Shania and Mary were a team, and for those outside that sacred circle it was at times not easy. "My dad was making his money and my mom was spending it on this dream," recalls their son, Robert Kasner. "Everything had to be perfect before she went out with Shania."

Without Mary's money and energy and belief, there might never have been a recording artist named Shania Twain. Mary's belief in Shania was like a first love, untempered by fear or doubt or suspicion. She did not have the sophisticated business sense of some of Nashville's managers, but those who had that in full measure did not have her single-minded passion.

Mary may have been from a small town in northern Ontario, but over the years she had enough contacts to get Dick Frank, a Nashville music attorney, to fly up to Ontario to hear twenty-six-year-old Shania. The lawyer arranged for her to meet Norro Wilson, one of Music City's premier independent producers. Norro had been a fixture in Nashville since the late fifties, first as a singer, then as a songwriter, and now as a producer. Mary paid Norro to cut three sides with her protégée. That led to a record deal late in 1991 on Mercury Nashville to be produced by Norro and Harold Shedd, then a top executive at the label.

Norro got songs from Nashville's songwriters and produced a mainstream Nashville album. Although Norro believed in Shania, she did not have the signature voice of a Reba or Wynonna or Patty Loveless, voices so unique it was as if they were signing their names onto every note. She had energy and ambition and beauty. Norro was enough of a realist about the new Nashville to realize that was the new money in town; if you didn't have it you might not get anywhere.

When Shania's first album came out, Mercury sent her out with two other new acts on the label, Toby Keith and John Brannen, on a sixteen-city tour. This "Triple Play," the brainstorm of Luke Lewis, the president of Mercury Nashville, turned into a nightmare of clashing egos and clogged logistics. It was bad enough to compete against scores of other new acts without having to go onstage and compete against your own label mates for media attention and applause. In this battle Toby Keith was the one winner, his debut album proving a hit.

In the midst of this promotion, Mary received a call from Mutt Lange. Mary had no idea who he was. Mutt said that he had seen Shania's video and was impressed. That was significant in itself. He had not heard her album, or seen her perform. Mutt was a man of the technocratic musical age, who thought of a singer's voice as little more than a vial of sound, to be mixed with other vials of sound and then packaged with images that were as much inventions as that alchemy of sound. Something in that video impressed the British producer enough to make a cold call, eventually impressing Mary enough to let him talk to Shania herself.

The singer and the producer talked much on the phone before meeting at Fan Fair in June of 1993. It was Shania's debut before this great American audience, but she knew already that her album was not making it. Her first single had gotten no higher than number fifty-five on the *Billboard* country chart. In the end, the album sold slightly more than a hundred thousand, making serious inroads only in a few markets such as Salt Lake City, Seattle, and Denver.

Insecurity is the natural condition of most artists. Shania could count well enough to realize that if something dramatic didn't happen, her career in Nashville might never go beyond her first album. Thus, she was primed to be receptive to the entreaties of a rock producer, who felt that he could do for her what he had done for Bryan Adams, Def Leppard, and others. Mutt was in his forties, sixteen years older than Shania. He had long hair, an unassuming manner, and a reputation as a first-rate rock producer.

Mutt had something else that made him irresistible as a producer. Money. He was a millionaire and was willing to put up his own money to produce Shania's album the way he wanted to produce it. He went in and cut a deal with Mercury that essentially made him partners with the label. "Mutt bore the risks as much as we did," recalls Luke Lewis. "That's a beautiful relationship to have with a creative person."

Mutt then set out to produce *The Woman in Me,* probably the most expensive album in Nashville history. The couple went off together on a vacation and ended up writing songs together. Mutt didn't call in Nashville songwriters; he looked no further than Shania, working with her songs for the album. There is no better way to a songwriter's heart than to praise her songs. Mutt could not have wooed Shania as well with diamonds and gold as with the prospect of recording her album with her songs. In the midst of this artistic marriage, the producer and his artist fell in love and married.

The Woman in Me took a year to produce. Mutt had a brilliant sense of the distractions and interests of the audience. He built hook after hook into each song, little flourishes and touches, as if he could never afford to risk boring the listener. He sprinkled touches of R and B, dashes of Cajun sounds, a bit of pedal steel here and there. If he had been a chef, his restaurant would have featured an international cuisine that tasted a bit like southern cooking, a touch of French, something Italian, and Chinese and Japanese too—a smidgen of everything for the price of one meal.

When Luke heard the album the first time, the president of Mercury knew that what he had was as much Mutt as it was Shania. "You can't take away [Lange's] contribution to the record," he reflected. "I don't mean to be mean, but you could play this record with no vocals and it would be an entertaining and interesting record."

Shania did not mine the dark truths of her past in her songs. Her songs weren't quite ditties, but they did not have the depth of the songs that other women singers such as her idol Dolly Parton had written. She sounded in places like a heated-up version of Karen Carpenter. There was another element in her songs, the macho female of the nineties carried to a new place. She didn't stand by her man. She kicked his butt, or rather *their* butts if "Any Man of Mine" didn't put up with her bad-hair day, or showed up late. She asked, "Whose bed have your boots been under?" and kicked them out of her bedroom.

Shania gave the women a few male-bashing anthems, but the men hardly minded. They were too busy looking at her calendar or watching her videos on CMT and TNT. John and Bo Derek were enlisted to turn Shania into a perfect "10." The calendar shipped out to country radio was a bit of soft erotica, a welcome gift to the fellows at corporate country radio.

It had always been the perceived wisdom in Nashville that the women who bought most CDs didn't want to buy some sexy hussy. Enter Shania. The videos were subtly erotic. The first video, "Whose Bed Have Your Boots Been Under?" was at first hardly shown on CMT, though later it was played heavily. "The CMT has a committee largely of women and I think their official response was that the video was redundant and boring," says Luke Lewis. "We felt that they felt it was a little too sexy and that's why they didn't want to play it much. CMT played it only rarely until the record took off and they deserve absolutely no credit for the success."

The first single, "Whose Bed Have Your Boots Been Under?" was the most country song on the whole album, a Trojan horse that Mercury decided to put out first before they hit radio with the other singles. With CMT refusing to play the sexy video heavily, the first single stalled out at number eleven on the *Billboard* country chart. The second single, "Any Man of Mine," had its own sensuous video to go with it, and after almost losing the single, it moved up the *Billboard* chart to reach number one in July.

By Fan Fair '95, *Any Man of Mine* was already number four on the *Billboard* country album chart. The more knowing Nashville hands were convinced that Shania was only a fluke whose album would soon fall off the list. That afternoon of the Mercury show a score or more of Nashville producers, songwriters, and managers scored backstage passes for the sole reason of seeing what Shania looked like. Shania was a beautiful woman, but no more attractive than many other artists performing at Fan Fair, but Mutt and the Dereks and Shania had done their thing brilliantly, constructing this incredible image of a foxy, no-nonsense mythical female.

The creation of this extraordinary image, a perfect mesh of sensual, suggestive music and sensual, suggestive photos and videos, was Shania and Mutt's great creation, her magical metamorphosis. She and her minions controlled her image with merciless strength and persistence. Much that was unpleasant, unseemly, unglamorous was buried from view. There was one startlingly truthful picture, though, that appeared in *Entertainment Weekly* in August 1995 to illustrate an article on the Canadian singer. At the front of the article ran a typical Shania shot. Shania, the macho siren, wore skintight black jeans with the zipper in front. The zipper ran from just below her trademark visible navel all the way down to her crotch. The top three buttons of her six-button black jean blouse were unbuttoned, a provocative V-line falling beneath her breasts. She held a guitar behind her neck, her head tilted slightly forward, her full lips as moist as her eyes, her mouth open.

The other photo in the article was a 1987 snapshot of Shania when she was still taking care of Mark and Darryl. The two boys had the dark features of their half-Indian heritage. Behind them sat a lean, white-faced Shania, her hands on her half-brothers' backs. Her shoulder-length hair framed a small, mousy face that looked as if she had indeed been brought up deprived. It was a strong-willed face, looking straight on into the camera with her thin lips tightly clenched. If the two pictures had not been placed in the same article, few would have recognized that they were the same person.

Any other performer with a big album would have immediately gone out on the road as opening act for one of Nashville's stars. When *Any Man of Mine* took off, Shania discussed doing just that, insisting, however, on the kind of lighting and sound and treatment that opening acts almost never receive. As the months went by and the album continued to maintain residence as number one, Shania's people raised their ante as to what would get her touring. Her associates discussed going out with Wynonna. Shania would go on first, but the two women would share star billing. Shania's management backed off that idea. "I came to the conclusion that there was no way I was gonna be able to compete showwise with Reba, Wynonna, etc., and if I can't compete with them, then I'm not gonna make an impression," she told the *Journal of Country Music*. "I thought, 'Is there really room for me to get out there and do my thing? How am I gonna stand out above the rest?' Maybe not going out there is the way to stand out above the rest."

Some thought that Shania did not go on tour because she could hardly sing. But of course she could sing, and had sung publicly for over twenty years. But she could not simply go out there and sing with a backup band, for she would never re-create the sound on the album that the audience desired. To match her virtual past and her virtual album, she and her advisers had to create a virtual act, a spectacular stage show in which Shania would stand in the midst, surrounded by dancers and lights and spectacle, just the way Mutt surrounded her voice with his musical engineering. That was how she could propel her career to yet a higher place.

There were those who would travel on with Shania to this new place, and there were those who would not. In the fall of 1995 Shania received her first major award, the Canadian Country Music Award for Female Artist of the Year. When she walked onstage in Hamilton, the cameras panned to Mary Bailey sitting crying in her seat. Soon afterwards, Shania dropped the manager who had been like a second mother to her. "Change is normal," Shania told the *Toronto Star*. "I like to go forward. I'm not a stand-still kind of person. I don't get caught in a comfort zone."

Mary wasn't caught in a comfort zone either. She was as emotionally devastated as if she had lost a child. Mary may not have had the worldly sophistication to lead Shania to the places she wanted to go, but she had given her heart and soul to Shania. Shania moved on to Jon Landau, best known as Bruce Springsteen's manager, signaling the direction that she wanted her career to go. The Canadian singer might have negotiated a new relationship with her first manager so that Mary could continue in some diminished role. That did not happen.

Shania was simply gone, out of Mary's life as if she had been nothing but an illusion, an image on a video. "I love her talent, I truly do, and I loved her like a child, like a daughter I never had," Mary reflects. "Because of my love I probably allowed things to happen that strictly as business, I never would have accepted. I know this industry very well. I looked at her like an athlete going for the gold. When you see people who are that completely focused and determined, they sometimes fail to realize that no one achieves their objectives alone. I understand that.

"It took a tremendous amount out of me emotionally. There are not enough words, it's beyond the call of duty what I did for her and her career and no one can take that away from me. It was not about money. I believed when no one else did and I mean no one. We had some very tough times. People asked me if it bothers me that she never mentions my name and I say no, not at all. I did not become involved for the glory. I did it because I felt the world had to see this exceptional talent. I truly loved her and I have nothing negative to say. She has now found happiness with Mutt, as well as overwhelming success, and through this, I hope will evolve the person I know is inside."

Shania was not touring, but she was as busy as Reba or Wynonna or any of the other stars of Nashville. She was out promoting herself, traveling around the country and the world with an entourage and security like a rock star, not a country singer. Never before had there been a performer in country who spent her days in endless self-promotion. There were pop stars such as Barbra Streisand and Mariah Carey who never or rarely toured, but they did not spend their days the way Shania did, moving from fan appreciation days to controlled interviews, from charity events to awards shows, rarely singing. Even if Nashville felt that she was not quite one of them, she was succeeding brilliantly, no one-hit Billy Ray Cyrus but a bona-fide phenomenon, who won the Grammy Award for Best Country Album of 1996, and ACM Awards for Top New Female Vocalist and 1996 Album of the Year.

Shania saw herself almost as a living advertisement, each photo, each quote, each video a disciplined effort to enhance her image. She was competing with MTV chanteuses, advertising sirens, and movie stars, and her sexy image had to be brilliantly projected. It took five hours to fit her skintight bell-bottom pants for the video of "If You're Not in It for Love, I'm Outta Here." She had no use for the homespun Nashville jive. "Listen," she confided to the *Village Voice*, "the audience has sophisticated ears—and eyes. The audience that watches any kind of television and listens to any kind of audio gets the top quality just through ads. Hey, they have to be able to go from a Coke ad or a Janet Jackson record to my record and not notice the difference in quality. There's no reason we shouldn't be at that level. That's absolutely been my goal from the beginning."

Shania saw her music as aural marketing, a little something for everyone. "Our job in country music right now as artists has to be to keep those listeners that would just as soon turn over to a light rock or adult contemporary station," she said. "We have to give those people what they want to hear in order to keep them there. They love to hear the rock influence, the blues influence, all the influences that are also considered very American. We've got a R&B genre, a light R&B, '70s rock stations, and AC stations that we could put out of business if we were clever enough to keep that audience."

Shania lived what appeared to be a strange, disjointed existence. She told the *Toronto Star* that she saw her husband only about three days a month. Their home was a twelve-thousand-square-foot estate on three thousand acres outside Saranac Lake in upstate New York, distant from Nashville, Britain, New York, LA, and the Canadian heartland, a place where she could live in isolation and solitude. Mutt never gave interviews, and he was this mysterious figure floating in and out of studios, in and out of Shania's daily life.

Shania ran hard and harder, knowing the great burst of initial success and excitement would not last, but hardly able to savor the moment. She didn't feel comfortable spending much money, though she was immensely wealthy. When she cooked a meal for Mutt, she prepared barely enough for the two, not comfortable with waste. She had become a vegetarian, and she ate minute quantities of food, knowing that she had to stay almost impossibly lean. She seemed at times not to be able to appreciate the moment in which she was living. When she received her first platinum record at a party in Nashville, she spent the evening playing Shania Twain. A few days later she watched herself celebrating on a television clip of the event. "Wow, I enjoyed that night," she thought, as if referring to another person. "That was fun."

Most people in Timmins were so proud of their most famous citizen that they paid little attention to the rude caricatures of their town that accompanied so many of the interviews that Shania gave. Shania had no bigger booster than her hometown newspaper. Despite that, in April, two months before Fan Fair '96, the *Timmins Daily Press* published a front-page article asserting that "the *Daily Press* has learned that Twain has woven a tapestry of half-truths and outright lies in her climb to the top of the country charts." It is one of the axioms of country music that no one knows you like the people you grow up with, and the two reporters, Dawn Liersch and Brad Hunter, had tracked down Shania's biological father, Clarence Edwards, and her grandmother, eighty-five-year-old Regina Nutbrown. Beneath the tabloidlike headline ("Shania Confesses She Might Not Be Native") was a sad, familiar tale of divorce, broken families, and twisted memories.

In Shania's response published that day in the *Daily Press*, the singer said, "I've never had a relationship with my biological father. . . . Although I was briefly introduced to Clarence a couple of times in my teen years, I never knew him growing up." Shirley Caby, Clarence's common-law wife of twenty-five years, says that her husband saw his daughter several times a year, usually at holidays, and tried to keep up more of a relationship but had been pushed away. "I never felt the need to seek the love or support of another family because I had it from the Twains," Shania admitted in her response. Although Shania asserted that "there was some Indian heritage in his [Clarence's] family," the *Daily Press* reported that "Edwards does not have any Native blood nor did Twain's mother." For her part, Caby says adamantly that her husband has no Indian blood.

The *Daily Press* had pulled at one single strand of Shania's story and her lawyers and publicists reacted as if the whole mythic image of Shania risked unraveling. The Canadian star threatened a lawsuit against her hometown paper, and took away the contract to print her fan club letter. In the end, after lengthy negotiations, the paper printed a front-page "clarification" stating in part that "The *Daily Press* accepts Ms. Twain's statement that there is a widely shared misunderstanding about the identity of Ms. Twain's natural father. . . . The *Daily Press* sincerely regrets any suggestion that Ms. Twain lied."

Shania had been advised to speak frankly about her past, but she had not done so, and her early years were rising up to haunt her. She had done her best to raise her two half-brothers, but their lives were turning up dark pathways, risking haunting her image as well. On New Year's Eve, police arrested Mark and Darryl for impaired driving and taking a vehicle, charges for which they were fined and had their licenses suspended. That would have been enough to have straightened up some young men, but in May, a month before Fan Fair, Mark was accused of breaking his girl-friend's car window and hitting a police officer in the face with a backpack. Later that month police arrested the two brothers at a car dealership in Huntsville, Ontario, for trying to steal cars. Mark was sentenced to six months in jail.

Shania did not have to exaggerate the truths of her past. She stood as close to the roots of country music in her past as did any artist, but she was the ultimate creation of the new country music of the nineties. As she stood signing autographs this evening, she was receiving a lesson in the emotional truths of country music. Life was not a ditty, not a disco single, not a romp. Life was in these faces, in the joy these people felt as they had their moment with her. She was here this evening, truly here, and there was something real and unaffected in this moment, something that did not have to be honed and shaped to fit an image, something that was not a calculated construction to please the most people. It was the great lesson of Fan Fair.

9

"Ten Thousand Angels"

Mindy McCready stood alone at the center of the great stage holding a microphone in her hand. Mindy had never performed before such a vast audience, indeed had hardly ever performed anywhere. As she waited for the applause to fade at the RCA/BNA Fan Fair show, she knew there were those watching to see her exposed, hoping that her voice would prove a pathetic echo of the sound on her BNA debut album.

Her first single, "Ten Thousand Angels," was rising up the *Billboard* charts to number six. Her video was a sensation on CMT. Her album was the fastest-selling debut album by a female country artist in five years. Nonetheless, the new technology could tune up a croak into a nightingale's lament. On Music Row they whispered that she was a twenty-year-old piece of blond fluff, a navel-flaunting Shania clone who would be blown right out of Nashville as soon as the country audience got a close listen to her music.

Mindy began to sing, and out in the vast reaches of the audience, no sound was heard. Her mouth moved and her hands gestured, but nothing. Out in the stands she appeared so terrified that she had been rendered speechless. Then, her microphone was belatedly switched on and a strong, intimate voice flowed out across the audience, a young voice that seemed to be living the lyrics.

The song told the story of a young woman who is attracted to a young man of such sexuality and guile that she is afraid she will go off and sleep with him. In an age of AIDS and increasing moral conservatism, the dilemma was a real one, and many young people who heard the song identified with the lyrics and with Mindy.

> I can tell he's gonna ask me to dance
> but that's not as far as he wants to go.

On the two giant monitors a stunning image appeared: a five-foot-eight blonde at one moment looking childlike, the next the Marilyn Monroe of country. She wore skintight, light blue, soft leather pants and a matching halter top, her midriff exposed, and white heels. The new generation of women singers were almost all impossibly thin, living on regimens that would not have satisfied Mahatma Gandhi. Mindy had dieted down to 110 pounds, and as thin as she was she worried that she was still too fat.

> Lead me not into temptation
> heaven help me to be strong.

Out here on this stage, Mindy was alone, but only she knew how alone. This was to have been *her* night, but so far it had been a merciless week. Her former manager was suing her. His lawyers had insisted on taking her deposition yesterday, the very day when she was supposed to sign autographs in the RCA/BNA booth. If she hadn't shown up, she would have been jailed for contempt. The lawyers had gone on and on and on, in part she felt to ruin her day. She had sat anguished, trying to focus on the endless questions, thinking, "I'm disappointing fans and nobody's telling them I'm not going to be there." She had stood up hundreds of fans who had waited for up to two hours. Even now she couldn't say what had happened.

Mindy's relatives had come up from Florida. For the most part that was more a burden than a support. As she sang, Mindy's forty-one-year-old pregnant mother, Gayle Phelan, stood behind her on the stage, her eyes wet with tears. Her mother had always hugged the spotlight. Now, instead of simply watching her daughter, Gayle stood being videotaped with Mindy in the background. Gayle was a beautiful, statuesque woman who had even more natural charisma than her daughter. Only Mindy understood all the burdens of that relationship, how it haunted her and everything she did.

To the side of the stage stood her new manager, Stan Moress. The man talked the best of games, but Mindy felt that Stan's ultimate loyalty was to Joe Galante, the chair of the RCA Label Group, and not to her. She liked Galante a great deal, but she was under no illusions here either. She knew that Joe needed her, but if she didn't succeed she would be gone. As far as the other artists and their comradeship, she had seen that was a joke. For the most part, they didn't like one another, and they didn't wish one another well, and the women were the worst.

Mindy had David Malloy, but even that she couldn't talk about. David was not only the coproducer of her album but her forty-three-year-old lover. She had not had ten thousand angels around her when that affair had begun and she had moved in with him. Galante had told her she should keep the fantasy alive. Let all the pubescent boys out there lust after her without thinking she was living with a man her father's age. It was a pathetic cliché, the middle-aged, divorced producer lusting after the ambitious teenager, and she knew that was something else that had to be kept secret.

> Help me break the spell that I'm under
> got my feet and hold me tight.
> I need ten thousand angels
> watching over me tonight.

Out there in the audience sat Mindy's grandfather, William "Bill" R. Stancel. Other than David, her grandfather was the most important man in her life. At least she did not have to hide him or pretend that her grandfather was not here this evening. As a child, her grandfather had often told her how he had sung one gospel song on the radio when he was growing up called "Ten Thousand Angels." The first time Mindy heard *her* "Ten Thousand Angels," she knew that she would record the song and it would be her first single. And she knew that she would sing it for her grandfather.

The performers this evening all sang mini-sets. Mindy sang just this one song. That was how careful the label was marketing her, not taking any chances that she could not hold the audience for several songs. It was enough. At the end of her song she had her sixteen thousand angels out there, standing and applauding with fervor.

As Bill Stancel watched his oldest grandchild up onstage, he thought back to when Mindy was a little girl in Fort Myers, Florida, and how he had baited her hook when they first went fishing. Bill had brown, leathery skin that was part his Cherokee Indian heritage, and part years in the orchards of South Florida and the hunting fields of Georgia and the South. He had sparkling, inquisitive, mystical eyes, a hunting guide's stealthy manner, and an unfocused anger that ran in the men in the family. Next to him sat Joan Stancel, his wife, a devout, sweetly demure woman who had acceded to the will and whim of her husband for half a century.

Bill figured women had their place, and it was in the kitchen and the bedroom, not out in the world, but with Mindy it had always been different. From the time she could walk, his little Mindy was special. He would go over to her house, call out her name, and off they went in Grandpa's truck, full of flats of mangoes or cantaloupes, taking the fruit from store to store. He set her up there on her special seat. Wherever they stopped, the storekeepers shook their heads in awe at this little girl who couldn't have been two years old, talking a blue streak.

Mindy's mother was twenty years old when her daughter was born. As a teenager, Gayle had been a beauty queen. Her stop-in-your-tracks good looks had attracted Tim McCready, her husband two years her senior who had himself a good job as manager at

Winn-Dixie. He adored his wife and left most of the child's rearing in Gayle's hands.

Mindy was hardly two years old before Gayle had Mindy memorizing the Gettysburg Address, the Twenty-third Psalm, and the Pledge of Allegiance. Gayle loved having Mindy recite and hearing people tell her how smart her daughter was. And Mindy just loved doing it. In the car she sang "Old McDonald Had a Farm," using a hairbrush as her make-believe microphone. She had a gift for mimicry, doing a perfect imitation of her mother's fullest, fakest smiles; flashing her eyes like the minister's silly wife; or shaking her head the way Farrah Fawcett did in *Charley's Angels*.

Gayle wanted Mindy to do her part around the house. At the age of three she had Mindy making the beds, telling her that she could figure out how to do it by herself. She had her washing dishes too, though Mindy couldn't see above the countertop.

Gayle took her daughter to a Christian day school. Little Mindy was soon ordering her schoolmates around. In elementary school, she was so hyper that Gayle started giving her paregoric, thinking that might calm her down. Mindy just couldn't sit still.

Mindy had two little brothers, Josh and T.J. Her mother didn't have the same interest in her baby boys as she first had in Mindy. She delegated Mindy to take care of them much of the time. Her father was working long hours and seemed to want to spend little time with his three children.

Her mother sought perfection, spending hours applying her makeup, directing Mindy to keep the house impeccable, insisting that her daughter act like a little lady. Mindy sensed that something was not right, though she didn't know quite what. She rolled her eyes when her mother did something she considered especially crazy, and then, Mindy recalled, her mother smacked her across the face. Her father was full of anger, too. He abused his children, beating them out of his frustration and fury.

Gayle said that in her house "firecrackers were going off all the time." Boredom was banished, routine exiled. Theirs was a life of endless dramas and noise, excitement and energy. Sometimes it was like Roman candles, Mindy strutting around the sofas in the living room doing her imitations, singing, jumping around. Other times it was a string of firecrackers, guests moving in and out, the boys shouting, Gayle ordering her children about. Still other times it was cherry bombs of deafening intensity and danger, fights and struggles, and name-calling, and pitched emotional battles. Occasionally it was emotional dynamite, shattering the very foundations of their lives.

When Mindy was eleven, her parents divorced. Tim wanted Gayle back. When Gayle and the children returned from a trip, Tim had a dozen roses and two enormous boxes of his ex-wife's favorite Hunt's Pudding packs sitting on the kitchen counter. Later Tim showed up at the house, attempting to win his wife back not only with gifts but with words. "She doesn't care about you," Mindy told her father as Gayle watched. "We love you. We want you to love us and you keep buying her things and you didn't buy us anything."

Tim had been handy around the house. With her father gone, Mindy took over many of his chores. Mindy could do just about anything, including driving a car, and Gayle sent her out running errands. She was too young to have a license. She could hardly look over the steering wheel.

Gayle ran a nonemergency ambulance service out of her house. When the phones rang, Mindy often answered, speaking in a commanding adult voice, assigning a driver to one of the three ambulances. Sometimes when the phone rang in the middle of the night and her mother was asleep, Mindy took the call herself, driving the ambulance through the dark streets of Fort Myers. She began taking more of the calls, sometimes going off with her mother but often alone, rolling 250-pound patients onto gurneys, driving between hospitals and homes.

Mindy had an authoritative way about her, as persuasive to her mother as it was to the patients on the ambulance service. Mindy was Gayle's talisman, her good omen, her best friend, confidante, and aide, and then her mother would turn on her. When Gayle didn't let Mindy have her thirteenth birthday party, she wrote her grandmother, Joan, a note. Joan lay on her bed crying, wondering what in God's name she could do.

Mindy loved sitting next to her mother at her makeup table

hearing Gayle's stories. She loved wearing her mother's clothes. Mindy could see how obsessed her mother was with finding a new husband, the clock of life ticking away like a bomb. Gayle started taking Mindy out with her to the singles bars. With her mother's clothes and makeup on, the two women looked like sisters, and nobody ever asked Mindy her age.

Gayle was not out here looking for a night's dalliance. She grasped tightly onto her chip of beauty, ready to place it down on one last roll of the wheel. She pushed the leering lounge lizards and make-out artists away, and sat waiting for Prince Charming to arrive. As for her daughter, she didn't bring the fourteen-year-old Mindy to introduce her to romance but to make it easier for Gayle to sit there.

Prince Charming arrived in the nick of time. His name was Thomas Phelan, and he was everything Gayle had dreamed about. He was handsome, with the long, lean looks of a model stepping off the pages of *GQ*. He was well-off, a pilot for United Airlines. He was romantic, with tales of exotic ports of call. He was nine years younger than Gayle. Best of all, he wanted to marry Gayle and move in with her and her three children and make a real old-fashioned family.

If Gayle and Tom were to have a real old-fashioned family, then Mindy had to be a real old-fashioned fifteen-year-old. Gayle laid out the tight clothes of childhood for her daughter and asked her to don them. Gayle thought she was giving her daughter a gift, but Mindy refused to revert to a life she had never known. She started sneaking out at night, jimmying the window up, and running off with her girlfriends. Gayle didn't want her daughter even to talk to boys on the phone until she was sixteen. To celebrate her fifteenth birthday, Mindy wanted to go out of town with a boy. Gayle told her no, but Mindy went anyway, and her mother called the police to stop her.

Mindy found herself cut off from the sisterly relationship with her mother, distraught over her mother's new husband and his relationship not only with Gayle but with her two brothers. She fled from the house, living weeks at a time with her father, grandparents, or her uncle. She would come back and forth, still working for the ambulance service. Tom came back and forth too, living for a while with his wife, and then after some epic fight, going off again. Tom was with Gayle only two years when they divorced. They remarried a few months later, and continued their tormented love. Mindy was afraid to tell her grandfather about their problems, afraid that he would pick up a gun and go over there, or have a heart attack.

At the age of fourteen, Mindy had her first boyfriend, a seventeen-year-old from a good family. He was the first of her rescuers. She lived with his family, getting away from her tortured life at home. The young man became obsessed with Mindy when she sought to move away from his suffocating embrace. Mindy had never lived as a child, and she did not do so now. She met her second boyfriend while she was working for the ambulance service. He was a twenty-six-year-old police officer. Mindy lied to him that she was eighteen. Gayle would have none of this. She went over to the sheriff's office and gave them a large unrefined piece of her mind. "Do not let him come to my house again or I want his job," she told them. "My daughter is sixteen years old. I don't have a husband here to help me. It should be against the law."

Tom returned to his own condo so he could move in and out at will. There were no weapons that could not be used in their anguished love. Gayle was so angry with Tom that she asked Mindy to break into his apartment and take anything valuable that she found. Mindy had learned to think that the law was just another kind of license that one didn't always need. She had the natural stealth of a cat burglar, and she jimmied open the window, and carried away Tom's valuables.

Mindy performed in public for the first time when she was three, singing a gospel song at the Pentecostal church the family attended. In elementary school, she started taking vocal lessons from a retired college professor. After her parents' divorce, her grandparents decided that their darling granddaughter should sing at *their* church. Mindy tried out, and as well as she sang, she was turned down. Mindy figured it was because her grandpa didn't wear a fancy suit to church and didn't put on fancy airs, but it may have been in part because Mindy was now a child of divorce.

Until her parents' marriage ended, Gayle had played gospel and Christian music around the house. Now Gayle started tuning in to country radio, discovering that the music was her spiritual autobiography, the songs speaking to her pain and passion.

Mindy listened to the music too, and as she became a little older she started going out to karaoke bars. Her girlfriends pushed her forward, daring her to sing. "Go, Mindy, do it!" they yelled. Mindy sang Trisha Yearwood songs and Crystal Gayle songs and Reba songs and Wynonna songs. The audience applauded but no more than they did for others who came forward to sing to the recorded background music.

Mindy graduated from high school at the age of sixteen with the vague idea of developing a career as a country singer. Meanwhile, she worked as a waitress at a resort hotel, occasionally getting up and singing a song or two. Mindy's uncle believed in his niece, and he bragged about her to one of his neighbors, Richard "Dick" Haskins, an elderly businessman who was part owner of the Quantum Publishing Company in Nashville. Haskins met Mindy and was so impressed that he immediately offered to help her career. Mindy had found her latest rescuer, not the promise of passionate romance, but a passionate musical career and a life away from Fort Myers.

Mindy finally had contact with someone who seemed to know Nashville. The man was wealthy, knowledgeable, and generous, taking Mindy and Gayle out on his yacht. Gayle was a creature of instinct, and she took an immediate dislike to the businessman. "Mom, just be nice to him," Mindy insisted. "Just be nice. Mom, he's loaded. He's going to do all these things for me."

Gayle masked her doubts, lit up her two-hundred-watt smile, and started conversing merrily with Ruth Haskins, the businessman's wife. "Dick is just looking so forward to this because he loves to create things," bubbled Mrs. Haskins.

"Well, I have news for you," Gayle interjected. "I created her."

Eighteen-year-old Mindy trusted more in Haskins's promises than her mother's doubts. As Mindy set out with Haskins for

Nashville, Gayle made Mindy make one promise: that she would give it a year. If she didn't get a record deal she would return home and go to college. Gayle had seen enough of the world not to want her daughter to sing in raunchy clubs, hit upon by drunken barroom cowboys and lowlife hustlers. Mindy wasn't worried. Haskins seemed to have everything to protect and shepherd her, including his own bus on which he and Mindy drove up to Nashville.

On her very first day in Music City, Mindy met Norro Wilson at Quantum Publishing. At fifty-six, Norro was one of the oldest premier producers in Music City. His career as a song plugger, singer, songwriter, and producer went back to the 1950s. "You remind me of my grandpa," Mindy told him, hardly a comment guaranteed to ingratiate her with the veteran producer.

Norro listened to Mindy's karaoke tape, rummaged through the Rolodex in his head, and thought that in all his years he'd never met a young woman who not only had such a killer voice but was so confounded good-looking, and with such a personality. He had just finished producing Shania Twain's first album, and the Canadian singer didn't come close. He decided that he would start working with Mindy, taking her around, see if he could get her a deal.

Mindy was still staying on the tour bus when Haskins presented her with a contract to sign. Without her father or an attorney going over the document, Mindy signed the contract. With that Haskins set Mindy up with a job as a receptionist at his publishing company, rented her an apartment, paid off her car loan and advanced her other money. That was a big break by itself, not to have to scrounge around for a job and a place to live. Her second week in town Mindy and Norro had lunch with Tony Brown. Mindy was so new to Nashville that she had no idea how unusual it was for an eighteen-year-old amateur singer to be sitting around with the president of MCA Nashville.

Norro started taking Mindy around to showcases and parties, trying to make her presence known. He took her to the Wildhorse Saloon, the large country dance club in downtown Nashville. Mindy was mind-boggled at the sheer size of the club, all these people jammed into the place, and was perfectly content to sit on a barstool watching a young singer, Chely Wright, singing out there on the distant stage.

"Hey, Mindy, come here a minute, I want you to meet someone." The man Mindy had come to call "Papa Narcy" motioned her over.

"This is David Malloy, Mindy. You know that Eddie Rabbitt song 'I Love a Rainy Night'? Well, this fellow cowrote that and a slew of others, and produced Eddie too."

"Oh, my gosh," Mindy said, looking in awe at Malloy, who stood there with a shy, embarrassed grin on his face.

"I've known you since you were thirteen, David, and have I ever brought you anybody, a singer?"

"No," Malloy replied.

"Well, I'm telling you this girl right here, she sings. She's got a card."

Mindy might have been impressed, but the whole town knew that Malloy was a has-been. His dad had been a leading engineer. As a songwriter David had started getting cuts when he was still a teenager. He was best known as the producer for Eddie Rabbitt, one of the pop country acts that succeeded primarily in the wake of the film *Urban Cowboy*. David had left town in the mid-eighties when a more traditional country music started making inroads. He had the idea of succeeding in pop music in Los Angeles. That hadn't worked out, and he had returned to Nashville, a divorced man with two kids. He overextended himself building a studio and he lost everything. He reeked of failure, his clips grown yellow, his tomorrows in the past. He had a writing deal at Giant Records, but he was on nobody's list of people you went to in Nashville if you wanted something to happen.

"Well, maybe she can do some demos for us over at Giant?"

The mere idea that these two longtime Nashville music professionals should be spending time promoting Mindy's career was a perfect indication of how much the industry had changed. A mere five years ago, no one would have wasted time with an eighteen-year-old blowing into town clutching a karaoke tape as if that were some kind of résumé. Mindy would have been told to go home and start paying her dues. She should start singing in clubs, go out there and live and learn and feel and come back five years later, if she came back at all. Now youth was king and queen and all the court, and as crazy as it might seem, Mindy had a chance.

Norro and David viewed Nashville from different ends of the artistic spectrum. Norro was producing George Jones, one of the greatest traditional country singers of all time. That was Norro's kind of music, but he saw how the world was changing, and he figured he better change with it. There were still rednecks, as Norro saw it, but they wore $150 cowboy hats, Guess! jeans, $200 pairs of boots, and drove themselves in spiffy $28,000 pickup trucks. They drank cocktails, and not too many of them either. And they sure didn't want to listen to some fool hillbilly crying sad songs into the dark night. They didn't hear them anymore either. Country radio played these light, up-tempo, danceable songs. It was country disco. That's what it was. And if Norro didn't start churning it out, he knew that he wouldn't be producing any longer.

David was different. He had gone to LA to strut his stuff in the big world, and the main noise he remembered from those years was the sound of doors slamming in his face. He had returned to Nashville with chips on his shoulders as big as epaulets. He could hardly believe what had happened to Nashville in his absence. It was like the Yukon gold rush in Music City. Practically everyone was making out, buying Mercedeses and Jags, flying around in private jets and driving around in chauffeured limousines, practically everyone but David Malloy. He felt like an untouchable.

His dad felt so sorry for him that he lent David money to buy a little studio on Music Row and see if he could get something started. He hung his shingle out and hustled whatever he could. He had never been a fan of old-time country. Now that Nashville music was again becoming infused with pop sensibilities, he figured he could make it big again if he could only get a break.

A few days later, Mindy and Norro came over to David's small, windowless office at Giant Records off Music Row. David listened to Mindy's tape. The voice wasn't mature, and the interpretation sounded lame, but David heard something. He played the tape for friends. They didn't hear it. Nonetheless, David started working with Mindy in his studio. David was a relentless, driven perfectionist. Hour after hour, session after session, night after night, he had Mindy standing before a microphone singing.

During those endless sessions, Mindy and David began a romance. Mindy was the same age as David's daughter and seven years older than his son. Mindy was no mere teenager. David learned quickly enough that behind that wispy blond veneer stood a forceful, dominating woman. Sometimes she seemed older than David, full of world-weary wisdom and savage insight.

For two decades David had seen would-be country stars show up in Nashville from tiny towns across America. They waxed sentimentally about good old Nowhere, Oklahoma, and wonderful Roadstop, Texas, but they worked so hard in part because they would do anything not to have to go back there. Mindy had promised her mother that if she didn't make it in Nashville in a year, she would return to Fort Myers and go to college. A year was a blink of an eye. It was nothing. But that was her promise. David saw that Mindy wanted to succeed as desperately as anyone he had ever worked with, desperately wanted never to have to return to live in her mother's world.

When David looked at the contract Mindy had signed with Haskins, he was appalled. He was no attorney, but as he read the contract, he saw that Mindy had agreed to pay the Florida businessman 25 percent of everything she earned for nine years if Haskins renewed his options. David believed the contract so unfair that he pushed Mindy to talk to John Mason, a leading music industry attorney.

Mindy was used to a life in which firecrackers were going off all the time, and Nashville had become a yearlong Fourth of July. The year would soon be up and she had nothing going. She was thinking about talking with this high-priced, high-powered lawyer about getting out of her contract, but she had no idea how she was going to pay legal bills.

When her paternal grandfather died, Mindy told her employer that she was going to the funeral. She drove out to the airport but the plane was full. Instead of trying to get on another flight, she decided to stay in Nashville. She had some free time, and David pushed her to go and see John Mason.

In Fort Myers, Haskins called Mindy's home, expecting her to be there for the funeral. "I don't know where she's at," Gayle told the businessman. "Maybe she's at Disney World or something." Mindy had seemingly lied about going to the funeral, and she was fired from the publishing company.

Mindy had no job, no future, no free apartment. She moved in with David, who was rescuing her from Haskins, offering both love and career.

"I'm gonna get a record deal, David, I am, I am," Mindy kept telling David.

"No you're not, Mindy," David replied softly. "Not now. Not so soon. It takes years."

"I gotta get it. If I don't, my mom's gonna make me come home."

Eleven months had gone by, and Mindy seemed further away from signing a deal than the first day she walked in and talked to Norro. A month from now, she would have to go back to Florida. In a folder at Malloy Boys Studio, Mindy found a song that David and Tim Johnson had written. Daryle Singletary, the other artist that David was producing, had sung the song on a demo tape. Mindy listened to "Tell Me Something I Don't Know."

"I want to sing this song," Mindy told David.

"Well, OK," David said, acceding to this as to almost all her wishes. "Let's work on it."

For three days Mindy sang the song over and over. They had worked hard recording songs before, but nothing like this. Again and again Mindy sang it, changing the phrasing, repeating verses and choruses, David working on the soundboard piecing together the multitude of versions. When it was finished, David played the song for his dad. Jim Malloy had seen and experienced about everything in Nashville, and he wasn't moved easily. "I think you can get yourself a deal with this one," Jim told his son.

David knew that you didn't get a record deal with one song. You had to have a slew of songs, better yet if you'd written them yourself. You had to sing them in public at a showcase before industry bigwigs. That was the way you did it.

David had no time for that. He had to call in all of his chits. He got two musician friends to come in and add guitar and steel guitar. He didn't have anything to pay them, but they understood. That was the way Nashville worked sometimes.

Then David started calling around the labels, setting up meetings. Most labels were becoming like pricey boutiques that only had a few of each item. So he looked around to see which label might want a new young woman singer. He figured his best bet was Atlantic, since they had only one woman on the entire label. David set up a meeting with Rick Blackburn, the Atlantic president. The executive wanted to hear Mindy at a showcase, to get a real feel for her singing out there in the world of live music. David couldn't wait around for that.

David sent out tapes to Jim Ed Norman, the president of Warner/Reprise Nashville, and to Scott Hendricks, the new president of Capitol Nashville. Neither man was interested, and time was running out. In two weeks Mindy's year was up, and she swore she was leaving. David called Thom Schuyler, the senior vice president/A&R at RCA Nashville. He had known Thom for years, but even so he asked for just ten minutes of his time.

"I got one song here," David said when he walked into the office. "And that's all I'm gonna play you. If you don't get it, man, three songs won't make a difference."

David tossed a tape to the A&R executive, who punched it into his tape deck and listened intently to "Tell Me Something I Don't Know."

Schuyler shook his head in awe. "Joe needs to hear this," Schuyler said, referring to Joe Galante.

Mindy had a few Sunday-go-to-church outfits, but she didn't have anything special enough to wear to her meeting with the chair of the RCA Label Group. So she and David went out and bought a sexy red dress. David called in more chits, asking Tim Johnson, his cowriter on several songs, to come along to play guitar. As they walked into the RCA/BNA building off Music Row, Mindy was sick to her stomach. "God, I really hope I don't hurl in the middle of this," she confided to David.

Joe Galante had long ago decided that small talk was the refuge of small minds and slackers. He made little attempt to make Mindy feel comfortable. Joe was a small, compact man, given to sly, sardonic smiles.

Joe listened to Mindy's first song, his face expressionless. That he was listening to her at all proved how much he understood the new realities of Nashville. Indeed, he had helped create those realities. Joe was one of the first people in Nashville to do market research. He went for youth and for acts with pop sensibilities. As he looked back on it, he believed that in Nashville "we started signing acts and lowering our standards. The hurdles to get on the label weren't necessarily a great singer with great songs. Maybe it was a good singer with great jeans and a hat."

Joe and the other label heads had created this new star-making machinery, and it was threatening to chew them up. He doubted that "some of the people that come through today will get respect and that's what leads to a shorter career." He listened to songs all the time, and he had a sense that the lyrics didn't matter the way they once did, that "it's more of a hook, more top forty formulas." He had pushed for youth, signing acts in their mid-twenties. That seemed young enough, for country music wasn't kiddie music. It was about life, and how could you sing it if you hadn't had a life?

When Mindy finished singing her third song, Joe looked at her as if some great gulf had been overcome. "Are you ready for this?" Joe asked, knowing that this woman sitting on the couch was only nineteen years old. "Do you even understand?"

"No, I don't understand at all."

Joe shook his head. Nashville had no place any longer for crazed characters like old No Show George Jones, who in his drugged days missed about as many shows as he played.

Joe believed that "we're strip-mining this business, taking these kids that are so young that they haven't even played a club, and yet we're trotting them out there trying to make them superstars and the whole format has dropped down in age and dropped down in quality and rushing for the gold mine." Nashville took these kids, pared them down, remade them in the image of the moment, stripped away any kernel of individuality that might be germinating, media-trained them half to death, and worked them relentlessly, ceaselessly, and then as likely or not, dropped them.

"You're gonna be on the road," Joe said. "You're gonna get no sleep. You're gonna have to eat at gross joints for several years. You're not gonna make any money. Do you want this that bad?"

Joe was not exaggerating. Even if Mindy ended up with a gold album, selling half a million copies, a big success for a new act, she would still be struggling. Once the label subtracted all the expenses, including recording and tour support, she might end up with no more than twenty or thirty thousand dollars. That was the reality. That was how badly the equation was skewed against the artist.

Mindy thought for a moment, an image of the future flashing through her head. "Yeah, I want it that bad. I want to sing that bad."

"Well, OK, uh, we'll talk to you soon."

Out in the car, Mindy started to cry. "Oh, David, I was terrible. I sucked. I couldn't keep my pitch. I was so nervous. Nobody's going to sign me. I'm going to have to go home."

Early the following week, fifty-one weeks after Mindy arrived in town, Schuyler called David on his mobile phone and said that the label wanted to sign Mindy.

Stan Moress kept calling and leaving messages on Mindy's answering machine. Stan was hungry for a promising new client. For a quarter century, he had been one of the top managers in Nashville, but he had learned that the bonds with an artist could be severed in an instant. He had walked down the aisle with Lorrie Morgan to give her away at her wedding. That's how close they were, and she had fired him twice in six years, the last time only a few months ago. Clint Black had been his other big-time client, and Clint had just fired him too.

Stan was yet another outsider. He had first started to come to Nashville from Los Angeles in 1970. Stan, like so many others, was enchanted by Nashville's world of country music, and he had moved to the Tennessee capital. After all his years in Nashville, Stan still had the patina of his past life in LA. He wore cotton and linen, not jeans and wool. He had a former public relations man's take on the world, believing that there was no hyperbole too big not to be believed, no compliment too large not to be swallowed whole.

Stan welcomed Mindy into his office with expansive warmth. Stan had the best shot at managing Mindy. He had been best man at Joe's wedding. He knew David from all the years he had managed Eddie Rabbitt. Stan figured that Mindy was taking his measure, and he was doing the same.

The stakes were high. The potential rewards were enormous, but the odds were brutal. It might be several years before Stan started earning his commission of 15 or 20 percent. Meanwhile he would be spending not only time but some of his own money. He had to be incredibly careful, and he and his manager colleagues were no more likely to take a chance with a daring, edgy artist than were the labels.

Stan knew that Mindy could sing well, but that was no better than half of it. Image. Personality. Drive. Perseverance. Luck. That was the other half. Stan told Mindy some of his sad stories of managing for three decades, all the promises that had been made, all the ego games and betrayals.

"I'm different," Mindy said, her voice full of confidence.

"Well, what makes you different?"

"I'm different, that's all. Help me get where I need to go and I'll work with you. If I don't like it, I'll tell you. But I won't not try it."

When Mindy left that day, Stan wanted to manage her. He felt her energy. He experienced her charm. He sensed her ambition. As he saw it, this was a woman who would settle for nothing but the top, a woman with a voice and personality and looks that could get her there.

Stan was a man of spectacular gestures. He had a door in a frame delivered to David's studio. On the door he wrote a note: "Dear Mindy, We would like to open the doors for you on Sixteenth Avenue. Love Moress Nanas."

Most of the money that Mindy received for signing her contract with BNA went to John Mason's law firm. Mindy prayed that the whole nasty business with her former manager would go away and she could get on with her new team, including her record label, her new manager, Stan, and her coproducers, David and Norro.

Mindy and David started immediately looking for songs for her album. Mindy was not a proven songwriter, but she chose the songs that others had written as if they were part of her autobiography. She could be so abrupt with songwriters and song pitchers that she offended them. "Don't play me any of those cheating songs," she insisted. "My attitude is if they cheat, they die. I don't like those songs and I'm not singing them."

She chose "Maybe He'll Notice Her Now" because it reminded her of the way her mother had tried to attract her father when they were going through all their troubles. She liked "Guys Do It All the Time" because she could imagine herself out with her girlfriends, drinking and joking and making their boyfriends mad. That was fine, but she didn't like these women-with-an-attitude songs that most of the women artists were cutting. As she saw it, these songs were stupid, man-bashing, and she wanted none of that either.

For all that had been happening to her, Mindy had never sung her country songs in public before. She did so for the first time in October of 1995 during CMA week. This was a time when the circles of success were sharply drawn. In the innermost circle sat those artists nominated for the CMA Awards in their special seats in the Grand Ole Opry House during the live television broadcast. Outside that circle sat the other major artists and young signed performers, most of them seated in the auditorium as well. Still further away were the young acts performing at the SRO showcases, the convention of bookers who this week were choosing acts for state and county fairs and theaters across America. Then came a more modest showcase in which singers performed before 249 winners of a radio station contest. In the outermost rings stood singers playing in the clubs and honky-tonks for a few dollars a night, hoping to get a break. Beyond them on the fringes of the fringe stood street singers hustling for quarters.

Mindy made her public debut in a dining room at the Opryland Hotel before the winners of the radio contest. This hotel was so enormous that with a few more additions the management would have had to hire safari-clad guides to lead guests to one of the nearly three thousand rooms, past the indoor 12,500-square-foot lake, skirting the Dancing Waters with water spurting up twenty-two feet in the air, over the catwalk above the junglelike vegetation. By the time the new three-hundred-thousand-square-foot convention center was finished, the Opryland Hotel would be able to boast that it was the largest hotel/convention center under one roof in the civilized world.

The radio contest winners had been given little time to explore the many wonders of the Opryland Hotel. For much of the day, the group had been sitting listening to one act after another. It had long since become one gray mush of sound. There was no spotlight, and the immense chandeliers left the temporary stage bathed in the same dull light as the rest of the ballroom. The room was acoustically dead, the music dropping like stones in a lake, disappearing into the rumble of conversation.

Mindy got sick to her stomach beforehand. She was just another unknown, with less experience as a performer than anyone here today. "Here's Mindy McCready, someone you will hear about soon," the emcee announced, his professional resonances hardly hiding his boredom.

The crowd gave Mindy a smattering of applause. All of the other young performers had tried to connect, reaching out to the lethargic group with aggressive friendliness, trying somehow to strike some resonant chord. A Texas boyhood. An army brat's upbringing. A small-town background. Make a story of your life. That was the idea. Connect somehow.

Mindy stood there. "I signed my contract today," she said finally. Someone in the back of the room applauded, the sound dying out, lost in the vast room. Mindy could think of nothing else to say. She was a nineteen-year-old woman who had never performed in public, and she was suddenly confronted with the reality that she was supposed to entertain. For the first time in her life, Mindy was out there on a stage by herself. Until now, Mindy had survived in the shadow of her mother's beauty. Gayle had been the star, her stunning looks bringing a bounty of attention wherever she went. But not now, not any longer. She nodded to David, and her little band began to play.

Stardom is a mistress that goes where she wants to go, and leaves when she pleases, transforming the ordinary into the extraordinary, the mundane into the marvelous. There may have been better performers on this stage that evening, but no one lifted the audience out of its listlessness the way Mindy did. Half a dozen people got up from their seats and took Mindy's picture, memorializing the moment. Afterwards, a line formed around the table where Mindy was sitting.

"Congratulations on signing your contract," said a grandmotherly woman, who rushed up to be the first in line.

"I want you to know this is my very first autograph," Mindy said as she signed the woman's program.

Becoming a country star is like running for the presidential nomination, starting in living rooms and coffee shops in Iowa and New Hampshire, working up to television studios and Rotary Clubs, to national television and the convention, picking up supporters along the way, never stopping, never missing a moment's opportunity. First came the message.

In the studio, David spent so much time that the album cost $230,000, more than twice what many albums cost. This was all money advanced to Mindy to be paid out of record royalties. Since Mindy had never worn makeup before, her label hired experts to teach her how to do that. A clothing consultant picked out $10,000 worth of outfits. A choreographer who had worked with Gloria Estefan was flown in from Miami. An $80,000 video for her first single was put together.

The great acts of the past projected some semblance of themselves, be it a tortured Hank Williams, a homespun Loretta Lynn, an emotional Patsy Cline. These new "baby" acts of the nineties took what was called "media training." These one-on-one seminars often stripped away all the burrs and blemishes, leaving a bland, smooth finish to which nothing negative could stick. Mindy was taught how to push an impertinent question away, and how to project the soothing image that would make no enemies and sell albums. Mindy listened hard and well, and left discarding most of what she had been told; she was the same bold, blunt, often profane young woman she had always been.

Most country acts made their money primarily not from album sales but by touring most of the year. At this point, most young acts put together a band, start playing at clubs and honky-tonks, and work their way up to opening for one of the major acts. That was known as paying your dues. Joe and Stan had a different strategy for Mindy. She had no experience performing, and they were not going to take the chance of ruining her elaborately and expensively achieved image by doing a lackluster job on the stage. They planned to have her wait to appear in concerts until 1997, as late as a year after her first album came out.

Mindy's career would only take off if country radio played her singles and gave her a chance. Mindy headed out on an extensive radio tour, visiting 160 radio stations in about a hundred cities.

Many station program directors and managers had grown tired of the endless circus of new acts knocking on their doors, seeking their blessing. The winds of economic change were blowing with hurricane force, and they had little time for polite chitchat. The giant corporations that owned most of the stations cared nothing about country music and everything about profits. A day hardly went by when one station or group of stations wasn't swallowed up, some analysts predicting that by the millennium fifteen corporations would own almost all the radio stations in America.

The name of the game was ratings, not music, and as the country audience began a slow decline, the stations did whatever they could to keep their audiences. They cut their playlists down to thirty or forty top hits. They went for up-tempo songs. They sped the music up 1 to 3 percent. They hired consultants who did extensive research, polling listeners, playing snippets of new songs for them. They gave away money and tickets. And they complained as much about the often mediocre music coming out of Nashville as Nashville did about the radio industry's narrow, pedestrian, unadventurous tastes.

Some new acts were embarrassed by the whole process, believing that sucking up to uninterested disc jockeys and radio executives had nothing to do with their music. Mindy, however, realized that this was part of the other 50 percent of life as an artist in the new Nashville. She had inherited a full measure of her mother's charm, and as she traveled from city to city, station to station, she was like some baby-kissing, sweet-talking southern pol, remembering names, proffering gentle compliments, ingratiating herself with radio people from Florida to Oregon.

With her album about to come out, it would have been expected that Mindy would sing at a showcase at the Country Radio Seminar, the annual convention for the country radio industry. These showcases couldn't make a career, but if you bombed they could help destroy it. Mindy didn't sing. Instead, she did radio interviews and attended the RCA Group dinner.

Each year Joe had the RCA/BNA dinner on the *General Jackson,* a replica side-wheeler that plied the Cumberland River. The executive invited many top radio people, and once he got them on board, the boat cast off taking them away from the other label parties for the evening hours.

The ship was full of the stars of the RCA/BNA labels, including Aaron Tippin, Lari White, Lorrie Morgan, Martina McBride, John Anderson, and Alabama. These performers didn't spend much time at radio stations any longer, and the seminar attendees acted like any other group of fans, asking for their autographs, taking photos with them. For some of the other young, recently signed artists, this was an intimidating enough specter to have them cemented to their seats.

At times, Mindy could be brutally caustic about some of these radio people, but not this evening. Mindy worked the room with aplomb. She sat on the laps of radio executives, exchanged pleasantries with their wives, remembering every name and station call letters.

"Oh Pat, gee, it's great seeing you," she said, giving a hug to Pat Puchalla, a music director of KKCB in Duluth, Minnesota.

"Ken, wow, you're here," she said, turning to Ken Peiffer, operations manager of WJOD Country in Galena, Illinois.

After dinner, Mindy sat at her table watching the leading artists on the label each sing a couple of songs. The highlight of the evening was Lari White singing "Amazing Grace." Mindy, like everyone else on the boat, got up to give the RCA artist a standing ovation. Mindy knew that next year she could be up there like

Lari. Just a year ago Lari had been nominated as a Star of Tomorrow for the TNN/Music City News Awards show. Her first album had gone gold, and her second album was just coming out.

The new album sold poorly, and a few months later Lari White was dropped from the label. It was just another lesson in the ways of the new Nashville.

Joe and his staff decided that Mindy's first single would be a ballad, "Ten Thousand Angels." That went against the Nashville adage that if you wanted to break a new act, you started with an up-tempo song. But "Ten Thousand Angels" just seemed right. It was youthful. It was Mindy. The video was dynamite.

BNA was spending a near record million to a million and a half dollars on Mindy, most of which she would have to pay back out of her royalties. The radio promotion and distribution staff knew that Joe wanted this to happen, and they better come through. Mindy had met most of the BNA people. She had made them believe in her and wanted her dream to succeed. It seemed, though, that every week the country charts became more brutally competitive, with more singles out there for fewer and fewer slots on country radio.

Joe had as strong a team in the field as anyone in Nashville, but even they could push only so far, and at first the single only nudged its way up the chart. While that was happening, Joe was out visiting radio stations. He kept hearing the same sorry lament; "Ten Thousand Angels" wasn't country enough, it was a ballad, new female artists were coming out of radio's ear. Joe was betting much of his capital on Mindy, and he watched as the single almost died twice. His staff kept pushing and arguing. Finally, the calls started coming in from people out there listening to the radio requesting the song.

Mindy was working as hard as if she were out on the road performing, heading out week after week to the radio stations. She was in Florida at the end of April when her album came out, and she planned to spend the weekend with her family in Fort Myers.

Whatever painful memories she had of growing up, Fort Myers was still her hometown, and what these people thought and felt and said about her mattered more than anything. Thus, as she drove with David and Stan to an event at Spec's, a local music store, she was nervous beyond nervous. At the store a cluster of people waited for her, plus a camera crew from a local television station.

Many of those waiting were friends and neighbors. "When you were one month old, I changed your diapers at this Wendy's when you were with your grandparents," one woman said proudly as she clutched Mindy's hand. Mindy's relatives had come in large numbers, and within the joy of this moment there was the deeper sadness in knowing that some of them were only here because she was Mindy McCready, recording artist. She felt her father had given her so little in time or emotion, but he was here now with his new wife. Her paternal grandmother was here too, the grandmother who had spent so little time with her. Her mother was here with Tom, and her aunt with her boyfriend.

Mindy realized that people were starting to treat her differently, with awe or deference, watching their words. She knew that she hadn't changed. She found it bizarre, as if she had suddenly left the human race. Of all the prices she knew that she would have to pay for stardom, this was the one she had never been told.

As Mindy stood talking to a group of fans, Tom Baldrica, the regional sales representative from Atlanta, rushed up excitedly. He had made Mindy's success one of his big causes, and he was a major reason why her single had just reached number nineteen on the *Billboard* chart.

"Guess what, guys? I just got a call!" Tom enthused. "There are ten thousand reorders. Imagine. The album's only been out three days. Incredible! It's happening!"

"You know when people hear it they're going to reorder even more," David interjected.

"You're speaking to the choir," Tom said, giving David's arm a squeeze.

In all her career, Mindy would never have such a welcoming, enthusiastic, uncritical crowd as the 150 people spread around Spec's. She was so nervous, though, that she could hardly speak. David got out his guitar and stood behind Mindy, ready to sing.

Mindy started to sing "Boys Do It All the Time," a song from her album that she had sung scores of times before. She was halfway through when her mind went blank. She stopped dead short, then apologized to the audience. "I'm sorry, I just don't know," she said. "This one I think you guys know," Mindy said. "It's 'Ten Thousand Angels.'"

The audience yelled and applauded fervently when she finished. "You guys don't know how wonderful it makes me feel to be able to look out and see you listening to my song," she said, breaking into tears. "Well, I have time now, two years if you want it, to sign or anything."

When Mindy finally left, she drove off with Tom, David, and Stan to have dinner. Every minute of her life seemed to be planned. She had no time to relish her hometown triumph before she had something else to do. Tom told her that a two-minute conversation with her had been a prize at a Louisiana radio station. "I don't understand," she mused. "It's so weird. I mean why would anybody call in to win two minutes talking to me?" Tom dialed the number. "Rebecca, how are you? This is Mindy, Mindy McCready." Mindy talked to the woman for five minutes as if they were close friends, then handed the phone back to Tom.

Up in the front seat Stan was complaining about his back problems and bragging to Tom how great Mindy was. Mindy had heard about enough. "Stan, I'm gonna push my foot in your ass, and then if you don't shut up, I'm gonna push it in your mouth."

Stan turned and looked back as if Mindy had just given him the Everest of compliments. "You're so fantastic," he said, not a quiver of irony in his voice. "You're wonderful, kid."

"Stop kissing my ass, Stan!" Mindy fumed, blowing out through her teeth.

After dinner, Mindy went back to her mother's house, where she and David were staying. Her album was selling awesome numbers. By rights this should have been one of the sweetest evenings of her life. Mindy may have been living 836 miles away in Nashville, but she was learning that she couldn't leave home; her home and its problems traveled with her. Her brother, T.J., had become so alienated from his mother that he was living with

Mindy and David in Nashville, and he wouldn't think of coming back to Fort Myers for the weekend. And down here the endless psychodrama continued, Mindy no more than a phone call away.

Late in the evening, the family gathered in the living room with its overstuffed sofas, the scene of so much that was good and bad in their lives. Mindy had always had insight far beyond her years. She suspected that her mother had gotten pregnant in part to call attention to herself, and to hold Tom to her. Now instead of celebrating her success, the family sat talking about their problems. Mindy had an appearance at Wal-Mart the next day. She should have gotten a decent night's sleep, but she stayed up talking with her family until four in the morning.

"Tom, the problems that you have with your mother are so deep-rooted," Mindy told her stepfather. "They start way back when your father died when you were a child. You need to go and see how you really feel and deal with your feelings. You really need to understand."

Tom was not the kind of man who cried, but as he heard Mindy's words he cried, the tears running down his face. Mindy left Fort Myers thinking that she had done some good, that maybe her mother and Tom would get along better now, but she had only arrived back in Nashville when she got a phone call. Her pregnant mother and Tom had gotten in a fight and they had both ended up spending the night in jail.

After her dramatic moment on the great stage at Fan Fair, Mindy headed back to her bus, at the center of a cocoon of managers, agents, relatives, friends, dressers, makeup people, and assorted hangers-on. David ambled along at the back of the group. He had so looked forward to this evening. He wanted Mindy to feel the adrenaline rush of performing before a great audience, believing that once she felt it she would want it again and again and again. She had loved her minutes on the stage, and she walked down the back stairways full of exhilaration and excitement over the world that lay ahead of her.

Outside the bus stood a line of radio contest winners waiting for autographs. There wasn't a moment any longer when there wasn't somebody wanting something from Mindy: fans wanting autographs, journalists wanting interviews, charities wanting her time and her name, relatives wanting money, old acquaintances wanting new friendships, her old manager wanting his cut, agents wanting to represent her, promoters wanting her to perform. It was a line that went on and on beyond the horizon of the horizon, a line that would not end until she was no longer a country star.

10

"Blue"

"Hate to bother you . . . Yeah, tell me about deadlines. I know . . . But listen, there's this rumor going round here that LeAnn Rimes is going to be the cover of *Time* next week. . . . I know, I know it's crazy her album isn't out yet. . . . Yeah, well, that's what I figured but you know . . . "

Holly Gleason sped out I-65 in her Toyota talking to a friend at *Time* in New York on her cellular phone. Next to her sat Mandy Barnett singing the Patty Loveless hit "That Kind of Girl." Mandy had a voice of such power that even though she was trying to hold it down to a murmur, Holly had to shout to be heard. Holly didn't mind yelling. Just a few hours ago Mandy had been so depressed that she seemed incapable of singing a single note.

In the afternoon, Mandy had been at the media center on the fairgrounds. She was sitting in one of a score of interview booths, separated from the rest of the world by a sickly green curtain, talking to a reporter about her career. She was only twenty years old, and for this moment she had been struggling and sacrificing for almost a decade.

Her first album, *Mandy Barnett,* had been released to stellar reviews. Two months ago the *Nashville Tennessean* had headlined its article on Mandy: WRITTEN IN THE STARS MANDY BARNETT BOUND FOR SUCCESS. So it had seemed. Since then she had been going around the country playing at shows and festivals. Wherever Mandy went, she was treated as the newest and youngest star in the country firmament. Thus, Mandy was primed for a busy schedule of autograph signings and personal appearances during Fan Fair, primed to meet the fans, to bowl them over on the great stage at the speedway, to sign thousands of autographs, and to tell scores of reporters her story.

That was the idea, but all anybody wanted to ask about was LeAnn Rimes. LeAnn's first single, "Blue," was the talk of the industry, already number sixteen on the *Billboard* country singles chart, and her album wasn't even out yet. "What do you think about LeAnn, Mandy?" "How does it feel to have a thirteen-year-old kick your butt?" "You both sound like Patsy Cline, right, hon?" "Have you ever seen such excitement as what's happening to little LeAnn?" "Gee, Mandy, like to get your comments on LeAnn's album."

Mandy had been sitting in her booth at her Asylum label signing autographs when a woman came over and started yelling, "She's not thirteen years old! How can she pretend to be thirteen years old?"

Mandy wanted to die. She didn't hate LeAnn. She hated being compared with her. It stunned her how brutally insensitive so many reporters were and even many fans. Couldn't they understand what she felt? Didn't they see the way she practically winced every time somebody mentioned LeAnn's name? Didn't they get it that she didn't like being treated like some old-timer ready to head to Branson after crowning the new star? Couldn't they imagine what it was like one day being this teenage sensation, a symbol of the youth movement in country music, and the next day being treated like this has-been who never was?

When Mandy came out of that wretched little booth after her last interview, she could have screamed. She could have stood there in front of a score of country music reporters and cursed the world in which she lived. As she was waiting there half ready to let loose, she saw Holly Gleason. Holly had given Mandy media training for her album. The thirty-two-year-old publicist had a tongue on her that could be every bit as sharp as Mandy's. She spoke so fast that it was like a 33 played at 78. She could be abrupt and dismissive, but Mandy felt that Holly was one of the few people in town who truly got her, understood her, and cared about her.

"How you doing, Mandy, kid?" Holly greeted the singer.

"Fine. I guess," Mandy sighed. She was simply unable to hide her emotions. That was a noble attribute when Mandy was onstage, but it was a detriment when she was supposed to be selling this perky, upbeat image of herself.

"What do you mean, you guess you're OK?" For all her brashness, Holly had a rare sensitivity to the performers with whom she worked. She had once been a junior golf champion and a music journalist, which gave her insights and empathy into the lives of performers that few other publicists in Nashville had. She knew that something was wrong. Mandy wasn't even one of the publicist's clients, but that didn't matter. Mandy was hurting, hurting terribly.

Mandy could hardly speak. "Well," she began slowly as if she had a terrible confession to make. "Everybody, all they want to ask about is LeAnn Rimes."

"Well, you know, that's not a big deal," Holly said, though it was about as big as a deal got in the life of an artist. The ship of stardom had only a few rooms, and if LeAnn took one of the staterooms, Mandy might be left behind. "LeAnn's a thirteen-year-old girl with a big record, and you're a talent that's there for the long run. And you don't need to get sucked into that game."

"Really?" Mandy said, mulling over Holly's words.

"Yeah, really," Holly went on, her voice almost angry, trying to break Mandy out of her dark mood. "I mean, if you can't see the difference between what she does and what you do, then you really need to get someone to explain it to you."

"Well, OK."

Mandy was a hefty, full-blown woman of 160 pounds with as beautiful and expressive a face as any singer in country music. She didn't act like she thought she was pretty, and on her video running on CMT she looked far bigger than any of the new generation of lithe, young woman stars. She led with her fists and her tongue, trying to fend off the pain of her life with a brash, bold, vulgar veneer. But she still hurt, and today she hurt worst of all. Maybe she was only twenty, but sometimes she was twenty going on seventy. Other times, she was a little girl of excruciating naïveté and vulnerability, whose emotional life was an open wound.

Holly knew how crazy Mandy could get, going off on one of her binges. She decided that she better not let Mandy be alone this evening, especially when she was supposed to be performing at the Asylum Show at Fan Fair the next morning. So she invited the singer to join her later at the Grand Ole Opry Trust Benefit out at Opryland where Holly's client, Patty Loveless, was performing.

> I'm not the woman in red
> I'm that kind of girl . . .

As Holly sped out toward Opryland, Mandy was totally into her singing. She didn't need an audience to get into her music. She just loved to let her pipes do their thing. Holly had warned Mandy to dress up. Knowing Mandy's mood, she might have shown up in cutoff shorts, a T-shirt with some kind of weird message on it, and no makeup. Instead, Mandy had gotten herself together, dressed up in her best young-diva-of-country mode. She wore spiffy new jeans, leather Roman sandals, and a dark denim shirt. She had done a killer job on the makeup too, the foundation perfect, red lipstick, subtle mascara, and that wonderful thick curly black hair, brushed up like a hundred-dollar perm.

When Holly got off the phone, Mandy stopped singing abruptly, like a needle pulled off a record.

"They're not doing a cover, Mandy. I told you."

"Well, why are they saying it all around town?"

"Because it's Fan Fair," Holly said, shaking her head knowingly. "Stuff takes on a life of its own. It's a supercharged time. People want this sensation, this sizzle. They want to believe it."

"Hhhhhhh," Mandy said slowly, as if this was something she wanted to remember and to think about again. "Geez, Holly, I don't know about meeting Patty," Mandy mused out loud. "She'll think I'm a gherm, nothing but a gherm."

"Gherm" was Nashville's term for devotees of country music so passionate in their love for the music and its artists that they would go to almost any length to get near their favorite star. There was a little gherm in everybody, and Mandy didn't want to end up gherming her favorite woman singer. Patty was as authentic a voice of country music as there was, and almost any country artist who loved and felt country music loved and felt Patty's music.

"Why will she think you're a gherm?" Holly asked, taken aback by Mandy's latest fear.

"She just will. I mean, it's that kind of a week. You know how it is."

Holly drove her car as if it moved ahead on its own accord while she attended to more important things like talking to New York on her cellular phone, or discussing the nature of gherms with the distraught artist sitting next to her. "First of all, Mandy, Patty will be thrilled to meet you. She loves your record. When she did *48 Hours* last month, she held it up to the camera and said this is probably the best young country singer today. She plays it on her bus all the time. So I don't think you're this geek if you go up and say, 'Patty, I love you.'"

That was enough to calm Mandy's fears and to make her excited again. She had been trying to make it for almost half her twenty years, nearly a decade devoted to getting an album out. In those years she had been beaten up and beaten down in as about as many ways as Nashville meted out its punishments.

The first time Mandy performed in public, she sang "Because He Lives" in an Easter program at the Holiness Church in Crossville, Tennessee. She was only five years old, but she hit each note square on, wringing every bit of emotion out of the lyrics, filling the worshipers in the pews with the spirit. Mandy loved that moment, and afterwards went walking around the house grasping a Mr. Microphone, singing her soul out.

Like so many child prodigies, be it tennis, gymnastics, or music, Mandy was an only child. Her father was a contractor, her mother a bookkeeper. They were devoted to their daughter, taking her to sing with gospel groups and driving her to Nashville at the age of nine to record a cassette that her parents gave away by the score.

Dan and Betty Barnett weren't stage parents, pushing a reluctant daughter toward the spotlight. Mandy wanted to perform. One day she heard a Patsy Cline song, and she had to have every record Patsy ever made. Patsy had cut only a hundred songs, and Mandy knew almost all of them. She became obsessed with country's greatest diva. Ten-year-old girls might like Karen Carpenter, or Linda Ronstadt, but not earthy, emotional, passionate Patsy Cline. At times, Patsy had been guised up in glamorous photos and stylish clothes, but she remained this hard-drinking, tough-talking life force, who sang a love song like her soul was on fire. Mandy loved Patsy. Mandy did not copy her songs, but she did emulate the stunning emotional feel.

At the age of ten, Mandy won a regular role singing in the summer at Dollywood, Dolly Parton's Smoky Mountain country theme amusement park. One Saturday evening two years later, her parents took her to perform at the "Midnight Jamboree" from the Ernest Tubb Record Shop after the Opry on WSM. If any other twelve-year-old had ever performed on the live radio show, no one could remember. Afterwards, Billy Strange, a guitarist who was also an arranger and producer, came up and said that he was so impressed he wanted to sign Mandy to a production deal.

Mandy didn't like the songs that Billy was having her demo, but she was too young to have much say. When Billy played the tape for Bowen at MCA Universal, the executive was ready to sign Mandy. There was one small caveat. He didn't want Billy involved. Betrayal is often in the eyes of the beholder. What to one person is duplicity to another is only opportunity. It only took a day or two before Mandy and her parents agreed to leave Billy behind.

Mandy sang two demo tapes at Universal before Bowen left the label and went to Capitol Nashville. Mandy went with him and continued recording demos. Her mother dropped her off at the studio in the morning, and her father picked her up in the evening. She went through one producer and A&R executive after another. Nobody seemed able to figure out just what tack to take with Mandy's music.

Mandy didn't know anything about business, but even she was startled as the total spent rose to four hundred thousand dollars. And she still didn't have her album. That was the Bowen way. Signing all these production deals. Doing all these demos. Seeing what worked. Throwing away the rest. And all Mandy wanted was to get a record out there.

Mandy hated high school. The best parts of it were the plays and shows that the school put on where Mandy could strut her stuff. In one show she danced fifties rock 'n' roll. She was a plump five feet four, and most young men couldn't have lifted her off the floor. But her six-foot seven-inch partner picked her up and flung her over his head like she was an anorexic ballerina. When he danced with her at the senior prom, he managed to slug her in the face, leaving her as the only girl at the ball with a black eye. That was bad enough, but just as she was coming around, the principal announced the senior queen as none other than Mandy Barnett. She waltzed forward, black eye and all, to put on a tilted tiara.

Upon graduation from high school, seventeen-year-old Mandy moved alone to Nashville. She didn't know very many people, but she kept making demos and having meetings at her label. She didn't have much money, and when she had her eighteenth birthday in September 1993, she decided to get a job. In high school, she had taught a mentally retarded young man how to do laundry. She thought that was the kind of work she might like to do. She was so brash and quick and unforgiving that she seemed hardly the person for a job that required patience beyond patience. If you challenged her, hit upon her, put her down, she might tear your head off and blow you back with foul invective. If someone was needy, she had limitless time and concern. She wasn't Princess Bountiful down to work with the less fortunate. She had the same empathy for these people that she brought to her singing.

So she went to work in a group home with eight women, all of whom had difficult behavior problems. Mandy worked eighty hours every other week. She brushed their teeth. She helped the women dress. She drove them to their workshop. She cooked and fed them dinner. She helped them bathe. She got them together in the living room singing "Oh How I Love Jesus," each in her own key, each at her own tempo. She pulled them apart when they got in fights. And at night she put them to bed. She still loved to sing, but she knew too that she loved taking care of people who needed to be taken care of, and she could always do that if the singing didn't work out.

Mandy felt that her record career was coming along too. She was having upbeat meetings at the label. Things were going so well that the A&R staff called and set up a luncheon meeting for her at Cakewalk, a good restaurant on West End Avenue just down from Liberty headquarters. Nashville, like Hollywood, is the kind of place where the length of a meeting is usually a function of how important you are, but all that matters is the last five minutes. The executives made their small talk over their meal, gossiping about the industry and other projects. Then when they were finished, one of them turned to Mandy. "Well, we've got forty acts on the roster and we're getting ready to drop a few of them," he began, then paused. "And you're one of them."

Mandy stood up, took out a five-dollar bill, threw the money on the table. "Don't feel sorry for me!" Mandy yelled, holding back her tears until she got outside. She wanted to get drunk, but every bar she went into asked for ID. So in the end she drove home to her parents in Crossville.

"Hey, Mandy, you see in the paper there's this Patsy Cline audition. If there's anyone that can do it, you can, Mandy."

Mandy was half asleep. She didn't even know how her former classmate had gotten her phone number, and here he was raving at her.

"What in the world are you talking about?" Mandy replied, fuming with irritation.

"It's at the Opry. I don't really know what it is. But it's a Patsy Cline something."

Mandy lay in bed trying to go back to sleep. Finally, she woke up and decided that maybe she better check this out. She called the Grand Ole Opry office and learned that there was an audition for *Always . . . Patsy Cline,* a major production that would play at the renovated Ryman Auditorium. You were supposed to bring a résumé, an eight-by-ten photo, and a karaoke tape.

Mandy had publicity photos, but they had been taken when she was twelve years old. So she found a picture in which she was sitting in a graveyard smoking a cigarette, wearing an old dress with a daisy on it. It wasn't quite a publicity photo, but it would have to do. She put on a nondescript dress and a pair of clogs and headed to the Hickory Hollow Mall to get a Pasty Cline tape. At the record store, the clerk shook her head: "Sorry, girl, but all of them Patsy Cline impersonators have cleaned us out. Might still be something back there."

Mandy settled for a tape of Patsy's most obscure cuts and headed over to the Opry. After she handed over her photo and wrote out a résumé on a piece of paper, she was given a number. As she walked into the theater Mandy saw a sight that was like some kind of stoned nightmare. Four hundred and fifty women dressed as Patsy Cline. There was a cocktail dress like the one Patsy had worn on Arthur Godfrey. And there was her cowboy outfit. And there was a killer Patsy Cline wig. Several women had already played Patsy in smaller productions of *Always . . . Patsy Cline*. And all of them running around warming up warbling "Sweet Dreams" or "Crazy" or "Walking After Midnight." Mandy was about the only one who wasn't trying to look like Patsy.

"Man, this is a freak show," Mandy said to herself, sitting down to watch. The director was cutting off some of the Patsy wanna-bes before they hardly had one excruciating note out of their mouths. When Mandy heard her number called, she wanted at least to get through the bridge to "Some Day You'll Want Me to Want You," so she could let it all out. She had hardly finished the first verse before the director killed her off. She figured it was all over. They called her back again, however, to sing other Patsy songs. And at the end of the long day, they asked her what size shoe and dress she wore.

The next day she returned to do a video audition. And the day after that, they called to tell her she had the part. Two days later, they gave her a wig and a costume and brought her down to the Ryman Auditorium to film an interview for *CBS This Morning*.

The two-person play opened two weeks later. Tere Myers portrayed Patsy's friend, Louise Seger, and Myers had almost all the speaking parts. Mandy not only sang Patsy's songs but inhabited her being. Those who had known Patsy, and there were still many of them in Nashville, sat there with tears in their eyes, wondering how in the world an eighteen-year-old kid could capture Patsy so convincingly.

The show was a hit, selling out the three nights a week that it played at the Ryman. Mandy was only being paid five hundred dollars a week, a pittance for what the production was taking in at the theater. But she was flush. She had kept her job at the home. There she was paid six dollars an hour, nine hundred dollars a month.

"Do you want me to get you some coke?" Mandy was sitting in her dressing room at the Ryman with one of her friends from the show. She had never taken cocaine before. Her mentor, Patsy, had been of a generation when in Nashville uppers were the thing. Then cocaine had come in for a while. Now the drug of choice in Music City was Prozac.

"Yeah, I guess so," Mandy said. She was willing to try about anything. The first time she snorted the white powder, she liked it. She liked beer and whiskey. She liked menthol cigarettes as well, two packs a day. She liked food too, and she started putting on weight, gaining thirty or forty pounds. She started going out at night with her new friends—crazy, long, drug- and booze-filled nights. She had people hanging on her saying they were her friends, then hitting on her for a line of coke. She was too young to drink, but she was a star, and she could get what she wanted. They ran from club to club, from Tootsie's and the Merchants to the World's Inn, Nashville's best-known gay bar.

Mandy didn't know what she wanted, but she wanted something she didn't have. She felt that nobody cared about her at the Ryman. They all said how much they cared. But she felt "they couldn't care less if I OD as long as the fucking show got done."

One evening in the midst of the performance, she got in a fight with her dresser, a brawl that ended only because Mandy had to run back onstage. After the show she ran through the long night hours, singing in karaoke bars, fighting in clubs, dancing in the dawn streets of the city.

Omens come in many forms, in this case as a blue liquid. One night a drag queen gave Mandy a little bag of coke. She snorted it and woke up the next morning with this strange blue liquid in her nose. Mandy knew it was time to cool out. Her second year playing Patsy, Mandy backed off her late-night friends. She was earning a thousand dollars a week now, double her first-year salary, and she quit her job in the home in Donelson. With all the publicity over playing Patsy, Mandy got a new record deal with Asylum Records, and in February of 1995 began cutting her own album.

Mandy wasn't into ditties. Neither were the songwriters whose music she chose for her debut album. The album was song after song by the finest writers in town, including Jim Lauderdale, Rodney Crowell, Kostas, and Willie Nelson, song after song interpreted with passion, power, and subtlety. "I predict the album will hit country music like a freight train," Dan Gordon said on the ABC Radio Network, shortly before the release. "Get on the train, don't be hit by it."

Mandy and Holly hurried through the crowded corridors backstage at the Grand Ole Opry, pushing past guitar-carrying musicians and performers, friends and reporters. A piece of the stage of the old Ryman Auditorium is embedded in the stage of the new forty-four-hundred-seat Opry House. Something of the old spirit is embedded as well. There is a whole row of dressing rooms, whereas in the old Mother Church of country music, there were four. Backstage there still is a neighborly, Sunday-go-to-meeting spirit, and little room for the high-flying egos of stardom. This was not an Opry night, but there was still some of that comradely feeling that for so long has been part of the Grand Ole Opry.

Mandy and Holly stood in front of the number two dressing room. Holly knocked on the door and waited until a young woman opened the door. "Oh, my God!" the woman exclaimed. "Why, it's

Mandy Barnett. What a privilege to meet you."

Mandy stood there as if there must be some other Mandy the poor woman was talking about.

"This is Deany Richardson," Holly said, breaking the silence. "She's in Patty's band."

"We listen to you all the time on the bus."

"You do?" Mandy said shyly. "No kiddin'."

"Yeah. We think it's incredible." Deany was a marvelous fiddle player herself who did not hand out such compliments like dessert mints. She turned back to the room where the rest of the band was sitting. "Look who's here, guys!"

Shortly afterwards, Patty Loveless walked into the room. The thirty-nine-year-old singer was a stunning woman, who to a sad, disillusioned twenty-year-old seemed the essence of womanly stardom. "Hi, Patty," Mandy said shyly.

"Well, hi, Mandy. What ya doin' here?"

"Well, you know it's Fan Fair and I sort of kind of wanted to meet you," Mandy said, turning into a dreaded gherm. "I think you're a great singer. You're the best."

Patty brushed the compliment aside. "Well, that's great. I mean it's a lot coming from someone that sings as well as you do."

"I know you gotta get ready, Patty. Ready for your show and stuff."

"Yeah, well, just hang around."

Mandy sat and watched as Patty and her band practiced the Appalachian harmonies of "Thousand Times a Day." This was something the audience almost never saw, how if you cared about your music, you cared about it all the time.

When Patty and her band walked to the stage, Mandy and Holly followed behind. The Grand Ole Opry House has onstage bleachers and a large area to the side of the stage where backstage guests stand behind a rope, watching the performance and other artists who wait their turn on the celebrated stage. It was there that Mandy and Holly stood as Patty walked onstage following Tim McGraw.

Mandy had never heard Patty perform live before, and she was mesmerized by the Kentucky singer's music, oblivious to the scores of people milling around. Music was Mandy's drug of choice, the drug that never failed. As she stood there, she could have been anywhere, in her apartment or car, lost in the folds of the music. Suddenly, Mandy turned as if jolted awake. "Oh, my God!" Mandy exclaimed. "Oh, my God!"

"Yeah, I know," Holly whispered gently into Mandy's ear. There not twenty feet away, surrounded by an entourage, stood LeAnn Rimes. Holly was sick. She had hauled Mandy out here so she wouldn't even have to think about LeAnn, and now this. "Are you all right?"

"I'm fine. I'm fine. I've got to get something to drink."

"What?"

"I've got to get something to drink."

Unlike Mandy, LeAnn wasn't out here to schmooze and to hear her favorites sing their music. There were photographers taking pictures of LeAnn with the stars as they came off the stage. It was a brilliantly calculated move. LeAnn's first album wasn't even coming up until next month, but this evening she was being anointed as friend and equal of the country music royalty.

Although LeAnn was only thirteen years old, the singer had been waiting for this moment most of her life. She had wanted stardom with a hunger beyond hunger practically since she could talk. She and her parents, Wilbur and Belinda, were living in Flowood, Mississippi (population 2,800) when six-year-old LeAnn entered a talent contest singing "Getting to Know You." Wilbur had so little faith that his only daughter would win that he didn't wait for the results but went out coon hunting with his dogs. When he got back to the house and saw a trophy sitting there twice as big as LeAnn, he started to cry. "I'm going to be a singer," LeAnn told her parents. "I'm going to be a big star one day." Wilbur sold his coon dogs, never hunted again, and the family moved west to Dallas largely so that LeAnn could have her chance.

Even then, LeAnn was already twice a star. She was a star as an only child is a star, the sole focal point of her parents' love and attention. She was doubly a star because she was a late, unexpected blessing. Wilbur and Belinda had been high school sweethearts, marrying when they were seventeen years old. For twelve years they tried to have a child. They had about given up when Belinda turned to prayer, asking God to bless her and Wilbur with a child. Six weeks later Belinda became pregnant. As Belinda saw her, then, LeAnn was "a blessing from God."

Belinda and Wilbur were not typical stage parents, pretending they were selflessly pushing their child ahead when they were selfishly fulfilling their own sad lives. It was LeAnn who wanted stardom, LeAnn who pushed her parents. Belinda believed that her daughter was born "to touch hearts . . . through her voice. I don't know where it's going to end, but I know she's here for a purpose. People come up to me and say it's not normal that she sings like that, and I say I know it isn't. It's a God-given talent."

At one moment LeAnn was a little girl. The next moment she was a mature, consummate performer, weighing her opportunities like an assayer measuring gold dust. As much as LeAnn's parents talked about God, this all seemed beyond the fundamentalist faith of the Rimes. In some ways it was similar to the ways that the Tibetans chose the next Dalai Lama. The monks went through the villages of the Himalayan highlands looking for the baby who had the sacred sign. Then with his parents' blessing, they took the infant to the palace in Lhasa to be brought up by monks as the next spiritual leader.

The Rimes believed they had been given something greater even than a daughter. In Dallas, Wilbur sold equipment for an oil company, and Belinda worked as a receptionist, but their other full-time job was making LeAnn a star. LeAnn took as her models Barbra Streisand and Judy Garland. Both women were enormous, passionate, emotive performers bigger than any song, any role, any moment.

LeAnn wanted to act. Her parents flew their seven-year-old daughter to New York to try out for the lead in *Annie 2*, competing against girls twice her age. She made it to the final cut, losing out to a twelve-year-old, in part she believed because she was considered too young to carry the show. If she had won the role, she might have had a career not only on Broadway but in Hollywood as a child star, never singing country music. As it was, LeAnn next appeared for two rounds on *Star Search*. She won the first week, but was left in tears the second week when the pianist did not shift keys during her song, and LeAnn faltered.

Until then, LeAnn had no interest in country music. "Baby," her mother told her, "we can't be flying back and forth to New York every time there's a tryout for a Broadway show. Maybe we can go through the good, clean country venues and see what happens." Country music, then, was a vehicle for her stardom.

LeAnn became a regular at Johnnie High's Country Music Revue near her home in Texas, over a six-year period performing there 389 times. The Rimeses chauffeured their daughter from performance to performance. Belinda worried and fretted about LeAnn and what this all would do for her, watching over her clothes and her friends, trying to give her a semblance of a normal childhood. As for Wilbur, he was out front monitoring the sound system, checking the details of her professional life, protecting her from the raw realities of show business.

Back in the dressing room a little girl played house with her Barbie dolls, or took a nap on the sofa. Then an hour before she went onstage, this amazing metamorphosis took place. The child donned her stage clothes, put on makeup, and transformed herself into LeAnn Rimes, country star. And a star she was, in this revue that was a Texas-style version of the Grand Ole Opry. The audience was passionate in their love for country music, and they embraced LeAnn, buying her family-produced album by the hundreds.

Those performances honed LeAnn's onstage persona, but more than that the show was a school in old-time country music manners. If you worked for High, you lived clean and you played clean. You didn't hightail it out of there after a performance either. You went out front and signed autographs for everybody who wanted them signed and then you left.

High thought of his revue as a little bit of church, a little bit of music, but the songs weren't hymns. LeAnn got up there and belted out songs of love lost and love found, of betrayal, and games of romance. She wrote her first song at age nine, "Share My Love," about sentiments more suitable for a woman three times her age.

One love song she sang on her homespun Texas album was, as she said, "something about a man and a girl falling in love or something. I don't know." She was a ten-year-old girl of surpassing innocence, singing songs a decade beyond her years. "Dad would explain that it was a sad song, and I would sing it that way," she explained. "I don't think I have to experience anything to sing it."

Onstage LeAnn not only sang but dressed far beyond her years, wearing lipstick and blush, tight-fitting little dresses, and adult hairstyles. Country music was supposedly for adults, and LeAnn had little choice but to sing adult-rated music. There was something unsettling about LeAnn belting out lyrics from movies she would not have been allowed to attend, and dressing like an adult. There was something almost unseemly, especially since the audience was so oblivious to the contradictions, relishing the purity of it all.

LeAnn was such a star in Dallas that on her twelfth birthday she took a stretch limo to the Palm, a celebrity hangout in Dallas, where her mug hung between Warren Beatty's and Ann-Margret's and her caricature hung from a wall. Afterwards, it was home in the limo to the Rimeses' modest apartment in Garland that was more like a backstage setting than a home. The apartment in Garland was in one of the new ghettos of American life. Immigrants and American-born residents mixed uneasily, everyone from Hmong refugees to Indian computer experts, most families hoping to move up and out. The mantel in the living room was a shrine to LeAnn's fame, pictures of her with other members of the Texas aristocracy of celebrity, including Nolan Ryan and Jerry Jones. The dwelling had no room for most of LeAnn's fifty-two trophies or her four hundred CDs and tapes, an eclectic mix far more heavily into pop and rap than country.

School for LeAnn had become just another bit of unpleasantness that she had to pass through before heading out to perform. In her school in Garland, she was an outsider. She did not come from the well-off homes of some of the girls and she was a country singer, with a world that reached far beyond that of any of her peers. On the last day of school in the sixth grade, LeAnn went to her locker to pick up her things and found eggs smashed against it.

She feared two girls especially, both of them from wealthy families, feared that they hated her so much that they would beat her up. That may have been an exaggeration, but it was enough to get her mother to pull her out of school and set up a home-study program through Texas Tech.

LeAnn and her parents had begun to get even more serious about the business of stardom. They met Lyle Walker, an attorney and part owner of a New Mexico recording studio. Walker offered to finance a second album for LeAnn and split the profits. The 1993 album, *All That,* sold an extraordinary fifteen thousand copies in the Dallas area. LeAnn already had a manager, Marty Rendleman, a well-connected public relations specialist. Now she took on a booking agent, Barbara Rice, and together the threesome took LeAnn to the next level. The booking agent pushed her client's price up to $3,500 to $5,000 for some shows, an amount that would have delighted many new acts in Nashville.

LeAnn flew up to Nashville to sing for Jimmy Bowen at his house. "Come back when you're eighteen," the president of Liberty told the twelve-year-old, advice he had not given Mandy Barnett when he signed her. In February of 1995, a whole team of executives flew down from MCA Nashville to hear LeAnn sing in her own bailiwick. They were accompanied by Narvel Blackstock, who managed his wife, Reba McEntire. The group offered a formidable package, a signing on Decca (a label of MCA Nashville), and management by Starstruck Entertainment, Reba's company.

Another Nashville executive, Mike Curb, chairman of Curb Records, heard LeAnn's album and also wanted to sign the performer. Curb had been lieutenant governor of California when he was only thirty-two years old. The fifty-year-old executive had moved to Nashville only two years before. He represented the one independent label truly competing head-on with the major Nashville labels, an intrusion that had won Curb few friends. His business relationships at times ended in multimillion-dollar suits. He was a conservative, a proponent of family values, as long as they did not get too much in the way of a good business deal. As a candidate, he had raged against the sordid fare churned out by the decadent Hollywood crowd. After he left politics, he produced such stellar films as the 1992 epic *Last Dance*, advertised as "an erotic thriller featuring hot young dancers with the hardest of bodies."

Curb could only compete against the majors by employing every bit of that shrewdness that had once made him the boy wonder of California politics. When he flew down to meet with LeAnn, he took not some high-powered, intimidating entourage but his two daughters. He introduced himself to the Rimeses as a family man. Belinda decided that "Mr. Curb was a religious man who cared about family," and he was the man for her LeAnn.

As success loomed on the horizon like a great city rising out of the desert, the Rimeses were afraid that their daughter and their life would be pulled away from them, sucked into the labyrinth of power and fame. The MCA Nashville people had gently suggested that they would bring in a producer to put a professional sheen on LeAnn's efforts. There was an amateurish quality to the production of LeAnn's record that made much of it sound as if it had been made thirty years ago. It was, nonetheless, full of that quality of "inspired amateurism" that one of Nashville's greatest producers, Jack Clement, called the essence of country music, a quality that was being scrubbed out of Nashville's music like a dirty stain. Thus, anybody in Nashville would have brought in a new producer, anyone but Mike Curb. He had brilliantly gauged the Rimeses' psyches and told them that Wilbur could produce LeAnn's album and continue to comanage her. That as much as anything else decided the matter, and LeAnn and her parents signed with MCG/Curb.

LeAnn went back into the Clovis, New Mexico, studio with Wilbur, recut some songs from her album, added others, and put together her first major album. She was only thirteen years old, but already had a schedule befitting a major star. In 1995, she played 107 dates, most of them in Texas. As the release of her Curb album loomed, LeAnn's father cut both Rendleman and Rice from the team, and Walker came even more fully into the picture, managing LeAnn along with Wilbur. Dropping the two close associates was part of the price of stardom, jettisoning excess baggage even if they happened to be human beings.

★　★　★

Blue was the title of LeAnn's album, and "Blue" was the first single, released just before Fan Fair. The song was unlike most of the songs manufactured in the Nashville music factory. Bill Mack, the songwriter, had pitched it to Patsy Cline in 1962. Patsy told Mack, "Send the damn thing to me," but he never got around to it, and in March of the following year Patsy died in a plane crash. In 1967 Kenny Roberts recorded the song on Starday Records. After that Mack let the song sit in his desk for years before deciding to pitch it again, possibly to Reba, who was a Patsy Cline fan.

Mack was himself as much an anachronism as his song. He had written some hits over the years, but was best known as the Midnight Cowboy on the Bill Mack All-Night Trucking Show on WBAP 820 in Arlington, Texas. He was one of the last of the real deejays, choosing the songs he played without benefit of consultants or computers, a spirited mix of the old and the new, keeping the truckers alert as they drove down the endless highway. The Midnight Cowboy played his old song for Wilbur, who thought the sad, beaten tone too downbeat and mature for his little daughter. When LeAnn heard the song, she knew it was for her and talked her father into putting it on her locally produced album, *All That*, singing with the intonations of Patsy Cline, adding her own yodel.

Curb knew that it would be difficult to make a hit out of "Blue," LeAnn's first single. Twenty years ago a song could break in one major market and move from there to half a dozen markets, building to become a national hit. There were so many singles out there now, and the system was so fast paced, that it was almost impossible to do that anymore. By the time a song started hitting nationally, it was already being dropped by other stations. Worse yet, most stations automatically added the newest single by the major stars, no matter how lame the song might be, narrowing even further the room for new artists.

For years the charts in *Record and Records* had been the all-important record of a single's rise. *R&R*'s charts were based on what each reporting station said they were playing, and they were susceptible to manipulation, but were often a sensitive gauge to the future of a top single. The new system at *Billboard* monitored the stations and was an accurate rendering of what songs were played and how often on the reporting stations.

Curb knew that his best shot at breaking LeAnn out was to get a number of the stations reporting to *Billboard* to play "Blue." He attempted to hire some top independent promoters to push the song, but was told they could not work the song because a major label had threatened to fire them if they did.

Nashville did not like what it could not control, and at first Music Row viewed LeAnn's single as a freak happening. Some people bad-mouthed the song and tried to destroy it. At least one important deejay reported receiving phone calls from Nashville telling him not to play "Blue."

The song, like most art that matters, was either loved or hated. The single sold a hundred thousand copies the first day it appeared in stores, and there were two hundred thousand more orders. Radio listeners called their country stations by the thousands, asking for "Blue" to be played again and again. Others called hating it. The first time Gerry House played it on WSIX Nashville, he got nothing but negative calls, including one complaining that "it sounds like Patsy Cline yodeling from her grave." It was that large negative contingent that largely prevented the song from being played on some stations. In the end, the single rose only to number ten on the *Billboard* charts and number twelve on *R&R.*

LeAnn saw none of the backstage machinations of Nashville. She was riding the whirlwind of success. For her debut at Fan Fair, she wore a formfitting black gown, and when she sang "Blue," thousands of fans sang along with her. Afterwards, she was surrounded by scores of reporters, well-wishers, publicists, and others, each seeking a moment of her time.

LeAnn was nestled within this cocoon of celebrity, and she acted as if she had finally found her natural home. Her father stood nearby wearing a "LeAnn Rimes Entertainment Inc." T-shirt. Wilbur had the satisfied look of a man who knows that his years of efforts have paid off. Nearby sat LeAnn's mother, the worry lines on her forehead growing by the day, fretting over her daughter's future and how would she ever protect her. She wanted to hold

LeAnn close to her, soon worrying about "these older men who are hitting on my daughter."

Now on the side of the stage at the Grand Ole Opry, LeAnn stood bathed in the patina of celebrity. This was a light that sometimes flickers away as quickly as it arrives, but it glowed as brilliant as klieg lights around LeAnn. She had the body of a twenty-year-old, displayed in form-fitting clothes. The promotional video that had been distributed to radio and reporters had her decked out like a country Lolita, in suggestive poses and heavy makeup. That was part of the unsettling fascination with her, this child-woman, an innocent little girl one moment, the next dressed to play a voluptuous country diva.

LeAnn had come out here in part to be photographed with these stars who a month ago did not even know her name. They knew her name now, and as the artists walked offstage they seemed to want to be photographed with LeAnn as much as she wanted to be photographed with them.

After Patty finished singing, Holly followed the singer and her entourage as they hurried through the curtains, doors, and corridors to her dressing room. As Patty changed out of her stage clothes behind a curtain, Mandy appeared in the room. Her mascara was running, and Holly figured that she had been in the bathroom crying.

"So Mandy, are you enjoying Fan Fair?" Patty asked, her voice carrying from behind the curtain.

"Well, it's OK," Mandy sighed, crouched up in a chair next to the makeup table, her body language signaling terminal despair.

"Yeah, it's really tiring, isn't it?" Patty replied matter-of-factly.

"Mandy's had a real bad day out there," Holly said loudly, thinking that maybe Patty could help Mandy a little.

"Wow!" Patty exclaimed, coming out from behind the curtain, turning to face Mandy. "What happened?"

Mandy stared at the floor. "Everywhere Mandy goes, they throw LeAnn Rimes in her face," Holly said.

"Oh, Mandy, you can't worry about that," Patty said, dismissing it as if it were no more important than a piece of lint on her sweater. "They're always going to compare you to somebody."

"Yeah, I know," Mandy replied, her voice stripped of emotion. "But it was Patsy Cline and now it's some thirteen-year-old girl."

Patty appeared sometimes as this wispy woman who could be blown over by the winds of ill fortune. But she had a core of toughness that she did not display to the world like an award pinned to her dress. She had started performing as a teenager, and she had struggled in ways that only she knew.

"You know what I think is so cool about you, Mandy?" Patty asked rhetorically.

"What?" Mandy asked, perking up a little, looking up.

"I love Patsy Cline and when I listen to you sing, it's like she's still alive. It's eerie. But it's Patsy singing these real cool, real new songs. It's like she's contemporary. You've brought her back to life, except it's something else now."

Mandy sat up in her chair and savored this awesome compliment from her favorite living singer. "Really?" Mandy said, not so much seeking more compliments as wanting reassurance that Patty was speaking her own truth.

"Really," Patty said. Then she turned to Mandy, speaking quietly, as if these were the words the young singer had to remember.

"You're real good. And you just need to do what *you* do and not worry about the rest of it."

Patty paused a moment, looked Mandy in the eyes, and spoke as if she were trying to burn these words into her consciousness. "And it's hard sometimes. I know. But you know, Mandy, you really don't have any choice. Do you understand? You really don't have any choice."

Thursday,
June 13, 1996

11

~

"River of Time"

12:18 P.M.

Only 130 members of Wynonna Judd's fan club made it out to the Roy Acuff Theater at Opryland. They sat in the first rows of the 1,469-seat theater beneath a gigantic poster of Wynonna's face that stretched from the top of the curtain to the bottom. The picture— that great mass of fiery red hair, the enormous eyelashes, the catlike eyebrows with their quizzical tilt pointing down to her long narrow nose, and the painted lips—was so overwhelming that it could have been either a religious icon or a device created by the Wizard of Oz in the Emerald City to captivate and confound his believers.

On the stage sat two ornate faux leopard sitting chairs that looked like leftovers from an old Tarzan movie. In front of the chairs stood Arch Kelley III, Wynonna's husband. Arch was the father of Elijah Judd Kelley, born out of wedlock in December of 1994. Wynonna had finally married forty-three-year-old Arch in January after getting pregnant again and was now waiting the imminent arrival of their second child. Arch wore a black Nehru coat, black pants, and thick-soled black shoes. Wynonna's husband looked like a priest or a minister in some obscure religion.

Wynonna was talking to her fans over an amplified speaker-phone from her farm in Franklin a few miles away. The more the thirty-two-year-old singer spoke, Arch appeared less the man of the cloth and more Wynonna's liveried lackey. "Now, folks, you make sure that Arch doesn't disgrace himself, make a fool of himself," Wynonna said. "You hear that, folks. Embarrass me again."

The event today had been advertised as "Arch and Elijah to Auction off Wynonna's Personal Belongings." Seventeen-month-old Elijah was not old enough to stand up here pounding a gavel. He was, however, being brought up in the light of celebrity, hauled in for occasions large and small. When he was carried onto the stage, he smiled and strutted his stuff for a few moments before Arch handed him off to a caretaker.

Arch had been a yacht salesman before he got involved with Wynonna. He and a professional auctioneer got things off to a spirited beginning. They had what appeared an impossible challenge. Only a tiny crowd had shown up, an ominous sign not only for this auction but for Wynonna's career. The two men had so much to auction that almost everyone out there would have to be bidding.

"Wynonna's personal belongings" were a bizarre accumulation that if they had not belonged to the star would largely have ended in the hands of Goodwill. Seven autographed crates of popcorn. One microphone headset. Award plaques. One Gibson Epiphone six-string guitar. One wooden choker. One Harley-Davidson bomber jacket. One wooden rocking chair. Fireplace utensils. Autographed albums. One queen-size Peacock Alley all-season blanket. One pink painted clay pot.

Arch held up the personalized license plate used on Wynonna's '57 Chevy. "Two hundred dollars." "Five hundred dollars." "A thousand dollars." These fans had come to walk away with their piece of Wynonna's life.

"Fifteen hundred dollars." "Seventeen hundred dollars." "Two thousand dollars . . . Sold for two thousand dollars."

Karen Cushing squealed with excitement, hugged her husband, and accepted the congratulations of several fans seated nearby. The couple had driven the 175 miles from Louisville this morning with the full intention of taking home something that Wynonna had touched or worn or used. Karen had been following Wynonna since the mid-eighties when as the Judds, Wynonna and her mother, Naomi, had such a bracing impact on country music.

The Judds had stood for traditional moral values, refusing to sing drinking songs and ballads that made light of adultery and other sins. They made people feel good about being good, and as a young woman Karen had identified with the teenaged Judd. When Wynonna went solo in 1992, Karen's parents were going through a divorce. Karen could feel what Wynonna was going through. She had written her a letter. A year later Wynonna had replied, saying that she had carried Karen's letter with her that whole year. Karen couldn't even remember what she wrote. She just knew it had been from the heart.

Since then Karen had been an active member of Wynonna's fan club, collecting everything she could about her idol, listening to every interview, reading every article, chatting about her idol on-line on AOL. She had found her fellow fan club members to be overwhelmingly sincere and generous, and she had come to count two of them among her closest friends.

In Louisville, Karen stayed home taking care of their two boys while her husband worked as a federal prosecutor. The Cushings were not wealthy, but Karen saw this morning as an opportunity she couldn't bypass. She bid on the headset that Wynonna used on her first tour, keeping with it until she won for $2,100. She grabbed an autographed album for a measly $200. She bought enough of Wynonna's clothes that she could have practically walked out of there in full outfit, starting with a $500 pair of boots, a $500 tour jacket, a bolo tie for $600, neatly accessorized with a $1,500 diamond necklace and a $370 bracelet. Best of all she won the prize of prizes, an item not even mentioned in the item list, a tour of Wynonna's house that went for $6,100. In all she spent $14,720, and from beginning to end her husband didn't blanch.

As her fans knew, Wynonna's life was a never-ending melodrama that made the soap operas seem as exciting as *Sesame Street*. These fans didn't want simply some item hanging on their wall, a trophy of their moment with Wynonna, they wanted to be with her. The second biggest item, after the house tour, was also not mentioned in the auction brochure: dinner with Wynonna. There was no timidity about the bidders, worries about what they would say, how they would behave. As they saw it, Wynonna was one of them, only on the same enormous scale as her portrait that dominated the entire theater.

"One thousand dollars."

Charley Hicks, a thirty-year-old painting contractor from Scottsburg, Indiana, started the bidding. He and Tina, his twenty-nine-year-old wife, had driven down this morning just for the auction along with Ryan, their two-year-old son. As the amount went up, Charley kept right on bidding. Tina turned red. She loved Wynonna even more than Charley, but this was money to them. This was weeks of work.

"Two thousand dollars."

"Three thousand dollars."

And still Charley kept in there. It was so much money now that it hardly mattered. It was like talking about the national debt. "$3,300." Charley wanted this for Tina, no matter what. "$3,450." He had won. "$3,450."

Charley also won the bidding on the brass fireplace utensils for a hundred dollars. He and Tina didn't even have a fireplace, and he figured they could set the utensils next to the microwave. That at least was something he could afford, but he had no intention of spending $3,450 to win such a grand prize. The other fans drifted out of the theater after paying for their items, in all raising $55,000 for the Animaland Animal Shelter in Franklin.

From the porch of her farmhouse in the countryside outside Franklin, Wynonna could see the cars passing by, many of them visitors to Fan Fair gawking at her. So much of her artistic and personal quest had been in search of freedom, love, and happiness, but even here she could not get away. The first cut on her first solo album was about a woman who "wants to walk to no particular destination" and is "going to do what it takes to keep this smile on my face." She had kept that smile on her public face, but she had paid a price in blood and soul.

Wynonna did not have freedom, but she knew no emotional boundaries, and she often walked over the lives of others. She called her new album *Revelations*. In the album notes, she thanked the Lord "for helping me to face the truth," but so much of her life had been lived not to face the truth but to avoid its calamitous consequences. "Everywhere I look the sun is shining," she sang on her second album, "but it's always raining here inside."

It had been thirteen years ago that nineteen-year-old Wynonna had sat on the leather sofa in the office of her new manager for the first time. "You and your mom are going to be making ten thousand a night, Wy," Ken Stilts had told her, and she had laughed at him in disbelief. "No way would anybody pay me that!"

Wynonna was a wild, unruly young woman whose temper was salved only by the sweet balm of music. Her mother, Naomi, a thirty-eight-year-old nurse who looked like Wynonna's sexy older sister, sang harmony. Naomi's voice melded brilliantly with her daughters', but it was only on their songs that Naomi played backup.

Naomi was one of these natural aristocrats of show business who come most alive when the spotlight shines on their countenance. Wynonna sang but Naomi held the spotlight, creating not a series of songs but a show, with patter and pace and her own homespun philosophy. She created the saga of the Judds that in a few years became one of the most compelling, most inspiring stories in country music.

Naomi told how as a seventeen-year-old in Ashland, Kentucky, she had been seduced one evening by the rich boy in the town. She became pregnant, married Michael Ciminella, her seducer, and brought Wynonna into the world. For Wynonna, what could be a more inspiring, noble model than a mother who sacrificed her worldly ambition for her daughter. Naomi and Michael had a second daughter, Ashley, and moved to Hollywood, where Naomi worked as a millionaire's assistant and as a model.

The marriage ended, and Naomi brought her two daughters back to the hills of Kentucky. There in a house with neither television nor telephone, mother and daughter listened to the Grand Ole Opry, sang together, and discovered their musical roots. The

Judds moved back to California, then returned east again to settle in Nashville, where Naomi worked as a nurse. It was there that Naomi made contact with the Nashville music industry, including Ken Stilts, a charming, life-loving, successful entrepreneur who dabbled in country music. Ken set up an audition that led to a contract with RCA/Curb.

The Judds were the songbirds of family and home, only lyrics of virtue and goodness passing their lips. During eight years, the Judds won most of the major awards in country music, sold albums in the millions, and performed as headliners before immense, enthusiastic audiences across America. During those years the drama that took place after their performances transcended anything that happened onstage.

Wynonna and Naomi had a love-hate relationship on a scale rarely seen. This was not merely affection tempered with dislike, but a passionately felt bond of blood and concern, and vicious disdain and manipulativeness. On their bus journeys across America, Wynonna ran out of control, heading out into the night on her Harley-Davidson, running with strangers, showing up late for concerts and meetings. Naomi was a woman of guile and shrewdness, knowing how to rein her daughter in, to plunge a knife of guilt and remorse into her heart.

As their manager, Ken was the mediator, believing that for a time he was the only person in the world Wynonna respected. The phone rang at two in the morning. It was Naomi calling after a concert in Las Vegas to complain about her daughter's latest outrage. Ken was half awake listening when the operator broke in, saying that he had an emergency call. Ken told the operator that he knew who the emergency was, and when he got through with her mother he would call Wynonna back.

"As strong as Wynonna was and as talented, she was equally weak in smarts because she had never had to think for herself," Ken reflected. "Naomi always did that. Naomi practiced total mind control over Wynonna. When she was not in her daughter's presence, she would joke about how she could control Wynonna, how she was so much smarter than Wynonna."

Wynonna struck back at those who sought to control her. Food was her friend and her weapon. When during a sold-out week in Las Vegas, Ken warned Wynonna about her burgeoning weight, she walked over to the dessert buffet and took two pieces of cake. The contrast between voluptuous Naomi and her fat daughter was overwhelming. Wynonna would never be like her mother. On the long bus rides, she ate and ate some more.

The tempestuous drama of the Judds might have gone on for more years, but Naomi was stricken with chronic active hepatitis. Naomi was a maestro of emotion. She did not simply walk off the stage with one last soliloquy. She and Wynonna traveled from city to city for twelve months and 124 concerts, saying good-bye. Night after night Wynonna and Naomi stood together onstage, wringing the last emotional decibel out of the saga of the Judds.

Backstage the other drama continued. One Sunday morning in the fall of 1991, Martha Taylor received a phone call from Wynonna. Usually this was the kind of call that went to her boss, Ken Stilts, as the Judds' manager, but Ken was sick. Wynonna told Martha that when the Judds arrived home from tour on their bus, Naomi had gone crazy, fighting Wynonna and her boyfriend. When the couple wouldn't leave Naomi's condo, she ran out of the house, got into her Mercedes and bumped Wynonna's car.

Martha hurried over to Naomi's condo and found her sitting there in her pajamas, her acrylic fingernails broken back and bloody. Naomi's storm of emotion had spent itself, and she sat calmly eating soup the maid had prepared for her, clutching a spoon with her bloody fingernails. The next day when Naomi and Wynonna went to see their Christian therapist, they insisted that Martha go along, to mediate between the two women.

In December of 1991 the Judds gave their final farewell concert in Murfreesboro, Tennessee. At times, Wynonna and Naomi had looked like garish country Barbie dolls in their flashy dresses and flashing petticoats. This evening the rich colors of their clothes seemed fitted to the richness of their onstage personalities. At times their endless quarrels and reconciliations and avowals of endless love had reeked of self-indulgent excess. This evening one could not hear a note without realizing the bonds of mother and daughter.

"Life is all about embrace and release, embrace and release," Naomi told Wynonna at the end as her daughter's eyes welled with tears. "Now you must spread your wings and fly, my darling, and go toward the light. Go toward the light."

Wynonna got back on her bus and headed out into the world alone. For a few nights back in the stateroom, she tried to stay awake all night long, finally falling asleep sitting up. Then she began to go to bed to sleep, but when she slept, she dreamed. Often she dreamed that her mother died. And then came back again. And again she died. Time after time. Night after night.

By any standard but her own, Wynonna had success beyond success. Her first solo album, produced by Tony Brown, sold three million copies. *Wynonna Judd* was the biggest-selling studio country album ever by a woman. The solo album was an enormous critical success, called by *Rolling Stone* "easily the most important release by a country artist so far this decade." Her second album, *Tell Me Why*, a year later in 1993 sold over one million.

Ken had pushed Wynonna back out on the road because he felt she was a great artist who would be even more successful by herself than with her mother. Ken felt for Wynonna. He watched as she searched for love and freedom, riding out there along a chasm of despair. She was so insecure that she always had to have a man. One man was rarely enough, as if the sheer quantities of her pursuers would make her insecurities go away. The newest arrival was Arch Kelley III. Ken was backstage in Tahoe soon after the couple met. "Are you and Wynonna planning on getting married?" Ken heard someone ask.

"Well, she's going to gross about ten million dollars next year," Ken recalls Arch saying. "So what do you think?"

As much as Ken cared for Wynonna, he was not about to jeopardize the millions of dollars that Wynonna represented to him by tattling about Arch's indiscretion. Though Ken took Arch's words literally, Arch's boast may have simply been the camouflaging of his own emotions. That's what Wynonna did to people around her. They began by caring for her with depth and concern, but she often managed to abuse them so that they turned cynical, getting whatever they could out of her.

Wynonna had eaten out of anger at Ken for attempting to control her. Now she ate as if food were the only sacrament left to her. Food was warmth and caring. Food was her mother holding her and rubbing her feet as they drove through the night. Food was a lover who never betrayed her, a friend who was always there.

When she looked back on those years as the Judds, Wynonna had come to feel that all those people who said they had cared for her had thought of her as nothing but a product. Wynonna Judd cut into pieces for sale, CDs, concerts, T-shirts, magazine articles, TV specials. It wasn't about music. It was about money. She looked at Ken, who had been a big daddy to her, shepherding her down the road, listening to her woes and her grief. As she saw it now, he was the one who had pushed her out on the road by herself. She had loved him, but he was like the others, out there for money.

Wynonna was almost thirty years old and she was still in some respects a child, in thrall to her manager and to her mother and to her fans. She had been, as she repeated again and again, "booked and cooked." Early in 1994 she decided to take the most dramatic step of her professional life: to fire Ken Stilts.

When Wynonna announced that she had hired John Unger to be her new manager, there were a few gentle guffaws and some outright anger. Unger, the son of a Chevrolet dealer in the suburbs of Philadelphia, had not grown up listening to the Grand Ole Opry. The forty-year-old Princeton man had come down to Nashville to attend Vanderbilt Law School and had never left the Tennessee capital. All of his professional life he had worked for a prestigious Nashville law firm doing corporate work. Only in recent years had he added a few clients in the music business.

John knew nothing about managing a country star, but he and Wynonna lived under the same emotional sign. He was feeling booked and cooked too, his days measured out in fifteen-minute billing segments. He had written his senior thesis at Princeton on Joseph Conrad's search for identity. John felt that he, like Wynonna, was a work in progress, out there searching for meaning in a strange, menacing, beautiful world. When he couldn't decide whether to go with Wynonna, he happened to be listening to a Mary Chapin Carpenter album. "I take my chances, I don't mind working without a net, I take my chances every chance I get." He listened as if he were hearing a philosophy lecture or a sermon. Music could move people. It could change lives. He decided that he would resign from his firm and become Wynonna's manager. He signed on for a salary, not for the percentage that most managers earned.

Wynonna told John that she wanted a team of people around her who would tell her the truth and help her build a strong new career. In 1994 the architectural plans of her new life had hardly been sketched when Wynonna became pregnant, putting everything back a year, making 1995 her new "comeback year." Her press conference was one of those "oops, sorry" moments. "Uh, I don't mean to let you all down, but something has come up."

Wynonna told Oprah Winfrey in front of millions of viewers that she had not even thought about an abortion because she had seen what happened to Patty Loveless when her former husband told a tabloid reporter about the country star's secret operation. "And I'll tell you why—no, because my biggest fear—Patty Loveless, do you remember that?" she said. "My biggest fear—and Mom knows this. I was never a good liar. . . . But if I went and had an abortion, my biggest fear would be that I would be sitting in an interview one day and someone would stick a microphone in front of me and say—which would, by the way, discredit everything I've ever said before—'So do you want to tell me about that abortion you had back in da-da-da-da-da.'"

It was a shameful business comparing Wynonna's decision with Patty's, and only Wynonna knew how shameful. In the spring of 1987, Wynonna was seeing several men, including a singer.

The singer lost contact with Wynonna when she moved. He finally tracked her down at Ruby Tuesdays in Green Hills, one of her favorite restaurants.

"What happened to you, Wy? You just disappeared," the man said. Then to make a joke, he added: "What happened, did you get pregnant?"

Wynonna started crying.

"Why didn't you tell me?" the man asked Wynonna, shaking his head in dismay. "I would have been there for you."

★ Garth Brooks signing a T-shirt during his twenty-three-hour marathon at Fan Fair '96 (Laurence Leamer)

★ Garth Brooks, the biggest selling solo artist of all time, driving alone in his pickup truck in Nashville. (©1994 Nubar Alexanian)

★ A show at the Nashville Speedway at Fan Fair '96. (Eric England)

★ The fans don't mind the heat. (Eric England)

★ Waiting for autographs. (Eric England)

★ Almost everyone has a favorite country star. (Alan L. Mayor)

★ For a quarter century, rustling up grub at Fan Fair. (Eric England)

★ What better than an autographed guitar? (Laura Levine)

★ Friends who meet each year at Fan Fair. (Laurence Leamer)

★ Tony Brown, the president of MCA Nashville, and Elise Loehr in a private moment backstage. (Eric England)

★ Vince Gill in his Hawaian shirt opening night at Fan Fair. (Alan L. Mayor)

★ Vince Gill with a fan in his booth. (Eric England)

★ Emmylou Harris on her tour bus in Paris, with guitar player Albert Lee, left, and the author, right. (© 1995 Nubar Alexanian)

★ Emmylou Harris with Rodney Crowell and Trisha Yearwood, left, in a Madrid restaurant. (Laurence Leamer)

★ Arch Kelley III,
  Wynonna's husband,
  auctioning off her
  belongings for charity.
  (Laurence Leamer)

★ "Wy's Collectibles,"
  Wynonna's booth at
  Fan Fair. (Laurence
  Leamer)

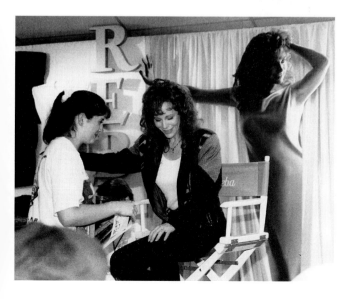

★ Reba McEntire on
  her temporary throne.
  (Laurence Leamer)

★ Mindy McCready in front of her bus at Fan Fair '96. (Eric England)

★ Shania Twain with a fan during the special Fan Fair session for the disabled. (Eric England)

★ James Bonamy blows out the stops during the Epic/Columbia Show. (Eric England)

★ LeAnn Rimes making
her debut at Fan Fair
'96. (Alan L. Mayor)

★ Mandy Barnett on
stage for the first
time at Fan Fair
'96. (Asylum)

★ Alan Jackson knocking them dead during the Arista Nashville show. (Eric England)

★ Alan Jackson's booth. (Eric England)

★ Scott Hendricks, center, president of Capitol Nashville, backstage at Fan Fair. (Eric England)

★ Ronnie Dunn during Brooks and Dunn's performance at Fan Fair '96. (Eric England)

★ On stage at the Arista Nashville show, Kix Brooks, left, talks with label president Tim DuBois, center, while Ronnie Dunn, right, has his own conversation. (Eric England)

★ Mary Chapin Carpenter at the 1996 CMA Awards. (Alan L. Mayor)

★ A youthful Mary Chapin Carpenter when she performed at open mike nights in Washington. (Juli Musgrave)

★ Patty Loveless
performing on the great
Fan Fair stage. (Sony)

★ A fan kisses Patty
Loveless in her
booth. (Laurence
Leamer)

★ Linda Hargrove
singing at Tootsie's
during Fan Fair
'96. (Eric England)

★ Ron Wallace singing at
County Q, a demo
studio. (Eric England)

★ BR5-49 performing nonstop at Robert's Western World. (© Rouda; all rights reserved)

★ Harlan Howard, one of country's greatest songwriters, in a favorite pose: drinking, smoking, and talking. (Donna Marie Jones)

The man may well not have been the father of the child, but he knew that he could have been and he was willing to take responsibility. He did not have that resolution tested, for in late August of 1987 Wynonna, using the name Connie Sims, had an abortion in Nashville. The singer who thought he was the father had a record deal, but he was broke. His truck had bald tires and a hole in the floorboard. A business associate called one of the tabloids. He was offered twenty thousand dollars to tell his tale. That was all the money in the world to him, but he turned it down.

The tabloids didn't have the abortion story, but Wynonna was now a queen of the tabloids, her picture splashed across the *Star* and the *National Enquirer*, the headlines exercises in shame. During her pregnancy she gained far too much weight, seventy-five pounds in all. She sought help from a Christian therapist, who tempered the unforgiving truths of psychology with biblical passages.

Wynonna attended Christ Church in Brentwood, a Pentecostal congregation that took its Bible straight and strong. Rev. L. H. Hardwick Jr. had risen from driving a bakery truck to becoming pastor of this glorious church on a hillside outside Nashville with over six thousand members of all ages and classes and races. Reverend Hardwick believed his church to be especially blessed to make of Nashville a New Jerusalem. There was no finer proof of his special calling than that he ministered to so many stars of country music, none of them higher in the firmament than Naomi and Wynonna Judd. The 175-member church choir had sung backup at the Judds' farewell concert, bringing yet more fame and honor to his church.

Thus it had seemed a curse of biblical proportions when Wynonna became pregnant. There were those among his congregation who looked on Wynonna with unforgiving eyes and would have cast her out of the church and its sheltering harbor. There were those too who looked on Reverend Hardwick as a rank hypocrite, rationalizing the sins of the celebrated. The reverend continued to welcome Wynonna as she arrived late Sunday and sat far up in the balcony, leaving a few minutes before the end of the service, rushing out to a limousine that waited below.

Wynonna could no more cast off her cloak of virtue, as spotted as it was, than jump out of her skin. She did not like carrying that burden. She did not like hearing from mothers with sixteen-year-old daughters who felt betrayed. "For some reason, I guess they decided that I had to be the role model, or the scapegoat, in terms of sex or something," she reflected. "I found that interesting."

Wynonna went back in the studio and poured all her energy into finding songs and recording what she meant to be a transcendent album, taking her career to a place beyond the beyond. In December of 1994 she gave birth to Elijah. Afterwards, she went back with her producer, Tony Brown, to the studio. Wynonna saw the newly fickle nature of fans, how a Billy Ray Cyrus could be an enormous artist for one album, and then practically disappear off radio. She had the natural insecurities of the creative to the nth degree, and she worried if her audience would still be there for her.

Tony was a diplomat, adept at dealing with the will and whim and uncontrolled egos of performers. Yet he had no artist at MCA Nashville who put him through a tenth of what Wynonna did. By some measurement, his time was as valuable as Wynonna's. Yet often he waited in the studio with the band when Wynonna arrived and said she didn't feel like recording. The band had to be paid, and Wynonna and Tony went off for what the producer called "four-thousand-dollar lunches." Wynonna could rationalize that these lunches came out of her royalties. She couldn't seem to understand that the cost was not tallied only in dollars. These band members were artists in their own right who could not perform at their best under such uncertainty.

Wynonna, Naomi, and Ashley sat in a bed in a suite at their hotel in Chicago, wearing the hotel bathrobes, munching on room service food, watching the first night of the mini-series on their lives on CBS based on Naomi's best-selling book. Tomorrow the family would be appearing on *Oprah* to promote *Love Can Build a Bridge*. Until a few days ago, Wynonna had refused to go on the talk show. For months her manager and publicist had been preaching to her that she had to establish a separate identity for herself. And all of this—the best-selling book, the mini-series, the *Oprah* show—helped to cement her feet in the past. Perhaps it was a mistake, but no one except Wynonna understood the emotional power of Naomi, and so Wynonna was here.

Wynonna's sister had more shrewdly distanced herself. Ashley was a rising young actress who could have played either her mother or herself in the mini-series, but she had stayed away, not even visiting the set. "I can't watch this anymore," Ashley fumed, throwing up her hands. "It's awful. I can't believe this." Ashley left the room. Wynonna stayed and watched her mother as a teenager, so innocent and sweet tempered. She was unable to resist the entreaties of a rich older boy and ended up pregnant with Wynonna.

Wynonna watched all her foibles and excesses portrayed, the endless psychodrama of the Judds spread out there for all America to watch. Michael Ciminella had been watching the mini-series too. Two months later he came forward and gave the only interview he had ever given about his marriage to Naomi. He told the *Daily Independent* of Ashland, the small Kentucky town that he and Naomi had once called home, that he was not Wynonna's father. Naomi had tricked him into marrying her "because she thought my family had more money" than the youth who had impregnated her. "She has spent her career saying what a horrible person I was when she, in fact, is the one who didn't stand up and do what is right," he said. "She let me take the rap for something I did not do."

Love can, indeed, build a bridge, but a bridge whose planks are rotted with falsehood is a bridge that threatens all who attempt to pass over. Wynonna was thirty-one years old. She was a mother. She was an artist. She needed her own true life, her own true story. Wynonna learned that close friends and relatives had known the truth about her father for years. Everyone had known, it seemed, but her. Ciminella believed that she was silent about the revelation because her mother would cut Wynonna off if she talked about it. John Unger and others advised her to step forward and tell her own truths about Naomi and her life. She dared not attempt that, to try to build her own bridge to an adult life. She dared not try to walk free without the crutches of blame and dependence.

Music had always been Wynonna's one sure escape. She took that pathway again, asserting herself in an album for MCA/Curb that in the end contained not one song that the Judds might have recorded. Wynonna had been the incomparable voice of the Judds, and willfully leaving that music, she left much of what was natural to her. Some of the musicians who heard the songs felt that Wynonna had gone over that vague unmarked border into music that was totally pop.

Wynonna was not a songwriter, and she searched through Nashville and Los Angeles for songs. She sat in Tony's office meeting with one important songwriter after the next, detailing the kind of songs she wanted. Trey Bruce came walking in. Trey, along with Russell Smith, had written "Look Heart, No Hands," a number one Randy Travis hit.

"Trey, this is the idea," Wynonna told the songwriter. "I want it to kind of have a little rhythm-and-blues feel. I want it to have Nashville homespun, earthy lyrics that everybody can understand. I want to sing songs about endless hope so that people don't think I sit up in a penthouse and eat bonbons all day. You know, like everything's rosy."

As Trey walked out the door, another songwriter, Dave Loggins, was waiting to go in. Loggins had written "She Is His Only Need," Wynonna's first number one single. He had a superb sense of Wynonna's artistic sensibilities. Trey waited for his songwriter friend to hear Wynonna's spiel, and then the two of them went off together.

Dave had appeared upset at his meeting, disappointed that this wasn't the same Wynonna he had known. Nonetheless, the two songwriters tried to write a song. It didn't work out, but a few weeks later they got together to try again. This time they succeeded. Dave had been a performer himself, and he thought he knew a fine song when he heard it. So did Trey. They were sure it had everything Wynonna wanted.

Dave sang the song on the demo tape they played for Tony. The producer confirmed everything the two songwriters had thought. "I love it," Tony shouted. "I'm gonna mail it to her house."

It was Wynonna's song, and they never heard from her again. In the end, Doug Stone took the song and made it the title cut of his new album, *Faith in Me, Faith in You*. The single rose to number thirteen on *Billboard*'s singles chart, though Trey figured that if Wynonna had recorded the song, it would have been number one.

The Loggins-Bruce song had come and gone from the charts, and still Wynonna hadn't finished her album. Tony couldn't even reach Wynonna sometimes. He called out to the house. Nobody answered. He'd leave urgent messages, day after day after day. The president of MCA Nashville ended up having to drive out to Wynonna's farm to talk to her.

Winter was falling on Nashville, and Wynonna had been recording her album for close to a year and a half, and she still wasn't finished. Tony booked his time months in advance. He had Vince Gill coming into the studio. Wynonna wanted to drag the producer and the musicians back in the studio some more.

Tony knew that Vince would have waited a few more days to go into the studio. For Tony, however, it was not simply a matter of time. He had to clear his head and be ready to give Vince everything he had to give to the man and his music. Beyond that, it was fun working with Vince. And it wasn't fun with Wynonna, not anymore.

Tony decided to ask Don Potter, the associate producer, to take over. Tony felt that the man hadn't received the credit he deserved, and this would be a great opportunity for him. Wynonna, however, would hear nothing of it. As upset as she became, Tony refused to back down. In the end, he dumped "Free Bird," a song that Wynonna had cut for the Lynyrd Skynyrd tribute album, onto the album as the tenth cut, and moved on.

John Unger believed in music as one of the last great honorable arts. He believed in Wynonna as a great honorable artist. Most of all, he believed in this new album. He had even been responsible for naming the album. *Revelations*. That's what the music was to him. *Revelations*. He listened to the cuts hundreds of times. He truly listened, savoring each word and nuance. *Revelations*. As often as he heard the songs, he still got goose bumps. He thought they could sell ten million copies. He thought that it could be the biggest-selling album ever.

When John had been in his law firm downtown, he had put in long hours, but that had been nothing compared to this. He was married. He had a son at home. He had a life, but he was endlessly on call to Wynonna's will and whim. He woke up in the middle of the night thinking about Wynonna. As hard as he worked, he had discovered an indolent quality in Wynonna that he never expected. She was lazy. She thought that her talent gave her a free pass. He kept telling her she was wrong; everything mattered, from the grandest plan to the smallest detail.

John promised his wife and son a Christmas vacation in Hawaii. They were ready to go when Wynonna called and asked him to stay a few extra days. It was one of those moments when a person's destiny and meaning stand there encapsulated in a single act. John stayed those extra days. When the story was told in the corridors at MCA Nashville, no one thought quite the same of John any longer, nor quite the same of Wynonna either.

Launching an album on the scale of *Revelations* was like a military campaign in which before the first planes are launched and the first salvo fired, everything and everyone must be in place. This was Wynonna's first album in three years, and the stakes were gigantic. At MCA Nashville, Reba's pop-oriented album *Starting Over* had just been roundly panned by the critics and proven a commercial disappointment as well. Nashville's most successful label needed Wynonna's album to work. Already there were ominous signs. Wynonna had managed to alienate herself from Tony, the most respected producer in Nashville. She and her manager had gone above the heads of MCA Nashville to complain to the top executives in Los Angeles. They might have done so with a modicum of subtlety, but that was not their style, and they returned to Nashville over burning bridges.

An expensive video had been shot to go on CMT and TNT, a crucial component in the launching of any new album. Wynonna had not liked the way she looked and insisted that the video be discarded. And now came the pregnancy that would limit her ability to promote the album, and with it the splendid event that the *Washington Post* had so indelicately called a "shotgun celebrity wedding."

Wynonna had wanted a private ceremony at home, befitting not only a twice-pregnant bride but a singer seeking publicity for her new album, not more tabloid fodder. Instead, the ceremony took place at Christ Church, followed by a reception at Naomi's Trilogy restaurant. The event garnered immense publicity for Naomi's restaurant, but for the bride it was more pie-in-the-face notoriety. BRIDE WYNONNA'S TWO-RING CIRCUS, the tabloid headlines waxed sarcastically. 200-POUND PREGNANT SINGER TRIPPED AS SHE WALKED DOWN THE AISLE. HUNGRY GUESTS FLED NAOMI'S RESTAURANT TO EAT ACROSS THE STREET.

Wynonna was one of the few acts in popular music with a stature and audience large enough to warrant her album making its debut a one-hour, prime-time television special. In the week before the album's February release, she taped an hourlong CBS special at the Sunset Studios in Nashville. The producers constructed a new set to hold an audience. A soundstage was remade, filling the space with white fake pillars suitable for a B movie on the fall of Rome. Seating was for four hundred in the round. The audience had won their seats in a lottery by calling Wynonna's 900 number. They had come from as far away as Colorado and Nebraska, and had begun waiting at the side entrance at nine o'clock in the morning for the seven o'clock performance.

With Wynonna everything was a drama, from the most mundane questions to the most enormous questions of her personal life and career, an unending, exhausting psychodrama that involved everyone who came within a few feet of her, including, this evening, her fans. As always, Wynonna was late. She sat in her dressing room so insecure, so petrified with the idea of again appearing before an audience, that she could not bring herself to walk out front.

The audience was revved up again and again, each time being told that the show was delayed. It was close to nine o'clock before the seven-piece band and three backup singers finally took their places and Wynonna walked onstage to a standing ovation. She was three months pregnant. That, added to her already substantial weight, made her look less like the diva of country than one of those temporary pillars, set down in the middle of the stage and covered with a garish mishmash including a gold and black brocade coat, a lime green shirt, black pants, and shoes. Although she had been sitting in the dressing room for hours being coifed and primped, a button on her blouse was undone, a fact that one of her minions in the first row finally noticed.

"I'm so nervous," Wynonna said, not in the predictable ingratiating manner of a professional celebrity but as she might utter a whispered confession to a friend.

"Wynonna, you are bad, baby!" a woman shouted out from the front seats.

"You go, girl, you go," Wynonna replied, turning toward the fan.

Wynonna's audience had become an entity that she treated like a good, loyal, but at times unruly friend, part of her intimate entourage that she had to please. As much as she loved her audience, she could tell it to step back, to stop trying to force its way into the rooms of her life where no one but her mother and sister entered.

"We love you, Wynonna," a woman's voice called out. It was one of the ritual imprecations of country music, not simply an avowal of devotion but an insistence on a response. Affection was hard currency. The fan had plunked her money down and she wanted full value. "I love you too," Wynonna replied as she had replied ten thousand times before on a thousand evenings.

"Where's my mama?" Wynonna asked, a slight tinge of desperation to her tone, only happy when she saw the reassuring presence of Naomi in the second row. In her wine-red tailored designer suit and black pillbox hat, Naomi looked less like Wynonna's mother than a Belle Meade matron with friends in the music industry.

"It's been a long time, but I'm back, baby," Wynonna asserted. "You can't keep the Judds on the farm. I'm really sweaty. I forgot how hard this is. I'm really sweaty."

Wynonna had cast her net across all the seas of popular music in search of the ten songs on her album, each song a chapter in her idealized spiritual autobiography. Wynonna's new album was called *Revelations,* but it was not so much an inspired vision of her life but aspiration, representing the world in which Wynonna wanted to live. In the years she had been singing, Wynonna had sought love among the roadies and the band members, sought it in bars and buses, losing again and again. She began the evening by singing "Heaven Help My Heart," a song of a woman's yearning for love. Although the album had not even come out yet, some women in the audience already knew the words, and they sound-lessly mouthed them with her, as if this were their song too.

At her most youthful, Wynonna had not been an athletic per-former, a female Garth jumping around the stage. Now weighed down with child, she stood stolidly anchored to the stage. It didn't matter, for she had more gestures in her voice than most dancers have moves. She didn't so much sing the song as inhabit it, to live every moment and nuance. She had one of the most powerful voices in popular music, and as strongly as she sang, it was as if only a tenth of its power had been touched.

When she finished, she was not satisfied. "When I'm practic-ing at home, I'm so into it but out here . . . " The words drifted off into silence.

"We're like family," a fan assured her.

"You want to do good for family. I'm a professional. I'm a Judd. I can do anything."

"Yes!" a voice shouted out. "Yes!"

"You sit there in your comfortable chair. It's my butt on the line in front of a hundred million people." Wynonna did some breath-ing exercises that she had learned from Deepak Chopra, the author and guru. And then she sang the song again.

All during Wynonna's singing, Arch paced back and forth hold-ing Elijah in his arms. Periodically, he tossed his son in the air or bounced him around, trying anything to keep the little boy awake except pouring coffee into his pudgy mouth. Arch had golden hair and the slightly spoiled, petulant handsome face that had spelled years of trouble for Wynonna. He wore the black Nehru suit, his coat buttoned to his throat, that was practically his public uniform.

As the minutes went by, Arch tossed his son higher and longer, and Elijah became more and more irritable.

When Arch finally brought Elijah forward to be filmed while Wynonna sang a song to him, the child was in no mood to be pushed and prodded any longer. "This is how me and my mommy got into this," Wynonna mused. "Do I really want to do this with him? Is this something too big to handle?" The audience applauded and ohhed and ahhed at Elijah's every move and gesture, like adoring relatives.

Elijah looked like the last of the Cabbage Patch dolls. He had inherited his mother's strong will in full measure, and hours past his bedtime he wasn't going to be guided anywhere. While Wynonna sang "My Angel Is Here," her angel was anywhere but here. He crawled up the stage steps, pulled himself up to his feet, and waddled toward the boom camera and away from any shots with his mother.

They tried again, but Elijah was too tired, and Wynonna realized that they would have to shoot the scene again the next day. For the next song, Wynonna knew that there would be no second chance. Bette Midler had flown in from Hollywood, or "Hollyweird" as Wynonna called it, for this one day. Wynonna and Bette had performed together to stunning success at the VH-1 Honors; in the world of celebrity, that qualified Bette as a "new friend" to be invited to perform on the CBS special.

After the makeup artist and hairstylists had worked her over again, Wynonna placed herself at stage center facing the stage exit that led to the dressing rooms. When Bette bounced up the stage steps, the audience jumped up in fervent applause, gasping at how fantastic she looked, exuding energy, and youth, and stardom.

This tiny woman in a yellow pantsuit that sculpted her curves stared across the set at a Wynonna who looked at if she had just come back from a shopping spree at The Forgotten Woman. Bette Midler began singing one of her signature songs, "Love Is . . . ." She had sung it countless times before, but the woman was a sterling performer, and she was into the song as if it were the first time, gracefully handing off the second verse to Wynonna.

"Love is . . . " Wynonna boomed out. "Ah, I don't got it right. I forgot."

Bette looked toward Wynonna as if she had just smelled a rotten odor. In Hollywood there is only one unforgivable sin, and that is to forget your lines, especially when you have an idiot-box monitor at your feet running the lines by as you sing them. Bette was a professional and she was professionally irritated. Bette had gone from singing in the Continental Baths on the West Side of Manhattan to idolizing largely gay audiences and from playing Tzeitel in *Fiddler on the Roof* to adoring largely Jewish audiences, to singing schmaltzy inspirational ballads taken to heart by Middle America and starring in family movies produced by Walt Disney. Anything was possible in America, but you had to remember your lines.

"I've been in that fucking trailer so long, I don't know what I'm doing," Bette said, the Divine Miss M reverting to her pre-Disney vocabulary. In her seat Naomi jumped back as if she had been slapped. The Judds hadn't sung certain songs if they were too raunchy or risqué, and they certainly didn't spew forth profanity with the cameras rolling.

The two singers started the song a second time, and again Wynonna blew it. "You want to go out and familiarize yourself with the material," Bette said, unable to resist speaking the obvious.

"You're tough," Wynonna said, as if she deserved a special pass.

While they waited to begin again, Bette bantered with the audience. "I only know a couple country songs," she said. To Bette "country" meant everything outside New York and LA, or before a certain era. She proceeded to sing "Pistol Packing Mama" and "Dance with a Dolly with a Hole in her Stocking."

For the third time they attempted the song, and for the third time Wynonna blew it. "You don't know what it's like," Wynonna said, shaking her mane of hair.

"You don't know what it's like to love somebody," Bette sang, as if Wynonna's words had been a lead-in. "You don't know what it's like . . ." Bette had brilliant improvisational skills, while in her own moments of uncertainty Wynonna's only recourse was to open herself and her life to view.

The fourth time Wynonna finally made it through the song.

She left the stage so Bette could do her solo. "Did you let a clam?" Bette said to the piano player, no happier with the musician than she had been with Wynonna. Then she turned to the audience. "When I got out of the plane this morning, I had no idea what I was in for—it's a quagmire."

After Bette left, Wynonna returned to the stage. Almost half the audience had left as well, to Wynonna a silent rebuke. "I'm trying to please everyone," she said. That was nothing less than the truth. She was trying to please her mother and Naomi's vision of what her daughter should be. She was trying to please the producer and the director. She was trying to please God and those who thought they were godly. After all, she had married Arch and ended that supposed shame. She was trying to please her audience, these people who were her fans. Everyone.

Wynonna sang the last song to be recorded for the evening, and the audience applauded with fervor. They didn't want her to go. It was almost midnight. Many of them had been here for fifteen hours. She decided that she would sing one more song, just for them, for the two hundred people still here. She was exhausted, and singing a last song was an act of enormous generosity and grace.

"Has my mommy gone?" she asked, thinking that she and Naomi might do a duet. But her mother did not return. She would have to sing a solo. Five minutes passed. Then ten minutes. And she still could not decide what song she would sing. It was as simple a decision as choosing what shoes to wear when she got up in the morning, but she filled each moment with anguish and uncertainty.

Finally she turned to her guitar player and backup singers and sang:

> Flow on river of time
> Wash away the pain and heal my mind.
> Flow on river of time
> Carry me away
> And leave it all far behind.
> Flow on river of time.

There was probably no one left in the room who did not know "River of Time," a song that Naomi and John Jarvis had written for the Judds. On their album, the mother and daughter sang it together, but Wynonna had always been the voice that carried their music, and the song was complete without her mother's harmony. She sang out with sweet melancholy, reaching within for all the emotional truths she found there. The song was like a benediction, and the audience, her audience, folks from Kentucky and Indiana and Texas and Colorado and Florida, swayed silently with the music, swayed back and forth, lost in the healing balm of her music.

"Good night and God bless you," Wynonna said, and walked off the stage.

The most important group in America to help sell Wynonna's album—the twenty-three hundred country radio stations—were having their annual Country Radio Seminar at the Opryland Hotel just as Wynonna's album was coming out. Some of the older broadcasters could still remember when many radio stations had been owned by individuals. In those days disc jockeys sat at turntables with stacks of 45s, spinning the songs they wanted to spin.

Most stations had been taken over by great corporations. The deejays played songs chosen by a small number of consultants after researching and testing, the mix tempered by computer programs. It was a brutally competitive world out there. For the three days of CRS, the broadcasters attended seminars on such subjects as "Better Profits and Ratings from Better Copy and Production" and "The Art of Managing and Motivating Air Talent."

Nashville introduced the broadcasters to the new Nashville acts at a series of showcases held each evening in the cavernous Jefferson/Adams Ballroom. The powers of the music and radio industry did not deign to descend to mill around the floor, sucking beer from bottles, feeding on beef sandwiches and greasy potatoes. They were up in the hospitality suites or at private dinners, leaving these showcases to the common hordes, standing around, or sitting in groups, the performers at times little but background sound for the gossiping and backslapping camaraderie of the industry.

This evening the showcases had gone on for over four hours straight, one act after another trying to make some sort of impression, to break through this enervating reality. By ten-thirty the free booze and food had taken their toll, but the broadcasters had learned that just down the hall in a smaller ballroom Wynonna was giving a performance.

The great stars of Nashville showed up at CRS during the day to cut radio interviews, or at night to perform at private parties put on by their labels. But they did not perform like some desperate newcomer.

For Wynonna, however, the ratings of the CBS *Revelations* special were disappointing. They were poor in part because the concert footage was interspersed not with honest revelations about herself but with silly babble about family and home that those around Wynonna called "Judd Speak." Disappointing too were the initial reports of sales and radio play of her first single, not even close to the numbers Wynonna's management had hoped for. Thus, suddenly and dramatically she had decided to come here.

The broadcasters filed in, filled up the seats up front, or stood in back lined up at the bar scarfing mixed drinks. The helium balloons were the only things buoyant in the room. "I'm just praying tonight that I can fit in your format," Wynonna said, a tinge of desperation in her voice. "I can't tell you how much you mean to me. I'm vulnerable to you. You know that. I think music is a healer. So help me on my journey."

Wynonna sang songs from *Revelations,* but she had a cold and her voice sounded stricken. "I want to be perfect because you're paying attention to everything I do," she said. "But I'm not completely comfortable and—" The microphone suddenly shut off, and she stood mute, trying to contain her irritation. The interruption gave a couple in the first row the chance to get up and start to leave, but as they turned to go back up the aisle, the sound came on. "Sit down!" Wynonna commanded. "You're not leaving! You're going to hold it!"

Even as Wynonna talked, the crowd in the back of the room continued their own conversations. "One thing I know I was born to sing. I tried to have a regular job. When you find something that you love, that inspires you to do it. I'm not going to give up. I get mad. I get frustrated at the ways of the world. But I'm not going to give up."

"1995 was a year of revelations," Wynonna told an interviewer for *Close Up,* the CMA publication. "1996 will be a year of revolution." Despite her immense intentions, much of her album had a mannered, overproduced quality to it, distant from country, yet not acceptable to the hip pop world she was courting. Her album was not this transcendent event that she had hoped it would be, neither artistically nor commercially; in the end it was more a millstone than a milestone. The album rose only to number two on the *Billboard* country charts, and fell back, in its first months selling less than half a million copies.

John Unger tried to pick up the pieces of his idealism, but they did not fit together any longer. He realized, as he looked back on his more than two years as Wynonna's manager, that in that entire period Wynonna had been pregnant every time she had performed. She was the queen of the tabloids, not the queen of music.

John felt spread-eagled, pulled this way by Wynonna, then wrenched the other way by Larry Strickland, Naomi's husband, and soon jerked in a third direction by Naomi herself. He was growing tired of it all, tired beyond tired, his voice often a dull monotone, struggling to make sense of not only Wynonna's life but his own.

From his own perspective as the Judds' former manager, Ken Stilts looked on Unger's discomfort with wry amusement. He thought that it was only a matter of time before Unger would be gone, Naomi and Larry would likely be managing Wynonna, and the Judds would probably be back on the road again.

Wynonna's new offices in Franklin were under construction. Her house was under major construction. Her life was under construction. As pregnant as she was, Wynonna had little choice but to go out on tour to support the album. Her last performance before giving birth was in May at Wolftrap, an open-air theater outside Washington, D.C. She was over seven months pregnant. To cover her bulk, she wore a purple harlequin's costume that had everything but a clown's pom-poms on it. And she sang like a vessel of endless emotion, pain and love and poignant feeling.

At the end of the concert, Wynonna gave a little talk to the audience, looking out beyond the seats to the grass where thousands more sat on blankets and camp chairs. "I just free-fall into my gift," she said. "I was afraid of performing. It's the one thing I've been able to hang on to all those years. I got fed up and then one thing I want you to know . . . "

". . . IS HOW CRAZY I AM!" a man shouted.

"I'm going to get up and kick your butt," Wynonna fumed. "Thanks for reminding me."

Wynonna's head turned up toward the hillside beyond the furthest seats. "Our journey isn't complete until we gave thanks. Let's be in the moment. Take a breath."

Wynonna sang the last song of the evening. "Live with Jesus" was a gospel song from her first album, a song far from the music she was recording now. It was a gospel song that she could have sung with her mother in that old house in Kentucky:

> Hard times is all I see
> Lost the ones that's dear to me
> But I'm gonna live with Jesus in the end
> I'm gonna live, I'm gonna live
> I'm gonna live with Jesus in the end.

Out at Fan Fair Wynonna had a double booth that was supposed to look like an old-fashioned store, with an old oval Coca-Cola sign, a gas pump, a sign that said "Auction Today," and above in large lettering the words "WY'S COLLECTIBLES." The booth had T-shirts and coffee cups to sell. Since Wynonna was not coming to the fairgrounds, Naomi had been scheduled to appear. A hand-printed notice said that she was sick and would not be coming either. Most of the fans hurried past, not even bothering to read the notice, moving onto booths where there were real stars and excitement, and they were not asked to believe in things they could not see and people they could not touch.

★ ★ ★

That evening after the auction Wynonna, Arch, and little Elijah drove in a chauffeured limousine from Franklin to Naomi's new restaurant, Trilogy, off Music Row. Every true fan of the Judds knew all about Trilogy, a shrine to the famous duo. The foyer was an elaborate, overwrought vision of pastels and elaborate flower displays, leading to a whole series of small rooms including Naomi's Parlor, Wynonna's Formal, and Ashley's Corner.

Trilogy was known to its employees by its nickname "the Tragedy." The restaurant was running through chefs the way other restaurants ran through ketchup. Naomi had insisted on exquisite expensive silverware and place settings rarely seen in restaurants. The fans who made a pilgrimage to the restaurant paid their expensive tabs, but some thought it only fair to spirit out some silverware or a plate as a souvenir far more authentic than any of the cheap stuff found in the shops over on Demonbreun Street.

Wynonna, Arch, and Elijah arrived only a few minutes late, which for Wynonna was like arriving at brunch the night before. There waiting for them were Charley and Tina Hicks, and their two-year-old son, Ryan. Earlier today at Wynonna's Charity Auction, they had won this dinner with Wynonna. He and Tina hadn't brought the clothes to wear to some spiffy Nashville restaurant. So after paying they left the auction and made the 213-mile drive back to Scottsburg, changed their outfits, and returned in time for their $3,450 dinner with Wynonna.

Charley had been around pregnant women before, and he had the feeling that Wynona was so many months along that at any moment she might deliver right on the linen tablecloth. "I don't want to make you uncomfortable, Wynonna," Charley offered graciously after they had only been there together a half hour and the food hadn't even been ordered. "Anytime you're ready to leave you just tell us."

"You bought and paid for this," Wynonna replied. Wynonna knew that $3,450 had to be the most expensive dinner she ever heard of, and she wasn't about to cut their evening short. "We want to make you have a good time."

The Hickses could hardly think about ordering food. The waitresses kept bringing course after course, crab cakes and some strange little cheese thing for appetizers, twelve-ounce prime ribs with all the fixings, champagne and wine, and a silver tray that had a dozen different desserts if it had one, from fruit tarts to the darkest chocolate cake you ever saw, to these neat little bowls of puddings. Chuck and Tina did their best, but they were so excited that they left as much on their plates as they ate.

Arch and Chuck had their man-to-man talk, but most of the evening Wynonna's husband took care of Ryan and Elijah, who would have liked to run wild together through the rooms. Ryan had been brought up to be a Wynonna fan. He had her picture in his room and had his favorite songs, especially "Girls with Guitars." He had been there in April when the Hickses had seen Wynonna perform in Terre Haute. In the midst of the show, an usher had plucked Ryan out of the crowd and set him down onstage, where Wynonna had sung to him and half a dozen other kids. This evening, Ryan was more interested in Elijah than Wynonna, though she gave him a guitar pick and an autographed picture.

In the midst of the evening a little man with a goatee came bouncing into the room, gave Wynonna a hug, and introduced himself as Tony Brown, her producer. The Hickses had never heard of Tony Brown before, but they were impressed as he ticked off the names of stars he had produced and walked back out of Ashley's Room to go off to finish his dinner. Charley and Tina took so many pictures of the evening that they could have worn out their camera. After dinner, Wynonna took the Hickses to a back room where she signed CDs and photographs for them.

"Anything else you want me to sign?" Wynonna asked.

"Not really, Wynonna, but would you be so kind as to talk to my mother. She is a big fan."

"Hi, this is Wynonna calling from Nashville," Wynonna yelled into the phone. "You don't believe it's me you're talking to, ask Charley and Tina. Why, we just had dinner."

Wynonna handed the phone back to Tina. "It's her you're talking to, Mom."

Charley and Tina couldn't think of another question to ask, and didn't have another scrap of paper to be signed. Wynonna and Arch said good-bye to them at the door, and the Hickses left to return to Indiana. Wynonna, Arch, and little Elijah headed back home too in their limousine, just another evening in Nashville.

12

~

"Left Hand of God"

At the Sony Columbia booth a long line stood waiting for free CDs. Most of the fans were given promotional CDs of the song "Bound and Determined" sung by Ron Wallace. The back of the CD case said that the song would be "available on the upcoming Columbia Cassette/CD *Bound and Determined*." The fans who left with CDs had no idea that Ron's album was never coming out and Columbia was passing them out rather than throwing them away.

Last year Ron had been at the Columbia booth signing autographs and photos, anticipating the release of his first album. Now Ron was a few miles away at County Q, a demo studio that had become almost a second home to him. County Q was an old house converted into a small studio. Here songwriters came with a band and a singer to have demo tapes made to be played for record labels, producers, and artists. This had become serious business, with the quality sometimes only slightly less than that on a finished album.

There was no better demo singer in Nashville than Ron. He had just walked in the door. Ron was looking at this song for the first time. He would run through it with the band, then nail it, all within an hour. Never in all his most morbid speculation had Ron ever imagined he would be back singing demos. A few months ago he had been over at several new high-tech studios around town recording his album. Now he was sitting here on a busted couch in a rambling old house with stained blue carpets waiting to go into the studio. A few months ago he had been feasting on catered food during his recording session. Now he was chomping down on an Italian submarine from Subway down the road, washing it down with coffee in a Styrofoam cup.

Ron was thirty-three years old. From the time Ron was thirteen, all he'd ever cared for was music. He didn't play baseball. He didn't go to the senior prom. He preferred to strum his guitar, write songs, and sing. His dad was a long-distance truck driver with a fine voice, and his dad was a country music fan.

Ron loved the raw, vital sound of Merle Haggard. He got into Waylon Jennings and Hank Williams Jr. too. When Ron was growing up in the late seventies, they were cranking, playing some mean strokes. He dug southern rock too, groups like Lynyrd Skynyrd and Marshall Tucker. He got into such happening bands as Styx, REO, and ZZ Top. His musician friends liked country and rock, and he saw no reason why he couldn't play both.

Ron was just an underage kid when he started playing in bands around his hometown of Independence, Missouri. By the time he got out of high school, he was a full-time musician, working in bars in Kansas City. It was a living, but Ron saw where that road ended. These other guys were twice his age. If they weren't drunk by the second set, they were high on speed. He felt that he had been born to play, but not like this, not with a bunch of burned-out dudes in these dreary little clubs, measuring out his life in beer tabs.

If you were a Wallace man, you served in the armed forces. In 1982 Ron joined the air force and was shipped out to the Philippines. By the time he got back stateside, he was hungry to get back into music. He heard that Branson, Missouri, was beginning to happen with old-time country acts. So he drove down there and got himself a six-shows-a-week gig. That wasn't what he wanted either, but he met his wife there. Her name was Rose Stoner. She was Japanese American, her mother a country fiddle player from Nashville.

Ron sold his PA system, borrowed some money, and drove with Rose to Nashville. Music City was always full of young musicians arriving in town knowing nobody, desperately seeking a way to make a few bucks so they could just hang in there. They were the ones nobody ever seemed to talk to, the ones lugging their guitars from club to club, sitting in the receptionists' rooms at publishers' offices trying to get appointments, hanging out at Douglas Corner, the Bluebird Café, and the other clubs, trying to meet the people who could make it happen.

The first contact the new arrivals made was usually with each other. Each year or so the new arrivals became a generation, helping one another get gigs, watching one another succeed or give it up and go back home. Ron had hardly arrived in town when he got together with a couple musicians and auditioned successfully for a gig at the opening of a new restaurant, Panama Red. It was only fifty bucks for a weekend playing Jimmy Buffett covers. Standing up there singing "Margaritaville" for the tenth time, he thought to himself, "Man, this is what I came to Nashville for?"

That, as it turned out, was one of the better weekends. Ron got up early each morning and drove out to the Hickory Hollow Mall to wash windows and mop floors before the stores opened. Then he tried to write songs and promote himself along Music Row. In the evenings, he drove his truck, delivering meals for The Cook Out. Then maybe afterwards he had a gig somewhere. As for Rose, she had grown up in a musician's family. She knew that glory fell to the singer, not to the singer's wife, and there was usually little enough of that. She worked three jobs to help make things go.

A musician had so many ways to lose, and so few ways to win. Ron knew that the club scene was usually a one-way road to oblivion, but that was all he could find. He got a five-nights-a-week gig in Donelson, a little town outside Nashville. That was money every week, but he knew what usually happened. You started drinking a few after the gig. You woke up late the next day. And by the time you got it together, it was time to head back out to the gig.

Ron started singing demos for free, and it was as if they were doing him a big favor. He then started getting ten dollars a song. He had a richly subtle voice that could go from nuanced ballads to full-blown country rock, capturing the essence of whatever song he was given. As the tapes made their rounds of the record labels, Ron started getting more calls. He was eventually up to the full demo scale of about fifty dollars for one song in roughly an hour.

The years were going by, and Ron didn't want to be remembered as a great demo singer who never got a deal. It had been seven years already. At nights he was gigging at the Pink Elephant, another of Nashville's little clubs. Other singers who had played and hung out there were getting signed. Tracy Lawrence and Tim McGraw came strutting back, talking about the albums they were making, and old Ron was just playing away night after night on the same bandstand.

Everyone had advice for Ron. Everyone had something they wanted him to change. Ron was six feet two, and that was about the only thing that nobody complained about. He had shoulder-length blond hair. He didn't have it brushed and pampered like some Hollywood star. The hair just hung there. Some of his critics said that the hair had to go, that it didn't work for a country artist. He was not handsome, but he had strong features that were a perfect blending of his truck-driver father and his poetry-writing mother. Others said that he should pay more attention to his image, watch how he dressed, wear tight Wranglers and a cowboy hat. Still others put his music down, saying he was too rock 'n' roll, that he might attract attention with his music in LA but not in Nashville.

Listening to all his supposed well-wishers, Ron felt beaten upon. He lived through his emotions, and his emotions were letting him down. He got up there each evening and sang from his heart and his soul to an audience that was only half listening. During the day he wrote songs about love and loneliness, opening his emotional veins. Time and again he was rejected, his feelings dismissed, a tape deck fast-forwarded to the next cut, a boisterous group at the Pink Elephant walking out in the middle of his song, a telephone answering machine that never had the messages he wanted to hear.

Ron started taking antidepressants, but the other drug that lifted him up was his own determined will. He decided one day that he wasn't going to listen anymore, to none of it. He wasn't an image. He was going to sing what he wanted to sing, and write what he wanted to write, and be what he wanted to be.

Ron didn't care what people thought, and suddenly people began caring about his music. He started getting calls from A&R executives saying how much they loved his voice, but they had only heard him singing other people's songs, in whatever style was demanded of him. They had not heard Ron Wallace singing, not the way he knew he could sing. So he borrowed twelve hundred dollars from his brother, got together a band of his friends, and cut five songs at County Q.

Paul Worley heard the demo tape and was impressed. Paul was a successful musician who had become a producer and publishing executive. He came out to the Bullpen Lounge at the Stockyard, a club where Ron was playing Sunday nights. Afterwards he came up to Ron. "I get it," he said. That was all he had to say.

Paul signed his new protégé to a publishing contract at Sony Tree, giving Ron a monthly draw. Ron knew that when Nashville started buzzing about your music, the louder it was, the shorter it tended to last. Moreover, he was thirty-one years old, and if it ever was going to happen it was going to happen now. Ron couldn't understand why Paul kept procrastinating, telling him to wait. Then one day Paul called and told him the news; he was the new executive vice president of Sony Music Nashville, one of a three-person team to lead the label. The first thing Paul was going to do was sign Ron to a deal and produce his album on the Sony Columbia label.

As happy as he was, Ron was disappointed to learn that his album wasn't supposed to come out until the fall of 1995, a year and a half after signing his contract. As a first-time "baby act," Ron stood in line behind all the other artists on his label. The delay gave Ron many months to look for songs and to continue to supplement his advance and songwriter's draw by singing demos. It was good he had some extra income, since he had two little girls at home now, Jacy and Mikenzi.

As Ron sought out music for his first album, he remembered a song he had sung on a demo session. He had been over at County Q doing a demo for three songwriters, John Greenebaum, Troy Seals, and Eddie Setser. Troy had sung on the work tape. Most of the time Ron listened to the work tape like a workaday professional. Then he walked into the studio, sang the song, and half an hour later could hardly remember the lyrics. This time he had heard and felt the song like any listener, moved by the sentiments.

John Greenebaum had the idea for the song. John had written many songs, but Ron could tell that few of them meant as much. In the mid-eighties John had been so burned out that he decided he had to get out of town. He and Mary Grant, his wife, got a U-Haul and drove north, settling finally in Milwaukee. Songwriters had nobody thinking of their future but themselves, and writing songs was the only way John was ever going to make much money. He ended up cleaning apartments and lawns. One day he was sitting home eating a bologna sandwich for lunch, listening to a television preacher talking about rich folks sitting at the right hand of God. A song came to him about a working man getting up in the morning realizing that his lot was to be "the callus on the left hand of God." When he returned to Nashville, he and one of his cowriters, Troy Seals, wrote the song in a morning, and Eddie Setser wrote the music.

The song had been pitched all over town. Nobody had taken it, and the publisher had suggested that the lyrics be rewritten. That's what Ron was supposed to sing. The song was now about a teenager supposedly with calluses on his pink young hands. Country music was the one popular music aimed specifically at adults. That did not mean it was like those late-night commercials on television selling hits from the sixties and seventies, playing on the nostalgia of the middle-aged. No, country music was about the lessons taught in the university of life, the one school that everyone entered. Ron was old enough to get it now, to know what love and loss were all about, family and yearning, life and death, booze and loneliness, joy and emptiness. It made him heartsick to have to sing a song from which the heart had been cut out, and know that was the version that might get cut.

Ron sang the new lyrics, but he remembered the old lyrics. Soon after he signed with Sony Columbia, he called the publisher and put a hold on the original version of "Left Hand of God." Ron was thirty-two years old, and he wasn't singing songs aimed at teenyboppers. Nor was he hunting for fancy songs to appeal to the upscale audience the CMA and marketing people bragged about. He wanted songs for people like his truck-driver father. Four of the songs on his album had truckers in them. The trucker seemed a free spirit barreling down the interstate, but he was working for the man, traveling from point to point, far from his family and his friends, far from life as a person wants to live it. These were songs that a trucker could push into his tape deck to carry him a hundred miles down I-95. They were songs that a waitress in a diner in Kansas City could punch into a jukebox to help her through her shift.

Ron started looking for a manager. He figured with his record deal, he could get a top manager. He got through to them, but they hardly listened. They said to call back when his album was about to come out; then they would talk. Ron wasn't into humbling himself before men who wanted to wait and see. So he settled on Dennis Lord, an attorney who had never managed a country act before. At least Dennis cared about Ron Wallace.

Ron headed out on an eight-week radio tour, visiting the station managers, program directors, and consultants at country stations all across America. That was something that every first-time artist did, meeting the people who would decide whether to play his album. Ron was a little too old for this. He held his tongue. He didn't tell them how he felt about radio no longer playing greats like Merle Haggard and Johnny Cash and Willie Nelson. He didn't admit that he thought much of the stuff they played was as fluffy as cotton candy. He tried to appear fascinated when a program director talked about his new Toyota or bragged about his latest ratings, but Ron wasn't very good at sucking up to people he didn't know.

Ron had more of a musician's than an artist's soul. That is, he felt that his professional life was the time onstage and the rest of it was nothing, whereas a modern country artist worked almost as hard offstage as on. He had a musician's mercurial temperament too, moaning when he didn't have a gig, and moaning soon after he got one.

Ron put together a band to go on the road once the album came out. His band mates were all buddies of his, and he was proud that he was giving them a chance too. He started lining up a number of dates. The problem was that he could only get about five hundred to a thousand dollars a night, and it cost close to four thousand a night to put a band on the road. That extra money had to be fronted by his record label, added to the money he would have to pay back out of royalties. By the time the album came out, he figured he would be a half million dollars in debt to Columbia. A half million dollars. A fortune. Plus he was another fifty thousand dollars in the hole to Sony Tree, his publisher. That would have to be paid back too out of song royalties.

At night Ron lay in bed awake, worried about what was going to happen. He knew that he was no pretty boy, nothing like the images appearing in the videos on CMT. He was already long in the tooth, in the way they counted things these days. "God, how am I going to compete with that?" he asked himself as he tossed in bed.

Ron knew that this was his one chance. He had mortgaged everything he loved and cared for on this album. "How stupid can you be?" he reflected, lying there next to his sleeping wife. "Basically what you've done is gambled with the lives and futures of your children. It's gonna work out. But what if it doesn't? What then?"

Record labels prepared the way for a new album by releasing a single or two before the album, trying to create a buzz. In August of 1995 Columbia shipped "I'm Listening Now," Ron's first single, out to radio. Radio ratings were going down now, and the last thing most stations wanted was to play another unknown artist.

Ron went into the label and called radio stations everywhere, trying to get them to add his song. The radio people were all friendly enough, but Ron didn't know what they were really think-ing. He felt that the promotion department at Columbia was only halfheartedly behind him, and the song only reached sixty-five on the *Billboard* singles chart. Then Ron learned that the label was moving on to the second single, "Left Hand of God." That was a daring call, going with a spiritual ballad that might become either a working person's anthem, or just as likely get almost no airplay at all on upbeat, up-tempo country radio. Ron started calling the radio stations again, but the song didn't even make the *Billboard* chart.

The advance copies of the album sat in the warehouse. The artwork was ready. The first video was already out there. The next time Ron went into the label, he was told that Columbia had decided to hold back his album to reevaluate things. First it was a month. Then two months. Three months. Six months. They wanted him to go back in and cut four new sides and do a new video.

Ron felt he was being beaten half to death from the sheer neg-ativity. Everyone had a take on what *he* had done wrong. This song wasn't country enough. That song was too country. This cut wasn't radio friendly. That song was rock 'n' roll. At home, well, he had no home any longer. Rose had had enough of the tortured life of Ron Wallace. She was gone, and they were getting divorced. He was no fly-by-night daddy and he won joint custody of their two little girls.

Ron was so down, so desperately down. He thought about checking out, ending it all, but those two little girls held him firmly in life. He got back on his pills, and slowly he started coming around. He cleaned up the house and started doing some demo work. At least he had people who still wanted him for that. At Sony Tree, the publisher signed him to a new deal but made him sign away any money he might make on radio play, credited against his debt.

At the time of Fan Fair, Ron was supposed to go back into the studio and start cutting new sides for his album. The closer it got to the date, the more anxious he became. He knew that Paul, his producer, believed in him, but he didn't feel that any other execu-tive at the label did. Whenever he walked into the Sony offices, he felt like a foster child foisted onto the label. He knew that they weren't cutting new songs if they didn't have some idea of bringing his album out. But he had an ominous premonition that it was all waste and pretense.

As the day got nearer, he kept thinking that he didn't want to do it. He didn't want to cut some songs just so they could get played on the radio. He wanted to sing about things he believed, things he knew to be true. As he saw it, everything was backward now. Music didn't make the business anymore; business made the music. He couldn't be somebody he wasn't. He was too old. He had lived too long, felt too much, loved too intensely, and hurt too deeply. He just couldn't do it anymore, play the game, walk the walk and talk the talk.

Ron set up an appointment to see his producer. Paul was a former musician, and Ron could talk to the executive the way he could to nobody else at the label. Ron saw how Paul was hurting doing the things he had to do as a label executive. Paul was a good man, but he was not strong, and the game went to the strong and the uncaring.

"I want to be released, Paul," Ron told the Sony executive. "I want you to let me go."

"We're going back in next week to cut some more sides, Ron," Paul insisted, startled at Ron's request.

"I've been thinking a lot," Ron replied firmly. "And I figure, why go spend money on something that's not going to fly? I really don't feel this is a place where I need to be."

Paul sat silently for a moment. Then he began to cry. Ron was the first artist he had signed. An artist starting out on a label didn't ask to be released. It just didn't happen. The truth didn't find its way into the music as often as it once did, and it didn't find its way into the lives of Music City as often either. But the truth was sitting there across from his desk, and Paul still had ears that could hear it, and a heart that could feel it.

Ron got his release from Columbia, and he walked with the firm strides of a man who knew the direction he was headed. This afternoon he might have been out at Fan Fair signing autographs or in the studio cutting new sides for his album. Instead, he was here at

County Q cutting demos. He was just a working stiff singing demos for fifty bucks a shot. He was writing songs again, trying to get a cut. He was sniffing around, looking for a new record deal too, though so far nothing was happening.

Maybe Ron was nobody, the way the world saw things. But he had a cut out there, on *Common Ground,* a compilation album of songs of faith, love, and inspiration. The other singers were well known, but no song on the album was as powerful and as meaningfully sung as Ron singing "Left Hand of God."

> So I guess my lot in life
> Is working on the sweat shift
> Wearing out the leather gloves
> On this backbreaking job.
> Some may say this ain't
> No way to make a living
> But somebody's got to be the callus
> On the left hand of God.

13

~

"Gone Country"

2:40 P.M.

Tim DuBois wanted the Arista/Nashville show to be the most popular, the most talked about event of the entire week. As the label president looked out on the vast multitudes stretched to the rafters of the great bleachers, and shoehorned into every square foot of ground, he thought that again this year he had pulled it off. He had succeeded in large measure because this afternoon wasn't like Scott Hendricks's operation over at Capitol Nashville, where his biggest star, Garth, hadn't performed. Nor was it like Tony Brown's MCA shop, where neither Reba, George, nor Wynonna had shown up. This was Arista/Nashville, and every major artist would be here to sing this afternoon and to make their presence felt as part of Tim's label.

Tim was holding his two-year-old daughter, Jamie Grace, in his arms. He had ended his twenty-three-year marriage in 1990, and a year later married for the second time, to Pam Smith. At the age of forty-eight, he had a full, neatly trimmed beard, warm eyes and a gentle manner. He might appear like a daddy on an afternoon lark proudly showing off his latest offspring. Tim, however, was working this afternoon the way no other label head did during their show this week. Now he was standing in the midst of the stage, overseeing the work of the sound crew, making sure every detail was ready and in place. Alan Jackson, who was just arriving up the back stairways, was the first artist Tim had personally signed to the label. Tim could say the same of everyone who would be performing this afternoon, from Brooks and Dunn to Pam Tillis.

The fledgling label had gone in six years from nothing to sixty million dollars in sales. Tim knew that part of his achievement had been due to his exquisite good luck in starting just as country music was beginning to surge in popularity. Arista's success, however, had not been a lucky fluke that pushed Tim along in the midst of the parade. Tim was up front leading. Even now he only had eleven artists on his label, and his lean, focused operation had become the model of what a country label should be. Tim's label stood at the hard commercial center of country music. Tim was never heard to utter a bitter word about country radio; he had a phone sitting on his desk on which country radio executives could call him directly.

The sound of gold coins tinkling into the Arista coffers had alerted scores of outsiders to the prospect of coming to Nashville. It looked so easy, and maybe it was for a short time, but it wasn't easy any longer. There were over twenty-five labels now, many of them subsidiaries of the major companies, all having set up shop in Nashville, all trying to do much what Tim had done. It wasn't easy for the new players, and it wasn't easy for Tim any longer either.

Tim sensed changes taking place in Nashville, even in his own shop. He still knew everybody by name. He tried to act as openly and directly as he could, but there was a bitchy, competitive spirit alive not only out there at the other labels but even sometimes at Arista/Nashville. Maybe it had grown too big to be like a big family. Or maybe somebody had left the doors open too long and the cold bitter air of the new Nashville had blown in, but Arista was not quite the same, and Tim knew it.

Other executives would have just shrugged their shoulders and figured that was the price of success, but Tim was a different sort.

He often quoted Norro Wilson's adage: "I'm an emotional man in an emotional business." He had to feel it to get it. He had to believe. He had to care. He was a wealthy man now, with a new young family. He was no good if he didn't care. He knew that, and he wondered sometimes how much longer he would head the label.

Tim was a man of instinct in everything he did from signing acts to hiring employees. He didn't believe in résumés. He believed in looking you in the eyes and taking your measure. Tim didn't believe in memos either. He picked up the phone and talked to you or came barreling into your office to speak his mind.

The roots of country music are not only place but feeling. It was a nurturing past that was Tim's most precious inheritance, and one profound source of his love of country music. He had grown up in Oklahoma, the state that is a virtual hothouse for growing country music talent. Tim was brought up on a little farm outside the tiny town of Grove (population 1,200), in the northeast corner of the state. His father had purchased the property from his father-in-law, for three generations now the family farm.

Tim's parents were schoolteachers. His mother taught first grade while his father was superintendent at Turkey Fund, a title that suggested a more elevated rank than the realities of life in Grove. They were parents who believed that schooling began and ended in the home, and they taught their three sons well and true. His mother, Jessie, a woman of joyous optimism, never spoke ill of another human, always looking forward to a better day.

There are those who think that negativity and cynicism is a sign of intelligence. But they have not lived on a farm in the hills of Oklahoma where the winds blow fierce and long and those who survive the long winters with their spirits intact are a special breed. Tim's eighty-two-year-old parents were still alive, and his mother's optimistic spirit was alive too in the life of Tim and the way that he did his work in Nashville. Tim's father was a man of the most profound honesty that often gets broken by the world, but this virtue had a sanctuary in a schoolteacher's life. Tim was a truth teller too, but he tempered his honesty with shrewdness, even as he carried his father's values into the world.

The three DuBois boys were the kind of talented young men who usually fled the small towns of America, heading for cities full of opportunity, returning only for holidays and reunions and funerals. Tim and his brothers stayed close to Grove. His big brother, Ed, was a scientist and professor who spent most of his professional career on the West Coast. But when he suffered heart trouble, he returned to live in Grove, dying there six years ago, an event the merest mention of which brings tears to Tim's eyes. His little brother, Randy, six years his junior, lived in Grove, a hospital administrator and a respected citizen. His parents lived there too, having moved into town after deeding the family farm to Tim and his brother. Tim returned home only to visit. Nonetheless, country music, to Tim as to Tony Brown and Scott Hendricks, was ultimately the musical soul of small-town and rural America, an America that Tim knew still lived in fact and spirit.

Tim left Grove to study at Oklahoma State, where he received a master's and his CPA certificate, hardly the standard training for life in Music City. While working as an auditor and analyst in Texas, the heavy lifting of accounting, he became interested in country music. Back in Grove, his tastes had been more to the Beatles and the Eagles than Hank Williams and Johnny Cash. He started writing songs more as an avocation than with any serious idea of becoming a professional songwriter.

Tim was of an academic bent, and he began teaching at Tulsa University, later at Oklahoma State. He was married and had two young children, but he still found time to pursue his interest in music. He met a young student named Scott Hendricks in the recording studio at Oklahoma State, and started working with him putting demo tapes together.

Tim's right side of his brain was as developed as the left. Whatever he did, he analyzed, auditing his own creative spirit. When he became serious about the idea of becoming a songwriter, he didn't just pack up and move to Nashville. He went to the library and read everything he could about songwriting and the music business, and he kept tinkering away at his country songs, shipping them off to a publisher in Nashville. One of them with the inspired title "A Good Old-Fashioned Saturday Night Honky

Tonk Barroom Brawl" made it to the Top 40. Tim took that as a sign that he was ready to pack up and head east to Music City.

When Tim and his family moved to Nashville in 1977, he wasn't the kind to hang around Maude's and other drinking spots with the songwriters and song pluggers. He was a craftsman keeping at his bench, turning out one song after another. He was not an inspired songwriter, but had ample qualities of wit and sentiment that found their way into his songs. In 1981, his biggest year, he had three number ones, including "Love in the First Degree" and another memorably titled song, "She Got the Goldmine (I Got the Shaft)," a politically incorrect anthem for any man going through a divorce.

Tim could have had a middling career as a songwriter, but in 1985 he joined a friend of his, Larry Fitzgerald, in his management company. Tim had superb commercial instincts. He put together Restless Heart, a harmony-based group that had many top singles in the mid-eighties. This was the most exciting, innovative time in country music in years. Tim and Restless Heart's coproducer, Scott Hendricks, churned out an easy-listening country pop sound that had nothing to do with the inspired sounds of the groups revitalizing Nashville's music.

Tim discovered that managing was a sorely inadequate term to define the grab bag of duties that fell to him. He might negotiate contracts at 10:00 A.M. and end hand-holding at two the next morning. He might push for more promotion money for an act, and then push to get the act to get out of bed. Tim was an astute judge of human character, watching the process of stardom etch its mark on the most modest and unassuming of singers. The best managers were either like his partner Larry, who was usually able to keep a Zenlike emotional distance from the ups and downs of it. Or they were an intense, mercurial sort who essentially gave up their own lives and took on the coloring of the artists they managed. Tim was neither of these, and in 1988 he left managing, feeling like a free man.

When Clive Davis offered Tim the opportunity to start the Arista/Nashville label, he knew it was an opportunity that you get once in life, if you are incredibly fortunate. He wasn't walking into an established company, burdened with staff and artists over which he had no say. He bought the first pencils and letterhead stationery, and he signed all the artists. Clive was his boss, and above him the Bertelsmann AG German conglomerate that owned RCA as well. Clive was blessedly ignorant about country music, and as likely as not would leave him alone.

Every night there are showcases in Nashville where new artists are trying to make enough of an impression to get a deal. Tim was the ears and the soul of his tiny label. He always seemed to be there, even at places that none of the other top executives in town would have gone to, nor few of their underlings, going almost anywhere in search of new artists.

Tim had hardly made his deal with Clive when the word was on the street, and he started receiving tapes and calls. Tim was too new even to figure in the equation of Music Row, but a label was a label. One of the first tapes he heard had something he liked, and he called the singer's manager, Barry Coburn. "Hey, mister, I really like this tape. When can I see him play?"

"Next Tuesday at six o'clock at Douglas Corner."

"No go," Tim replied. "I'll be in LA. When's the next time in Nashville?"

"No time that I know of," Barry said in his intense, fast-paced manner. "He's only ever played showcases three times. And I gotta tell you, Tim, I've got some interest."

Tim changed his plans and the next Tuesday drove over to the Douglas Corner Cafe, a bar over on Eighth Avenue South that was one of the better places in town to hear music. Several nights a week early in the evening, Douglas Corner was a setting for showcases. The sets usually lasted not much more than a half hour, and the record company executives were out of there while they were nursing their first beer. It was a tiny world, and Tim's competitors were all out there in the darkened room too, checking out this artist this evening. They had all heard his manager's impassioned spiel. They had agreed to show up this evening, though they were jaded enough not to expect too much.

As Tim sat at a table, Barry sat crouched over in a corner, watching nervously for the set to start. Barry was a New Zealander, with the brashness, and quickness of mind and word, that

Americans associated with native New Yorkers. Barry had very little money, and he was fiercely hungry for success, and success to him meant getting Jimmy Bowen, the president of Universal, to sign his artist. Bowen was the most powerful man in Nashville. He was the one face card in the room. Twice before he had paid for showcases, and Bowen hadn't shown up. Once he had set it up right across the street from the studio where Bowen was producing, but still he hadn't bothered attending. Tonight, he was here, however, and tonight was Barry's chance for his big score. What Barry didn't know was that Bowen was negotiating to buy Universal Records, and he would have passed on Patsy Cline and Hank Williams if they were showcasing this evening.

A lean, lanky six-foot-four singer with long flaxen hair worked his way through the crowded tables to the front and started singing with a backup band. The man's name was Alan Jackson, and he sang nine songs in a row. The crowd wasn't just record company executives but people off the street, and although Alan received a good response, this evening was hardly the stuff of legend. As the set ended, Barry was even more nervous than when it began.

An executive from Warner Brothers was the first person to come up to Barry afterwards. "Now don't get a big head because Bowen's here." As the man walked away, Tim hurried forward. He was a man of instincts. He wasn't much of a poker player, or maybe he was, but a player who never bluffed. "Mister, I want him," Tim said. "We've got to meet."

"Well, that's great," Barry replied quickly.

"This is wonderful. I love him. He's great. Can we meet tomorrow morning?"

That next morning at nine, Clive Davis's office called and asked if Mr. Coburn could meet with Mr. Davis and Mr. DuBois at two o'clock at the Arista offices in Nashville. The British-sounding voice on the phone put Davis's secretary on hold, and came back almost immediately to say that Mr. Coburn would be able to make the appointment. Davis's secretary hung up, hardly imagining that the very proper voice on the telephone agreeing to the meeting was Jewel Coburn, Barry's wife.

Barry was ecstatic that things were moving along so fast. He called Alan at home and told him excitedly about the meeting that both would attend.

"Can't do it, Barry," Alan replied languidly. "I've got grease all over my hands. Been tryin' to fix this boat trailer. Banged my head. It's bleedin', man, can't do it."

"Alan, you've got to come."

Barry didn't know whether Alan was going to make it or not. At five minutes to two the singer strolled in, wearing a cream-colored jacket, a big cowboy hat, and boots, and looking a country star. Davis was wearing a double-breasted designer suit that looked as if it had been knitted out of hundred-dollar bills. When Barry was nervous he talked nonstop in staccato rhythm, and he was so nervous today that he could hardly sit there. But he had hardly reckoned with Clive, who didn't believe in conversation as much as he did in lectures. "Well, I'm glad you're both here," Clive said. "Tim tells me that you've been a little—sort of hesitant about signing with us." Clive spoke as if this was slightly short of treason. "And I want to tell you all the reasons why you should."

Clive launched into a fifty-minute soliloquy that was a mini-history of pop music, in which he always stood firmly in the middle of the stage, from Bruce Springsteen to Paul Simon, Whitney Houston to Barry Manilow. Barry tried to say something, anything, and Clive ran verbally over him, leaving his words splattered on the ground.

When it was finally over, Clive paused a moment as if expecting them to stand and applaud. When he did not hear Barry begging to sign with Arista, Clive spoke again. "So, now you see all the reasons why I think it would be a really good idea for you to sign with Arista."

Barry sat there silently.

"Well, what do you think?"

"Let me think about it."

Clive acted as if he surely must have misheard. "Well, what do you need to think about?"

"I just need to discuss it and think about it."

Everyone got up at once as if the chairs had been wired and said their good-byes. "I'm, uh, pleased to meet you, Mr. Davis,"

Alan said, speaking his first full sentence of the afternoon. "Uh, uh, I'm glad I, ah, didn't know about you. 'Cause if I had I sure woulda been too scared to come."

The two men, the singer and his manager, left. Alan walked along Sixteenth Avenue South, shaking his head in bewilderment. "What are you doing, Barry!" Alan exclaimed. "That man offered me a record deal and you didn't take it right there."

Barry hadn't wanted to appear too eager. The next day Barry called Tim back and signed with Arista.

Up on the great stage at Fan Fair the pedal steel emitted a taunting, whining, belligerent sound as if to say this is country and if you don't like it, you better turn off your radio, click on the remote on your CD, or pull out the cassette in your tape deck. Then Alan stepped forward and started singing his 1995 number one hit, "Gone Country."

> He commutes to LA, but he's got a house in the
>   valley
> But the bills are piling up and the pop scene just
>   ain't on a roll. . . .
> Lord, it sounds so easy, this shouldn't take long
> Be back in the money in no time at all.

The song was written by Bob McDill, one of the greatest songwriters in Nashville. Bob had been writing in Nashville for over a quarter of a century. Everywhere he went, he saw that Music City was not the same place he had come to so many years ago. Bob didn't like a lot of the music he was hearing on the radio, but he liked that Nashville was losing its narrow self-serving provincialism about what made a country song. He liked the fact that successful songwriters were making so much money, but he didn't like the fact that the scent of lucre had brought so many impostors to town, looking for a Nashville buck. And he especially didn't like the fact that so many of these outsiders spoke with northern accents.

Bob wrote a song about what he saw happening in Nashville, a song that he figured didn't have much chance of getting cut. He was a man of immense artistic calculation, and he stitched a catchy chorus onto his verses that would carry the song. His publisher pitched the song to Alan.

Nashville was terrified of anything that even scented vaguely of controversy. Alan said that he would have been afraid to record "Gone Country" earlier in his career. Even now he sang this song of social commentary while pretending it was something else. He called it "just a fun song actually, celebrating how country music has become more widespread and accepted by all types of people all over the country." "Gone Country" became not simply a hit, but one of the seminal songs of the nineties, a brilliantly evocative take on the new Nashville.

> Yeah, he's gone country, a new kind of walk.
> He's gone country, a new kind of talk.
> He's gone country, look at them boots.
> He's gone country, oh, back to his roots.

Alan was a good ole boy from Georgia, not one for making proclamations about the state of country music, but he didn't like the country lite they were serving up as the real thing in Nashville. "There's some good stuff out there, but it seems like everything now is slide guitars and Hammond organs," he told the *Journal of Country Music*. "It's like the old country sound is kind of disappearing. I hate to see that. Not everybody needs to sound like a George Jones record. But that's what I've always done and I'm going to keep it that way—or try to."

Alan was real country, his songs resonating with the great old themes. For the most part, the thirty-seven-year-old singer let his music do the talking for him, not liking to say much onstage or do interviews with pesky journalists. Less than a decade ago he had been sitting out there in the vast crowd, looking up, realizing that he was among "the real fans . . . the ones who listen to country radio . . . good people . . . and they love music." He had traveled so far from those days that he was the one star to arrive by helicopter, to be gone hardly touching a fan. He had to say a few words, though, especially to this Fan Fair audience. "It's good to

be here at this Fan Fair show to thank all you fans for coming out,"
Alan said. "And I'd like to thank Arista Records for their support
keepin' those records out there. Somebody sent a note back, and
they said this one's their song, 'Livin' on Love.'"

> Livin' on Love buyin' on time.
> Without somebody nothin' ain't worth a dime.
> Just like an old-fashioned story book rhyme
> Livin' on love.

After Alan had written the song, he said to himself, "Boy, that
sounds just like my mama and daddy's life." His daddy was a Ford
factory worker, and he and his kin had lived on little but love. That
was the one great lesson of his life, that love was the richest treasure of all. It imbued the best of his lyrics with passion, and it
inspired his life. With all the immense wealth and celebrity that
came his way, he was trying to recapture the sense of family and
security that he had known as a little boy. His parents were celebrating their fiftieth wedding anniversary, and they were the
repositories of memory, witnesses not only to what life had been
but to what it still was, if he could work his way back to it. That was
not only *his* lesson, it was the lesson of country music of his time,
of those seventeen thousand people there before him, of going on
in life and in music but holding and nourishing what is good and
true.

Alan was born in the tiny town of Newnan, Georgia, big
enough to have rich folks in their big old houses and poor folks in
houses like the Jacksons'. Alan's grandparents had divided up their
farm years ago, and most of the children had stayed in Newnan on
their few acres. Alan's parents' house had started out as little more
than a shed that they had kept adding to over the years as they
kept having kids. They had four daughters, and finally Alan. He
may have been the pampered last-born only son but there still
wasn't enough room for him to have his own bedroom, and he
slept in the hall until his big sister went off to college.

Alan had the feeling sometimes that, as he said, he "grew up in
a time warp . . . thirty years behind other people." And in a sense

he had. His father, Eugene, was a mechanic who tinkered with cars and machinery on or off the job. In most of urban America, the idea that part of a man's upbringing was to learn about cars was long gone, but in Newnan it was still considered part of a man's natural knowledge. Alan picked up on that, fixing cars on his own, he and his dad rebuilding a 1955 Thunderbird when Alan was only fifteen.

There are few things greater for a boy than to have a father who is truly his model of what a man should be. That yardstick is always there, judging not only his own growth and limitations, but those of others around him. "My father might be the only truly good man I've ever known," Alan said when his career was first starting. "He's as honest as they come. If I turn out half as good, I'll be happy."

Alan was a small-town boy, and he always would be. He knew every pew in church, every kid in school in Newnan. When he graduated from high school, some of his classmates headed off to college. As much as they vowed their love of good old Newnan, most of them didn't return much, or when they did they were different. Alan was still hanging around taking odd jobs, over the years doing everything from driving a forklift at Kmart to selling used cars. One day down at the Dairy Queen he got to talking to a pretty young thing who was still in high school. He sidled out of the booth, went outside, and hid in the backseat of her mother's LTD four-door that she was driving. Once she peeled out of there and was driving down the road, Alan jumped up and scared the living daylights out of her. In many places, his joke could have got him shot, but in Newnan, it got him a date. Four years later, when Alan was twenty-one and Denise nineteen, the couple married.

If Alan and Denise had been like most couples in Newnan, they would have soon been saddled with mortgages and car payments and kids, and never would have left. Alan didn't have much going for him, except for a far-fetched desire to make it as a country singer and a pesky dissatisfaction with the tedium of his workaday life. One of his friends had a dream as crazy as Alan's, not country music but flying one of those big jets so far above. When they were still in school, his friend started taking flying lessons over at the airport; one day he left town, and the next thing Alan heard his friend was flying for an airline.

Denise was a caring woman who believed in her husband's dream. She was working as an airline flight attendant. One day in the summer of 1985, Denise was flying out of Atlanta when she saw Glen Campbell waiting for a plane. Alan never would have walked up to the singer and ask for advice. Denise did, and Glen pulled out a business card and told Denise that if her husband was serious, he should contact the singer's publishing office in Nashville.

Alan and Denise moved to Nashville. He got a job sorting mail at the Nashville Network while Denise continued to work. A year later Glen Campbell's publishing company signed him on as a songwriter, giving him a draw of a hundred dollars a week. He started going out on gigs with a band. Onstage, he had no patter, no wit, no banter with the people. He was both shy and quiet. He was shy, uncomfortable in new surroundings, around people he didn't know, things he didn't understand. He was quiet too, with the rare quality of a man who felt he should only speak when he had something to say, a quality that made him admire old-time movie stars such as Jimmy Stewart and Gary Cooper whose presence was statement enough.

In 1988 Alan and Barry got together for the first time. Barry had been a concert promoter in New Zealand and Australia, working often with American artists, including Emmylou Harris. When foreigners loved country music, they often loved it not only passionately but with scholarly knowledge. There was probably no other manager in Nashville who had Barry's awareness of the most obscure country singer, or anything like his collection of thousands of vinyl records, cassettes, and CDs. That love of country music and an immense ambition were what he had in common with Alan. Beyond that they were men who would never have shared a beer, a human experience, or an evening together. They even looked mismatched, Alan's lean frame making him look even taller than six feet four, while Barry was this nervous little wisp of a man.

Barry and Jewel, his wife, had shown up in Nashville with the idea of making it in publishing and managing. It was a daring ambition, but they knew that America was one of the few places in this world where things weren't so wired that an immigrant had little chance. They were greeted no worse or no better than most outsiders. They set up their modest shop and began working energetically. Jewel answered the phones and, to make extra money, even catered lunches.

Alan kept coming into the office pestering them about why he couldn't get a record deal. He was pushing thirty, half a decade older than guys like Clint and Garth who already had their deals. He had been turned down by about everybody in Nashville. Barry kept grooming him, getting him to work on his unformed songs, setting him up with cowriters, propping him up. Barry approached managing Alan like the D-Day invasion, mapping the enemy territory, preparing his troops, working endlessly on his game plan, holding off until the weather and conditions were right for his advance. Alan just wanted a deal.

One day Jewel was riding through Nashville with Alan in his pickup truck. Alan had a courtly manner to women, especially the wife of his manager. He enjoyed talking to Jewel, even confiding in her at times.

"Barry really wants this to happen," Alan said in that slow measured manner of his.

"Yeah, he does," Jewel said, as if there could be any question.

"Well, I do too," Alan replied, turning toward Jewel, his brilliant blue eyes looking directly into hers. Jewel had been a successful singer in Australia, and she understood ambition and what it required to make it on the great stages of the world. All it took was one look into Alan's eyes for her to see that this singer was like her husband. The man driving this truck was going to let nothing stop him.

Barry pushed Alan to work on his songs. They were little more than snippets of ideas and emotion. Alan worked hard both by himself and with cowriters. He jelled into a compelling writer of straightforward country songs, so much so that Alan wrote or cowrote nine of the songs on his first album.

Alan went into the studio with two producers, Keith Stegall, a singer/songwriter, and Tim's friend, Scott Hendricks. The second single and title song of his album written with Mark Irwin was "Here in the Real World." The song was a perfect verbal signature for a man who knew that "No, the boy don't always get the girl here in the real world." The song rose to number one on the charts, signaling the debut of the rarest of stars in the new Nashville, a traditional country singer. Alan won the ACM Award as Top New Male Vocalist of 1990. Alan headed out on the road opening for the Judds, an inspired combination, his album certified platinum in a little over a year.

The ride that Alan was on kept getting faster and faster. When he got off his bus for a few days, he could still feel the momentum of the travel, and he was hardly rested before he was off again. His second album went platinum in six months, his third album platinum in less than three months. He was soon a headliner in his own right, singing before the same vast audiences as the other superstars of country.

Alan was a talented singer, but without Tim and Barry he probably never would have become more than a midrange artist with a gold record or two. At the beginning Alan was the entire Arista/Nashville roster. Tim knew that it was imperative that his first artist succeed. He poured his savvy and marketing money into the effort. As for Barry, he brought all his energy and expertise in making Alan happen.

Opening acts rarely were allowed to use the giant onstage video screens. But when Alan opened for Randy Travis, Barry shelled out money to Randy's manager so that Alan could be seen on those mammoth screens. Barry observed every minute detail of the performance, figuring out what would work when Alan started headlining. The manager knew that Alan wasn't going to jump around the stage like Garth, and he didn't try to copy that, but focused on Alan's own uniqueness. Maybe Alan just stood there and sang, but surrounded by those video screens and mumbling modestly about his beloved father, he created his own sensation.

If not for Garth, Alan might have become the most celebrated male country singer of his generation. As much as he had wanted to succeed, he did not have Garth's overweening ambition. He had no grand idea of himself. He didn't think that his music was anything

more than good times and true emotions. If he had a model of success, it wasn't Garth but George Strait, who stayed out there on his
Texas ranch, venturing forth only to sing and to record, hardly ever
doing interviews or taking part in all the hoopla in Nashville, the
charity benefits, awards shows, and media appearances that most
singers made part of their lives. Alan was almost too country for the
national media and the crossover audience, and he wasn't about to
walk halfway across the road to meet that audience. That simply
wasn't the way he was.

Barry enjoyed playing the big-time manager more than Alan
enjoyed playing the big-time star. Barry was full of the most monumental plans for Alan, pushing the artist ahead, telling him what
he should do. Alan didn't like to talk to the media, and Barry was
the one who had to say no, often baldly enough to irritate
reporters. Alan didn't like to take time away from his family to do
charity gigs. Barry often took the blame for Alan's own decision.

Alan saw himself as a man not simply consumed with his career
but one who wanted to do some fishing, work on an antique car,
spend time with his family, lie around at home. Barry thought that
Alan was sometimes lazy. He felt he had to prod Alan awake, get
him up and out, chasing that neon rainbow a little further down
the road. "I was the guy that was saying, 'Well, I don't agree with
you on that, I think you need to write better songs,'" Barry
recalled. "I was the one that forced him to write songs. I mean, I
used to threaten to put people on the bus to write with him unless
he wrote, and people he didn't like, mind you. That was the only
way I could get him to write the songs."

Barry considered himself Alan's one honest critic and goad. "I
think he probably felt that he had reached the point in life where
he didn't want anyone telling him what to do or anyone criticizing
him," Barry reflected. "And I was the only one that would. If I felt
that the show wasn't that good and he was really just lazy on a particular night—and he wasn't like that very often—but if I saw a bad
show, I'd tell him. I never held back. I'd say, 'I thought that was
pretty bad. I think you could have done a lot better there. You
weren't really communicating.' And he'd go, 'Oh.'"

When a performer is starting out, he is totally beholden to the manager. As the singer becomes a star, it is the manager who becomes insecure that he will be replaced. Some managers deal with this by the foolhardy, futile method of backing off, cutting down what they consider their unappreciated efforts or spending more time on other projects. That's what Pam Lewis did when she feared that Garth would one day retire; Garth rewarded her by not renewing his contract. Other managers become fawning lackeys, feeding the artists' growing ego on morsels of praise. Barry, for his part, was oblivious to this change. He did just what he always did—if anything, more forcefully.

Barry's chorus of complaints rankled Alan. But the thirty-five-year-old singer had come a long way with Barry, and they stayed together like many long-term marriages, held together with mutual interest and lethargy.

In March of 1994, Alan was scheduled to go out to Bradley's Barn Studio in Mount Juliet to take part in a tribute album in which George Jones would sing duets with some of the major country stars. For many artists, one sincere compliment from a peer means more than a standing ovation from a whole arena of fans. Thus, there was an extraordinary anticipation and nervousness about this recording session with the man considered by many the greatest living country singer and one of Alan's idols.

On the morning that he was supposed to record, Alan heard a visit to the session advertised on the radio as the prize in a radio contest. The singer called Barry, upset at the prospect of the studio being surrounded by hundreds of fans. He sought to back out. Barry called the producer, furious at the prospect of this private session turning into a mini Fan Fair, offering to set up security for the session. Barry had only been trying to create a situation in which Alan would feel comfortable, but he got the blame for arrogantly insisting on security for his superstar. For Alan it was a moment of abject humiliation. To his colleagues he appeared like a sixteen-year-old whose parents have hired a baby-sitter to watch over him. Alan could not tolerate silent shame, and soon afterward, he fired his manager.

As Tim stood on stage watching Alan perform, the Arista/ Nashville president was as astute a judge of the process of stardom as anybody in Nashville. He had seen it as a manager, and now he saw it as a label head. The new ones were cute when they started. They came sidling in as if they feared they didn't have an appointment and might get booted out. They would do anything you asked them to do, sing free at Tower Records, sign hundreds of autographs, perform every last charity benefit.

By the time they had sold half a million albums, they thought they were stars. They stood out there each night in front of those worshipful fans, and they started believing it, every cheer and hoot and clap. They got jealous of other acts and became insecure that it was all about to end. They'd had all their lives to do their first album, and then they had to put together the second in a year. They had sung because they loved to sing, and now they were out on the road forty weeks a year, and sometimes they sang when they didn't want to sing at all, and on occasion they turned downright mean. He had seen it so often. He didn't blame the artists. It was just human nature. Tim had just signed a new act, BR5-49, a hip retro band that was the buzz of Nashville. The boys had been playing for tips, and as their manager they had taken on none other than Barry. Tim would have bet the family farm that in the end BR5-49 wouldn't be any different from Alan out there or any of the other acts.

"I wrote this song quite a few years ago when I first ran away from home and I was homesick," Alan said, standing there in his jeans and cowboy hat while a great line of amateur photographers moved slowly past the stage taking pictures. "I've traveled a lot of places I thought I'd never be, all over the world—well, not all over the world, but parts of the world. And one thing I find that wherever you go, there's one place you call home."

Alan had written many songs, but "Home" was the one that meant the most. He wrote the song soon after he arrived in Nashville. There was a homespun, ragged quality to it that would not have passed muster at most of Music City's publishers. But life didn't always rhyme, and the words were deeply true and deeply felt, and out in that vast audience deeply felt, resonating with seventeen thousand lives:

> My mama raised five children, four girls then
>   there was me.
> She found her strength with faith in God and
>   love of family.

If Alan was lazy before he fired Barry, his former manager would have considered him even lazier now. The singer took on a second manager who didn't last, and then a third. He didn't tour as much as many of the superstars of country; in 1995 he gave 104 concerts, taking in over twenty million dollars. He sold his song catalog for thirteen million dollars, and cut a multi-million-dollar deal with Fruit of the Loom. The man wasn't hurting for money. On his off dates, he had plenty of time to sit around and write songs, but he didn't have Barry nagging him and he didn't write so much anymore. He preferred tinkering with his collection of old cars or fiddling with one of his boats. His forthcoming album was his first all-new work in almost three years, only half of which were songs he wrote or cowrote.

None of this seemed to matter. He had the biggest fan club in country music, with 150,000 members, and earlier this week he had won the TNN/Music City News Award as Entertainer of the Year, and for the fifth time in a row, Male Artist of the Year.

Alan was the kind of man who felt a grain of sand in his boot like it was a pebble, and a pebble like it was a boulder. He was about feeling comfortable, getting rid of all those grains of sand. He had pushed away Scott Hendricks from coproducing after his second album because Scott had become one of those grains of sand. Anyone who stayed around Alan knew not to push him too hard, not even to ask him things about which he was bound to say no.

Alan would like to walk into Wal-Mart or over to Pizza Hut and not have people looking at him, asking for his autographs all the time. He understood why they did so, but he was not a man like Garth who relished the fan's attention as a sign of his own value. He was still shy around people he didn't know, and he created his own islands of privacy. He had money that was like winning the lottery of lotteries. His T-shirt deal alone brought him a seven-figure advance. He had a private jet to take him back and forth.

To a degree unlike any other artist in Nashville, Alan built a network of his own private islands. There, isolated and protected, he sought to replicate the sense of family and peace he had when he was growing up. Outside Music City, he had a great home on fifteen acres of land. On a hill above Center Hill Lake between Nashville and Knoxville, he had an exquisite custom home that he called the "Real World," where he liked to spend much time with Denise and their two little daughters, Mattie and Ali. Down in Gulfside, Florida, he had a third magnificent modern home with great ceilings and tinted-glass doors. Outside Nashville, he was building an enormous, 29,000-square-foot home, to replace his older Music City residence. Today he was giving the fans what they wanted. But he would soon be gone, flying off in a helicopter to one of his houses while everyone was still sitting there at Fan Fair. No matter how high Alan built his walls around his homes, no matter how far back from the clamorous roads of life, he could not reconstruct the life he once knew. The great houses were his residences, but Alan knew that he only had one home.

> No there'll never be another place in this world
> that I'll call home.

As Alan left the stage, Tim hurried over to embrace the man who had been the beginning of his great success at Arista/Nashville. Alan shook hands with other Arista executives, and then he was out of there, even before the next artist had begun to sing. BlackHawk. Pam Tillis. Steve Wariner. Michelle Wright. One Arista/Nashville artist after another came forward to sing a mini-set. Tim greeted each with a warm hug and congratulations after they finished singing.

Out on the infield it was blistering hot. The fans had their own cardboard fans, which had been passed out to the vast audience, and the fans flickered back and forth by the thousands. In the onstage bleachers, several people had brought water guns, and periodically spirited battles broke out on this scorching afternoon. Few of the people onstage were older than their mid-forties. Country music was a young person's profession, not only the young stars of the nineties country but the managers and label heads and other executives. The oldest people up here were the men moving the heavy equipment onstage, their T-shirts drenched with perspiration. Back behind the stage, those guests with backstage passes sat in an enormous open-sided tent. Some looked at the monitors showing the performances while others ate hot dogs and chugged beer and soft drinks.

As the lineup of Arista artists continued, Kix Brooks and Ronnie Dunn slowly made their way from their bus, through hundreds of well-wishers, toward the stage. These backstage passes were supposed to be given to industry people, but the hundreds scurrying to meet Brooks and Dunn appeared no different from the fans up front. Brooks and Dunn, the biggest-selling duo in country music history, had given themselves plenty of time to stop along their route to sign CDs, guitars, posters, napkins, and whatever else was thrust into their faces.

As they finally pushed their way up the stairs and onto the back of the stage, Tim hurried over to greet the two men who were his greatest creation, and other than Alan Jackson, Arista/Nashville's biggest success. Tim had what Bowen called "an accountant's mentality." He had looked out on the country music world in 1990 and noticed there were so few duos that the CMA was thinking of dropping the category in the annual awards show.

Tim set out to put together an act just the way he had put together Restless Heart in the eighties. Tim heard a tape of Kix Brooks, a singer/songwriter over at Sony Tree. Kix had a voice that he thought might work. But he couldn't figure out a second voice.

One Saturday afternoon in the fall of 1990, Tim and his old Oklahoma buddy, Scott Hendricks, were driving to Knoxville to attend a University of Tennessee football game. Tim started talking about his problems putting together this duo. "I've got this guy named Kix Brooks and here's four songs," Tim said as he punched up a tape in his deck. Then he put in another tape. "Here's the other guy." The two men listened closely to the second tape of a prominent songwriter.

"What do you think?" Tim asked.

"You know, I swear, I don't hear that. I just don't hear it. I mean,

I know he's a great singer and a great songwriter, I just don't hear the blend. I don't hear the combination and I just don't see it."

As Scott talked, he pulled a tape out of his pocket. "One more time, I'm going to bring this up," Scott said. Scott had been the engineer for the winner of the Marlboro Talent Competition, a nationwide search for country singers. The winner happened to be another Oklahoman, Ronnie Dunn. Tim had been impressed every time Scott tried to play something of the man, but not for a duo. This time Scott played four songs that Tim hadn't heard before, including "Boot Scootin' Boogie," "Neon Moon," and "She Used to Be Mine."

"You're absolutely correct," Tim said, delighted at how wrong he had been.

Kix and Ronnie both wanted solo record deals, but their chances were about over when Tim heard their tapes. Six-foot, four-inch-tall Ronnie was thirty-seven years old, and though he had a wonderfully evocative voice, he had a face like that of a hungry eaglet that even his full beard couldn't disguise. Kix was two inches shorter, two years younger, and much better looking, but he didn't have a tenth of the voice Ronnie had. Nashville was full of people singing their sorry song, men in their mid-thirties who had come to town looking to be stars and ended up hustling around writing songs for those who had gotten their record deals.

Both men were trying to make it in Nashville, but they didn't know each other, and Tim took them to lunch. Nashville wasn't big on fancy power lunches. Tim drove them to a little Mexican restaurant with a few tables well off Music Row. The two men were wary, for they saw the man across the table as more the end of their dream than the beginning of a new one. Both had struggled in the bars and honky-tonks for years, and they were not the kind of performers who liked sharing a microphone.

"Why don't you guys get together and write some songs," Tim told them as his way of gentle matchmaking.

The audience had been sitting out in the heat and the sun for close to three hours. They appeared drained, every ounce of emotion and enthusiasm sweated out of them by this endless onslaught of performers. Then up on that great stage Ronnie and Kix walked forward, and the audience erupted as if they had not heard a single song yet today. Fans stood all across the vast expanse of the infield, raising their hands in V for victory. The line of photographers started moving faster, like a great snake that fears it won't eat unless it crawls ahead.

Forty-one-year-old Kix was the great showman, sitting on the stage, shaking hands along the perimeter of the stage, as he sang. Today, however, forty-three-year-old Ronnie was his equal, a musical messiah dressed totally in black, working his will over the seventeen thousand fans spread out before him. As the backup band struck up a rock beat, Ronnie yelled at the crowd: "I want you to stand and applaud. All the way from the bottom to the top. You guys got it. Yeah. Do it. Over there. Over there. Do it."

As Ronnie pointed down to the front rows, the audience stood up, raising their hands about their heads. As he pointed his finger upward, the crowds rose, a great human wave rising across the infield and back up to the farthest reaches of the stands. Wherever his finger pointed, the audience stood up screaming. He was controlling these thousands and thousands of fans as if they were one organism.

"Rock my world . . . ," Ronnie sang. "Stay with me now."

"Rock my world," the crowd sang in unison.

"Rock my world!"

"Rock my world."

Ronnie turned back to the stage for a moment, a demonic grin on his reddened face at what he had wrought out there beyond the stage. Tim looked at Ronnie and smiled slightly. It didn't get much better than this. There are two kinds of egos in the world, the producer and the artist, the writer and the editor, the actor and the director, and Tim knew where he stood. He was the power behind the power, the string that pulled the string.

When Ronnie and Kix had first started performing together, they saw that they were opposites in their onstage personae. Ronnie's hero was Merle Haggard, and he stood there like The Hag and Johnny Cash and all the old greats of country music. He sang his songs, believing that the words and sentiment and his rendition were enough to hold his audience. Over on the other end of the stage about as far away as he could get, Kix jumped around, bounced up and down, his guitar a prop, singing only a part of his act.

Tim had not put together a duo, as country music had always defined the genre, one person singing lead on each song, the other harmony. For the most part, Ronnie and Kix each sang his own songs, with almost none of the rich harmony that had been the essence of classic country duos such as the Louvin Brothers and to a lesser extent the Judds. In any duo, there is usually one lead voice, but in Brooks and Dunn the difference was startling. Ronnie might have become one of Nashville's greatest, deepest songwriters. As a solo singer, he might have become a legitimate heir to the mantle of George Jones. Kix had neither ability, and some critics were so brutal as to say that "Kix Brooks cannot sing to save his life" or that "Brooks's voice came close to disappearing." Ronnie wrote the songs that became most of the duo's hits. Ronnie sang most of the songs, while Kix ran around onstage. Brooks and Dunn looked, as Nashville's wags said, "like an organ grinder with his monkey on a long leash."

The two men were equal in ambition and hunger, and they went out in the world with a brilliantly calculated sense of what would work. As the duo was taking off in 1991, Ronnie told Jack Hurst of the *Chicago Tribune* that the mood of their songs was "like my heart's broken, but I'm not going to kill myself about it. On the other side of them swinging doors there's a good time and some beautiful woman who's just waiting for me, so if you're planning to hang with me, heartache, you better get ready, you're in for a rough ride. . . . It's like life. You can talk yourself into staying down if you want to, but there's also a positive side to everything. There's maybe just a hair of chauvinistic rebelliousness to our songs, but it's not the old traditional, all-out, closed-minded kind. We like women. Heck, we love 'em."

Brooks and Dunn's first number one hit was Ronnie's haunting "Neon Moon," a classic honky-tonk song. ("I spend most every night beneath the light of this neon moon.") The song that made them one of the country sensations of the nineties was another of Ronnie's songs, the upbeat "Boot Scootin' Boogie." ("I see outlaws, in-laws, crooks and straights all out makin' it shake doin' the boot scootin' boogie.") It was as natural for the line dancing of the new country as Billy Ray Cyrus's "Achy Breaky Heart." Although the duo had no desire to be known as, in Kix's words, "the disco ducks of country," engineers in Los Angeles made a pumped-up dance version of the song that was shipped out to country and noncountry dance clubs.

Brooks and Dunn had an image as these good-time-loving party dudes, an image they fostered every way they could. Merle was Ronnie's idol, and Merle was a ballad man, but the boys didn't mess much with ballads in their show. They heated things up with up-tempo songs and kept it going that way all night long. They got Miller Lite as their tour sponsor, and that was a perfect match. Theirs was a young, heavy-drinking party crowd in the pickup trucks spinning out of the arena lots full of half-loaded ticket holders.

Kix and Ronnie had an in-your-face attitude about them that appealed to the audience, but not always to the wider world. The first time they went on *The Tonight Show*, Ronnie tried to appear like Jay Leno's buddy by slouching down in his chair. Instead, he came off as this arrogant know-nothing. The talent coordinator vowed he would never have them back; and she didn't until they were so big they couldn't be ignored. When they went on the David Letterman show, they were offended that David asked them who was Brooks and who was Dunn. They didn't seem to realize that most of the viewers didn't know either, and it was a reasonable question.

As enormous as Brooks and Dunn became, there was still that gaping discrepancy between the two men onstage that was disguised by enormous flashy sets, video screens, and showbiz razzmatazz. In February of 1993, they appeared at Billy Bob's, the giant Fort Worth club. Ronnie had such a problem with his throat that he spent much of the day with a specialist. The doctor shot him up with steroids and told him he wouldn't know for sure if he could sing until he started to perform. The club was sold out. The previous year the duo had canceled, and Ronnie wasn't about to be the one to do it again. When he stepped out on that big stage before 5,700 honky-tonkers, he knew it was no good, but he soldiered on for seventy minutes, trying to hide his plight as best he could.

The next day Ronnie read the *Dallas Morning News* review that he would remember beyond any criticism he ever received. "It was absolutely embarrassing," wrote Michael Corcoran, "but as the club had been sold out for days, you could say he was blushing all the way to the bank. When their goofy, cheery facade was stripped away due to illness, the duo's songs proved unable to stand on their own."

It wasn't Kix's voice that was stripped away, and that long evening in Fort Worth was a lesson in how carefully the Brooks and Dunn image had to be maintained. Ronnie admitted that he was "neurotic," a term that most country artists would not use to describe themselves, no matter how accurate it might be. As half of Brooks and Dunn, he was living something that wasn't true. He knew, even if most of the audience didn't, that he carried so much of the musical burden of the group. He had wanted to be like Merle Haggard once, and he was about as far from that as a man could be. Nonetheless his journey to stardom resonated with the great themes of country music.

Ronnie's mother was a hard-shell Baptist in a family of Baptists, hard, true believers, who followed their church's dictum to the word and to the letter. He loved his mother deeply. From her he got that Baptist faith, with its spiritual passion and its guilt, its sense that one is always falling short. His father was a hard-drinking man, a lover of good old-time country music and good old times. His old man played guitar backing country groups coming through Abilene. He could get mean when the liquor was in him, and when liquor was in him he couldn't seem to keep a job in the oil fields. The family wandered from town to town, job to job, thirty-five different places in Ronnie's childhood. Ronnie loved his roustabout father deeply too, and from him he learned to love music that his old man played around the house with his friends, strumming on a guitar, singing out those songs.

His father was a wild, crazy man. His mother was washed in the blood, a woman of deep faith. There was the classic southern soul in all its glorious contradictions, the Bible held forward in one hand, the bottle clutched behind the back in the other. In *The Mind of the South*, W. J. Cash writes of "the two currents of Puritanism and hedonism [that] continued to flow side by side to opposite quarters, crossing often, certainly, but never to the production of an impasse, never beyond the possibility of amicable adjustment." As a boy growing up, Ronnie could not listen to country radio for a half hour without hearing that "amicable adjustment" from songs that sang of family and faith, love and hope to those that talked of adultery and betrayal, shame and wantonness.

In the South in which Ronnie grew up, the devil was no mere metaphor, no High-Church Episcopalian intellectualizing. *Satan Is Real* was the title of an album by the Louvin Brothers, arguably the greatest duo in country music history. On the cover the devil leered there in full regalia, pitchfork at the ready, above a bed of fiery coals. Ira and Charlie Louvin stood in their white communion suits in the midst of the fiery damnation, for all appearances trying to sing their way out of hell.

The devil was out there. You could see the struggle between God and the devil in Ronnie's kin and in another musical family, Jerry Lee Lewis and his cousin, Jimmy Swaggart. The devil grabbed poor Jerry Lee, sent him down chasing skirts, marrying his thirteen-year-old cousin. Good Jimmy, a preacher man, saved souls, but the lust in him ran deep. Good Jimmy met the devil in the form of a prostitute in the evil streets of New Orleans. The congregation, or much of it, took him back, for a man was of flesh and weakness. Let the heathen onlookers speak of hypocrisy. His followers knew that when their preacher man spoke of temptation and the devil's fatal pull, he knew of what he spoke.

The South was still full of extremes of good and evil, love and hate, rich and poor, that could drive a person to sin or song, the Bible or the bottle. Ronnie grasped for the Bible as a teenager, planning to become a preacher. He went to Abilene Christian College, where he studied the Word long and hard. He still loved music, and sometimes he went out and sat listening to rock and country at some of the bars, and sometimes he even played some devilish music. The teachers didn't wait for sin; they went out looking for it, and when they heard that Ronnie was playing in honky- tonks, they figured they had themselves a sinner by the scruff of his fallen neck. "You know our policy here, Ronnie," the dean told him. "You can't frequent those places and we hear you're not only going, you're playing music. You got a choice, either stop doing it, or you can leave."

Ronnie was a young man of the most abysmal shyness. Singing music was about the only thing he felt comfortable doing in public. That he could do, but as much as he loved the Lord he couldn't see himself preaching, standing alone before a congregation. So he told the dean he would be leaving, and the dean didn't bother trying to get him to change his mind and stay out of those heathen honky-tonks.

Ronnie moved to Tulsa where his family was living and got a job in a clothing store that featured the disco wardrobe of the day. Through that job he met many outstanding musicians and started playing on demo tapes. He came over to his parents' place one night and played his newest tape. "It's not country enough," his father told him, dismissing everything his son was doing.

For years his father had been on his case about music, as if his son was betraying everything that was good and true. For years, Ronnie had seen what drinking could do, the abuse, the swaggering bluster that he'd had to hear all those years. His father wouldn't let up. He kept ragging on him, putting him down, telling him the tape wasn't country. His father was a strong man who made a living with his hands. But that evening Ronnie stood toe-to-toe with him and fought him with bare fists until his old man lay sprawled beneath him on the floor.

Ronnie eventually made up with his father, and his life that next decade and a half followed close in the footsteps of his father. He didn't make his living in the oil fields, but he would have made more money doing that than playing in the clubs and honky-tonks that he did. He wasn't an alcoholic, but he got into that crazed musician's life, sleeping late, playing nights, abusing his body. He got married, had a couple kids, but he couldn't expect a wife to chase that neon rainbow with him forever, and they divorced. He had the sadness in his voice that he had earned tear by tear, and a life of endless nights in endless clubs. He hadn't even sent in an application for the Marlboro Contest. A friend had done that in a local convenience store, but he had gone ahead with it, and it gave him the chance he needed. He married again, to a woman he met playing at her family ranch, and he and Janine had set out together for Nashville.

In Music City, Ronnie and Janine had got to know Johnny Cash well enough that he invited the couple to live in his cabin outside the city. He came over one day and gave Ronnie one of his Man in Black stage suits, a gift of emotional value far larger than the considerable financial worth. "Don't tell June about it," Johnny said, asking the Dunns not to tell his wife. It was a great gesture, and Ronnie wore the suit on the cover of Brooks and Dunn's first album.

All those years he had struggled, and when Brooks and Dunn took off, Ronnie lost it for a while, his vision blinded by the light of the spotlight, his head permanently cocked toward the endless praise and applause. "My husband went crazy," Janine recalled. "Everything had to be done as quickly and wildly as possible. It was awful."

And so it was. As Ronnie stood on the great stage with Kix, he was more together than he had been back then. He still feared that it might go away one day, and he and Kix watched over their careers with minute, compulsive detail. They were business partners who pretended to be like brothers. They helped design their line of shirts, overseeing merchandise that in 1995 brought in about seven million dollars. They traveled like some armada, with six trucks, three buses, and a crew of forty-five who put up their massive stage shows. Night after night they went on, rarely stopping, returning home tired, Ronnie wanting to be alone with his new baby for a while, wanting to forget those endless nights and all the wages of success.

>My Maria don't you know
>I've come a long, long way.

Ronnie dug into the lyrics of "My Maria," the old seventies pop song that Tim had pushed the duo to record against Ronnie's wishes. As usual, Tim was right, and the song became a number one hit. The audience was into it, singing along, swaying with the music.

My Maria
Maria I love you.
My Maria
I love you.

As Brooks and Dunn turned away from the great audience, Tim stood for a moment looking out on the vast scene. This was one of the few times of the year that the artists got together, and for Tim it was like seeing his family together for an afternoon. Ten of his Arista/Nashville artists had performed today, more than any other label. They had gone on for over three hours, pushing the limits. Tim remembered how two years ago there had been torrential rain. The great crowd had been out there anyway, and the rain let up just before the first artist stepped out on the stage. Today it hadn't rained, and it had gone so well. Tim was, as he liked to say, an emotional man in an emotional business, and he left the stage as drained as the audience.

14

~

"I Don't Think I Will"

It was evening, but the heat beat down on the racetrack with all the intensity of a dog-day August afternoon as the vast audience waited for the Sony Epic/Columbia show to begin. The week was almost over, and the crowd sat waiting for the final label show as if it were the last course of a rich dinner.

Onstage the crews prepared the microphones, testing and retesting. Over on the side, just out of view of the audience, a group of six men and two women stood huddled together saying a prayer. At the center of the group, his head bowed like the others, stood James Bonamy, who was about to make his debut before an audience larger than he had ever sung to in his twenty-four years.

James had the perfect image for the hot young country demographics of the nineties. He appeared poised halfway between boyhood and manhood. He had sultry eyes and sensuous lips and smooth unblemished features. These were the benignly handsome good looks that were the stuff of fantasy to teenage girls who wanted their heroes sexy but safe. He could have been kin to Donnie

Osmond or David Cassidy when they had been teen sensations. Until recently the look was foreign to country music. Hank Williams was even younger than James when he had his first hit, but he seemed born old. So had most of the male stars of country music.

James was doubtless going to have his age lines soon enough, for he had already learned that in the brutally competitive world of the new Nashville, life could be merciless. One mistake and it might all be over. And James had already had his one mistake. His first single shipped to radio was "Dog on a Toolbox." It was a silly song. ("Sometimes I feel like a dog standin' on a toolbox in the back of a pickup truck going 'round a corner at ninety miles an hour in the rain.") No way was it the initial statement to make if Epic wanted James to be considered a serious new artist with depth and integrity. The label believed that the upbeat song could become a teen anthem, propelling James to platinum-level sales.

The song was catchy, and it started getting a lot of play. Then the label heard discouraging comments from some of the consultants who determined the playlists for major stations. They didn't like dog songs. Some of them had a rule that they didn't play songs that had "dog" in the title. James would need these powerful consultants if he wanted to succeed. If he alienated even one of them, their displeasure might prevent another song from getting enough plays to become a top single. Although people were calling in asking for "Dog on a Toolbox," and James usually got a rave response whenever he sang it on tour, the label decided to retreat and recalled the single.

James had that sweetly malleable quality of a new country artist. He accepted the embarrassing recall and ignored the fact that "Dog on a Toolbox" had become something of a joke along Music Row, a classic example of the mindless ditty that the industry was foisting on an indifferent world. His album, *What I Live to Do,* was out there in the stores, but it was not selling even well enough to make the *Billboard* Country Top Seventy Five. That was enough to lead many on Music Row to believe that James was on his way to that great graveyard of dead careers, gone before he had begun.

The label was discovering other problems marketing James as this sexy young thing. At first, he wanted to have a fish symbol on his guitar so everyone who saw or heard him would know that he was a Christian. The label executives knew that religious images could be unsettling to country music fans out for a night in a country dance club or turning in a few minutes of CMT. If the audience wanted Christian contemporary music, they would buy it and not tune in to hot young country. James saw the logic in this, but he and his band continued to have prayerful huddles before he went onstage, and he kept making a short witness in the midst of each performance.

The other problem was that James was married. The first manager who wanted to sign the singer made it plain that he better not marry if he wanted a career. Not only had he married, but he talked frequently about how much he adored his wife and sang songs about Amy Jane onstage. The female fans could hardly forget that he was married, for his wife sang backup in his band. Amy Jane was a pretty woman, with fresh, innocent features, unblighted by life, but onstage she wore heavy makeup that made her look older than her husband and more sophisticated than her twenty-three years.

A few weeks before Fan Fair, Epic invited all the major country music journalists in Nashville to meet James, have dinner, and hear him sing. The writers agreed to be there, and the label ordered tacos, enchiladas, and beer. The publicist called the reporters back, confirming the six o'clock session at the Mill, a small recording studio off Music Row. James was there a few minutes early, as was Doug Johnson, the Epic label head who was also James's producer and musical mentor.

When he was a kid, Doug wanted to be an artist. He saw in James a fulfillment of everything he had wanted to be. He loved James like a younger brother or a son. He admired him as a performer, but more than that as a young man of sterling virtue and modesty.

The two men were as similar as if they were of the same blood. Doug loved two things deeply, his family and country music. He lived for both of them. Doug had written or cowritten three of the ten cuts on James's debut album. Although the cynical take on this was that the producer had used his position to foist his own songs on the poor kid's album, that was not the way Doug Johnson worked. As head of A&R at Epic, Doug had a reputation as a man of elemental decency, qualities that some of his colleagues considered little more than foolish naïveté. He could not stand the kind of duplicity and double dealing that was rampant on Music Row. That's why he wasn't happy at Sony, and that's why he cared so for James and wanted him to become a major star. Of course, Doug was not unmindful of all the money and prestige that would come if James succeeded, but ultimately that was not what it was about.

At 6:15 P.M., Cyndi Hoelzle, the Nashville bureau chief of *The Gavin Report,* a trade journal that deals with radio, wandered into the room with her publisher in tow. She was the only guest to show up. The Epic staff waited a while longer, but James had been stiffed by every important journalist in Nashville. It was a moment that would have sent many young artists into a paroxysm of anger or despair at such humiliation. James, however, had a graciousness that did not leave him, even this evening. He fixed himself some Mexican food, opened a beer, and started talking music with Doug.

Doug had even greater reason to be angry. This was a slap at him, telling him that James wasn't worth the time, and neither was he. He may have been a vice president of a major label, but he wasn't important enough to warrant common courtesy. He knew enough about clout to realize that Tony Brown or Tim DuBois never would have been stood up. He, like James, let the matter slide. After munching on a taco, he started playing music, trading songs with James.

Doug and James were brothers of the soul and spirit. They loved to play together, but they were both so busy they rarely had time. As the two men sat on folding chairs in the little studio, they were as much into this as if they had been sitting in Doug's back-yard strumming away on a Sunday afternoon. James sang a song he had written, and Doug pitched a new song to his artist. In their own way, they were saying that what mattered was music, that in country music life and music were a seamless web, and that a man should sing what he believed and believe what he lived.

This evening at Fan Fair, James was the opening act, a position for which he had a lot of practice. In the last months he had gone out a dozen times opening for a big star, John Michael Montgomery. James had gotten the gig because his management company represented John Michael, but that hadn't made it any easier once he got onstage. The crowds hadn't come to hear James Bonamy. They were still settling into their seats or making their way down the aisles, treating the first act as a filler. The opening act was supposed to be good but not so good as to make the star seem almost an afterthought. James worked his half hour and then got off, at best revving the audience up for the dramatic appearance of John Michael.

This evening it was only fitting that James should be the first act out here, considering his standing at Sony and his mediocre sales. James came running onstage like a quarterback charging onto the field before the big game, and burst into the seminotorious "Dog on a Toolbox." Radio consultants might have hated the song, but the audience hadn't gotten the message, and they clapped and hooted.

To the side of the stage stood James's mother and father, Robert and Paula. His mother kept thinking about how upset she had been when her youngest son dropped out of the University of Alabama to pursue a career in country music. Neither Paula nor Robert had college educations, and Paula fretted that James was cavalierly throwing away a chance to be somebody. She wanted both her sons to have opportunities their parents didn't have.

Paula met her husband when they were working at a Sears store in Key West, Florida. He was Lebanese American and she had Cherokee and English blood. They believed in family and faith. They believed in America too, and that anybody had a chance. Now after all those years of pushing James to do his homework, he simply walked out of Tuscaloosa with the crazy idea of becoming a country music star. She could hardly believe that three years later James was standing up there on that great stage, jumping up and down, working that vast audience as if he had been doing this for twenty years.

The Bonamys lived not so much through their sons as for them. Robert sold new cars and later ran a used-car lot in Daytona Beach, Florida. This was a business in which the hours when a man wanted to be home with his family were the hours he had to be selling. Despite that, Robert almost always managed to be home for dinner, even if it was a late hour. The family sat down together, said grace, and ate their meal, for that was what life was about.

Beyond his wife and two sons, Robert had two great loves in his life, the Crimson Tide football team of the University of Alabama and country music. They were peculiar passions, for Robert had neither attended Alabama nor heard much country music when he was growing up in a Lebanese American community in Key West, but he had taken to both the football team and the music. He introduced his sons to coach Paul "Bear" Bryant's awesome record as Alabama's football coach, as if the Alabama football field were a plain on which life's lessons were taught. Country music had life lessons to teach too. Robert had a large country record collection, each album kept neatly in its sleeve, and he introduced his two sons to artists such as Merle Haggard and Conway Twitty.

The Bonamys' oldest son, David, had played high school football and had gone on to Alabama, where he had made the football team as a receiver. He was only 180 pounds, lucky even to be a reserve end. To his father, to be able to say that his son had worn that crimson uniform was an honor of unimaginable magnitude. As for his other love, he believed that only a God of infinite generosity could give him this too, to have James up there on this stage, playing country music. It was not exactly the country music that he loved to play, but the world was different now, and he counted his blessings, as if he were afraid they might one day go away.

James had not grown up devoted to country music, though he listened to his father's records. He had little choice, since Robert woke the family up each morning at seven with Merle or Willie or Hank or Johnny Paycheck blasting through the house. As he entered his teen years, James strayed from his father's country music and started listening to the rock 'n' roll that the other kids in school liked. When his older brother was punished by being sent to his room, it was as if he had been drawn and quartered. James, however, was delighted to spend time by himself, alone with his guitar. James was shy and quiet and found in music an identity.

James, like most teenagers, wanted to be cool. He enjoyed going out to the dirt track outside Daytona Beach and watching stock car racing, but when he came into school Monday morning, he was called a "redneck." James found it fun being out there at the track, but he was discovering one of the more peculiar aberrations of the human species. People often turned away from things they liked—be it people, ideas, music, or books—simply because they were afraid that their peers would think less of them for liking them. It wasn't until he was sixteen that James again embraced country music and started playing the music on his guitar.

James had been an athlete in high school, but he was not big enough to think about playing football at Alabama. He joined his brother there, sharing an apartment. He had never sung in public, but during his first year he got up in the middle of the night and drove to Birmingham to sing with the house band on the *Country Boy Eddie* television show. The program went on the air at 4:30 A.M., when many viewers felt the act of anyone singing live at that hour was talent enough.

James was allowed to sing one song. No one asked him back, but James returned a few weeks later with his guitar to sing the first song he had written. It was called "I'll Always Love You So." It was about his mother and was terrible enough to give motherhood a bad name. The producer gently suggested that if James returned, next time he should sing a cover song familiar to the television audience.

One evening during spring break in 1991, James happened to be in Orlando at Church Street Station. This was a large entertainment complex designed primarily for the tourists after their day at Disney World. Fridays the house band played to audiences of up to two thousand. James walked up to the guitar player and asked, "You mind if I sing a song with you guys?"

"Yeah, sure," the musician said. "Come back next weekend. You can sing at the late show."

James returned a week later. By the time he got up there, the crowd had thinned out to about five hundred. James sang some Alan Jackson and Garth Brooks songs. He did fine, but not so fine that the band leader asked him to join the group. He did say that next time in town, he could sit in with the group.

Back at college, James called his parents and said he was planning to drop out of college, move to Orlando, and sing at Church Street Station when he could. The Bonamys had seen other teenage lives smashed against the shoals of adulthood, and James's plan seemed quixotic at best. He said that he would transfer to a community college and get a job. The Bonamys gave him enough money to pay his rent but not enough to live on, believing that James should pay for his own dream.

James found a tiny apartment, furnished with a sofa and bed from his Alabama digs, and found a job in a gift shop at Church Street Station. He would gladly have dropped out of college altogether, but that was part of his deal with his parents, and he was a dutiful son. He went to his classes during the day, often writing lyrics in his notebook during the droning lectures. At night from six to ten he worked in the gift shop, writing songs on the backs of discount coupons. And every weekend or so, he got up there and sang a few songs. He made a tape, which he took to a local country radio station, trying to get them to play his songs.

It was a life that many young men would have found a dreary purgatory, doubly dreary because it was so unnecessary. He could have been up in Tuscaloosa partying with his brother, sitting in the student stands as Alabama went through another winning season. James didn't drink. He didn't smoke. He wasn't hustling pretty young women. He had few friends at Orlando. He kept his own counsel and his own time and worked learning how to sing and to write songs. He listened to country radio. He listened to albums. He played and sang by himself in his little apartment.

James intended to get to Nashville one day, but he wanted to be ready. In the fall of 1991, he auditioned to sing at one of the shows at Opryland USA, the Nashville theme park. He had been practicing copying the styles of leading country singers, and of the hundreds auditioning, he was one of the few to make the cut. The job didn't start until the following spring, but now even James's parents knew he had something going, even if it wasn't a college education.

"How're you doing?" James yelled as the applause from the Fan Fair audience died down. Country fans had a politeness gone from much of American life, and initially they had greeted James as they would any stranger, with a certain wary warmth. By the end of his first song, he had won them, and they were listening to him, not biding their time until the major stars stepped forward.

"How're you doing?" he shouted again, though he could tell by their response that they were doing just fine.

James segued into another mid-tempo song from his album, "She's Got a Mind of Her Own." That had been his second single. It had reached thirty-four on the *Billboard* Country Singles chart, and much of the audience had at least heard the song. Epic put an upbeat spin on things, but given that the label had pulled James's first single to please radio, James was just barely keeping in the game.

Standing behind James on that vast stage, Amy Jane was totally into singing backup. When James played honky-tonks, Amy Jane got her full share of sly looks from guys on the dance floor, most of whom didn't realize she was James's wife until he introduced her. Amy Jane was from White Oak, Texas, and despite her sophisticated look onstage, she was as small-town as a party line. Her father was the athletic director at the Pine Tree High School. He was everything a Texan was supposed to be, a quiet man who rode horses with his daughter and made extra income by shoeing horses. They were good Baptists, and the first song Amy Jane ever sang was "Jesus Loves Me." She had been more into singing contemporary Christian than country, but when she heard the Judds, she realized that you could sing country and still keep that spiritual quality.

Amy Jane was such a homebody that when she went off to junior college in Tyler an hour away, she sat in her dorm room crying, wanting to go home. Most of her friends had gone to school even nearer to home, and by those standards she was full of wanderlust. She was daring enough that when she heard about auditions for Opryland USA, she drove all the way to Arlington, Texas, to try out and was hired.

Amy arrived at Opryland the same time as James. The first time Amy Jane saw James, she was sure that he was playing in the pop music show. He was just too pretty to be singing country. The two of them ended in the same show. James pretended to be Garth and Lester Flatt, while Amy Jane sang like Loretta Lynn and Patty Loveless.

Amy Jane was engaged to a fellow back in Texas, and James was going with a student at the University of Tennessee. They found in each other a soul mate. Both came from loving families. Both were religious. Both wanted to lead good, honorable lives. They wrestled fitfully with their feelings.

Amy ended her engagement, but that did not mean she wanted to exchange one ring for another. On their first real date, James blurted out "I love you." Amy replied, "That's nice but don't expect me to say that word to you." Amy took awhile to realize what she had in James, and once she realized she grasped tightly onto him. They decided that they wanted to marry. The couple found a Baptist church they both liked and made the church a center of their life. And they vowed that whoever got the first record deal, they would work together to make one star in the family. Then they would work together to make a second.

Amy Jane kept working at Opryland, even after they married. James had gone on *Star Search* and gotten all the way to the semi-finals, getting some visibility that Amy Jane did not have. Much of the time, though, he was working as a carpenter. Nashville was booming, and there was plenty of work putting up houses.

On one of his off days, two women came up to James at Longhorn Steaks off Music Row where he was having lunch. They had seen him on *Star Search*, and they wanted to introduce him to John Dorris and Estillo Sowards, two prominent managers. James was rightfully suspicious. He had already met his share of hustlers who who would have signed his life and his career away, taking advantage of a newcomer's desperate desire to succeed. Dorris and Sowards represented John Michael Montgomery and Doug Stone. James grew especially close to Dorris and he trusted his son, John Jr., who took over day-to-day management. They got James his record deal at Epic, but that was only the beginning. They were successful enough to help James and Amy Jane buy a tract home outside of Nashville. They fronted James three hundred dollars a week, leased a bus for him, hired a band, and got him out there on the road. That would all have to be paid back one day out of the money he earned from records and performing.

James and Amy Jane tried to create a group of people in the band much like themselves, including two married couples. There were no heavy drinkers, no dopers, nothing but family people. James and Amy Jane had met Dan Kelly, the fiddle player, and his wife, Sonya Kelly, the guitar player, when they all were working at Opryland. Sonya was Amy Jane and James's closest friend, a special blessing on the road. Jeff Little, the piano player, traveled with his wife, Sharon, who sold merchandise during the show. Gary Lumpkin, the bus driver, had played guitar in various bands, but the money was better and more certain driving a bus. Gary was as much a member of the group as anybody, and James thought it would be kind of neat to have him play once in a while. James at times took over the driving, cruising down the highway, king of the road.

Now that James had a band, he had to work enough to give the musicians a living. As it was, with the bus, the fuel, the hotel rooms and all, it was so expensive to keep a band on the road that every night he played he was deeper in debt. He got a special deal from the bus leasing company by taking whatever bus was available. Often the stale stench of cigarette smoke and diesel fuel was hanging there in the air.

On one weekend sprint down to Chattanooga to play at Governors, a big old honky-tonk on the edge of town, it was poor solace to know that when Garth was starting out he had drawn only fifty people to the club instead of the two hundred who showed up this Friday evening. The room was full of women who were forty trying to look twenty. The men stood in their boots and jeans, checking them out. They all had something on their mind other than listening to this kid singing "Jimmy and Jesus." His parents had driven down from Nashville, and he sang the old Conway Twitty song "That's My Job," about a father's love for his children. His father sat there crying, and the audience stood there dancing and drinking, trying to boogie to a ballad. James soldiered on as if they cared.

Another week they drove down to Texas to do the circuit of Midnight Rodeo clubs. The clubs all had the same decor, and it was often hard to tell one night from the next. In Lubbock, there was a tornado warning, dark funnel clouds on the horizons, hailstorms beating a tattoo on the room, puddles on the concrete floor, water dripping down on the stage, and about thirty customers out front.

"It's so good being here in Amarillo," James said gamely.

"You're in Lubbock," somebody yelled over the storm.

For Amy Jane, there was a whole new kind of anxiety when James had large crowds and his natural magnetism drove young women by the score up to the stage and afterwards prompted them to wait for his autograph. Some women were shameless, wanting James to sign their bodies or their bras. Amy Jane had learned to stay away, to get on the bus and wait for her husband. She knew her James, and she knew that he wasn't even tempted. She didn't want to be a complaining wife like some of those she had seen or heard about. She just wanted to do whatever she could to help her husband become a star.

Monday before the doors at Fan Fair opened, Amy Jane had gone to Building C with James's parents to put together his booth. As they walked through the empty buildings, they saw the extravagant booths built for the major stars. Some of the performers spent twenty or thirty thousand dollars to have their double booths designed, built, and set up.

Amy and her in-laws found James's booth way off in a side corridor among such stellar names as Tug Boat International Records. To decorate the booth, they had gone out to Wal-Mart and spent less than two hundred dollars buying black cloth and some cowboy-appearing ornaments. For several hours they hammered away, stapled cloth, and nailed up a signboard with James's name on it. They were proud of what they did, but compared to many of the others, it looked like a 4-H booth at a county fair. In reality, James's booth came closer to the old-time spirit of Fan Fair than did the expensive booths of the major stars. Even five years ago, James's booth would have seemed like most of the displays at the annual event.

James spent the week moving between various signings and events, for the most part just slightly off the fan's radar screen. One afternoon he had the unenviable honor of sitting between Patty Loveless and Doug Stone at the Sony booth, looking less like a star than a buffer between the two artists and their long lines of well-wishers. In the end, some fans got James's autograph as well, for the more experienced fairgoers had learned to get the signatures of these new acts even if hardly anyone seemed interested. You never could tell. Reba had sat alone one year, and so had Garth, and those who had their early autographs valued them like precious gems.

Country music had never tried to hang out a sign saying the age group for which the music was intended. The young and the old line-danced together at the country night clubs and listened to much of the same music. In a country divided as much by age as by race or class, that was a great virtue. In America it was a remarkable idea that a song could be youthful enough to appeal to teenagers yet full of sentiment that could appeal to their grandparents.

In recent years, Nashville, in conjunction with radio, had begun producing music to drive the demographics to a younger and younger audience. Nashville was marketing the music more and more to the teenagers who haunted the malls and bought most of the CDs and cassettes. By so doing they were ridding country music of many older listeners, who tuned in to the music on the radio but rarely bought albums. The strategy was working. Since 1989 the proportion of teenagers listening to country had nearly tripled, from 2.8 percent to 8.5 percent. During that same period, according to the *Billboard*/Arbitron survey, the core thirty-five to sixty-five-year-old audience had dropped from 13.1 percent to 12.2 percent.

James was part of this wooing of the young. As the week went by, more people started showing up at James's booth, getting his autograph, saying hello. There were young people by the score, but there were their parents and middle-aged couples as well at his booth. Yesterday, the line at James's booth was about at an end when Casey Kidder, a fourteen-year-old from Hillsboro, Ohio, came forward clutching a T-shirt for James to sign. When Casey looked up at James's big eyes, she started to cry. James couldn't leave the teenager standing there wailing. He invited her back to his bus, where he gave her autographed photos and two CDs. "Anything else you want to stop you cryin'," he said to Casey, who could hardly believe her good fortune.

"Hello, friends! How're y'all doin' tonight?" James shouted. The second song had drawn an even bigger response than the first. He worked the stage, kneeling to the fans as they reached up, kicking his feet in the air, running back and forth. "It's good to be here tonight. We love you. We're looking forward to meeting everybody we didn't meet yet tomorrow in booth C309."

That brought a new wave of applause. "We've got a new single out," James said when the crowd quieted. "It's called 'I Don't Think I Will.' I sure hope you enjoy it."

> Hold it right there.
> Don't say a word.
> I hear a voice I've never heard.

Radio lived off a diet heavy with up-tempo songs, but ballads were usually the career-making songs. The audience wanted to believe in true love, if only for three minutes, and James sang his third and final song of the evening with passionate intensity. He believed in such a love, for, after all, wasn't that what he had seen in his own home and what he had with Amy Jane? His father choked up, holding back his tears. Doug Johnson had written the song, and as he stood on the side of the stage, he was crying. Doug loved James and he loved country music, and on this evening in the spring, he felt them come together in an exquisite moment.

"Thank you so much, I love you," James said, and walked off the stage to a thundering wave of applause.

The next morning James Bonamy drove to the last day of Fan Fair with Amy Jane and his parents. It had been a long week, but they were still on a high from James's performance.

"You know it's Father's Day Sunday," Robert said. "Last night you gave your dad the best Father's Day present any father's ever gotten."

The family rode on in silence, parked the car in V.I.P. parking, and walked toward the building complex where James had his booth. They turned a corner and saw a line reaching out of the building almost a city block long. They had no idea who could possibly generate such a huge crowd on the last day of Fan Fair. As they got nearer, the fans started shouting James's name and he knew they were waiting for him.

15

~

"Hometown Girl"

8:15 P.M.

At the very moment that Mary Chapin Carpenter would have walked onstage to sing her set on the great stage at Fan Fair, the singer sat in a great tent on the south lawn of the White House attending a state dinner in honor of Mary Robinson, the president of Ireland. Her escort was Francis Peter Gallagher, an Irish musician she was dating. Chapin had sung at President Clinton's inauguration and had been to the White House for dinners before. The Columbia Nashville artist was far more comfortable here among guests such as Caroline Kennedy Schlossberg, Meg Ryan, William Styron, Senator Edward Kennedy, Paul Newman, and Joanne Woodward than singing at Nashville Speedway in front of thousands of fervent country music fans. Chapin had only sung at Fan Fair once. It had been a monumentally unpleasant experience for her, schlepping through the fairgrounds, through the heat and the dust and the fans with their grasping familiarity.

Chapin was the least likely of country artists. It was not simply that she was a child of privilege and private schools. So were Kris

Kristofferson, an air force major general's son and a Rhodes scholar, and Gram Parsons, a Harvard dropout and scion of one of the wealthiest old families in the South. Both these artists sought to camouflage their past, shed the cloak of privilege, and forge new identities closely attuned to the world of country. Chapin, however, in most of her songs proclaimed herself an inhabitant of an urbane, introspective woman's world remote from the traditions of Nashville's music.

Chapin signed her Nashville record contract in 1986, at practically the nadir of country music sales. The tide was so low that a number of unique artists outside the country music mainstream walked unchallenged into Nashville, artists whose one commonality was that they were uncommon. Steve Earle, kd lang, Lyle Lovett, and Nanci Griffith all got record deals. Of this group only Chapin stayed on as a country artist, becoming so popular that by 1996 she had sold over eight million albums worldwide. She was equally a critical success, the 1992 and 1993 CMA Female Vocalist of the Year, and winner of five Grammy Awards.

Chapin neither grew up with country nor had the almost religious conversion that Emmylou Harris experienced, developing a deep, abiding faith in country music and a scholarly knowledge of its roots. Chapin had never liked country music especially. Though she now enjoyed some of the edgier acts, she was still far from a devotee of the genre. Most country artists made their homes or at least recorded in Nashville; Chapin lived in the Washington, D.C., area and produced her albums in a studio in Virginia.

What Chapin shared most profoundly with country music was her deep sense of loss of home and place and roots and belonging. It was a loss that linked this northern upper-middle-class woman who said that her ancestors had come on the *Mayflower* to the poorest southerner who had headed up that hillbilly highway.

Chapin was raised in Princeton, New Jersey, as idyllic a suburban community as exists in America. She was the third of four sisters; her brother, Chapin, died when he was an infant. To her, men would always be a peculiar, esoteric species they might not have been if her brother had lived to give her insight into the male sex. Her father was an executive with *Life* magazine, making the daily commute into Manhattan. She was one of the thousands of little girls with visions of pirouetting on ice at the Olympics, going out to the ice arena at all hours to train. When she was ten in June of 1968 and Robert Kennedy died, her father held her—as she would sing years later—"on his shoulders above the crowd to see a train draped in mourning pass slowly through our town."

A year later her family moved to Tokyo, where her father became publisher of the Asian edition of *Life*. Chapin was a child particularly vulnerable to the emotional insecurities of adolescence. She had suddenly been pulled out of her network of friends and a neighborhood to live in an exotic land.

Two years later the family returned to the United States, but life was never the same, and home was no longer home. Children can smell the death of a marriage even in air scented with the most extravagant of lies. Two years later her parents divorced, living separately in Washington, D.C. Chapin gave up skating in part because of the merciless pressure of competing. She went off to the prestigious Taft School in Connecticut, with new classmates who had their own tales of divorces and families living lies. "I used to believe . . . we'd grow just as tall and as proud as we pleased," she sang, "with our feet on the ground and our arms in the breeze under a sheltering sky." From the time she was a lonely teenager, Chapin did not believe that any longer.

Chapin sat here on the south lawn of the White House eating seared salmon, endives with roasted tomatoes, goat cheese, and Portobello mushrooms, and drinking California and Oregon wines and champagne, a menu infinitely preferable to the rude diets of Fan Fair. Chapin was not the only artist who disliked Fan Fair. Many stars felt they had been blackmailed into giving away a week of their lives for nothing. But they did it, shook the hands, signed the autographs, and sang their songs with smiles on their faces. Chapin not only did not show up, but she got away with it, the way none of the other women artists of country could, not Reba McEntire, not Faith Hill, not Lorrie Morgan, none of them. Chapin got away with it because her audiences were not the hard-core country fans here this week but upscale suburban/urban women more likely to buy Shawn Colvin or Tracy Chapman along with their Chapin than Shania Twain or Reba McEntire.

What Chapin shared most dramatically with the other women of country music was the freedom that came from being considered not as important as the men of country. The male country stars moved most of the product in the music stores and sold most of the seats in the arenas and fairs. Thus, Nashville paraded the men around as trophy artists, decked out in starched jeans and cowboy hats, their music often as limited as their outfits. For most of the history of country music women artists had rarely sold many records. So in the mid-eighties they were pushed off on the side to do their thing, and their thing was some of the most innovative country music of our time. From K. T. Oslin to Kathy Mattea to Rosanne Cash, they pushed the themes of the music to places they had not gone.

Chapin wrote an urbane feminist folk music in tune to the educated women of her age. There was no pedal steel, though perhaps an oboe or a flute. There were no easy crowd-pleasing avowals of eternal love, but words like "listless" and "whispered ecstasy." Her songs were a moral philosophy that millions of listeners, mainly women, hummed as their mantra of life.

In her musical persona, Chapin was the uncommon woman writ big. She was a savvy, independent woman of her time, who knows that love is rarely eternal but wants it nonetheless. She puts a dollar in a beggar's outstretched palm and hurries ahead holding her grand skim latte from Starbucks in the other hand. She lives on middle ground, successful, single, a woman who knows that "sometimes there's something missing." She struts alone into a bar in her dreams, watching Lyle Lovett and Dwight Yoakam fighting over her because "mmmmm I feel lucky today." She knows that there are always secret costs, and secret dues, and secret initiations in life, but she goes ahead because "I take my chances, I take my chances every chance I get, I take my chances."

President Clinton introduced Chapin and she moved gracefully forward to sing. Then she joined Mary Black, the critically acclaimed Irish singer, who sang some music from her native land. This was the artistic world where Chapin felt she belonged, singing before this glittery group of 380 guests, most of them prominent Irish Americans, not before rabid fans under the searing spotlights of the stage at the Nashville Speedway.

It was a Sunday evening in the winter of 1980, and twenty-one-year-old Chapin was singing the blues, wailing out, making up the lyrics as she went along. She was at the home of her closest friends, Reuben and Juli Musgrave. On most such evenings, Chapin and Reuben would have been down at Gallagher's on Connecticut Avenue in Washington singing folk songs. They called themselves "Junque Street," and they sang there for eighty dollars a night one weekend a month, standing on a tiny stage at the back end of this long, narrow dark room. It was just another bar with government workers, professionals, "Posties" (*Washington Post* reporters and editors), boozers, retirees, and the professionally lonely filling the tables and stools. But it was Chapin's and Reuben's musical home, and they cared immensely about it, cherishing each evening.

Reuben had been playing there longer than Chapin. He was an editor and consultant, who loved music so much that at the age of thirty-five he had decided to try to make a career performing. For a while he kept a part-time job as a copy editor at the *Washington Post*. He left that job to make his living, such as it was, totally from music. Reuben was a folksinger imbued with the prickly idealism and purity that are found so often among the music's adherents. Juli, his bride, was a nurturing woman who fancied making their home a musical Bloomsbury, where singers and songwriters could get together and celebrate their muse in word and song.

> These people are my best friends
> And if I can't be on their good side
> You know my life would probably end.

Chapin had brilliant improvisational gifts when she was around people who made her feel comfortable, and nobody made her feel more at home than Reuben and Juli. The three friends had met at Gallagher's. Sunday evening the pub featured an open mike night, when anyone could get up and sing a song or two. As a teenager when Chapin came home from the Taft School, she had sat around in her father's house writing songs that she recalled as "probably in adolescent angst. Moan for the guy you have a crush on, play your guitar like he's hearing it." Her father grew tired of the strumming and the wallowing songs of self-pity. Several years later when she returned from her studies at Brown University, he banged on her door one evening. "Would you just get out of here with your guitar?" he told his daughter.

Chapin headed down to open mike night at Gallagher's. She came in the back way, sang her songs with her eyes closed, and left as furtively as she had arrived, gone even before the applause had ended. Whenever she was in town, she returned and sang a few songs. She was a plump, disorderly young woman whose stringy long hair, baggy jeans, and sweaters and blouses with the shirttail out spoke of a person uncomfortable with her being. But there was a startlingly compelling quality to her. The male patrons, sitting over their beer and Scotch, looked up and listened intently when she took her turn, her melodies lingering in the air long after she disappeared out the back door.

Reuben listened to Chapin's commercial folk music, covering songs by Joni Mitchell, Joan Baez, Bonnie Raitt, and John Prine. It was close to the vein of music that Reuben was working, and he went up to Chapin one Sunday night and introduced himself. They were soon singing together, getting paid gigs at Gallagher's and elsewhere. They became an inseparable trio of friends even if Reuben was fifteen years older than Chapin and Juli five years older. Reuben was dating Juli, and Chapin served as a matchmaker, pushing the couple together. She was so close to the couple that she was there the evening that Reuben gave Juli an engagement ring. And at their wedding in the St. Joseph of Arimathea Chapel at Washington's National Cathedral, she was a member of the bride's party and sang a song she had written for them.

"Don't give me that finger, baby!" Chapin shouted, a momentary aside as she sang out, lyrics spilling out of her about her two friends and their evenings together singing songs. Reuben knew that Chapin was a superb talent, but as much as he valued her friendship, he found an inexplicable quality to the young woman.

When she had gone back to Brown that first year, he wrote her several letters, and she had never responded. It had seemed so strange, and he wrote her again asking what was wrong. Only then had she called, telling him: "Reuben, you mustn't worry if you don't hear from me for long periods of time. But that doesn't mean I'm not thinking about you."

Reuben began to realize that Chapin had lives within lives. Part of this was the way that children of divorce learn to compartmentalize their emotions, shuttling between their parents. Reuben saw her with both parents, her formal, austere mother and her more relaxed father, living with his new wife in a Washington suburb.

Chapin majored in American civilization at the Ivy League university, limiting her music largely to long late-night sessions by herself in her dorm room. She rarely performed her own songs in public. She was working hard at her writing, though, and she was learning that a person wrote best what she knew best.

Chapin next sang one of the few of her own compositions that she regularly sang solo when she and Reuben performed as Junque Street.

> Times I can remember
> it's always been so fine
> we sing til no more songs are left
> way past closing time.

The song was an exquisite piece of work. It was not about romantic love, for Chapin had not had a compelling love, and her love songs were more about yearning than unbridled emotion. It was not about pain, for what was her sorrow compared to what others felt? It was a song about her intimate life, about what mattered to her now. It was a lyrical testament to friendship. It was about people singing songs that said, no matter what their words, that life matters, that sadness was a gift too, and life was full of tiny losses and tiny gains. Reuben and Juli loved Chapin, and she loved them too, and this song helped to tie them so closely together that if ever they should part, it would be impossible to sever the bonds without cutting flesh and blood.

I sing a song of farewell
and memory is mine
as a northern city calls me back
but I leave my heart behind.

As the words ended, Chapin continued to play the haunting, emotive chords on her guitar. As she played, a whisper of another melody seemed to sound out of nowhere, like an echo of the song, carried back out of a world beyond. The sound grew louder, taking over the original melody, and Chapin began to sing:

Somewhere over the rainbow way up high
There's a place that I've heard of once in a lullaby.

It didn't matter who sang "Somewhere Over the Rainbow"; Judy Garland's rendition always hung there somewhere in the air. Not this evening. This evening Chapin was the only singer who had ever sung the song. The song had become nothing but a long lament. There was no place over the rainbow. There was not even a rainbow, only a few flashes in a darkening sky. It was so subtle and deep, slowed to a funeral dirge, full of terrifying poignancy.

Chapin always sang "Somewhere Over the Rainbow" as her encore at Gallagher's. Juli shuddered when she heard it. She had taken a job as the night manager at Gallagher's, and one evening she had leaned over the bar to Chapin and said, "Don't do it anymore, Chapin. You know how Judy Garland ended." And thus she stopped singing it.

If singing birds can reach so high
Beyond the rainbow
Why, oh why can't I?

Chapin spent intense evenings with her friends, and then she was gone off into another life. When she graduated from Brown in 1981, she moved back to Washington, where she continued playing gigs, much as she had while a student. She worked part-time at the Arca Foundation near Dupont Circle, the youthful hip/gay center of Washington. She lived in a room in a group home that was little different from her dormitory-like group house at Brown.

At Brown almost everyone had dressed in funky down-home garb. But when Chapin's classmates arrived in Washington for their first professional jobs, most of them metamorphosed into young professionals, wearing uniforms of suits and slacks that would likely be their workaday costumes until they retired. As for Chapin, if anything, she dressed even worse than she had at Brown, so purposefully disheveled that it was as if she were trying to turn her clothes into a philosophical statement.

Reuben cringed at the old painter pants and boots that Chapin insisted on wearing when they performed. She didn't get that some of the audience might take her dress as an insult. It was as if she didn't value them enough to wear something, anything, a caftan, anything but those dreadful pants and old shirt. Once when they had gotten a gig playing at a summer concert series at the C&O Canal in Georgetown, the organizer took one look at Chapin and said that she would never book Junque Street again.

Chapin was consumed with music, spending endless hours by herself working on her songs. She was disdainful about the compromises of pop and what she considered the crude banality of mainstream country music. In her sets with Reuben at one in the morning, when only the hard core and the drunks were sitting out there, Chapin pushed her partner to sing a nasty little parody of country music called "I've Got a Hundred Miles of Hard-on for You, Baby." Reuben got totally into it, capturing the cadences of a southern accent, mimicking every nuance.

Chapin knew she was not going to succeed as a pretty young thing, strumming a few chords on the guitar, singing silly love ballads. She taught herself to play guitar well, and she kept up diligently with her writing, honing down her songs to their essences. Up on the tiny stages at Food for Thought or Kramerbooks and Afterwords or the other little clubs and restaurants and bars where she performed for a few dollars a night, she started trying to trot out her own creations, like new children to the world. But the audience saw her as a Joni Mitchell/Judy Collins clone. "Sing 'Big

Yellow Taxi,'" they shouted. "How about 'Both Sides Now'?"

Chapin felt her blood pressure rising. It was likely time for a break and one of the Merit cigarettes that she chain-smoked. But she stood there and sang a new song to an uninterested room.

One night in February of 1982, Chapin was singing at a pub in upper Georgetown. During her break, a vivacious young woman came up to her. "I'm Ivy Harper," the woman said. "And you're wonderful! We've got this traditional Irish group. We call it the Hags. I'd love to have you join. We've lost our soloist, Grace Griffith, and you'd be perfect. We're doing the college circuit."

"Sounds interesting," Chapin replied. The next day she called to say yes, happy to pick up a new opportunity.

On her first performance with the Hags, Chapin drove up with the group to perform at Holy Cross College in Boston. On the long drive, Chapin was full of wit and candor, and Ivy and Chapin became fast friends. A few months later Chapin struck up a friendship with the newest member of the Hags, Erin McGovern, Ivy's childhood Nebraska friend, who was Chapin's equal as a musician. Chapin did not get along with the only man in the four-person group, a supremely able French fiddle player with an all-consuming interest in traditional Irish music. The fiddle player could not abide the way Chapin came bursting in at the last minute for their performances, rarely practicing with the group, sometimes not even adding harmonies to their songs. Then in the middle of the performance, Ivy pushed Chapin to sing a couple of *her* songs that had nothing to do with the music the group was supposed to be performing.

Chapin and the fiddle player became so bitterly estranged that Chapin quit the group but continued her friendship with Ivy. Chapin always seemed to have one special friend, and for a while it was Ivy.

On a Thursday evening in October of 1982 Chapin walked into the Class Reunion, a bar a few blocks from the White House that was a hangout of reporters, photographers, PR types, lobbyists, and politicos who liked to hang around the acerbic, gossipy world of journalism. She pushed through the usual crowd at the narrow bar and found the group brought together by Bill Danoff, a celebrated local songwriter whose credits including cowriting the John Denver hit "Country Roads" and the Emmylou Harris classic "Boulder to Birmingham."

Danoff was always trying to put people together and see what the chemistry produced. He called this group "Talking Eclectic" and it was indeed an eclectic group of songwriters, musicians, politicos, and bartenders. The idea was to sit here, drink heavily, talk hardily, and maybe even write a few song lyrics.

One of the regular participants, John Jennings, gave up his idea of writing a song this evening as soon as he saw Chapin striding up to the table. The thirty-year-old guitar player was an integral part of this Washington musical scene. He had had his own band, and played around with many of the major players. When he saw Chapin, he was smitten.

John bristled at the humiliating compromises of adult life. As fine a player as he was, John was more comfortable playing in what he and his friends called "the Starvation Circuit" than hustling to make it big-time. He had a natural and subtle musical sense, and he knew that there were at least half a dozen bands playing in D.C. good enough to make it nationally, if anybody had been looking. But John kept playing for twenty-five or so dollars a gig, running from Food for Thought to Mr. Henry's, wherever he and his buddies could get a gig.

Chapin joined him on the Starvation Circuit, playing her mix of folk music. John, like Chapin, was intense and passionate about music, and the two began a turbulent affair. In her musical partner, Chapin finally had someone who was her equal in intelligence, idealism, emotions, and musical self-absorption. And the very qualities that drew them together pulled them apart, in arguments nearly as bitter as their love.

Chapin often visited Ivy at home in the Washington suburbs and talked about her life. Since the Hags had broken up, Ivy was devoting herself to freelance writing for newspapers and magazines, and mothering her baby boy. At Ivy's, Chapin received regular doses of family and home and normality. Chapin tried to be a good and loving friend, one day bringing over a purple and white quilt for little Carlos Jr. Ivy was suddenly embroiled in all the duties of a young mother. Sitting at home concerned with diapers and dishes, she found it fascinating to hear Chapin's stories of life as a single woman and performer.

Chapin was full of sad stories of short-lived love affairs, of tortured family matters, confessions of lonely, unhappy days and nights. She would call late at night, or rush over to their home bursting forth in an overwhelming torrent of confession and agony, so much so that anyone who heard her thought that she would be struck down with despair for days. And then the next day she would be as bright and upbeat as a spring day, the memory of her anguish seemingly disgorged.

Hardly an evening passed when Chapin didn't give Ivy an impassioned monologue on John Jennings. John was the mentor who would help Chapin record her songs for the world. Sometimes he was the love of her life, and she spoke of him with romantic ardor. Other times she hated him, and she condemned him with words and feelings as strongly as she had vowed her eternal love.

No matter how angry Chapin might become, she and John had a brilliant musical rapport. Reuben had been Chapin's tutor before. Now John was leading her to places and musicians and opportunities she had not known before. As the months went by, those evenings at Gallagher's playing with Reuben in Junque Street seemed pathetic relics of her past. A wealthy patron of the bar offered to fund a recording of the duo. Reuben saw that as the great opportunity he had waited for these years, seeing himself and Chapin becoming the new Ian and Silvia, a prominent folk duo. Chapin pushed that idea away. She could not bring herself to talk honestly to Reuben, or even to ask Ivy's advice. Instead, she started putting down her duo partner.

"Reuben's guitar playing is a joke, Ivy," Chapin asserted one evening. "It's just delusion that he thinks he's going anywhere."

"Gosh, Chapin," Ivy replied, taken aback by her brutally caustic attitude toward her friend. "He may not be Eric Clapton, but he lives for music and has a great feel for traditional tunes."

"Yeah, I guess so," Chapin fumed dismissively, as if the matter was hardly worthy of discussion.

The two women changed the subject, but Ivy kept thinking about what Chapin had said. Ivy knew that she wasn't half the musician Reuben was. If Chapin was putting *him* down, God knows what she was saying about Ivy behind her back.

Juli had the disheartening premonition that Chapin might be merely using Reuben to advance herself. Onstage they were a duo, equals before the world, but offstage they were not. That was growing painfully clear. Reuben had neither Chapin's willful ambition nor her enormous talent, and Juli feared that she saw too clearly where their pathways were leading. She thought she glimpsed beyond the bend where their roads divided and Chapin headed off somewhere Reuben would never go.

Juli took Chapin out for dinner at Kramerbooks and Afterwords Cafe on Connecticut Avenue, where Chapin occasionally sang solo. "I don't want you to hurt Reuben, no matter what. Do you understand, Chapin?"

"Of course, I understand," Chapin replied. "I love you and Reuben. I would never never do that."

Chapin's romance with John continued for two emotionally tortured years. Finally, at the end of 1984, they realized that it was no good between them and ended their love affair. Three weeks later John was driving his car in his neighborhood in northern Virginia, just over the boundary line from Washington, when he saw Chapin's old car. Chapin waved her former lover over and rolled down her window.

"I feel terrible," she said.

"Well, I don't feel so good myself," John sighed. "But how can I help?"

"I want to make a record. Help me make a record."

John had never produced an album, but he took Chapin into his little sixteen-track studio in the basement of his home and started cutting tracks.

Chapin was still playing regularly with Reuben, but she was

getting all these other gigs, including spots at the Birchmere, the best folk and bluegrass club in Washington. After one of her evenings with Reuben in the fall of 1985, she told her longtime singing partner, "You know, Reuben, we should stop doing this regular Gallagher's thing."

Reuben looked squarely at Chapin, having heard the words he had been expecting for so long. He had his full quota of pride, and his reply was as quick as it was final. "Well, let's stop the whole thing."

The friendship ended that evening, not in recriminations and tears but in shrugs and silence, in two musicians putting their guitars away and walking different ways into the Washington night. Reuben had a baby daughter at home now, and the end of Junque Street was the end of much of his musical dreams. Juli was a fine photographer, and Chapin called and offered her the opportunity to do the cover on her album. Sometimes a small kindness is the greatest cruelty of all, and Juli turned Chapin down.

Ivy continued her friendship with Chapin. She heard the singer's sad disavowals that she never wanted her friendship with Reuben and Juli to end so badly. Ivy listened and gradually had the feeling that she was just a convenient repository for all Chapin's emotions. Confession is not the same thing as friendship, though Chapin counted it out like the hard currency of intimacy. Ivy had a husband, two toddlers, and a writing career, but Chapin rarely asked about her life.

After one falling-out, Chapin came over to the house to make her apology. When she knocked on the door, Ivy went up to an upstairs bedroom and sat on the bed. The knocking continued, but she just couldn't deal with her, not now, not today. Chapin left, and when she learned what Ivy had done, the friendship was never the same.

John believed in Chapin, and he recorded an album largely of Chapin's own songs. Chapin looked into her self for her songs, writing an emotional autobiography of a woman's life. The songs were often too long, and sometimes too precious, but her talent shone bright enough to interest several smaller labels, including

Rounder. Chapin was about to sign with the Boston-based label when her new manager, Tom Carrico, and his attorney partner, John Simson, got a call from Larry Hamby, an A&R executive at CBS Records–Nashville. Hamby had heard the tape and was willing to pick up the album and get it out into the market under the label's imprimatur.

In its initial release in 1987, *Hometown Girl* sold an embarrassing twenty-five thousand copies, enough to doom many artists' career. Roy Wunsch, the new president of the label, knew that all logic told him he should dump Chapin. Before doing so, he decided to hear her sing in person. He was impressed not only with her songs but with the way the audience related to her music. It was a gamble to let her cut another album, but Nashville was changing, and he had a hunch that Chapin was a direction worth heading.

Chapin and her brain trust had a justifiable mistrust of Nashville and what the powers of Music Row might do to her music. When she first started coming down to Tennessee to perform, the makeup artists attempted to do their thing on Chapin, piling up her hair, outlining her features in makeup. She and John joked about that but realized, as John said, that "country music is in many ways a cult of personality for people." Chapin could not continue standing onstage staring at her feet, mumbling half-heard asides between songs, looking like an unhappy graduate student. She lost weight, got a professional hairdo, started wearing dresses onstage, and developed her own persona and patter.

A singer such as Emmylou Harris considered an album a work of art that had to work seamlessly from beginning to end. Chapin and her producer didn't feel that way. To satisfy country radio, they threw a few songs on the albums that they thought of as mindless ditties. Up front Chapin was willing to make the kind of compromises that Emmylou would never have made. It was a more narrowly competitive world out there now, and Chapin understood what she had to do to succeed in that world. She did so while maintaining an image as an uncompromising purist.

The first song on her second album, *State of the Heart,* was "How Do," a song that John considered "crap but crap of a relatively high order, very clever crap." "How Do" did its job, becoming Chapin's first radio success, reaching number nineteen on *Billboard's* country singles chart. The song was about a woman who picks up a Texas cowboy in a Washington bar because she's "sort of in the mood to speak some French tonight." Ditty or not, the song introduced one major theme of Chapin's music. She almost single-handedly invented a whole subgenre of country music, the woman with an attitude. Here was this feisty, good-time-loving, butt-kicking, tough-talking, macho female, a woman with all the virtues of the traditional country woman but not putting up with male malarkey.

Chapin got some radio play, but the album was selling poorly. The business it was doing was primarily in the Northeast, hardly the hard center of country music. As Chapin's producer, John Jennings was as disappointed as the singer at the album's reception. He didn't know if it was going to work. Then one night they were playing at Poor David's Pub in Dallas. Afterwards, this old farming couple came up to the stage. They had driven a hundred miles to hear Chapin this evening. "We really love your songs," they told Chapin. "They're deep." John would never forget that evening and that old couple, and how they got it long before most others, and how he figured that one day others would get it too.

Roy Wunsch flew Irving Waugh, the producer of the annual CMA Awards show, up to Washington to hear Chapin sing. Waugh had been largely responsible for the idea both of Opryland and Fan Fair, and was one of the most influential people in the industry. Now he was playing a crucial role in choosing the artists to perform on the premier showcase in country music. Wunsch knew that Waugh would not possibly have Chapin on this year's show, but he wanted the producer to be introduced to her music now.

Seven months later, just before the 1990 CMA Awards show, Waugh called Wunsch at what since the Japanese takeover had become Sony Nashville, home of both the Columbia and Epic labels. "What was the name of that little girl you took me up to see in Washington?" Waugh asked. The executive producer had seen so many acts that sometimes they became like a parade of soldiers, one hardly distinguishable from the next.

"Chapin," the record executive replied. "Mary Chapin Carpenter."

"She did this song, 'Opening Act.' Think she'd do that on the show? I need something different."

"It's not even on her album, Irving," Wunsch replied. "But I'll see."

Wunsch knew that the producer's offer was not quite the gift it appeared. Of course, every artist wanted to be on the show. That was part of the problem. The Sony executive had other more prominent acts who wanted their shot on the awards show. The other artists would be royally unhappy. Chapin wasn't even nominated for an award, and unknowns did not sing full songs. Moreover, artists sang songs from their albums. That was the whole idea, to sell some product. Beyond that, the song that Wunsch wanted Chapin to sing was a cutting satire on the way headliners treated their opening acts. Chapin was already standing outside the fold. She might so alienate the audience that she could ruin herself in Nashville. That's how sensitive country music was to criticism.

Chapin turned the idea down. To her, "You Don't Know Me, I'm the Opening Act" was a foolish ditty that she had sung a few times primarily as a joke. A silly novelty song wasn't what *her* music was all about. The two men convinced her, and a week later she stood on the side of the stage wondering whether she was making a dreadful mistake.

"That was a nice career you had going out there," Ricky Van Shelton, a fellow performer, shouted as Chapin walked onstage.

Wunsch was almost as nervous as Chapin, but by the end of the first verse, he knew that she had them. The song resonated in the lives of most of the audience, and when she finished, she won a standing ovation. You had to be accepted to make fun of Nashville, and Chapin was accepted.

Retailers doubled their reorders of her album. Her fan mail increased four times. In New York City a few days later she did twenty-two interviews with the media. And all because of a song that she would never even think of recording.

★ ★ ★

Chapin had an image that she had no image. There seemed an authenticity about her that was lacking in many of the cowboys and cowgirls of Nashville, and the garish prima donnas of pop music. In her official biography she had gone from singing at open mikes to recording her first albums, her five years with Reuben in Junque Street and her time singing Irish music with the Hags all gone. She was real, hanging out in jeans and old shoes in her managers' office in Takoma Park, Maryland, on the back roads of the entertainment world. She was a proud Clinton Democrat, espousing no end of worthy causes from Earth Day to the Wilderness Society to AIDS to CARE. Her relationship with her managers, Tom Carrico and John Simson, was like no other business relationship in country music. They stayed as far from Nashville as she did. They shared her values. They believed in her both viscerally and intellectually. They were shrewd deal makers, working to protect what they saw as the integrity of her vision. It was almost impossible to envision Chapin without them.

When she was home in her apartment in Alexandria, Virginia, Chapin sat for hours and wrote her songs. She looked within herself and within her life, and she wrote what she saw and felt. Chapin, like many women of her time, had set out on a road marked freedom, a journey along unmarked roads with as many hollows as passages above the plains of life. Truth was always solace to those who would listen, and millions of women did listen. Chapin's sisters had babies now, and she was the maiden aunt on the cusp of middle age. In "Middle Ground," she captured the quiet anguish of a thirty-three-year-old single woman with a career and the unheralded courage of a human being who "could be safe and sound, Oh, to know middle ground." Chapin had her short-lived love affairs, but nothing seemed to last. There was a poignant aloneness in a song such as "When She's Gone," the tale of a woman who realizes that "when she's gone you won't miss her."

Chapin exhorted her listeners to go on, to dare, to care, to feel, to live. "Everything we got, we got the hard way," she sang. "Show a little passion, baby, show a little style." Those who cared and felt the most dared to go on, to live, and one day perhaps to love. "Come on, come," she coaxed musically. "It's getting late now."

Life was out there, up those uncharted pathways. "I take my chances," she sang. "I don't mind working without a net."

It had been a struggle trying to record *her* album. One evening label executives took her to dinner to tell her that on her third album, they wanted to add a duet with Joe Diffie, a Sony artist on the Epic label. That would give it a little oomph with the hard-core country audience. Chapin sat there crying, but her tears did no good, and the cut ended up on the album.

When the album was about to be delivered, she drove out to the house of a label executive with whom she felt an unquestioned rapport. They sat there in his living room listening to the songs. The executive told Chapin how honored he was to be one of the first to hear her album. "These are great, just great," he told her earnestly.

"Then why am I so unhappy?" she asked. "Why am I so fucked up?"

That was a question that perplexed all who were around her. Chapin drew everyone near her into the psychodrama of her life, even this label executive more used to dealing with questions of market share than those of emotional stability. He was discovering what many soon realized about the singer. People sucked into her life might at first be flattered by her seeming revelations, but they soon learned the emotional costs of being around her.

Chapin suffered not from mere unhappiness but from a merciless depression. That was her dark friend who came visiting unannounced. She didn't know when he would arrive, how long he might stay, or if he might never leave. Chapin could talk about mood-changing antidepressant drugs the way a wine connoisseur discussed the vintages of Burgundy. She admitted to the London *Daily Telegraph* that "she has suffered most of her life from clinical depression." "Early on, I thought I was just moody, but I've learnt to accept it as a part of me," she told the British paper in 1994. "I've constantly struggled with depression," she admitted to the *Vancouver Sun* a year later. "There are times it's gotten so bad that I don't even know who I am anymore. . . . Call it chemical imbalance or seasonal disorder or whatever—you find yourself in a low spot for some reason or other."

In her songs Chapin might sing about a woman throwing off the cloak of the past and dancing into the future, but as often as not she sat shrouded in darkness. At the end of December 1993, Chapin flew down to Hilton Head, South Carolina, to attend the annual four-day Renaissance Weekend, which with the election of one regular attendee, Bill Clinton, had become the most sought-after seminar in America. Chapin put on a tag with her name on it and mingled with such guests as Supreme Court Associate Justice Harry Blackmun and Federal Reserve Board chairman Alan Greenspan. Most of the guests were adept at the *pas de deux* of intimacy danced by the new President and his associates, creating a hardy illusion of spontaneity while giving away little of themselves. At the session in which Chapin spoke, she played it straight, talking about what mattered to her. She talked about her depression.

"Music has just always been the most important thing to me, and now all of a sudden I was in a position to have it be more than a hobby," she said, remembering her remarks right afterwards. "So I'm playing music and things are going great and my records are starting to sell, and it's like, gee, this is wild. So there I am, sort of in the midst of all that and the point I would describe is, be careful what you wish for, because all of a sudden I was just getting so stressed out."

Chapin found it emotionally exhausting to deal with the endless intrusions of fame. She could not abide people, attention, demands. That was in part why an event like Fan Fair was so bothersome in its demands. "It's the artifice that goes along with a lot of the 'star' stuff that I'm uncomfortable with," she confided to Robert K. Oermann in the *Nashville Tennessean.* "There's a sort of 'glam' factor to the care and feeding of a career in show business. I'm not saying that everybody's phony and unauthentic, or that it's all a bunch of bullshit, but there are times when I feel uncomfortable with it. I think my resistance to it comes from a desire to be invisible. I want to do good work and show up when I feel comfortable, yet disappear when I feel like doing that as well."

Chapin's fourth album, *Come On Come On,* sold triple platinum, making Chapin one of the premier stars of country music.

She could no longer choose to dance in and out of the spotlight at will, especially when her whole persona was that she was taking her audience into the private recesses of her life. Her producer, John, called her PBS documentary concert an "invitation to intimacy," and that was the image she was creating.

Despite all Chapin's fears of intrusion, she was standing on a stage creating the illusion of entry into the most private portions of her psyche. It was no wonder, then, that people felt they knew her and that she was living their life and they were living hers.

The road of success Chapin was traveling had no exits. She either went ahead or she went backward. Only a few years before, Chapin had stood on the stage at the CMA Awards show and satirized the sad lot of the opening act. Now she was the headliner, and her opening act was only one of her burdens. Night after night she was responsible for filling these great arenas, her success or failure measured in how many seats she filled. Her music was far better suited for a club, or a small theater, but success meant size, and her audiences often only got an echo of the experience they might have had in a smaller venue. The road itself was a merciless place for a single woman of a certain age, her days measured out in tedium and books and videos, living for the two hours on the stage each evening.

For all its drawbacks, success bought what Chapin wanted professionally above everything else: artistic freedom. She was now the biggest artist on the two Sony Nashville labels. With the eventual three million sales of *Come On Come On,* the new leadership at her label let her and John alone to create the album they wanted to create. The result, *Stones in the Road,* Chapin's fifth album, was in many respects her finest achievement. "Why Walk When You Can Fly?" she asked her listeners. But she also picked up darker colors on her palette, painting more with shades of black and gray.

Columbia shipped the album out in enormous quantities, promoting *Stones in the Road* with a powerful marketing campaign. The album received generally excellent reviews, winning the Grammy Award for Best Country Album of 1994. *Stones in the Road* became Chapin's first number one on the *Billboard* country album chart, staying there for three weeks. As the world looked at it, Chapin had traveled even further up that road of success. She knew, however, that hundreds of thousands of albums were coming back from the record stores across America, and it was a devastating disappointment. In the end the album sold only about a third of *Come On Come On,* hurting the profits at Sony Nashville and Chapin's relationship with the new leadership.

Chapin had begun as a singer with no idea of becoming a mainstream commercial artist. Now what a few years ago would have been considered success beyond success had become a failure that put the whole future direction of her career in question and made the burden of her next album enormous.

Erin McGovern, Chapin's friend from the days in the traditional Irish group, the Hags, had kept in touch with her musical comrade. Erin was back studying at the University of Nebraska, but as Chapin's career took off, Erin journeyed forth wherever within a day's hard driving she could hear the singer. Erin had the feeling that Chapin was lonely, and viewed Erin's frequent visits as a treat, a time to laugh and let down, two women friends hanging out. Erin was studying architecture at the university, although she was still playing and singing in a successful regional group. Chapin was not only a friend but her touchstone to the larger world of music.

In August of 1994, Erin received a call from Mary Beth Aungier, Chapin's road manager, asking her if she would like to go on the road as Chapin's guitar tech for the 1995 tour. The woman whom Chapin called her "Head Concierge" said she and Chapin had been talking about how they wanted more women in the crew and that Erin would fit in perfectly.

Erin didn't even have to think about what to do. The chance to go off with Chapin for a year broke the scale. She ran around Lincoln telling her friends, dropped out of college, bought new clothes and suitcases, and sat waiting around for Mary Beth's next call.

Erin wasn't much of a pusher. Eventually, she called Mary Beth at her office in Takoma Park. Mary Beth was never there, or at least never took her calls, and Erin kept trying. After the first of the year,

Erin left a more urgent call on Mary Beth's machine: "Mary Beth, I've got to know just when you need me. What's the deal?"

A few days later Erin came home and found a message from Mary Beth on her answering machine saying that Chapin had decided to go with Bob Dylan's former guitar tech.

Erin thought that she had learned most of the hard lessons about human beings that life has to teach, but she was devastated. She *believed* in Chapin, in the truths of her music, and the truths of her life. It stunned her that the singer could be so cavalier about another human being. From then on whenever she heard a Chapin song, she felt it resonated with hypocrisy and sham. "I take my chances, I pay my dollar and I place my bet," Chapin sang. Erin had taken her chances and placed her bet on Chapin, and she had lost months of her life and whole chunks of her faith in human beings.

Chapin hadn't called. She had left it to an underling. Erin thought about a lawsuit, or doing something, somehow showing Chapin that she could not treat another human being that way. But that was not Erin.

In March, Erin flew to Washington for a reunion of the Hags at the Birchmere. Chapin had been invited, but she never responded. The early evening following their performance, Erin and Ivy were driving around their old Washington neighborhood. Ivy turned the corner onto Connecticut Avenue when she almost struck a woman walking slowly across the intersection, a baseball cap propped on her head. The woman looked up startled, and Ivy realized it was Chapin.

Chapin waved the car over. Ivy and Erin got out of the car and embraced their old friend. It had been eight years since Ivy had seen Chapin. She recalled that one of the last times she had seen the singer, Chapin had tried to hit Ivy and her contacts up for money to help back her demo tape. Now she was famous and rich. As for Erin, she was one of these people who didn't consider that she had a right to anger. She tagged along with the two other women and their rich reminiscences.

"My house is right there, up the street," Chapin said. "Why don't you come on over?"

The three women walked up the pathway toward the imposing

yellow house that Chapin had recently purchased for $700,000. In the foyer, Chapin looked down. "Do you hate me, Erin?" she asked plaintively.

"No, Chapin, I suppose everything happens for a reason."

Chapin led them into the spacious living room.

"I'm sure you'll have a better career in architecture than as a guitar tech with me," Chapin said, as if to dismiss the whole unfortunate matter in a philosophical aside.

Erin wasn't buying. "Well, it hurt my feelings," Erin said. That was right too. It wasn't the time she lost, the embarrassment, the uncertainty. It was her feelings, her sense of betrayal.

Chapin turned to look at Erin as if she knew the direction this was going and didn't want to go there. "Well, here is my new painting," she said, turning toward the enormous oil on the wall over the fireplace in a baroque frame.

Erin was startled that Chapin could write songs of such deep moral statement and yet dismiss another's life or time. "Did I have bad breath or what?" Erin asked suddenly, a seeming non sequitur.

Chapin usually prepared in advance to answer difficult queries, but now she fumbled for an answer. "At first when Mary Beth and I talked about it, I saw myself like in the old days. I forget how big I am."

Erin and Ivy left that evening full of a sense of melancholy and loss. They had once admired Chapin so much that they had promoted her to everyone they met. They had championed her, and in doing so thought they were championing everything that was good and noble in music and life. Erin had that midwestern sense of language. A word was a word. It meant what it said. She found it hard to understand how the words of Chapin's songs and the words of her life could be so different. As for Ivy, over the past few years she had thought sometimes that she and Chapin would reconnect one day, that they still had so much in common. But Chapin had gone to a place so far from her two old friends that it was as if she had moved to a different galaxy, a brilliant distant star or a black hole.

Chapin's comanagers, Tom and John, had come all this way with her. They had gotten their share of midnight phone calls.

They had believed. She left them now too, and went with a high-powered Los Angeles company. John Jennings continued to coproduce Chapin's albums and travel with her on the road, but he moved down to Nashville to make his own career as a producer and singer, and he was not there for her any longer, not the way he once had been. As for Sony Nashville, she had no one there with whom she had a trusting relationship. She still had close friends like Wendy Franklin and her husband comedian, Chip Franklin.

On her 1995 tour Chapin went on the road with the Mavericks, the hippest band in country music, as her opening act. They could be a rude, difficult lot, especially Raul Malo, the lead singer. Chapin became so disenchanted with the group that she almost fired them. On the last evening of the tour, the Mavericks had their little revenge, horrifying her by prancing onstage during her set in boxer shorts. Their piano player ripped off his shorts to reveal that he was wearing a black velvet G-string that he had purchased at Victoria's Secret.

Chapin had once had a marvelous sense of humor, but she was not amused. Chapin was a musical philosopher who turned away from her own words. "I take my chances," she sang, but she didn't take her chances, not any longer, not when it came to Erin, not when it came to the songs she was writing for her new album. "Why walk when you can fly," she sang, though she was a swan traveling with clipped wings.

Chapin's last album had been such a disappointment that Sony Nashville was telling her what to do now, what songs to add to her new album. As she sat writing new songs for her album, she was putting on a great deal of weight. There was no longer the energy in her music, no longer the journey upward. She was a thirty-eight-year-old woman, struggling to maintain her stardom. There was a scent of nostalgia creeping into her songs, and nostalgia was the death of creativity. Her sixth album was coming out in the fall. The title song, "A Place in the World," was about a place no longer out there, somewhere up that distant road. It "could be right before your very eyes. . . . When I'm sure I've finally found it gonna wrap these arms around it."

★ ★ ★

It was Palm Sunday, and Chapin was sitting alone at an outdoor table at Starbucks on Connecticut Avenue a few blocks from her home. As she sat there, her nose in the *Washington Post,* Reuben and Juli Musgrave and their three children brushed past Chapin, walking into the café for coffee. They were out in their Sunday best after church. Reuben didn't play much anymore, but every Sunday morning he performed a folk mass at the Washington National Cathedral. He sang each Sabbath in the same chapel where he and Juli were married and Chapin had sung her song in their honor.

The couple rarely talked about Chapin and Junque Street any longer. These were the best moments now, these good simple times, the family together, out for a stroll.

As they entered the café, both Reuben and Juli saw Chapin there with her dog. They hadn't seen her for years. She was dressed the way she had when she had started out, in rumpled pants, a threadbare sweater, and an old baseball cap. As they stood waiting for their coffees, Chapin got up, pulled her cap down even further over her eyes, and shambled homeward, clutching her papers.

Reuben and Juli touched each other and thought how sad and lonely Chapin appeared, and how lucky they were to have each other, three children, and a life full of friends.

Out on the south lawn of the White House, Chapin and Mary Black were singing a few songs to end the evening. The final song was a traditional Irish song often sung in pubs at the end of the evening. Chapin knew the song because the Hags always sang it to end their performances.

> Kind friends and companions
> Come join me in rhyme.
> Come lift up your voices
> In chorus with mine.
> Let us drink and be merry
> All grief to refrain
> For we may and might never
> All meet here again.

"Weren't they wonderful tonight?" President Clinton asked rhetorically. "They made us all so happy. . . . I thank you Mary Chapin Carpenter. Thank you, Mary Black. Thank you, gentlemen. It was a wonderful evening."

As Chapin left the White House, the thousands of fans were still out there on the fairgrounds listening to country music. She walked among the guests in their tuxedos and fancy gowns, as far from the world of Nashville as she was from her first night at Gallagher's so long ago.

16

~

"You Don't Even Know Who I Am"

9:17 P.M.

Night had finally fallen, and the heat had disappeared like an intruder slinking away into the darkness. It had become one of those evenings of late spring when the world looks best from a porch, a stoop, or a seat at an outdoor concert. As the Fan Fair audience sat there enjoying the spring almost as much as the music, Patty Loveless walked onstage. At the age of thirty-nine, Patty was at the height both of her musical life and of her beauty. She was five feet six inches tall, with moist green eyes that looked as if they were on the verge of tears, reddish brown hair dyed from the natural brown, pouting lips and an expressive face that had a slightly exotic cast. She did not have the waiflike body of the young female artists of the new country, but a woman's nourishing form. She wore an elegant white pantsuit, the kind of outfit that until a few years ago would not have been considered appropriate dress for a country star.

Patty hated to be part of these massive shows where you did a couple numbers and got off hardly before you began. She called such performances "wire and fire." She wasn't the kind of singer who worked well that way. She didn't jump around the stage. She wasn't much good at making patter with the audience either. She just stood there and sang, and for the most part she liked to sing ballads.

This evening Patty came onstage singing an up-tempo number. Singer after singer had tried to flail the audience alive, but for the most part much of the audience just sat there.

"What a beautiful night," she said, after she had finished her first song. "There are a lot of country fans out there. On all the albums I've done I've tried to stay true to the roots of country music I grew up with, George Jones and Loretta Lynn. So we're going to do some real traditional country music right here."

No woman singer of her generation sang hard-core country music as true and as deep as Patty did. Both Wynonna and Reba had in some measure left the music, while Patty stayed where she was, her feet placed firmly in the tradition. Her band began, and it was like the sound of wind whining down from the mountainside. The audience was ready to listen and to feel, and by the time she sang the first note, a great expectant hush had come over the vast audience.

> You said you didn't want to see me
> But you've been lookin' for me everywhere
> And you know that you're gonna find me
> If you keep on drinkin' fast
> 'Cause honey I'm right there waitin' on you
> At the bottom of the glass.

Patty couldn't sing it if she didn't feel it, and she couldn't feel it if she hadn't experienced it, or seen someone else live it. She had felt this song back when she was sometimes drinking a quart of bourbon a day, mixing it with uppers and downers. On those dread days she had seen the devil in the bottom of a bottle. She was so hard on herself, harder than anybody else, and sometimes she felt she had become nothing but another sad little piece of poor white trash. That was over ten years ago now. She didn't drink much or do drugs any longer, but she was a witness to that time and to that life, as she was a witness to so much.

Patty was born the sixth of seven children to John and Naomi Ramey outside Pikeville, Kentucky, in January of 1957. Her cousin lived with the Rameys too, treated like another sister. Patty lived not along the macadam highways snaking through eastern Kentucky but up a rutted dirt road in Belcher Holler. As a child Patty slept in a bedroom first with her brothers and then with her mother. Her dreams were her only private room, the place she could go where no one could follow. She walked out by the creek bed and by the trees. She hiked up in the mountains and sat there scarcely bothered by the lizards and the snakes.

Patty grew up in a world full of terrible fatalism. Life blossomed in the sweet spring of youth. Adulthood was often like a dark shroud, hardscrabble days and nights, bodies broken down with kids and coal dust. Old cars often stayed where they died beside a house or pushed into a creek bed.

In the coal mine where Patty's father worked, the union complained about the company's lack of concern for the miners' safety. The miners, however, shared the blame. They often ignored precautions and new safety measures, sticking with the way they had always done things. They figured it didn't matter. Life would get you anyway.

Younger miners scrubbed the coal dust off after their shifts, but Patty's father was of a generation where the black soot was always there. Friday night he took a bath and washed himself with strong detergent powder, but it still stayed in his pores, his skin a pallid gray. John Ramey had gone into the mines healthy at the age of eighteen, and he left sick at forty-two, broken down with black lung disease. His cough sounded through the house, tolling the wages of his years. The family lived on Social Security until he got black lung benefits.

Patty was blessed with a wonderfully melodious voice. She was so shy, though, that when her mother asked Patty to sing, she stood alone in one room letting only her voice carry her to the next. Patty came from a big family, but she had no one she dared talk to about the things that mattered. She wasn't about to ask her father, and her mother seemed embarrassed about so much. Her mother had quit school when she was eleven, and she seemed shut off from so much of life beyond. Patty thought, "Well, it's like we don't want nobody to know our business. We don't want nobody to know truly how we feel."

When Patty had her first period at the age of nine, her cousin told her what it was or she would have been scared plain through. On another occasion she was watching a movie on TV with her mother. The couple started kissing, keeping at it until the man had his tongue in the woman's mouth. Soon after that, the woman was pregnant.

"See, there, you do those kinds of things, that's just what's gonna happen to you," her mother told her. Patty wasn't about to ask more about "those kinds of things," but when a boy kissed her, she was sure that she had gone and done it, gotten pregnant and ruined her life.

Patty wasn't much for boys, though. She was her daddy's daughter, and it was from him that she learned her love of country music. She loved her daddy and it hurt her so to see the life draining out of him. It wasn't just the black lung anymore, it was the heart, and when Patty was twelve, the family moved to Louisville in search of better medical care. That journey from the mountains to the plains, from the country to the city, was the epic journey that gave country music much of its soul. Almost every country artist had set out on that road. Jimmie Rodgers had taken it. Hank Williams had taken it. Patsy Cline had taken it. And now Patty Loveless took it, looking back on these years in Kentucky as a time of peace and security that she would never again know. There had always been food on the table, even if often it had only been potatoes and greens. And there had always been love in the heart.

"I'll always hold those days dear to me because they were the best days of my life," she reflected years later. "Those days that came after, you know there were some good days. But as I learned to become an adult, I was faced with a lot of tough times because of bad decisions I made. And I think to this day that maybe there was a part of me going, 'Okay, God said all right it's time for you to really learn about life. And for you to appreciate what you really have, it's time for you to learn about hardships just like your mom and dad did.'"

Patty was a poor country girl, and the Rameys moved into the poor part of Louisville. The day Patty walked into school, the other children took her measure. She spoke with an eastern Kentucky mountain accent, with the almost archaic intonations that remained in that isolated region. Her speech was riddled with grammatical errors. She dressed poorly even among the poor.

Children don't wrap their cruelty up and pretend it is something else, and they much prefer to kick someone who is lying down than go after someone standing up. Patty became a game target for her classmates. They mocked her clothes. They mimicked her speech. She did her best to get rid of that mountain speech, the cadence so slow that people figured she was dumb. They drove her deeper and deeper into her shyness, adding to her secret pain. After a while, she began to realize that she wasn't the only country girl that they made fun of, and these scorned children became her friends.

The Rameys had come down from the mountains, but the mountain life had come with them. They had friends from Kentucky and they had the music they had always loved. Saturday night Patty listened to the Grand Ole Opry while her mother washed the floors. She loved those old soulful sounds.

At the age of twelve, Patty drove over to Fort Knox with her mother, her big sister, Dottie, and three of her brothers to visit their brother, Wayne, who was in the army. They sat with Wayne at a serviceman's club, talking about life in Kentucky and half listening to a country band. "I got a daughter that sings," Mrs. Ramey said to the guitar player. "It looks like you need a girl singer."

"Well, bring her on up," the musician said. "Give her a try."

Patty always remembered how Dottie had looked that day, wearing a brown suit, the color matching her long dark hair. To her little sister, Dottie was as beautiful as any of those Hollywood stars. Dottie got up and belted out "Walking After Midnight." It was as if Patsy Cline had come in that door and walked up on the stage.

Patty's eyes swept the room. She saw all those soldier boys looking up there as if they had fallen in love. Dottie had a rich, smoky, evocative voice, and in this dark little club, she owned those soldier boys. Patty loved Dottie as everything she would like to be. That day Patty decided that she too would like to be on a stage, doing what Dottie was doing.

Dottie and her brother Roger Ramey often sang together as a duo. Roger was not much of a singer, but he had this bold drive that seemed left out of the genes of the other Rameys. When Dottie went and got herself married, Roger figured that his sister Patty could be the one to sing and get them a musical career.

Roger pushed Patty out onstage for the first time when she was twelve years old at a little country jamboree in Louisville. It was only a bunch of foldout chairs in a little auditorium, but as terrified as Patty felt, she could have been about to step out on the stage of the Grand Ole Opry. She broke into hives. She didn't belt them out like her sister, but the audience loved this little girl singing with the emotions of a woman.

Patty walked off that stage knowing she loved it, loved the applause, and loved the five dollars they put in her hand, the first money she ever earned. She and her brother became the Swinging Rameys, traveling around Kentucky playing at jamborees.

Patty remained an extraordinarily introverted young woman who among strangers found peace and openness only on the stage, lost in the folds of her music. She had a natural reticence that gave her dignity. Words meant much to her. She tended to use them sparingly, as if she had been given only so many. Her dreams were still her best friends, and she began turning those dreams into songs. She was only a child, but she was writing adult songs that seemed drawn out of the life of a woman who had lived and loved.

Roger believed that Patty was the bus ticket to their fortune. At the age of fourteen, they drove down to Nashville. Porter Wagoner was as big a star as there was in Nashville. That didn't stop Roger from barging into his offices and getting the singer to sit there long enough to listen to a few of Patty's songs. Patty sang him a song that she had recently written called "Sounds of Loneliness":

Hear the sounds of loneliness
Hear the sounds all around
Since you've gone and left me alone
I just hear these sounds from now on
And they grow louder and louder and louder.

The song was a lament that sounded as if it was echoing through the hills. A fourteen-year-old could get onstage and mimic the emotions of a singer thrice her age. But nobody can fake songwriting. Patty had poured all of her loneliness and pain into song. It was a testament to her life. Oh, how her father loved that mournful song. Whenever they sat in the kitchen, with Patty strumming the guitar he had given her, she played it for him. And whenever she and Roger performed and her dad was there, she sang it for him, and he was happy in the sadness.

Porter loved it, too. The country star thumped his hand on the desk and said that he was going to help her out. He introduced her to Dolly Parton, who performed with Porter and played on his syndicated television show. Dolly was already a major star, but she reached down to Patty and embraced her, teaching the teenager how to wear makeup and what to watch out for in the dangerous Nashville world. There would come a day, not far in the future, when Dolly would leave and go to Hollywood. There would come a day too when Dolly would appear this buxom cartoon figure, who had so much plastic surgery that it was impossible to tell what was real, what was half real, and what was only silicone and artifice. Patty knew the real Dolly was a country girl who treated Patty like a little sister, with gracious concern and goodness. That became young Patty's model of what a country star should be, part of Dolly's lasting legacy of those years.

At the age of sixteen, Patty started singing with the Wilburn Brothers, a successful country band. Their girl singer, Loretta Lynn, had just left them to go on to solo stardom. Doyle Wilburn, the leader, was slowly grooming Patty to replace her. He held her publishing contract too, for he knew that Patty could write a good country song. Patty traveled with the band on weekends and when school was out. Doyle looked upon Patty like a daughter.

He protected her in a suffocating embrace. At home her parents insisted that her brother chaperon her on dates, and on the road Doyle was another constant guardian. Traveling with the band she was an entertainer living in the spotlight, but back in Louisville she was just this shy teenager, rarely speaking in class.

In the world that Patty came from, there were good girls and there were bad girls. The road between them led only one way. A young woman got a reputation, and got pregnant, and that was the end of the story. Her family wanted something different for Patty. They wanted her to get out, to break away, not end like Dottie living with a bad marriage and good memories.

Patty had been brought up to obey, and obey she did. Upon graduation from high school, Patty moved to Nashville and continued going out on the road with the Wilburn Brothers. Doyle was like many successful Nashville performers, a twopenny entrepreneur with all kinds of businesses. When the group wasn't on the road, Doyle shuttled Patty between his various enterprises, having her wait tables at one of his restaurants, other times setting her down clerking in Music Mart USA, his record store.

Patty was eighteen years old, out on the road singing about broken hearts and passionate love. The pleasures on the road are for the most part quick and furtive, taken when and where you can. Patty noticed the new drummer, Terry Lovelace, from the moment he arrived. Terry came from the mountains of North Carolina, and before long the two of them got together. Twenty-two-year-old Terry was a simple, plainspoken mountain man, like many of the men whom Patty had known from Pikeville. He had a musician's soul, with no thought in life but to keep going from gig to gig.

Living a musician's life, Terry had had plenty of women, but from the moment he met Patty he knew that this was different. Twenty years later he could still remember every nuance of those days, how "naive and innocent" she was, "a babe in the woods," and how "she touched me in a way never before." He could tell that she "felt hounded by all these lecherous old guys." He had no great ambition in life except to love her, and when he was back at his home in Kings Mountain, North Carolina, he wrote her love letters.

Patty warned her new boyfriend that they had to be discreet, but their secret soon got out.

"I hear you're seeing this drummer," Doyle told her.

"Yeah," Patty replied, never much of a liar.

"I'm tellin' you right now, Patty," Doyle said paternally, "I'm not going to have it."

"You're not going to have it!" Patty exclaimed, for the first time standing up to her patron.

"No. I'm not," Doyle said definitively. "I don't want you to see him anymore."

Patty turned and walked away thinking, "I must feel for Terry, or I must love him, because I'm so angry."

Patty called it love, but love was sex and loneliness and friendship and excitement all compounded together. Beyond that, she was angry, not only at Doyle but her parents, her brother, all of them. "These people are going to stop telling me what to do," she thought. "I'm tired because people have been telling me what to do all my life." She didn't reflect that maybe Doyle was right, maybe Terry wasn't right for her, maybe she was on the verge of a great career that she was jeopardizing with a silly affair.

Patty called Terry and he drove up from North Carolina in his old Ford van to get her and bring her home to Kings Mountain. He would have stayed with her in Nashville if that was what she wanted, but she wanted out, to have her own life. And so on her nineteenth birthday, in the dead of winter, they drove east to North Carolina. She told Terry that Doyle had threatened her that if she left him, he would see that she would never succeed as a singer in Nashville. She didn't care anymore, or so she thought. She wanted what she called her own life.

For six months, Patty lived in what her Baptist church called sin. And for six months, Patty cried, wondering what she had done. Doyle asked her to come back, but she felt the tentacles of his control reaching out for her again, and she turned him down. She came from a culture of shame. She knew that she could not live like this for long, shacking up, disgracing her parents and all they stood for and believed. So nineteen-year-old Patty married Terry.

Terry didn't treat his wife any worse than did many of the men

he knew in Kings Mountain, and he probably treated her a lot better. He loved her. She was his proudest possession, and he wanted
her to become fully part of his world. For a while she worked as a
waitress in his mom's restaurant, while he played with his band.
When their girl singer quit, he figured Patty could take over. That
was about all he wanted in life, to play the drums in a band, to live
with Patty, to party with his friends, and to see his kinfolk.

The newlyweds lived in a trailer and played in a circuit around
North Carolina. The state had strict liquor laws, and for the most
part Patty and her husband played in illegal juke joints that served
liquor by the drink. The patrons were a rowdy bunch. Patty sang
covers of rock songs, a lot of Linda Ronstadt and Bonnie Raitt, and
the other hits of the day, occasionally throwing in a country song.
For Terry this was a good life, and he felt it was a good life for Patty
too. She wanted to be good and do right. She started to drink and
to pop uppers and downers. She aged the way many women aged
in Appalachia, as if they had been left outside, their skin weath-
ered. She had been somebody in Nashville, but nobody knew that
or cared.

Patty couldn't go home again, for she bore the darkness of her
life in her face. In August of 1979, her father called. "When do you
think you're going to be able to come home?" he asked.

"Daddy, I'm really working a lot and it's so far to drive and I
tried to buy a plane ticket, but I guess I'm trying to wait till things
get better."

Her father listened a moment. "Well, OK, try to make it home
if you can."

Patty went to her rehearsal for a club date. When she got home
the phone was ringing. "Patty, I got some news for you," her mother-
in-law said. "Well, your father died."

Her daddy was gone and she had not been there. That was a
pain that sat there at the bottom of the heart and never went away.

Twenty-two-year-old Patty became pregnant. She had
dreamed of a child, but not in this world. She was popping drugs
and drinking up to a quart of booze a day, and she feared for any
child she would bring into this sad world. She feared that her body
was this vessel of unhealth, and she might bear a sickly child

unable to stand up to the winds of life. She feared too for the life of any child of hers brought up in the emotional squalor of her life. She saw two choices in front of her, and she knew that both of them were terribly wrong. One was to have the child, and the other was not to have it.

The day Patty drove off with Terry to the abortion doctor, she did not do so as if this were an act of no consequence, merely a medical matter. Her grandfather was a Baptist preacher, and she had heard too many fiery sermons to do this easily, or ever to forget. She knew that she was doing something that she wanted kept secret, between her and Terry and God, something for which she knew she would have to ask God's forgiveness.

Even the booze couldn't hide the world from her anymore. The police started busting the clubs, raiding them and shutting them down. Once the police arrested her, put her in handcuffs, and shoved her toward the door and into the patrol car.

"What'd I do?" Patty asked.

"You're playing in the club here, lady," the sheriff told her. "You're aidin' and abettin'."

"So this pool table here is aidin' and abettin' too," she replied, spitting the words back at the officer.

It had been bad before, but at least they had work. Now they were shutting the clubs down all over the state. Patty got a job waitressing in Terry's mother's restaurant. In their trailer the electric heating bill was so high that Terry bought a little kerosene heater and taped plastic to the windows to try to keep the cold out. And Patty kept drinking.

Nobody hates the unworthy poor as much as the worthy poor. All her life Patty's family had been proud that they weren't like those others. They lived on black lung payments, not the welfare dole. They were churchgoing, God-fearing folks, not low-life no-goods. And now Patty, viewing herself as harshly as she ever had, felt that she was one of them, poor white trash.

The bottom sometimes is the firm place a person has to fall to before beginning to stand up. Patty woke up one morning with a hangover and saw the bodies of the people who crashed there when the party ended, saw the empty bottles and the dirty glasses.

She walked into the little bathroom in the trailer, looked into the mirror, and saw a terrifying apparition. That was *her*, Patty. That's what she had become. She was so thin and wan, she looked like death. She had done this to herself, and only she could stop doing it. She turned away from the bottles and the drugs, turned away from what she feared she had become.

Two years later in 1984 Patty was playing a club date, singing country music for a change. She felt the emotion she had felt the first time she had gotten onstage. She felt the sheer pull of the music. She knew that there was a new generation of artists in Nashville, singers like Ricky Skaggs and Emmylou Harris, who were going backward to go forward, reinvigorating the traditions of country music. This was something she knew that she could do and feel and be. She called her brother, who was working at a wax museum in Nashville, and asked him to manage her return to country music. Patty was now just another singer who long ago had almost been somebody, and she flew up to Nashville to try to begin all over again.

Desperation is sometimes a wonderful tonic, and Roger was full of brash daring. He was fortunate that Nashville was not yet a place where every portal was guarded by rent-a-cops or lawyers, unsolicited tapes thrown away or sent back, and unconnected singers shown the door. Roger had a demo tape made of Patty's songs and sent them out to the major labels.

Nothing excited Tony Brown, MCA Nashville's new vice president of A&R, more than hearing some wondrous new sound, a voice of mystery and passion, a song that touched the heart and the soul. Still, he did not have the time to listen to every wanna-be who sent him a tape or tried to set up an appointment.

Roger talked his way past the receptionist at MCA Nashville by pretending to be someone else late for his appointment with Tony. Inside the office, he asked Tony for time to hear only one song. He promised if Tony would only listen, he would never bother him again. Listening to her music, Tony realized that he was hearing a passionate new voice true to the tradition.

If he wanted to sign her, Tony had to play her music for

Bowen. The MCA Nashville president listened for a few minutes, hearing in this one voice everything he didn't like about country music. To him Patty's voice reeked of yesterday, full of that hokey head sound that he abhorred and had vowed to purge from country records. Beyond that, although he did not say this, when he met Patty he doubtless found that she dressed and acted like some backwoods hillbilly, an image as dated as her music.

"I don't care for her," Bowen told his subordinate. "But go ahead if you want."

Bowen had so little faith in Patty that he wasn't about to risk a whole album, but let Tony go ahead and produce a series of singles. Tony brought Emory Gordy Jr., his old friend from Emmylou Harris's Hot Band, into the studio with him to coproduce. Emory had been in the elevator the first day Patty and Roger came to the label. Patty weighed only 113 pounds, 10 pounds less than she does today. Emory could hardly believe that this pale, timid, scrawny thing fancied herself a potential star. Patty was hardly more impressed with Emory. She remembered how she had seen him playing bass for Elvis when she was thirteen, but she had just been with Tony, who had played piano for the king of rock 'n' roll. Tony was Nashville's spiffy Mr. Cool, and this strange little bass player stood there dressed in white overalls.

Bass guitar players are a self-effacing breed, producing the strong currents of music but rarely stepping forward for a solo. Emory's whole life was in his ears. He heard every subtlety of a song or a lyric. He heard spoken words too the way few people heard them. He took words at their full meaning, and was often hurt by remarks that others would consider nothing more than silly asides. As soon as Emory heard Patty's tape, he was a believer.

"She's from North Carolina," Tony told his producing colleague.

"Tony, she's not from North Carolina. I think this girl's from Kentucky. Bet you Pikeville, somewhere around that area."

There were no two truer music men in Nashville than Tony and Emory. Together they produced a series of heartfelt country songs, and one country radio station after another threw them in its discard pile. At her own label, Patty was in competition with such major stars as Reba McEntire, and the label promoted Patty's singles almost as an afterthought. One of the singles was "I Did," a song Patty had written as a teenager with a recitation added by Harlan Howard, one of Nashville's best writers. It was such a strong ballad, sung ringing with such emotional truth, that the single started moving up the charts.

The ballad had gone out to radio along with releases from four other new MCA Nashville acts, all of whom had albums out there in the record stores. Bowen came to ask Patty to allow the label to pull the single off the radio not because it was failing but because it was succeeding too well. "I have to be fair to the other artists," he told her, promising that he would give her an album deal and she could rerelease "I Did" as a single on her first album.

Terry had put Patty on the plane to Nashville. Once she got her deal, he built a little trailer, put all their belongings on it, and drove up to Nashville. The couple rented a little apartment. Terry figured he would be the drummer in Patty's band, but she seemed kind of vague about that. So to earn some money he got a job in a lumberyard.

When Patty packed up and left the apartment, Terry got himself a tiny room with bars on the window and a shared bathroom. He stayed there until the day they served him with divorce papers. That was when he decided it was time to leave. He packed up his trailer and drove back to Kings Mountain. He started playing with his band again, during the week painting houses with his brother. He kept all her letters, and he kept her clothes. He never met anyone else. He never married. And years afterwards if you asked him if he still loved Patty, his eyes teared up, and he said that yes he did and he always would.

The critics held Patty's first albums up with endless accolades, but they didn't sell particularly well. The one public legacy of the decade-long marriage was her new stage name, Loveless. Emory was there for her, first as her producer, than as her friend, and finally as her secret lover. It was her voice that had drawn him to her, and it was her voice that he loved as a perfect exemplar of her being. He understood better than anyone how "she just belts it out from the heart without overintellectualizing it" and how "with some people it's as if it isn't even coming through them, but through some kind of divine inspiration."

Patty had one of the most diverse audiences in all of country. People came early to a George Strait or George Jones or a Reba McEntire concert to hear Patty opening the show. In Nashville, among musicians, she was considered a singer's singer. In the gay bars of Southern California, the patrons loved to sing along with her most heart-wrenching ballads. And up in those hollows of Kentucky and West Virginia, she was played as an authentic heir to the tradition of Loretta Lynn. But Patty just didn't sell well.

Tony took over as Patty's lone producer. As his star rose in Nashville, Tony wedded his artistic sensibilities with shrewd commercial instincts. In Patty's case, that meant sending out as Patty's singles one upbeat, up-tempo number after another. The problem was that Patty's ballads made her truly a unique artist.

Patty found little time or energy to write songs any longer. She was having a conversation one day with her ex-husband, "telling him that in time it would ease up and get better." When she got off the phone, she wrote down some notes and wrote a song called "Go On" that made it onto her third album, *Honky Tonk Angels*.

Patty was what was supposed to be a success, but it was nothing like what she had imagined. When she had been with the Wilburn Brothers, it had been fun, not these days and nights of ceaseless pressure. She hated those long nights on a cramped bus, the nine or ten bodies stacked like firewood in the narrow bunks, the gas fumes hanging in the air. At its best her music was about deep and simple truths, and that was the kind of life she wanted to lead. Her days were cluttered with interviews, business meetings, meet-and-greets, photo sessions, and phone interviews, an endless series of obligations. She pushed as much of it away as she could, not because she was arrogant, but because she couldn't handle it all and keep the core of her life together.

In 1989 when Patty was in the studio with Tony recording her fourth album, *On Down the Line*, her sister Dottie was in the hospital. Dottie had two children, and had been married twice. She was so desperately thin that outsiders would have deemed her anorexic, but that was not the way Patty's family looked on life. She was just down with sickness. She had a broken heart and a broken life and she was withering away. One day she would be better, or she wouldn't be better, and there was only so much that anyone but God could do about it.

Patty adored Dottie, her model, her dream of what life could be. Now Dottie was a model of another kind. Patty was shy, withdrawn from so much, but Dottie was so far removed that she hardly touched the pulse of life. If Dottie was all Patty's promise, her big sister was now a dark rendering of aspects of Patty's own life. Patty was recording a ballad by Claire and Larry Lynch, called "Some Morning Soon." The song had that mournful Appalachian tenor to it. It was as if these words could not be said, only sung:

> The wind is cold, I walk alone
> My head is hanging low.
> The friend I found within myself
> Is the only one I know.

For most people, singers or not, the corrosions of life have blocked much of the connection between word and emotion. They still feel, but it is therapeutic: feel, hurt, emote, forget, move on. With Patty there was none of that. As Patty sang those lyrics, she thought of her sister and tried not to cry. She wondered if it was true, if Dottie had been driven to despair by her loneliness. She wondered if Dottie had ever opened up to anyone, even to her. Patty didn't see life with all the rationalizations of pop psychology. Life was simple and deep, and she heard those truths in the music she sang. And every time she sang this song she thought of Dottie and tried not to cry.

Fans thought that stars like Patty lived in splendor, but she was not selling enough records to be rich. She was not even a headliner, and with all the expenses of the band and her bus, she was living in a modest apartment in Nashville, going off to Emory's cabin in Georgia as often as she could.

In February of 1989, she and Emory went off to Galtinburg, Tennessee, where they secretly married. For a year and a half afterwards Patty coyly pretended that she was dating an unnamed figure in the industry. The trouble with the truth was that she did not want to hurt Terry, who still loved his former wife.

Emory was a kindred spirit, and they had as close a marriage as was to be found in Music City. In the studio he might yell and fume, but he did so only because they shared the common goal of making fine music. He, like his wife, was a shy man uncomfortable standing in the glare of publicity. He was painfully uncomfortable at the public part of his professional life, standing up to receive an award, making a little speech, talking to a music reporter. Emory, like his wife, lived within music, off in the studio producing, or listening to demo tapes. He was a painful perfectionist who did many things well, none more than producing his wife's albums.

Patty adored Emory, but, beyond her marriage, family was a curse as much as a blessing. Her eldest sister, Ruth, ran Patty's fan club. And of course without Roger she would not have come to Nashville when she was fourteen, and perhaps would not have returned. He was all the brashness she did not have, all the fire that with her rested inside. He believed in his sister so much that he pushed and pushed and pushed, and he sometimes upset people Patty couldn't afford to upset. Brother or not, Roger was like almost everyone else in her life, thinking he could dominate her. She had tried to signal to Roger in so many ways what she felt. As early as 1988 she had told a reporter, "I try to make my brother Roger understand when I have to be hard with him. I'm very close to my brother but he still wants to lead me sometimes. He still wants to make my decisions for me sometimes. But I think he's catching on."

Roger was not catching on, not in the way Patty wanted him to. The worst part of it was that he was not a sophisticated, smart-talking manager who could work his way with the powers of Nashville. Patty had the feeling that she wasn't getting the kind of deals she could have gotten if she had somebody else managing her career. As the days of their five-year contract ended, Patty was torn apart about what to do. If he had not been her brother, she would have let him go and gone on, but this was Roger. Patty was Roger's life, his identity, his future, everything. Patty tried to make things better by bringing in a comanager, but the two men didn't get along. Her career was simply not happening the way she and Emory felt it could happen. As the months until the end of the contract turned into days, she dreaded what she felt she must do. She knew that Roger wasn't healthy, and she had a terrible premonition of what would happen.

In May of 1990, at her lawyer's office, she tried as gently as she could to tell Roger what she had to tell him. "Roger, I'll give you a percentage just so you can operate out of your house and you can be president of Patty Loveless Enterprises."

Patty thought she was doing good and doing right, but Roger didn't see it that way. She knew that. He began to cry, and Patty felt shame and embarrassment and guilt. "Oh, my God," she thought, "I'm causing him to experience all this pain in front of all these people."

In her own mind, Patty tried to believe that she hadn't fired Roger. His contract was up and she had offered him an alternative. Although people in Nashville knew that if anything Patty had been too kind too long to her brother, the world did not all hear it that way. In some of the news stories, Patty became the singer who had fired her brother who had made her career. Even worse, her family blamed her, seeing her as this selfish, soulless country diva who had cast off even her own blood and kin. "Oh, my God, what have I done," she thought. "I've destroyed Roger's life."

Patty flew out of Nashville to go back on tour opening for George Strait. In exchange for singing songs of pain and loss like almost no one else, she was condemned to *feel* that pain in her own life like few others. Now she dreaded the moment she had to perform. Every night when she walked onstage, she felt ten thousand fingers pointing at her in condemnation. And every evening when she collapsed back alone into the bus, lying there balled up like a fetus, she cried as the bus rolled through the endless night.

Patty had Emory. She had her band. She knew that without them and their assurance that she was a good person, she would not have survived. Patty had felt that Roger was the source of many of her problems at MCA, but with him gone nothing changed. That was God's little joke on her. Wynonna and Trisha Yearwood and Reba McEntire were all selling millions of records on the MCA Nashville label, and she was pushed even further backward, this traditional singer in a happening world.

Patty didn't understand why MCA Nashville treated her like a foster child. "If this is the problem, all right, I've proved myself," she said to herself. "I've done probably the hardest thing I could have ever done in my life." She got a new manager, Larry Fitzgerald, who also managed Vince Gill.

At their year-end business meeting, Patty was sitting with Emory, her attorney, and her business manager, talking about her future. Larry walked into the meeting. "This is all bullshit," her new manager asserted. "What we need to do is to get her off of MCA and get her to a label where people love her and will support her."

Larry walked into Tony Brown's office at MCA Nashville and told the executive that Patty wanted out. *Honky Tonk Angel* had gone gold, but her two last albums had done less than half that and her career had the scent of failure all over it. She was still making money for the label, and on one level it was hard to justify letting her go.

Tony, however, had an artist's soul. He realized how painful it was for Patty to know that her efforts were shuttled to the back of the pile just the way they had been when she first arrived at the label. Tony also had a superb sense of public relations. If he let her go, he would seem a noble sort, his label a worthy home for those singers in Music City who cared most about music. When idealism and self-interest are bonded together, they are the strongest of all motives. Tony went in to talk to Bruce Hinton, then still the label president. Bruce had the cold business shrewdness that Tony lacked. Bruce put together a deal that would allow the label to profit if Patty succeeded at her new label.

Larry knew that in Nashville perception was everything. He could not allow Patty to seem tainted, damaged goods that MCA Nashville had gladly thrown overboard. Patty's problem at MCA Nashville was that she was just another girl singer on the label with the most spectacular list of female vocalists in all Music City. Larry looked at all the labels and decided where to go first. Over at Sony

Nashville, their Columbia label had a star in Mary Chapin Carpenter, but the Epic side had nobody.

Larry set up a meeting with Roy Wunsch, the president of Sony Nashville. "If you're interested, I won't go anywhere else," he told the executive. "I want to do it in one day. I'll come over with my attorney. I want her out of MCA and on your label before anybody in town knows about it."

By the end of the day, Patty was the newest Epic artist. She was ecstatic to have a chance at a new label, representing the best possibilities of success for the struggling Epic label. She went into the studio and began to cut songs for her first release. As happy as she should have been, she held a secret that threatened her entire career. Patty carried down with her from Kentucky that secretive, suspicious mountain spirit. Life here below had not taught her to trust any more easily. Back in 1990 a doctor had discovered a red spot on her vocal cords. That was something she might have confided to Larry or at least to Emory, but she had not. She had a woman's stoicism, silent bearer of pain, and she had struggled on, telling no one.

In the studio Emory could tell that Patty's voice wasn't as strong as it once had been. He pushed her ahead, trying to get a first-rate performance out of his wife. The rap from the naysayers on Patty had always been that she had trouble with pitch. Now in the studio Patty moved back and forth across the notes like a drunken driver weaving back and forth across the center line.

Patty's voice felt to her "like a busted speaker." Every time Patty stepped out onstage, it was as if she had been handed a bum microphone that might hiss, drown her voice in feedback, or go dead in the midst of her first song. She felt that it was God's judgment on the wrong that she had done. During the summer of 1992 she kept running between stage and studio pretending that it would get better. She made frequent visits to the office of Dr. Robert Osoff, a vocal specialist, who propped her voice up with steroid tablets and cortisone.

In October Patty was scheduled to film a television special on the women of country music when she asked Larry to accompany her to Osoff's offices at Vanderbilt. Neither of Larry's two clients, Vince nor Patty, needed much hand-holding or constant assurance.

Larry didn't think much of it when his new client said that she was having some voice problems. At the clinic, Osoff showed them devastating videos of Patty's vocal cords. There was the tiny red dot on her vocal cords back in 1990. And here two years later were her vocal cords now, with this enlarged blood vessel that looked like a varicose vein. It was a terrifying juxtaposition, but nonetheless Patty wanted to postpone the required operation until January.

"You have a voice here too," Dr. Osoff told Larry. "She'll listen to you."

"My God! This is serious!" exclaimed the usually taciturn manager.

"Well, I've got all these dates on the book, all these. . . ."

"Patty, the short term doesn't matter here."

Although Patty went ahead and sang in the television special, Larry canceled all Patty's engagements until the end of the year. There was no more terrifying thought to a singer than that her voice might be gone. Patty had tried to push the idea away, imagining by sheer force of will that she would heal herself, but that had not worked out. The singer entered Vanderbilt Hospital where Osoff performed an operation. It was almost as frightening afterwards as before, not knowing whether her voice would come back. In the end, as Patty slowly discovered, her vocal cords were restored. She had a new, well-founded confidence that her voice was a strong instrument she could now test to its limits.

Back in the studio the singer and producer went to work. In this album Patty and Emory explored every nook and cranny of that emotion known as love. It was love in all its joys and perils, blue love, new love, old love, lost love, found love, mother's love, daughter's love. Patty and Emory listened to hundreds of demo songs, discarding almost all of them. Although love makes Nashville's songwriters go round, most of the love songs they heard didn't resonate inside her. Although country music is often accused of emotional excess, in the best of the songs there is a daring, disciplined emotional restraint. Those were the songs Patty and Emory chose. When matched with the disciplined emotional restraint of a fine country singer, that led once in a very great while to three minutes of what some would call greatness.

In the midst of the recording, Patty called Doug Johnson, vice president and the A&R head of the Epic label. Unlike most of the other label executives, Doug still had something of the fan in him, an awe at the achievements and perils of an artist's life. Doug was a song man. He had found a song by Burton Banks Collins and Karen Taylor Good called "How Can I Help You Say Goodbye." It was based on Collins's experience saying good-bye to his beloved grandmother. The song was an exquisite piece of work, and he thought it was right for Patty. She and Emory thought so too, but now Patty was telling him that she wouldn't be able to do it.

"Doug, I can't sing it. I can't get through it. Every time I sing it I break up just before the last verse."

"Just gotta keep trying, Patty," Doug offered consolingly.

"I don't know if I'm ever going to be able to sing it. I don't know if I'm ever going to be able to perform it live. I don't know if I went on TV if I could get through it."

Doug had heard all the criticisms of country music exploiting sentiment. He knew that those who said that an artist like Patty Loveless didn't feel her music had no idea. Burton, the cowriter, sent a letter to Patty telling her why he wrote the lyrics and what the song meant to him. She kept the letter in her purse like a talisman and took it with her into the studio.

Patty sang the first verse about a woman watching her best friend die. She sang the second verse about a woman getting a divorce and saying good-bye to her husband. She sang the third verse about a woman saying good-bye to her dying mama. And she sang the final chorus, sang it for her father, sang for how much she loved him, how profoundly she grieved him, how much she missed him, sang it as if she had lived every moment, every nuance, lived and felt and gone on.

> How can I help you to say good-bye?
> It's okay to hurt, and it's okay to cry.
> Come let me hold you, and I will try.
> How can I help you to say good-bye?

The staff at Epic believed that *Only What I Feel* was Patty's finest album, and they promoted it energetically and creatively. The album was already on its way to becoming platinum when "How Can I Help You Say Goodbye" was released as the fourth single in the spring of 1994. As a country single the song had everything wrong about it. The radio consultants who tested new songs reported that it researched poorly. It was too long. It was too down. Moreover, Patty's successes had come with upbeat, up-tempo songs. But the searing ballad moved up the charts, a startling riposte to the light fare of hot young country radio, an affirmation that people out there felt and cared as much as people always have. The song placed Patty's career on a different plane and was nominated as CMA single and video of the year.

Reba was the only woman superstar of country music, and though Patty aspired to join her, the two women were traveling down two different roads. Reba traveled along superhighways with her truckloads of equipment, delivering to her audiences a spectacular stage show. Patty still continued down those country byways, standing there alone singing her songs.

Reba always delivered, but sometimes Patty didn't connect. Sometimes she seemed to be holding back, unable to pull out of herself. This evening that was no problem, and Patty held the audience in her gentle grasp.

Patty stood on the Fan Fair stage singing "You Don't Even Know Who I Am," a ballad that had helped to define her career. The songwriter, Gretchen Peters, was the privileged daughter of a CBS television producer and author. She had been brought up in suburban New York City, a world far from Pikeville, Kentucky. Gretchen had found her way to Nashville, and her uncompromising songs had found a home here. A few years back they would have been considered pop or adult contemporary, but Patty's gritty rendering transformed the ballad into a song that few country music fans would deny.

Gretchen's song was one of the main reasons that Patty's second album for Epic, *When Fallen Angels Fly*, won the CMA Award as 1995's Album of the Year.

> She left a note in the kitchen
> Next to the grocery list.
> It said, you don't even know who I am.

These should have been good times for Patty. She had just been named Female Vocalist of the Year at the Academy of Country Music (ACM) Awards in Los Angeles. The label had given her a party at Cheekwood Mansion to honor her awards and her second platinum album. Patty used the party to honor all the fine songwriters who had contributed to her achievements. The label dinner party afterwards in a private room at F. Scott's, one of Nashville's upscale restaurants, should have been a triumphant ending of the evening, but two of the tables stood empty. Sony Nashville had become a dispirited organization, unable to take full advantage of Patty's critical success and awards and honors, and a number of staff people had not shown up. The label had probably the worst morale of any major company in Nashville. Patty saw the empty seats, and the party was as limp and depressed as the label itself.

As she stood on that great stage at Fan Fair, Patty was faced again with family tragedy. Her beloved sister Dottie was at Centennial Medical Center in Nashville. Dottie was only forty-nine years old, but she was broken down and worn-out, lying shriveled up in that hospital bed. Patty had risen out of that world of poverty and pain, but her family was a constant witness to that past, always standing somewhere nearby, with their problems and attentions. Dottie was the shadow image of Patty, the woman she easily could have been.

Patty wanted something as far from stardom as the earth from a mountain peak. She wanted a child with Emory. That was not happening, and as Patty saw the world, that was perhaps God's judgment. She wanted to rise to the level of a superstar too and stand on that same high plane with Reba. That would make these years of struggle, the endless nights in her bus, the ten thousand smiles, the hundred thousand handshakes, all add up.

But the road that led up there passed through a thicket of journalists and media, through reporters with their mikes sticking into her face and into her life, through spotlights that shone on her as much offstage as onstage. That was a journey that she turned back from, often retreating into the shell of her shyness.

On an evening like this, she could tell how much the audience cared about her music. She brought an emotional authenticity and honesty of such depth that almost everyone out there in that vast audience gasped. They weren't jumping up and down. They were sitting in silence pondering the words and the emotions. This music was about the searing, uncompromising truth of Gretchen's song. Her voice was this vessel of truth, carrying the words out into the world.

> And I go to work every morning
> And I come home to you every night
> And you don't even know who I am
> You left me a long time ago.

Patty lived her life through her music. When she sang the way she did this evening, she was in control of her life up here on the stage. But the songs always ended. When Patty walked offstage to a standing ovation, the world was again with her. There was Emory, standing to the side, always so discomfited in these crowds, yet he was here this evening, knowing she needed him. There were the Sony executives and the distributors and the radio big shots, all wanting a hug, a handshake, a moment's recognition. She greeted them as she had to. Then a phalanx of security led her down the backstage steps and toward her bus.

Patty walked with her eyes locked forward, never making the mistake of recognizing someone and having to stop. She was so tired and worn by the routine of stardom, by poor Dottie, by all of it. It all came to her, an avalanche of feeling. And as she sat in the bus trying to compose herself, scores of fans pressed up close against the bus, shouting out her name, insisting that she greet them.

"Patty! Patty! Patty! Patty!" Louder. And louder. And louder. "Patty! Patty! Patty! Patty! Patty! Patty!" She sat in the blessed darkness of the bus, trying to compose herself. "Patty! Patty! Patty!

Patty! Patty! Patty!" She knew that she would have to go out there soon. "Patty! Patty! Patty! Patty! Patty! Patty!" She would sit in the stairwell, and sign autographs for all her fans, but just a few moments. "Patty! Patty! Patty! Patty! Patty! Patty!" Just a few moments.

17

~

"One Woman's Life"

The night air was a blessed balm, but the heat and the sun and the press of bodies had been enough to tucker out most of the fans and send them back limp and weary to their motels, hotels, and campers. Only the most energetic headed along I-65 to downtown Nashville in search of more country music.

Until a half dozen years ago, this part of downtown Nashville near the Ryman Auditorium had been largely a slum, and some of these storefronts still had the hardscrabble aura of the depression. Here on Broadway between Fourth and Fifth Avenues stood Tootsie's Orchid Lounge, the most famous honky-tonk of all.

Linda Hargrove was singing on a tiny stage in the front window. Behind her up those rickety stairs was a tiny room yellow with age like an ancient temple. If one looked closely through the gloom, there was a Willie Nelson album cover on the wall, laced with names, next to falling wallboard. Years ago the Grand Ole Opry stars made their way up there up the back staircase through the alley leading directly from the Ryman's stage door. Patsy Cline,

371

Webb Pierce, and Ernest Tubb sat there between sets, drinking and talking to such songwriters as Willie Nelson and Harlan Howard.

Over two decades ago the Opry moved away, and the bar no longer was a regular hangout for singers and songwriters the way it had been when Linda first came to town. Linda knew that if it was going to happen again, she had to get her music out there, though Lord knows it was unlikely that anyone from a record label would chance into this bar during Fan Fair.

Lower Broad wasn't the place you came looking for a future. Since 1974 when the Grand Ole Opry moved out to Opryland, Lower Broad had fallen on hard times. Gruhn Guitars, the famous old guitar store, had stayed put on the corner of Broadway and Fourth. Friedman's Pawn Shop, another classic establishment, was on the block too, along with a modest competitor, L and L Pawn Shop, and Adult World, a girlie show.

The whole block was one Adult World. You could come to town, buy your guitar at Gruhn's, purchase your outfit at Robert's Western Wear, drink and play for tips at Tootsie's, Robert's, or the Wagon Burner, eat at Jack's Bar-B-Que, pawn your guitar at Friedman's where they'd put it in the window just where it had been at Gruhn's a few months before, and end up at the check-cashing office on the corner of Fifth, wiring home for money to get you back where you came from.

There was hardly a bar in Nashville down here and throughout town that didn't have somebody picking, playing for a few bucks or for tips—or maybe for nothing at all. Most of the players were twenty years younger than Linda. She had seen the singers and the songwriters come to Nashville over the years, packing their guitars and their dreams, singing their songs to anyone who would listen. She had been one of them once and now she was one again, just looking for a chance.

Linda tuned her guitar, strummed a chord, and began to sing:

> Mother always warned me 'bout the devil
> And I know that he wears a sweet disguise.
> But I'm too weak from fightin' off temptation
> And there's a trace of heaven in his eyes.

Linda had a voice that was a vessel of memory and emotion, carrying the story of her life out into that dark room. She had a rich southern accent, bending the syllables so they seemed almost to break in two. She was forty-six years old. She had none of the girlish qualities of most country singers her age. She wore tight jeans and a blue blouse, hardly disguising her matronly body. She had straight brown hair, a large, long nose, ample eyebrows that were like exclamation points set on their sides, and a long, narrow mouth. She did not look at all like anybody's image of a country singer, but then she never had.

Linda had grown up in a middle-class home in northern Florida, liking the blues and rock 'n' roll. As a teenager, she played a mean guitar, mimicking Joan Baez and Bob Dylan, not Kitty Wells and Tammy Wynette. Her major instrument, however, was the French horn she had been studying with a scholarship to Troy State University in Alabama. She had dropped out and had been playing in a rock band in Tallahassee while trying to write rock music.

Linda kept catching phrases of country music songs as she restlessly worked the car radio dial looking for the Beatles or Rolling Stones. She heard snatches of country songs on jukeboxes in bars. Almost despite herself, she listened to music she thought she despised.

Linda was a child of the new America, and she was attracted to country music "by the clear simplicity of it and how in good country songs, everything fits together." To her it was "true American music, that's the magic of it." These country songwriters and singers were given only a few basic colors on their palettes and a series of small canvases; the best of them could paint most of the hues of human emotions and the rich colors of American life.

Almost every song Linda sang resonated with her past or the emotional truths of her life, and this evening her singing opened the wellspring of memory. She remembered how she had moved to Nashville in July of 1970, and this song, "Fallen Angel," had been one of the first songs she had written. Linda drove into Nashville in her battered old Datsun, carrying a guitar and seventy-five dollars. She was scrawny, all bones and sinew. In her blue jeans, black T-shirts, and jean jacket she looked to the demure gentry of Nashville like a hippie chick, a member of the breed they liked to think of as pied pipers of sin and salaciousness descending on the pristine South, cultural carpetbaggers who had their outposts in almost every city and town.

Linda knew one person in Nashville, a man who ran a small recording studio. She slept in his basement when she first arrived. She met a few people in the floating community of musicians, some of whom let her sack out on their living room sofas for a night or two. Many nights, however, she slept in her Datsun, crunched up on the backseat.

Linda got a job at the Red Dog Saloon, a bar that had a clientele of hippies and bikers, two outcast communities that usually stayed far apart. The pay wasn't much, just tips, two sandwiches a day, and all the beer she could drink. The sandwiches were better than the tips, and the beers were better than the sandwiches. She starting drinking more than she ever had, drinking so much that she started gaining weight.

By wintertime Linda found a job in the bookkeeping department of a small record label. She got herself a fifty-dollar-a-month apartment down on Music Row. The job didn't last any longer than the winter winds that came roaring through the cracks in the wall, and she was out there again dependent on the kindness of strangers. Nashville was full of people who considered charity not professional largesse, money to be neatly calculated and written off on taxes, but simply the natural order of things. That is, they considered charity not charity at all. A manager let her stay at a cottage that he rented for the sole purpose of giving hard-up musicians and songwriters a place to sleep. It wasn't much. Linda kept her precious guitar hidden on the roof.

Linda met a successful country singer, Sandy Posey, and she began baby-sitting for her little girl, Amy. Linda played some of her songs and told Sandy of her dream of becoming a country singer. Sandy did not view country music like a Sunday chicken that could only be cut up so many ways. When Sandy went in to record her new album, she invited Linda to go along to pitch some songs to her producer.

Thinking back on that day, Linda cringed at how green she had been, not even knowing who Billy Sherrill was, or what a glorious opportunity she was being given. Billy, a Baptist preacher's son, was one of Nashville's top songwriters and one of the most successful producers. He wasn't in the habit of listening to tunes written by unknown amateurs, but listen to Linda he did this day. "We'll cut it," he said. "You come on over when we record it."

Linda showed up for the recording session, the first time she had ever been in a full professional studio. After they cut Linda's song, she hung around waiting to hear it played back.

"Did you write that?" asked Pete Drake, the pedal steel player.

"Yeah, I did," as if to say "What's it to you, fellow?"

"Well, you're a smart-aleck, aren't you?"

"Yeah, I'm a smart-aleck," Linda replied, and turned away.

Pete sidled back to her a few minutes later and set in again in that half-joshing, half-serious manner of his. "You got any more songs like that?" he asked.

Linda couldn't tell whether he was putting her down or not. "I got more and they're better than that."

"I'd like to hear 'em sometime."

Linda wasn't one to push her way through half-open doors. She left thinking she had merely been flattered, but Nashville was not a town where lying was considered high manners. For the most part, words meant what they said. When someone asked you to have lunch sometime soon, they usually meant that they wanted to see you again, not that they never wanted to have the misfortune of ever again seeing your blighted face. When Pete Drake said that he wanted to hear Linda's songs, he wanted to hear them.

Linda knew nothing about Pete Drake except that he played killer pedal steel. She wasn't about to embarrass herself by giving the musician a call. Two weeks later, she went back to her cottage and found that someone had broken in. The robber took her clothes, the last of her cash, everything but the guitar she had hidden up on the roof. She would have jumped into her car and headed down to Florida, but the car had broken down weeks before; she hadn't had the money to fix it, and the police had towed the car away.

Linda picked up her guitar and walked over to Marchetti's Restaurant. She had patches on her jeans, and she looked like a homeless waif, wandering the streets and byways. Some of her musician friends had arranged to let her sign their tabs for an occasional meal. As she sat there, Linda reached down into her pocket and found a quarter. A quarter. That was it. She played with the coin. Should she call her mom and ask her to wire enough money so she could get a Greyhound back to Tallahassee? Or should she call Pete Drake to see if he was joking or not? She figured that she could always call her mother collect, and she might as well see if she could get through to Pete.

Linda had found out enough about Pete to realize how unlikely it was that he would do anything for her. Pete was the best pedal steel player in Nashville. He had played on the four albums that Linda's idol, Bob Dylan, had recorded in Nashville. The year before he had not only played but kicked around town with Ringo Starr when he had come to record. He had recently returned from London, where he had recorded with another former Beatle, George Harrison, on his new song, "My Sweet Lord." He had his own publishing company and was producing several artists as well.

Linda dialed Pete's number and was immediately put through. "Where are you?" Pete asked, as if he had been sitting there for two weeks waiting for her call.

"I'm down at Marchetti's," Linda replied, as if she had nothing to do but to hang out.

"When could you come over?" Pete asked.

"Anytime."

"Well, why don't you come over now?"

Linda hitched her guitar around her neck and walked over to Pete's office. Linda sat down in a stuffed chair and played several songs, including "Fallen Angel."

> The truth remains a-shinin' through the darkness
> And Lord, you know I'm hung up on that light,
> So I'd rather tell you now than be deceivin'
> I gotta be a woman tonight.

Pete had a gentle face that looked out on the world with such goodwill that it was hard to tell what he really was thinking. He could stack his track record in picking hits up against just about anyone's, but he was known as much for his generosity to the aspiring, operating what he called the Drake School of Recording where he nurtured new songwriters and singers. Linda didn't realize it, but she had just passed his audition.

"Some of them songs need a little more work on 'em," Pete said. "But you're one heck of a guitar player. Got them licks, sounds like English players. That's the way Peter Townshend plays."

"He's one of my idols," Linda said, surprised that Pete could figure how she had copied some of the British guitarist's licks.

"Well, I'd like to publish your songs, Linda," Pete said slyly. "But I'm not going to pay you a draw."

There always was a gimmick. Linda thought, what good was it going to do if she didn't have some money coming in?

"Instead, I'll pay your way into the union and you can make money playing on sessions with some of the boys."

Linda was in high cotton. She knew she wasn't dreaming because dreams were rarely this good. Linda had never even imagined playing on records. After all, there was only one other woman playing sessions in Nashville, and she was a piano player. Linda didn't ask what session players got or exactly what Pete had in mind. She started packing up and getting ready to get out of there and go hopping and skipping down Music Row.

"You don't have any money, do you, Linda?" Pete asked as she turned to go.

"No," Linda shrugged.

"Well, you take this earnest money, honey," Pete said as he opened his wallet, took out a new hundred-dollar bill, and handed it to Linda.

> Ooo, fallen angel
> Tonight I'll leave my wings at home.
> Ooo, fallen angel:
> Even fallen angels hate to be alone.

As Linda finished the song, the beer drinkers looked up from their tables and struck their hands together in a few moments of obligatory applause. There were two tables where the music had pulled the couples out of their conversations, and they applauded fervently, as if they had happened in on a special moment.

"I put this on my first album in 1972," Linda said. Then she thought a second, realizing how little that meant to the faces before her. "You weren't even born then."

Linda looked to the back of the room where until recently Charlie Bartholomew, her husband, would have been sitting looking at her as if it were the first time he was hearing these songs. Now there were just faces. "I guess I'll do another one from that first album. 'Let it Shine.' Olivia Newton-John had a top ten hit of it."

In the back of the room, one woman clapped in recognition.

> A woman needs attention like the flowers need the sun.
> 'Cause without that attention, Lord, a woman feels
>   undone.
> And, Lord, I'm like a flower that's been standin' in the
>   rain;
> Hopin', Lord, and praying that the sun will shine again.

That evening in 1972 after leaving Pete, Linda treated her friends to a celebration's worth of beer, and the next week she was in the studio playing guitar. Pete threw as much work to Linda as he felt he could, but it was a men's club in the recording studios, and she never quite made it into the exalted ranks of the regulars.

Linda was like no other woman in the musical community. For the most part in Nashville, women either stayed home or they stayed in their place, and whether they were secretaries or stars, they dressed in dresses and wore makeup. Some women performers had started wearing jeans onstage, but they were Saturday night barn-dance pretty, a country mile from Linda's scruffy jeans, no makeup, and the raw vulnerability of her personality.

For a young woman, Nashville was a city of temptation. If Linda walked through life with the Bible in one hand, she held a bottle in the other. She hung out with her friends at the bars, and fell in and out of love with musicians and songwriters, exploring those emotions with willful abandon. It was all fodder for her songs, the highs and lows captured in three minutes of emotion. She couldn't get enough cuts or session work to make a go of it. By wintertime, she was out facing the street again, homeless without enough money to pay for a motel room.

Linda was friendly with many leading songwriters in Nashville who saw her not as a nasty intrusion on their little worlds but as a worthy addition. Just before Christmas she was hanging out over at Combine Music with Lee Clayton, a songwriter friend. For a few hours she didn't have to think about where she was sleeping that night and could pick away, singing songs.

The songwriter told her that Michael Nesmith was coming over to listen to some songs. Nesmith had been a member of the Monkees, an enormous but short-lived pop and television hit.

Clayton didn't shuttle Linda aside, getting her out before Nesmith arrived. They started trading songs. When Linda's turn came up again, she sang a song she had just written, "Let It Shine."

> Is there anybody out there who can shine?
> Anytime would be fine.
> Is there anybody out there who can flow?
> And would like to see a little flower grow?
> Shine on me. Let it shine.

In the midst of the song, Nesmith walked into the room. Linda kept on singing. Nesmith was a talented musician, far different from his image as a robotic Beatles clone. He was looking for songs for an album he was producing on the new Elektra record label, and when Linda finished, he cut to the matter at hand: "Hey, Linda, this is great stuff. Would you play it again?"

Linda said nary a word and sang the song again. When she finished, Nesmith shook his head in appreciation: "Wow, I really love the way you play that guitar. Good song too. I'm leaving today at two for LA. You think you could fly back with me and play on this record next week?"

"Well, I, ah. . . ."

"I'll buy you a round-trip ticket and I've got some friends you can stay with."

Linda had no place to stay in Nashville. Her Florida soul was chilled in the icebox winter of Tennessee. And she had always wanted to see Los Angeles. Three hours later she was flying westward with the most talented fourth of the Monkees.

Pete had warned her to be careful out there in the land of Charlie Manson, fearing that Nesmith was looking for a groupie, not a guitar player. Nesmith was a man not simply of his word but of more than his word. He found her a place to stay. He had her play on the album. He and Linda wrote two songs, "I'll Never Love Anyone More" and "Winona." Finally, at the studio, he introduced her to Russ Miller, one of the heads of his label. After hearing Linda sing, Miller flew to Nashville and cut a deal with Pete to produce Linda for the label.

Linda appeared on the cover of her 1973 album, *Music Is Your Mistress,* staring out between the metal slats of an old bed in a barn. She looked as if she were peering out from behind the bars of a prison cell. That was the dark metaphor of Hank Williams that cast its long shadows over country music, a shadow darker than night, life as a prison from which one escaped to either wantonness, booze, or the sweet lap of Jesus. It was a metaphor more for the men of country music than the women.

Linda's face on the cover had no makeup and an austere, sculptured look, as if she were pared down to her essence. Pete added strings, background choruses, and lush arrangements, but through it all Linda's voice and songs sang out with passionate intensity. In her music as in her life she had wit without cynicism, and strength with vulnerability. She sang of herself, more of her pain than her joy, more of her loneliness than her loves.

In country music the nights were usually dark, and the roads wended onward in eternal loneliness. That was the world that beckoned Linda, a world where even happiness contained a kernel of despair. She sang of the night she had sat alone in a New York City hotel room. ("New York City ain't the place a country girl should be; No, New York City ain't the place for me.") She sang of her suffering secret self. She sang of love found and she sang of lost love. She sang of her love of Jesus and how we must "try to live like Jesus, Lord, He said He was the way." That was half of her love, and the other half was music. The title song was sung to a man, but music was Linda's true mistress. ("Music is your mistress, music is your life. Music fills the need that you won't find in any wife.")

Elektra thought that the market for Linda's music transcended country music, and Linda promoted her album from college towns to clubs to auditoriums. She opened for other acts, from Mac Davis to Jackson Browne. She loved to sing, and the fact that the album didn't sell well seemed almost secondary. As she journeyed from gig to gig, she wrote more songs. She didn't like the way society seemed to put everything in categories, whether it be people or music; but unquestionably her songs were becoming more country, stripped down to their lyrical and musical essences.

Her next album was called *Blue Jean Country Queen*. On the cover Linda sat perched on the hood of a Volkswagen Beetle in her denim outfit, with a Grand Ole Opry tour bus behind. She had her own band now to travel from gig to gig, and an album that received fine reviews. There were songs of evil cities and mean streets, of love lost and gained, songs of exquisite vulnerability and quiet stoicism, old adages and modern sensibility. Critics compared her to Kris Kristofferson, who brought an Ivy League poet's prose and a roustabout's spirit to country music.

For Linda life had always been a matter of blessed timing, meeting Pete and Michael and Sandy, chance meetings that didn't seem like chance at all. Timing had blessed her again. She had gotten it right on this album. She knew it, and the critics knew it, and the public was slowly knowing it too. On the Fourth of July in 1974 she played Willie Nelson's birthday bash in Texas. She belonged on that stage, part of that cowboy country world. She traveled to New York and played at the Bottom Line. It was not that lonely New York City hotel room anymore. She was singing about emotional verities that were as true on Sixteenth Street in Manhattan as they were on Sixteenth Avenue South in Nashville. She rolled on from city to city. The band was expensive, and she was broke, but she rolled on, knowing it was all coming together.

Linda knew that she was right when the William Morris agency called and told her that she would be opening for the Eagles in Louisville and Knoxville. The Eagles were the hottest country-rock group in America. She believed that opening for them on their first major tour would do it for her, put her music up there on a stage where tens of thousands would hear it, and it was a stage from which she felt she would not soon depart.

Linda had been feeling tired. She saw her doctor two days before the first of the Eagles' dates. The doctor told her that she had hepatitis, and she couldn't sing or do much of anything. She might have said to hell with the doctor, to hell with the contagious nature of the disease, to hell with all of it, and gone on and performed. For Linda, though, truth was not something to be parceled out in three-minute musical lectures.

No, truth was something you lived and sang, in a seamless blend. Thus, Linda was lying in bed when the Eagles sang. By the time she recuperated three months later, her record was dead, gone, finished, and the Blue Jean Country Queen was finished at Elektra.

The next year Linda signed with Capitol. She knew that when she changed labels she probably should have changed producers. That was the way the business worked, but Pete had been so good to her, and you didn't push your friends aside. It was again a good album, and she scored a country top forty hit with one cut: "Love Was (Once Around the Dance Floor)," but that album didn't sell. She did two more albums for Capitol, but they just sat in the record bins. She wrote songs for other people as well.

Linda had lived in Nashville for enough years to understand the cycle of country music. Once it became popular the music drew all kinds of outsiders to its banner, outsiders who led the music further and further away from sounds and themes that were its essence. In the mid-seventies many people in town considered country pop performers like John Denver, Olivia Newton-John, Anne Murray, and Kenny Rogers as guests at the barbecue. They brought no dishes with them, chose the best ribs and the biggest ears of corn, and after eating their fill and then some, headed home, leaving little but a mess of dirty dishes and bones behind.

That journey into pop reached a garish epitome at the 1976 CMA Awards dinner. The impresarios of the event decided to have it take place outside the new Opry House at Opryland, the gentlemen and ladies of country music garbed in gowns and black tie, sitting in the frigid night air. They spruced up the evening with ballet dancers dressed as cowboys and cowgirls, and while they pranced across the temporary stage, the sounds of country pop blared out into the frigid night.

Linda came home and wrote a song about the evening. "I was appalled when I went to the ball, and I saw you with all your masks on." She warned: "That California tide will take you for a ride, and it will take our pride and try to use it."

That song was on Linda's third album for Capitol. The message went as unheeded as the record. She signed up to do an album for RCA. They hadn't listened to the words of her own song either. They asked her to discard her jeans, to wear outfits frilly and feminine and bright, and dress up her music the same way, to try to sound like Barbara Mandrell, the current queen of country pop. Linda tried, how she tried, but selling out is easier to do if you aren't any good, and the album was never released.

Six albums. Six years. A career over, and she thought it had hardly begun. Almost a decade in Nashville. She felt burned out, nothing left but ashes. She had always been ahead of her time in Nashville, and now in 1979 she was ahead of her time again, doing cocaine before most people in town. Coke kept her going. Coke and booze.

Linda was thirty years old. She was tired of it all. Tired of the men, the strutting musicians, the jealous songwriters, the insecure singers, tired of them all. Tired of the pain. A friend died, run down walking across Peachtree Street in Atlanta. A week later another friend, a bartender doing too much drugs, died in a car crash. And then there was this man, there was always a man. He left Linda for somebody else. Linda had a gun. She would kill him, kill both of them, and then end it. No, she wouldn't kill them. She wasn't going to kill anyone else. Just herself.

Linda took her pistol out of the closet. She took the cold metal into her hand and reached it up toward her head. As her hand moved upward, she felt a monumental force. This power beyond power took that pistol and tore it out of her hand and left her arm numb, unable to move. She stood there weeping, all the pain flowing out of her in a torrent of tears. She believed that God had visited her. She knew Jesus. All of the anguish, the thwarted ambition, the terrible emptiness fell from her. What was a record career anyway? What was all this endless, ceaseless striving? What was any of it?

Linda flushed the rest of her cocaine down the toilet, and flushed much of her old life away as well. She recorded a new album for a small Christian music company. She called the album *A New Song*, and her life was indeed a new song. For a decade she had sung of broken hearts and broken homes and broken dreams, and now she sang of God and Jesus.

Linda dreamed of finding a new man who didn't come into her life carrying a guitar and a fistful of songs, and find him she did. His name was Charlie Bartholomew. He was fifty years old, eighteen years older than Linda. Charlie was a man of gentle goodness, a Vanderbilt graduate working as a midlevel executive for a manufacturing company. He didn't come strutting in with all the signs of success. The meek may one day inherit the earth, but Charlie's bequest had not yet come in. At times he seemed almost too gentle for this world, but Linda found in the man's kindness a reservoir of peace. In 1980 they married.

Linda had hardly exchanged vows when Charlie was diagnosed with cancer. She nurtured him through his successful surgery. Charlie's illness was yet another stark lesson in what mattered in the world. He quit his job, and Linda and Charlie moved down to Monroe, Louisiana, where they helped friends start a new church. Linda and Charlie were born-again Christians, and they witnessed their faith out in God's world now, building His church as His disciples. They built with mortar and brick, and song and parable. Linda sang and played piano and Charlie took care of the administrative duties.

For Linda it was a glorious time of renewal. She had always been one for seeing omens in chance encounters, the naked hand of God and circumstance touching her life. Shortly before leaving

Nashville, she had written a song with Dean Dillon, one of the top songwriters. It sat there unrecorded until 1984 when "Tennessee Whiskey" became a number one hit for George Jones.

Linda took that success as an omen. She started listening more to country music radio. She heard Randy Travis and the Judds singing the kind of heartfelt country music she sang. She knew if ever she was going to make it again, her time was now. In 1986, she and Charlie moved back to Nashville. She was thirty-six years old. She was emotionally healthy, happily married, and felt strong. In Nashville they welcomed her back. She set out to make her way. It took time to get a publishing deal and to start getting tapes to the record executives. Linda had been there before, and everything was going fine, just fine.

Some days Linda didn't feel as well as she thought she should, and after four months in town, she went to see a doctor. He told her she had chronic lymphatic leukemia (CLL) and had six to eight years to live. She had been given a death sentence, with no chance of reprieve. She tried to keep writing songs, but the melody had gone. She tried to sing, but her voice faltered. She tried to pitch record companies, but her steps were leaden.

The doctors said that they could do no more for her. She and Charlie left Nashville to go and live with her mother in Coral Gables, Florida. They had almost nothing, she and Charlie, except their few belongings in storage and a ten-by-eleven-foot bedroom in her mother's home. The shadow of death was written across Linda's face.

Charlie had to earn some money to keep them going. He hadn't been much of a hustler when he was twenty-five, and he sure wasn't one now, in his mid-fifties. He got a job driving a school bus, and then found a position at Sam's, the giant discount warehouse. He walked those aisles in his red Sam's jacket. He was a good and caring guide to the shoppers, leading them to their chosen wares and then going home to his dying wife.

Linda had little to do but to wait and to think. She found a young doctor who did not know that hopeless is hopeless. He sent her to the H. Lee Moffitt Cancer Center at the University of South Florida in Tampa. The doctors proposed a bone marrow transplant. The specialist told her that she had a 20 percent chance of surviving this new radical procedure. That seemed a risk worth taking, if they could find a donor. Her younger brother, Mark, turned out to be a perfect match, and he agreed to be the donor.

The doctors had told her nothing less than the truth, but no warning could prepare her for what she suffered going through a protocol of marrow transplant, drugs, and radiation. They kept bringing new patients into the hospital, and they kept dying. She lay in her bed, her body bound down with tubes.

Music had always been such sweet solace, and each night before she left, Linda's mother set up her tape recorder so all night long, over and over again, it played scriptures set to music to bless her spirit. One evening she had a nurse turn the tape off, and she lay there in silence falling asleep. It was then she saw the angel of death coming in the window. It was not some vague premonition, but a cold spirit reaching to pull her away from life.

She tore the tubes off her body, got out of the hospital bed, and walked out into the hall. "It's the angel of death, come to take me away," she yelled at the nurse. They led her back into the room, and when they gave her a sedative she could feel life returning, like sweet rain upon the parched and barren earth.

Linda was one of thirty patients who passed through the bone marrow program, and she was the only one who survived. That seemed like bare compensation for the agony. There was nothing left, no song in her soul, no coins in her purse. It took her two years to recover. When she finally began to feel and think and care again, she decided that she would have to return to Nashville. She believed in a God who looked over everything from the ocean tides and the feathers on a robin's wing to the minute patterns of her life. She knew that she had gone through the fire for a purpose. The one great purpose she had in life was making heartfelt country music.

"I got a new song to do for you now," Linda said. Tootsie's was not like the Bluebird Café, where the audience was expected to be quiet and to applaud. Here a singer won her audience, and Linda had won this one. For the most part she had touched a resonant chord in this small audience in this dark room. "This is called 'We Feel Each Other's Pain.'"

> I catch the downtown bus in the morning heat
> Walk half a mile up a tree-lined street.
> Oh, it's quite the place to dream.
> But I've got fifteen rooms to clean
> Though I hurry up the driveway past the lawn
> Let myself inside and put my apron on.

Linda and Charlie returned to Nashville in November of 1992. Charlie didn't ask for much, and he had given it in great measure during those terrible trials; loyal and caring and true. He was sixty-two years old. He had almost nothing on which to retire. Another man might have said enough is enough; it was time for Linda to look on life as it was, not as she wanted it to be, to get a steady job somewhere. Charlie believed in her music, almost as much as Linda did, and her dream lifted him up above the drab ordinary world. He got a job at Wal-Mart. He wore a badge as a customer representative, and as he walked those endless aisles, he knew that Linda was out there singing and writing, sending her music out like a gift to the world.

This very song had come about as the two of them were driving up Belle Meade Boulevard, a road full of great old houses. This was the grand old Nashville, where the rich and the poor were different species, the served and the server. Linda knew that so much suffering was out there, but since the illness it was as if some embedded emotional vein had been opened up, and she felt and saw so much more. She and Charlie talked about that old world that day as they cruised along in her old pickup truck, and a song and lyrics came to her almost full-blown.

As Linda walked the byways in the Nashville she had known in the early 1970s, she thought sometimes that when she had started out she had been too young, a decade younger than the most popular women artists. Now in the 1990s she was too old, two decades older than the singers of the hot young country songs. It didn't seem fair, but she had never thought that fairness was one of life's givens.

When she had started out she had written many songs full of world-weary wisdom, pain, and grief. She had always sung them well, but she owned these songs now, and she sang with rich poignancy, as if she were the honest messenger. When she sang with other singer/songwriters at evenings at the Bluebird Café or at benefits for various charities, she was not as well known as many of the other singers, but no one sang with greater depth and passion, her songs resonating in the air long after she had left the stage.

> She sits at the table and she drops a coffee cup.
> As I sweep away the pieces she looks down and I look up
> And we feel each other's pain,
> Just as if we're standing in the same rain,
> Though we're worlds apart and that won't change.
> All the same we feel each other's pain.

Linda got a publishing deal, a monthly draw to help keep things going. She wrote new songs that she thought were as good as anything she had written. She had it all figured out. This time she wasn't doing it herself. She needed a team to work with her, some hotshot advisers and a manager. She wanted a record deal, and a book deal too. She had fallen to the depths of the pit. She had survived and could tell all that she had felt and seen and knew. She was ready to get it out there in song and story.

Linda knew that her new songs were strong, but she just couldn't get any cuts. The new artists didn't seem interested in her kind of song. After a year her publishing company let her go. She called people she used to know. They promised to get back to her, to hear her tapes, or hear her plans. People listened, or she thought they listened. Everyone seemed so nice to her.

But Nashville wasn't the way it had been twenty-five years ago. There was a killing kindness. They doled it out by the tablespoon until you gagged on it. They opened the door so that you could look within, and then they shut it behind you and you could find not even a keyhole. She thought sometimes that maybe there was no place for a middle-aged woman singer, but the songs were not stamped with her age, the songs were not lined with the years.

The producers and managers looked at the lines on her face more than the depth of her voice. They meant her no disrespect, but she was too old to please the youthful minions who bought Shania Twain and Mindy McCready at Kmart, too old for the videogenic age. There were other societies where the great chanteuses were women of a certain age, women who had lived, and when they sang of love lost, they sang from the depths of their lives, not out of youthful fantasy, but that was not America of the nineties, not the world of hot new country music.

"You've been great," Linda said to the audience when the applause died away. And in the end that was true. "I'd like to end with another new song for you. It's not been recorded yet. This one's called 'One Woman's Life.'"

> I ran into an old friend who I hadn't seen in years
> Shared as if we'd never been apart.
> And as we spoke I felt the flood of memory
> Swelling up within my heart.

Charlie was still out there. He was always out there, looking up at her even like tonight when he was home. He had been with her fifteen years. He always with her. And now at the age of sixty-five, the doctors had told him he had Alzheimer's disease. They said he had already had the disease for five years, most of the time she had been sick. It all became clear. The things he forgot. The ellipses. He had hidden it all. She knew that God had His purposes, but when she first learned about Charlie's illness, she wanted to get in her pickup truck and drive, just drive. If the earth had been flat, she would have driven until she had fallen off.

What was she to do? Sometimes she felt like a bayou, with no way out for her emotions. She had thought that God had saved her for a purpose, and she thought that purpose had been music. It was the only thing she had ever known deeply. It was the only way she had ever earned money. It was all that she had left, that and Charlie. She saw how Charlie dreaded meeting new people, being thrown into the restless throngs of Nashville musical life. Everywhere they went she watched out for him. He continued going to Wal-Mart, and she understood what he was doing for her, for their life. Other times, though, the man lying next to her in bed was gone. He was emptiness within emptiness.

In her songs Linda wrote about the tiny epiphanies of life. She saw now that the greatest heroism was the tiny private acts that the world would never celebrate nor even acknowledge. Charlie at Wal-Mart wearing his customer representative badge, answering questions when sometimes he couldn't recall what happened fifteen minutes ago. Charlie out there in the audience, there for her, there for her music.

Linda didn't know what to do. She was so tired, half sick herself, short of breath and energy. She didn't know where in God's name she would find the strength to go on. She had no money. She had spent everything to produce the tracks for her album. Everything. She had bet it all on one lottery ticket, and when she scratched off the number it wasn't even close. Last year she hadn't paid her taxes, and now the IRS wanted her house. They didn't care about Charlie. They didn't care that she hadn't replied to their letter because Charlie had hidden the mail away and she hadn't found it for weeks.

Linda told the manager at Wal-Mart about Charlie's disease. The man seemed to understand. He put Charlie on the front door as a greeter, and promised to keep him on as long as he could. But he said that Charlie had been wandering around the back of the store looking at the time clock. Linda had prepared a little book for Charlie telling him his hours, but that didn't seem to work. The manager said he had to cut Charlie's hours. Linda couldn't afford it, but she put Charlie in adult day care twice a week.

Those were her hours to write. She was writing songs full of darkness and despair, songs that once would have gotten a hearing in Music City, but she feared even playing them for publishers and producers. She needed to get a publishing deal. She needed at least that. Linda knew that in the new Nashville when they saw desperation in your eyes, most of them just walked around you and left you alone to die. She didn't know what to do. She had called about everyone she could. She had given her life to and for this music. She knew nothing else. She had so little time, so little time, and still she sang on:

> We talked about the choices that we made along the way.
> She told me all about her family.
> I told her my career had taken off and now it seemed
> It was more than I had dreamed.
> And I thought
> Add up all the tears and take away the years,
> and multiply them by the miles,
> then divide them by the trials,
> And you'll figure out the sum of one woman's life.

18

~

"Chains of This Town"

Robert Moore stood at the doorway of his honky-tonk three doors down from Tootsie's beneath a hand-painted sign saying: ROBERT'S WESTERN WORLD, HOME OF BR5-49. Robert looked like a geriatric Popeye. He had a little pot belly below which he hitched his pants, bulging biceps, and a manner that said he would treat you with respect until you double-crossed him, which you probably damn well would do, and then if you didn't get quickly out of his sight, he would as likely as not kick your ever-loving butt to the corner of Broadway and Second Avenue.

Robert was pleased to see a decent crowd down here after Fan Fair, not a tenth as many as would have been here if BR5-49 had been playing, but a decent crowd nonetheless, buying their fair share of $2.25 Buschs and even a few chili dogs.

Robert was the philosopher of Lower Broadway where he had spent most of his adult life. There was hardly anything known to human purview that he hadn't seen on these few blocks. When he took over running the Merchant's Hotel on the corner of Fourth and Broadway, he booted the no-account troublemakers out and turned it into a place where you could bring your lady friend, if your lady friend liked hanging out in a downtown dive. He took over running Tootsie's Orchid Lounge after the old lady died, and he turned that back into a success. The landlord kept raising the rent on him, enough to bleed him dry. You could just push Robert so far, and so he gave up the lease and moved three doors down and opened up Robert's Western World.

Until recently Nashville's music community hadn't understood what a mecca country music could become. The local establishment was more interested in continuing to sell religious publications, insurance, and health services than sullying the image of the Athens of the South by peddling the low-life sounds of country music. The result was that it wasn't until the last few years that the city had begun sprucing up downtown, setting off a real estate boom and creating a number of tourist spots.

There on the corner of Second Avenue and Broadway stood a spanking new Hard Rock Café. It was the kind of place to which Robert would never think of going and that he simply didn't understand. It was an emporium of burgers and T-shirts that had as little to do with country music as it did with the soul of rock 'n' roll, but the tourists lined up there every night as if they were handing out free beer. Up Second Avenue stood the Wildhorse Saloon, the newest venture from Gaylord Entertainment, the company that owned country music television and media about the way old John D. Rockefeller used to own oil. The Wildhorse wasn't wild, and it sure wasn't a saloon, leastways the way Robert saw it. It was an enormous place, featuring country line dancing, T-shirts, and live entertainment that turned every singer into a lounge act.

There were all kinds of new restaurants and tourist hangouts along the street, a Hooters, a sushi bar, souvenir shops. The tourists staying at the Opryland Hotel could catch the General Jackson, ride down the Cumberland River in that Disneyland version of a river steamer, spend an evening on Second Avenue, and ride back up again, without even glimpsing Robert's Western World and the few other honky-tonks.

Robert didn't like what he saw happening, and he knew they were raising the rents all along Lower Broadway, hoping to get rid of these dives, turning it into a place fit for tourists by the busload. On the corner of Fourth and Broadway they were putting up a Planet Hollywood. Across the river there was going to be a new football stadium for Nashville's new NFL team. Right there across the street between Fifth and Seventh Avenues, the city leaders were building themselves the biggest arena between here and Atlanta. They didn't have anything to go in it yet. That wasn't the way Robert did business, put up a building and then figure out what goes inside.

They were trying to get a major-league hockey team, though ice hockey was about as popular in central Tennessee as lawn bowling. They'd get it, though, or maybe a basketball team, something to fill the place. He could just feel them eyeing those two blocks between the Hard Rock and the arena, figuring by the time that arena was up, they wanted those disgraceful honky-tonks out of there.

Robert had learned long ago that when a rich man wants something, the poor man better get out of the way. Lower Broadway was the only home he ever had. There wasn't any amount of money that would get him to leave. He had this dream of turning Lower Broad into a hillbilly Bourbon Street, where folks would come and listen to real country music, not some gussied-up tourist version played in soulless rooms, but the real thing played in real places. Of course, that dream was built mainly on the boys in BR5-49, and now during Fan Fair they weren't here the way they said they always would be.

When Gary Bennett rolled into Nashville in his old Nissan pickup truck in the summer of 1993, he was raring to try his luck songwriting. Gary didn't know much about Music City, but word about the Bluebird Café had made it all the way back to Portland. The place was supposedly a hangout for all the great singer/songwriters trying out their songs and exchanging tips. He figured he would go moseying on in there, sit at the bar, wait his turn, sing a song or two, and one of the old pros would nod at him, and he'd be on his way.

Gary got his guitar and drove over to Green Hills to search out the Bluebird. The club sat in a strip mall. You could hardly make the place out, for there were about 150 singers/songwriters lined up already to audition for open mike night. For Gary, who thought that two people were a crowd, it was a pathetic sight.

Gary got at the end of the line and waited with the others. Some of them struck mournful Gary Cooper poses and others boasted in loud voices, as if their own words could scare away their doubts. Gary looked at the others, sizing them up as best he could. His eyes kept falling on one fellow. He was about Gary's age, but with restless confidence and savvy that Gary figured he would never have. The man could have been a western B-movie gentle-man bandit, swaggering up and down the aisle of a train, collecting wallets and purses, with a tip of the hat to the ladies, his victims feeling they had been given full value for their loss. Gary nodded a greeting to the man and prepared himself for the audition.

Gary was twenty-eight years old. At one moment he looked like Tom Sawyer with an aw-shucks incredulity open to whatever would meet him down that country road. Then suddenly it was an old man there, all bone and lines worn with worry, and the pallor of too many nights in too many bars. He had lost his front teeth, and when there wasn't anyone around he often didn't wear his front plate.

Gary spoke in what half the world figured was a southern accent. He was, in fact, born in Las Vegas and brought up in Cougar, a village of about a hundred in southwestern Washington in the forests at the foot of the great Mount Saint Helens volcano. It wasn't that Gary spoke southern but that he spoke slowly. Each syllable rolled around in his mouth before it came out and just hung there in the air, waiting for the next syllable to push it away. Words mattered more than time, and when he spoke, he made damn sure he was saying what he wanted to say.

Gary had been making a living playing in a country band, driv-ing sixty miles to Portland every night. He was making good money, a hundred dollars a night. The years were going by, how-ever, and if he was ever going to be anything more than a guy trudging between gigs, hauling his guitar and his songs, he knew that he better do something about it. He didn't have anything holding him down. He had been married and divorced twice. He wasn't walking up that fool's hill again. The fiddle player in the band, Donnie Herron, had left and moved to Nashville. He kept calling telling Gary to come, shop his songs around, and stay with him until he got his own place.

When Gary finally got in the door, he hardly had time to look at the bluebird motif over the little stage before he was called to whip through one verse and chorus of his song. They told him he had made the cut and was scheduled for a Sunday evening in February, and pointed him out the door.

Gary returned four months later with about forty other singers/songwriters. By then he knew that the chance that some high-powered executive would be sitting there waiting to discover him was about as likely as being picked up hitchhiking along Hillsboro Pike by the ghost of Hank Williams, but he went anyway. He was pushed and prodded like all the others, told to get tuned, and get ready, do his thing, and get off. Gary tried the other writers' nights at clubs across Nashville, but it was triple all for nothing. You didn't get paid. You didn't get noticed. And you sure didn't have a good time.

Gary could have started beating his head against doors, hoping someone would hear him, but that wasn't him, and he didn't figure it was worth it. Instead, he started spending time down on Lower Broadway. Gary was sauntering along one day when he heard the sound of Willie Nelson's classic song "Hello Walls" pouring out on the sidewalk from an open door. That was the kind of great old country music, first recorded in 1961 by Faron Young, he hadn't heard since coming to Nashville, and he gave it a listen. He started hanging out at the bars, nursing a drink along, checking out the scene. Most of the places were quite empty, but there were some good pickers, along with some drunken ones. Good or bad, they were playing what they wanted to play.

These weren't fancy folks sitting at the bar, down from the suburbs for an evening. These were the poor whites that nobody wanted anymore. Nashville didn't want them, fouling up the image of the new progressive South, scaring the tourists. The hot new country music didn't want them either; they were the creators of country music, but they pulled down the affluent demographics with their poverty.

The more Gary sat there, the more he realized that these were like the people back in Cougar. That's why he felt at home here. He knew that down here was the dead end of country music, a place of lost careers, and lost songs, but it just felt right. He was tired of trying to pitch his songs to a world that did not listen, tired of the songwriter evenings.

Gary came down toting his guitar, planning to walk from bar to bar until he found somebody who would let him get up and sing. He ended up playing in a band at Robert's Western World. The place was primarily a clothing store with a small bar. Gary stood on a little stage in the window, performing before an audience largely consisting of cowboy boots, saddles, and fringed shirts. One evening Gary noticed that working the door up the street at Tootsie's was a face that Gary recognized from the line at the Bluebird, the fellow who looked like he made his living cheating the rubes at three-card monte. Gary started talking to the man, who gave his name as Chuck Mead.

Chuck had arrived in town about the same time as Gary, and he was doing even worse pushing his way into Music City. Chuck had been less than enthusiastic about life as a doorman when before his first shift he had been told how to deal with customers who pulled knives on him. He had lasted a month as the bouncer. The only good thing he could say about the job was that he hadn't seen a flash of steel or had to disarm anybody. He went from doorman to playing two nights a week at Tootsie's, but the tips he earned hardly kept him in razor blades.

"Hey, man, you oughta come down to Robert's," Gary said when he heard Chuck's tale of woe. "You know, this weekend our guitar player can't make it. Can you come and play?"

"Well, sure," Chuck replied, grateful for the smallest of favors.

When Chuck walked into Robert's and got up on the little stage, he had the feeling he was playing in some bizarre hillbilly Kmart. He imagined that at any moment Robert would announce over the public address system: "Attention, Robert's World shoppers, for the next twenty minutes we are having a special on all lizard-skin cow-boy boots."

Chuck was used to playing in dark honky-tonks, but here the lights were turned up higher than at a 7-Eleven. Robert was trying to discourage shoplifters and was zapping them with every light in the place. A thief might get away with a gun belt or two, one of those holsters on the rack, or one of those cowboy shirts with the silver frill, but it didn't seem likely anybody would burst into that glass case with the bola ties and belt buckles, or get out the door carrying a saddle or one of the cowboy hats above the bar. The cowboy boots were safe too. There were three long rows of boots on shelves running all the way along the wall, sitting neatly like dawn in a humongous bunkhouse. Anyone taking a pair would have to pluck them down and run straight past the band.

This first evening there couldn't have been much of a shoplift-ing problem. Most of the time there were no more than four peo-ple in the joint. Chuck loved the old country tunes as much as Gary, though he was no more a southerner than his new buddy across the little stage. He had grown up in Lawrence, Kansas, home of the University of Kansas. His father was a teacher.

As a baby Chuck had practically been swaddled in sheet music, learning the old songs at his mommy's knee. Back in the late for-ties she had played with her parents and brothers in a country band. They were known as the Wynes Family. While his friends were having normal half-crazed teen years, Chuck was out with his family in small towns in Missouri, Kansas, and Iowa playing Hank Williams and Patsy Cline and Ernest Tubb.

Chuck attended the university for a semester, but he wanted to make music, not study, and he dropped out. He dropped out of country music too, but eventually joined a roots-type band, The Homestead Grays, that broke up in 1993. Chuck was thirty-two years old, damn near retirement age in a rock 'n' roll band, and pushing it in country music too. He didn't have anything much left in Lawrence, anything much but tattered pride and a good guitar, so he packed up, got in his old car, and headed to Nashville.

★ ★ ★

Gary and Chuck discovered immediately that one thing they had in common was that they were both deeply grieved by what they saw happening to country music. They listened to the radio and they despaired of what they were hearing, and what they were not hearing. They saw the situation almost in a biblical sense. Grievous sins were being committed in Nashville in the name of money and marketing. The music was losing its soul and spirit. The temple had been stripped of its gold, the altar pulled down. Young people turning on the hot young country on their FM radios were listening to false prophets who didn't know the true word.

Gary was a singer of ballads and Chuck a rockabilly man, and between them they knew most of the important repertoire of old-time country music. Gary loved the sad slow songs. He sang them with a voice that was a reservoir of such pain that he did not seem simply to be singing but giving living testimony to all the hurt that he had felt. He walked upon the precipice of tears telling tales that resonated with the lives of most of those in the room. It was an overwhelming paradox why people who knew such hardship in their own lives should choose to spend their few free hours listening to songs so often about the sadness of others. There was no better answer than that found in Ecclesiastes 7:3: "Sorrow is better than laughter; for by the sadness of the countenance the heart is made better." The heart was made better by these sad sad songs, and Gary was doctor of the soul.

As soon as Gary finished one of his ballads, Chuck, the rockabilly man, revved his guitar up, and set off on a fast-paced, foot-tapping, get-off-your-duff-and-dance-your-head-off kind of number, maybe an early Johnny Cash or a Carl Perkins song or one of those he had written himself. Chuck preferred singing happy songs of happy times, singing them with such exuberance that it seemed he might levitate, rising a few feet off the stage with his guitar. And Gary loved singing those laments, elegies to better times and better places, songs of despair and loneliness, of dark empty highways stretching into eternity. Between them, though, they captured the joy and the sadness, the good times and the bad, captured the hillbilly world while standing on a little stage in a room full of boots and bottles of beer.

Maybe there had been almost nobody there that first night, but Gary and Chuck had such a kick playing together that they decided to keep it up. They played many nights together, but they were still just another no-name, no-account pickup band. Chuck might like those good-time songs, but at times he had a hustler's desperate look in his eyes when the scam isn't working, and it was about time to run. He called his old buddy, Shaw Wilson, to ask him to move out from Lawrence and play drums with him at Robert's and in a two-person group they called Dos Cojones. "Man, it's happening," Chuck said, ever the promoter. "You can come down here and we're making thirty-five bucks, tips."

"Well, hell, I don't have a job," Shaw replied, seeing no reason to belabor the obvious.

Shaw, like Gary and Chuck, had been branded weird when he was a kid. The son of a career air force navigator, he had grown up on a series of bases, living in houses that looked as much in uniform as his father. It was the bizarre world beyond the gates of the base that intrigued him, those monstrous gleaming Cadillacs cruising down the highway outside Topeka, the sounds of Johnny Cash and Johnny Horton and Patsy Cline and other strange stuff coming over the car radio.

His parents had sung folk songs when he was a kid, but he had never picked up on that and it wasn't until he got his first set of drums that he became consumed with music. He had gone to college and had studied business, but he wasn't fit to be some bow-tied advertising man. He dropped out, ending up in Lawrence, Kansas, playing in various bands, doing what he had to do to make a living.

The college town was full of young men whose promise was fast becoming what might have been, young men who weren't young any longer. Shaw played in some decent local bands, but most of the time he was just keeping his nose a quarter inch above the water. He was thirty-four years old. He was living among a bunch of kids, cooking in a sorority during the day, playing in bands at night. College was out, and the best he could hope for during the summer was a job painting somebody's house. He didn't have much to his name except a good set of drums, and so he headed down the highway to Nashville.

When Shaw showed up at Robert's, he stepped around a drunken bum sprawled across the sidewalk, and entered the western wear store/honky-tonk. He set up behind Gary and Chuck, and got into it. Although the few customers couldn't see him hidden behind his drums, he was a worthy addition to the museum of physiognomy that was the group. Shaw was slightly south of handsome. With his razor-thin, rakishly curved mustache, slicked-back black hair, and studied diffidence, he looked like a fifties lounge lizard.

When the group took a break, they trooped out into the alley and stood there in the shadow of the Ryman. They smoked a cigarette or two, drank some beer, or sometimes puffed on a reefer and chatted a bit. That was the rhythm of a musician's life on Lower Broadway, a seductive serenade that drained the last of the ambition out of most of those who made their way down here.

It wouldn't have gone any further than this, another group of itinerant musicians thrown together for a few months. When they returned and got up on that stage, they noticed many of the same faces night after night, and new folks standing at the bar. They had found something, though they didn't know quite what it was. They liked the sound they were making, but they knew that it wasn't quite right, and they began tinkering with the group.

Chuck operated on some plane of logic known only to himself. They needed a bass player; then why not Jay McDowell, a guitar player who had never touched a stand-up bass all his twenty-five years on this blessed earth? The two men had met early in the year when Chuck heard Jay playing with Hellbilly, a rockabilly band that traveled around the Southeast on weekends. After that, Jay had come out to hear Chuck and Gary at Robert's one of the first nights they were there, and their singing had struck a resonant chord. Jay came back many nights, feeding the tip jar like everybody else.

Jay went out and got a loan on his car and bought a thousand-dollar stand-up bass. Jay could not understand why he was compelled to do this. Here he was playing guitar in a group that was doing better than the boys at Robert's, going off on paid gigs. He didn't even know if he could play the bass. He and his wife had just broken up, and here he was breaking up with Hellbilly to play for tips earning maybe fifty bucks a week. He was going through desperate times, and here he was willfully making them even more desperate.

Human lives resonate together sometimes as much as the strings on a guitar. Jay had never talked much with the three other musicians about their lives, but it was as if their emotional autobiographies had been written by the same pen. Maybe he was a decade younger than his new band mates, but growing up in West Lafayette, Indiana, he had felt just as much the outsider as they had.

Jay looked now about the same as he had as a teenager, like a member of the chorus in a road company of *Grease*. No one else in his high school oiled their hair and slicked it back. No one else liked the bizarre grab bag of music that he did. He was out there in a world of his own, a greaseball, punkabilly freak. He remembered when his family would drive down to his grandmother's place in rural Indiana Saturday night listening to the music on the Grand Ole Opry. His father, a computer programmer at Purdue University in Indiana, had brought up his son to love music, giving him a guitar and a set of drums. Jay had dropped out of college and for several years had made his living teaching guitar before driving to Nashville.

That first night up there on the stand, Jay felt stark-naked fear. He had been practicing alone for a few days, playing along with some of his old Elvis records, but it was different being up here, trying to wing it. He looked over at Chuck's hands on the guitar and did his improvised imitation of a stand-up bass player. It wasn't bad if you didn't know much about bass playing, but it wasn't good if you did. Jay felt good up here with the boys, and he kept it up night after night, and night after night he got better.

They still needed somebody who could play the fiddle, lap steel, and maybe the mandolin. The first and best choice was Donnie Herron, who had played with Gary back in Portland and had given his old band mate a place to stay when he first arrived in Nashville. The only problem was that Donnie was playing in Southern Exposure, a southern rock band that had a record deal on Curb. That didn't stop Gary from asking Donnie and giving him plenty of room to think it over.

Donnie had just had an operation on his elbow and was recuperating up at his mother's farm in upstate New York. He couldn't play his fiddle, but Chuck had lent him a six-string lap steel. So he sat up there on those cold February days, picking up a new instrument, playing along with a bunch of Hank Williams tapes.

When Donnie wasn't playing and talking to his mom, he was thinking about just what he should do. As a boy he had lived with his parents on a fifty-seven-acre farm in West Virginia, working it with horses when his father wasn't out driving a big rig somewhere. Donnie had been nothing but a little kid when his folks had hauled him off to a square dance and told him to stay put. He sat there staring at this ninety-year-old fiddle player playing the living daylights out of the thing. The old fellow got so into the music that he picked both his feet up off the ground. He was having more fun than every last one of the dancers.

Donnie just wanted a fiddle, and he talked on it so much that he got one for Christmas. Soon he was playing all the tunes about as well as the old men who taught him. He was still just a kid, but Friday night he played in a club outside town. The Farmer's Daughter had a floor that was half cement and half dirt, and it was a hard-drinking, hard-fighting, hard-playing kind of place.

There were still fiddlers in those hills, music up those hollows, but most of the young people were embarrassed by those old country sounds. In high school, Donnie didn't mind that many of his classmates shunned him. He loved those old fiddle players, and he preferred them to his smart-talking classmates. He loved to play with those old men, and listen to them, and learn from them. They were his best friends, and they were dying off. When his classmates were attending sock hops, Donnie was attending funerals. He would be with a fiddler one day, the old man playing his heart out, and the next day he would be gone. And when he played those sad country songs, he knew that these truths were his truths.

Donnie heard about this school down there in Levelland, Texas, called South Plains College, where you could major in country and bluegrass music. Donnie paid his way playing in bands in Lubbock and Wichita Falls. From there he traveled on to Bakersfield, the home of Merle Haggard and Buck Owens, two of the kings of country. He stayed there a good five years, playing in various groups and getting married. After Donnie and his wife split, he couldn't stand living there any longer. He headed north to Portland, where he met Gary and played in his band for about a year before driving east to Nashville.

Donnie liked old country songs. He liked bluegrass. He liked Bob Wills's Western swing. But he sure didn't like the stuff Southern Exposure was playing. They could call it whatever name they wanted, but it was nothing but early-seventies rock and roll. He much preferred to play with Gary and the boys down at Robert's. He'd come off the road with Southern Exposure, playing fairs and amphitheaters, with thousands of folks hooting and hollering, and he'd head down to that half-empty honky-tonk, and he just loved it.

Donnie had learned from those old fiddlers back in West Virginia that there was only one worthy reason to play music: because you loved to play it. That was an old man's wisdom and a young man's truth. It wasn't wisdom or truth for those hard years in the middle when a man had to make a living and make his way out there in the world.

Donnie's father had passed on years ago, and his mother was alone working the farm. She had every reason to think it was time for her son to start living in the world as it was, and not go running around looking for Lord knows what.

"Mom, I just don't know what to do," Donnie told her one evening. "I'm between a rock and a hard place here."

"Son," she said as she turned to Donnie. "You ain't got no bills. You ain't got no wife. You have to worry about nothin'. You do what you want to do."

When Donnie came back to Nashville, he gave notice to Southern Exposure and started spending his evenings playing for tips at Robert's.

During the day the five musicians often went off pawing through the bins at secondhand record stores, picking up old records. Country music wasn't that different from the rest of American culture. People lived long in America and they died young, most memory of their achievements gone, buried with their careers. The boys listened to the old songs and played the ones they liked, adding them to Gary and Chuck's own songs. They had no highfalutin notion of celebrating the roots of country music. It just so happened that the songs they loved ranged from Jimmie Rodgers and the Carter Family and the beginnings of country music in the late 1920s, through to about 1967, just before the pop country Nashville sound took over. They did them their own way, true to the spirit, but sung to their own beat and nuance. Gary and Chuck were very different songwriters, but their songs so seamlessly meshed with the old songs that most of the younger audiences didn't know the old songs from the new.

Sometimes when they were playing they felt the spirit of the Lord as much as if they were playing in the heavenly chorus. They didn't even have to talk about it. Gary would look over to Chuck as he stood up front plucking away on his guitar, and good old Donnie fiddling away would nod over to Smilin' Jay playing the stand-up bass, and back behind him on the drums, Shaw Wilson would get that funny look in his eyes.

Robert had started feeling that something pretty amazing was happening. There wasn't much of a crowd except on weekends, but there was a strange hillbilly spirit alive down here now. He didn't know what it was or where it would take him, but he turned the lights way down, moved the bar back, got rid of the saddle and most of the clothes, and put up a hand-painted sign outside above the window: ROBERT'S WESTERN WORLD: HOME OF BR5-49. That was the name the boys had given themselves. They had gone back to the old country TV show *Hee Haw* and chosen the phone number that the comedian Junior Samples gave out in his knee-slapping takeoff on a slimeball used-car salesman doing a TV commercial.

Since they had been appearing at Robert's, BR5-49 had developed their own fans. Some were regulars from Robert's days at Tootsie's. Others had chanced in and liked what they heard and what they were drinking. There was nobody here who lived a tax-deductible life. Some customers looked eternally doomed to sit here drinking beer. The waitress had a firm rule. If a regular customer passed out twice at the bar, he wasn't served any more beer.

Drunk or sober, these were working folks to whom this music res-onated with all the themes and stories of their lives. They liked nothing better than to stump the band, asking Gary or Chuck to play some old Roy Acuff or Webb Pierce song, but it was con-founded difficult to come up with something the boys didn't know.

One evening John Michael Montgomery came strutting into Tootsie's, where the boys were playing one evening. The country star told Chuck that he would give him twenty-five dollars for every Hank Williams song he could sing. John Michael left the club more than six hundred dollars poorer than when he arrived.

When Gary started at Robert's, he had taken a regular break with the boys in the band. Now that they were together as BR5-49, they played from around nine-thirty in the evening until two, four and a half hours straight. Most musicians would have considered that a merciless schedule. They got so into it that they didn't know if they'd been playing ten minutes or ten hours, so into it that it didn't matter if there was a big crowd or not. They weren't think-ing about record deals and fancy gigs. Not only were they happy but they knew they were happy, and they could think of nothing better in the world than night after night to play at Robert's Western World.

The decoration at Robert's was the same at it had always been, the most notable feature those long rows of cowboy boots, about all that was left of the western merchandise. It took a few drinks sometimes to figure out that the faces on the mural behind the bandstand were Roy Acuff, Dolly Parton, Marty Stuart, Hank Williams, and that woman with what looked like fangs coming from her mouth was Patsy Cline.

As the weeks went by, the crowds started to grow, students from Vanderbilt and Belmont, secretaries and mailroom staff from Music Row, urban sophisticates, fraternity boys and truck drivers, yuppies, retirees trying to look young and high school kids trying to look old. It grew so much that Robert tore down his upstairs office, set up another little bar, and turned the balcony into space for the overflow. Even that wasn't enough on the weekends, and the lines of people stood out on the street waiting to get in, a sight as rare on Lower Broad as a Rolls-Royce.

Chuck made the pitch for the tip jar, and by rights he should have had half the preachers in Tennessee sitting in booths, taking notes. "We live by these tips," he began, in his fervent last-evening-of-the-revival voice, his fedora tilted rakishly. "Now come forward, brothers and sisters, and give to your band." He looked down approvingly as a scattering of believers scurried to the stage, heads down, plunging green bills into the glass pickle jar. "You have been saved, saved, but what about the rest of you heathen out there?"

The boys—and that was what everybody called them—had almost everything they wanted, and best of all they knew it. Gary and Donnie lived in an old trailer that Robert had sitting on some land in East Nashville. It was a hillbilly haven if there ever was one, with rats running around beneath, but it was all they felt they needed. Robert had given it to them for nothing, and they thought of the old man as kind of a redneck angel, generous and good not only to them but to all the down-and-outers of Lower Broad, putting some of them up in his house.

They had plenty of money now, cash buckets of it, and they spent much of it on instruments, including a two-thousand-dollar mandolin for Donnie. They shopped at Goodwill and used- clothing stores for outfits that were as seasoned as their music. Chuck duded himself up in a kind of Hank Williams look, so that when the smoke was thick you could imagine it was old Hank up there wailing away. Jay looked like a fifties gambler, fresh from sitting behind a deck of cards in Vegas, while Donnie settled for bib overalls, hitched up as if he had just come back after a day in the fields.

There was nothing like this scene in all of Nashville. In the Tennessee capital as elsewhere in America, the young and the old, the rich and poor, the city dwellers and the country folks didn't like the same music, dance to the same tunes, eat the same food, or go to the same bars. The advertising industry knew that. The marketing people knew that. Music Row knew that.

Out there on that floor was a scene to bedevil the experts enough for them to drink their Maalox straight from the bottle. One weekday evening in August, a woman editor got up from her table of women friends and started dancing with a seventy-five-year-old farmer. High school students boogied with yuppies, and retired folks two-stepped with businessmen from Omaha and points west. Back near the bar a Japanese tourist pulled out his miniature video camera and scanned the room, before passing out warm sake from a flask to his guests. A Native American in a head-dress and war paint squeezed past the bar, and the regulars did double takes, as if they feared they had been drinking too much. Reassured that this apparition was an Indian in the flesh, they returned to their beers.

What the boys had above everything else was joy. On the evenings when they were right and the crowd was right, there was more joy in this narrow room than in all the corporate palaces along Music Row, more joy than in the state-of-the-art studios that dotted the town. There was joy in singing new songs that resonated with the themes of the old; joy in rediscovering the old songs, trea-sures lying in the attics and cellars of American culture; joy in dust-ing them off, burnishing them up, and playing for an audience; joy in seeing that old pickle jar filling with folding green, stuffed so thick with bills; joy in strolling out of there at two in the morning, the streets empty, the skeleton of the new Nashville arena rising dark against a somber sky.

The scene at Robert's had become the place to be for almost anyone who cared about country music in Nashville. One evening Emmylou Harris, one of the great heroines of the boys in BR5-49, hired the band for a private party to celebrate her daughter Meghann's sixteenth birthday. They were getting used to having prominent musicians show up, but it was mind-boggling to have one of the genuine legends of the music they cared about sitting up there in a broken chair in the balcony.

It was one-thirty in the morning. Meghann and her friends had gone. The only guest left was Emmylou's old singer/songwriter friend, Jamie O'Hara, sitting across the balcony. Down below Emmylou's longtime road manager, Phil Kaufman, sat alone drink-ing at the bar, calling out songs by her mentor, Gram Parsons, for the band to play. Next to Phil, Larry, the janitor, sat with his head in his hands.

Phil barked out another command. This time it was for "Hickory Wind." Gary knew the version that Emmylou and Gram did together to the last note and nuance. It was a classic. It didn't seem right to sing his version in front of Emmylou. Up in the dark balcony Emmylou nodded her wish that he should go ahead, and the band played the song.

> But now when I'm lonesome
> I always pretend
> That I'm gettin' the feel of hickory wind.

As Emmylou listened, she knew that though it was still Gram's song and her song, it was Gary's song now too, and BR5-49 would take it out into the world anew. Sitting here in the darkened room, she saw that the music she cared about was still alive, carried forth to a new generation.

Up on Music Row they dismissed BR5-49 as "retro." The strange thing was that the assistants to assistants, the secretaries and runners, were down at Robert's getting into the whole thing, coming back and telling their bosses what an exciting act they had seen. What it took to wake the mandarins of Music Row was not the fervent pleas of their underlings. It was a cover story about BR5-49 in *Billboard* in July of 1995. If the trade publication could write that BR5-49 "single-handedly transformed Lower Broadway into the hippest place in Music City," then the top record company executives figured they better make the jaunt down to Lower Broad.

The first label interested in the band wanted the boys to start out by ditching Mike Janas and Josef Nuyens, whom they had signed to produce them. The band wasn't having any of that. The next label executive wanted Chuck and Gary to bring in some of the best session players in town to give their music a professional Nashville sheen. Chuck and Gary didn't even have to think about that one either.

At Arista/Nashville, Tim DuBois's staff pestered him so much about BR5-49 that he went down to Lower Broad after work for a showcase especially for Arista. Robert kept the door open so any-body who wanted to could come in, and the show wasn't much dif-ferent from any other night at the honky-tonk. Tim sat there in his unobtrusive way, sipping a beer, looking no different from anyone else in the club. When BR5-49 finished their set, Tim got up, walked up to the band, and handed Chuck two twenty-dollar bills, symbolizing that he had bought into their music.

Tim signed BR5-49 because they were different, and he wanted to ride that wave he had seen down at Robert's, ride it as far as it would go. Tim could see that the boys had a vision of themselves as a hip, quirky group on the edge of things, playing in small clubs, high school auditoriums, small towns, and college campuses. He wasn't about to tell them the truth.

If they had wanted that, they should have signed with some rinky-dink independent label. He wasn't fronting them tens of thousands of dollars and putting his staff to work for them to sell a hundred thousand CDs and keep on playing part of the time for tips at Robert's. Arista didn't work that way. He only had nine artists on the whole label. He was going to do everything he could to make them an arena act, as big as his two superstar acts, Alan Jackson and Brooks and Dunn, playing before ten thousand fans at a time, selling albums by the millions.

Gary stood on Broadway in front of Robert's with his thumbs around the belt loops on his pants, swaying back and forth as if he were a sailor on a ship. The two weeks they had been recording the album, BR5-49 hadn't played at Robert's, but now they were back. Gary loved hanging out there, having a cup of coffee with Robert or Mattie, the bartender, or just sitting around saying not much of anything. It was all rushing so fast now that Gary woke up every morning feeling he was in this Cinemascope wide-screen Cecil B. DeMille movie, and he was one of the stars.

Robert was mighty proud. He knew that he had given the boys their chance, and without him there would not have been any BR5-49. The boys told everyone they talked to that they would never leave Robert's. Robert wouldn't have been a philosopher of the street if he didn't have a grasp on that slippery thing known as human nature. It wasn't that he disbelieved them, but he had heard those tales before over at Tootsie's when somebody got a bit of success. He had seen them looking him in the eye and say they were there forever, and that was about the last time they played there.

Of course, Gary and the rest of the boys were different, at least he hoped they were, but he knew that they wouldn't be there the way they had before. He'd already been bringing in other guitar players and singers and letting them stand up there on that little stage and sing their songs, dreaming of following along that pathway where BR5-49 had been. When the boys did play an occasional weekend, it was crazy, lines out on the street, the fire marshal counting heads and giving orders. The room was jammed beyond jammed, and the money was great, but the people whom Robert knew, the people who had made the honky-tonk their little club, for the most part didn't come any longer.

The band kept playing at Robert's whenever they could, but they signed with CAA as a booking agent, and they started getting paying gigs. In February the boys heard that they would be playing their first major gig, opening for Vince Gill at the cavernous Von Braun Auditorium in Huntsville, Alabama. The promoter was having trouble filling the seven thousand seats, and at the last minute he needed an opening act so he could have an intermission to sell drinks and merchandise. They drove down to Huntsville, hardly having time to worry about this evening. But at the sound check in the empty auditorium, they suddenly sensed what was before them. "And then he'll introduce these BR-500 fellows, and after that . . ." the stage manager said, as Chuck and Gary stood at the side of the stage. Shaw's eye was twitching, jumping back and forth like a crazed Morse code operator while he was back sitting with his drums. That evening the boys did fine, holding the crowd, delivering it to Vince in fine fettle. They didn't knock 'em dead, but they weren't supposed to, and they left that evening feeling right and good about the world. The boys got a new manager too— Barry Coburn, who had previously represented Alan Jackson—and for months had hung out at Robert's because he loved country music. Barry wasn't making his living earning 15 percent of a pickle jar of tips, and he pushed BR5-49 out in the world.

Many hoped that BR5-49 could lead country music back to its roots, opening the music to all kinds of singers and bands, neotraditionalists, roots bands, folk country. Waiting in the wings if BR5-49 succeeded were scores of other new groups that were part of a vague movement of alternative country known by some as No Depression. Logic and sentiment said that the band should have been at Fan Fair, meeting the fans out at the fairgrounds and playing every night on Lower Broad. That would have sent a message to the world that BR5-49 played music equally for the young edgy audience and for older lovers of the deep and the true in country music. Their new manager had this idea of making them the next hip thing in Europe. He had the band playing festivals in Scandinavia during Fan Fair.

Robert knew somehow that it was too good to be true, that it couldn't last, not something this good. When the folks at Fan Fair came asking for them, Robert didn't know quite where they were, except that they weren't where they said they'd always be. He had hoped that BR5-49 would save Lower Broad, but as he looked up and down the street, he could see that a great revolving ball was going up on the corner of Third and Broadway for the new Planet Hollywood that was opening in a few days. The great silver icon looked like a wrecking ball, and that's what Robert figured it was. Maybe it wouldn't have made any difference if BR5-49 had stayed the way they said they would. He didn't pretend to know. He kept that hand-painted sign above the door, but BR5-49's home was now somewhere else.

Robert's Western World wasn't just a honky-tonk on Lower Broad, though, it was a spirit and a sound that the boys in BR5-49 were carrying out into the world. It wasn't just their spirit and sound. It was Hank's and Webb's and Buck's and Johnny's and Faron's and Ernest's and Merle's and Patsy's spirit, revved up for a new world.

BR5-49 may have been the anointed ones, but it wasn't just the boys carrying the music out into the world either. It was scores of groups from Chicago to Portland, picking away in scruffy clubs and little bars. It wasn't about making platinum records and getting played on hot young country radio. It was about playing music that mattered to people, that was deep and true and fun and joyful. BR5-49 weren't here this evening and maybe they should have been, but the kinds of songs they cared about played out in the night, and people danced and drank, and celebrated not simply good old country music but life in all its shades and nuances, its darkness and its light.

Friday,
June 14, 1996
~

19

~

"Heartaches by the Number"

Harlan Howard sat on a barstool at the Sunset Grill. This tiny, windowless bar stuck into the recesses of the upscale restaurant was one of the few places left in Nashville where songwriters still hung out. And nobody hung out here more than sixty-eight-year-old Harlan Howard. He had been here for several hours already, drinking and talking to the bartender and anyone else who sat next to him.

There was a time when he put down nothing but White Russians, a volatile mixture of vodka, Kahlúa, and cream. For a while he had liked his own special milk shake of chocolate milk and vodka by the pitcher. Now he wasn't so particular, having the bartender mix the vodka with orange juice, Bloody Mary mix, or tonic. It didn't matter much as long as the drink was strong and the next one was sitting there when he had finished the last.

Harlan didn't care about Fan Fair. This had been the last day, and many of the major stars had already left town, spreading out across the United States to perform at fairs, festivals, great arenas, and theaters. Although few artists showed up the final day, many fans stayed around until the very end, as if there was something they had been searching for here and did not want to leave until they found it. At precisely three o'clock the last of the fans were pushed out of the buildings. Trailer trucks and U-Hauls rolled onto the grounds and crews began tearing down the booths. Some fans still did not want to leave the grounds, and the guards gently prodded them to the exits. Within a few hours everything was gone and there was an eerie emptiness to the fairgrounds, as if nothing had taken place.

Harlan wouldn't have cared about Fan Fair except that over on Music Row, people were busy with things other than what he considered the most important thing of all: hearing new songs. For Harlan it was a week to do nothing much but write songs. That was fine with him, for that's what he was supposed to be doing anyway.

Harlan asked the bartender for a pen and scribbled a few lines on a bar napkin. Over in his office two blocks away on Wedgewood Avenue, Harlan had a big old desk. The upper right-hand drawer was stuffed with bar napkins laced with his barely legible scratchings. Sometimes they sat there for months, years even, but they were his private treasure trove. The title was the thing. Once he got that the verses would come, the bridge, the rest of it. Maybe a month. Maybe a year. It would come. But first a title.

Harlan had begun to think how he wanted to be remembered. His wish was a simple one, grounded in the sinews of truth, like the songs he had written. He did not have a rich man's foolish vanity, thinking that by emblazoning his name on buildings, highways, and endowed university chairs, people would recall and think fondly of him long after he was gone.

Harlan knew that it was a man's deeds, not his name, that lived after him, and usually not even his deeds. He knew that because that's the way it already was with him. Outside Nashville few people knew his name, though he was one of the greatest songwriters not only of *his* time but of several times. In a world of endless fads and change, Harlan had managed to write hits during five decades.

Harlan knew that when people turned on the radio in the car or pushed in a CD or cassette in their living room, they didn't know it was a Harlan Howard song. Patsy Cline fans didn't care that Harlan and Hank Cochran wrote "I Fall to Pieces." Reba fans didn't care that Harlan and Chick Rains wrote her first number one hit, "Somebody Should Leave." The fans didn't care that Harlan had written Mel Tillis's first big hit ("Life Turned Her That Way") and twenty-three years later his daughter Pam Tillis's first number one hit as well ("Don't Tell Me What to Do"). When they listened to Patty Loveless singing "Blame It on Your Heart" they didn't care that Harlan and Kostas had written the hit.

Most people passed their three score and ten in a fog of life, seeking moments of illumination in the pathway ahead. When people sat in their car and heard his song on the radio, they might be worrying about the mortgage payments, listening to the kids fighting in the backseat, or the fellow might be thinking if he was going to get lucky later in the evening. In that precious moment he had to touch their hearts, and move them, and so he had for close to forty years.

Harlan's wish, then, was that a hundred years from now some people somewhere would be sitting around a campfire, or in a dingy bar, and they would sing one of his songs. Of course, they would not know that it was *his,* but that was not what mattered. They would sing it, and if it was a sad love ballad they would feel sad, and if it was a joyous song they would be lifted. And in that song he would be alive. It was only a wish, but it seemed likely it might just take place if a century from now people love the way they have always loved, and hurt the way they have always hurt.

For most of his life, Harlan had treated his body like an old truck that he abused and neglected. Then he cranked it up again and off he would go. As a young man, he saw dawn as he drove to work in a factory. For years in Nashville he often saw dawn as the end of another carousing night. He drank earlier than most. He didn't drink alone. He drank among friends. He drank to quell his shyness, not his thirst. He drank stronger. And he drank more. He smoked one cigarette after another. He had been divorced four times, and again and again had felt emotional agonies that close to felled him.

Two years ago, his body had just given up, from his feet to his head. He had a pinched nerve in his foot so he could hardly walk. The arthritis in his back was so bad it was like he was rusted out. His heart was giving out. His stomach didn't work right either. The doctors put him on painkillers. He was in such a daze that he signed things he didn't remember signing. He could hardly write his name, and he sure couldn't write a good country song.

Last year he had four operations to relieve his major problems. It was like waging four major wars in a year. His weight dropped from 213 pounds to 150. During one operation his blood pressure dropped to zero. Harlan had fine surgeons, but if he had not been so touched by life, with such a fierce will to go on, he would not have lived. He had not merely survived, mind you. His walk was a little slow, but he was back now, in spirit and form.

Young Harlan was tuning in the radio one Saturday night in a foster home on a farm in Michigan when he happened onto Ernest Tubb singing "I Wonder Why You Said Goodbye" at the Grand Ole Opry on Nashville's WSM. That evening a songwriter was born. Harlan started listening to the Opry whenever he could and tuning in to other country music. He wrote down the lyrics, making up his own lines when he couldn't take it all down. He began writing his own songs. The radio was his school, and he listened long and he learned well.

Of all the singers he heard no one touched him more than Ernest Tubb. The Texas Troubadour's gruff, manly baritone was distinctive, yet it was a disciplined, restrained voice in which the song always came first. Tubb was the greatest of the pure honky-tonk singers of the forties. The style developed out of having to sing over the rowdy patrons of bars and juke joints and dance halls. The crowd down there on those floors was not interested in dancing and drinking to tunes about cabins in the woods. They wanted to hear about love, lust, betrayal, booze, pain, and heartache, and Tubb gave them what they wanted.

Honky-tonk music was for adults who had lived and loved, not for a kid scarcely into his teens, but Harlan's life already had enough sadness to pour into a thousand country songs, and then pour it into a thousand more. He got his name from his family's home in Harlan County, Kentucky, but Harlan was born in Detroit, where Ralph Howard, his father, worked on the Ford assembly line for five dollars a day. His daddy stopped at those hillbilly bars after eight hours on the line, drank up his wages. One day she just couldn't take it and upped and left him, taking six-month-old Harlan with her, leaving their three other children with her husband.

His mother shipped little Harlan back one day in a taxicab, and he lived with his father in a tiny room on the fourth floor of a tenement. When the liquor got to him, Ralph went off on one of his binges, and four-year-old Harlan learned to watch out for himself for several days in a row. To survive he learned all the stealthy savvy of an alley cat, slinking away into the darkness from those who reached out to hurt.

One day when Harlan's daddy was gone and he was climbing those stairs, he saw an open door and a plate of meat sitting on a kitchen counter. He was so hungry that he scurried into the room, grabbed the meat, and ran out. Little Harlan was afraid that he would be arrested and put away, but the next day a box of food miraculously appeared before his door—peanut butter, and crackers and bread, all kinds of goodies. Soon after that the woman came from social services to take him away and put him in the first of his many foster homes.

Harlan was not an orphan, for he had a mother and father, but he had an orphan's psyche. Life was training him that when they didn't want you, they didn't want you. You better always be ready to pack up and leave. He had the morals of an urchin, stealing pennies and nickels from newspaper boxes, swigging milk from milk boxes. He was like one of the street kids of Rio or Calcutta, with their catlike eyes and feline manner, measuring joy in the quick puff of a cigarette butt someone had just tossed into the gutter. He may have been born in Michigan, but he was a son of the South, living largely in the colony of transplanted southerners, who felt the themes of their native region even more profoundly from a distance.

Christmas to Harlan was just another day. The December of

his thirteenth year he hitchhiked down to Miami Beach, where he lay in the sand and worked washing dishes. Outside Atlanta one evening, he was stuck out on a country road when he saw a farmhouse lit up like a Christmas tree. He crept up to the window and looked in and saw a scene of such bliss that the image stayed in his mind the rest of his life.

There was the father smoking a pipe, sitting in the living room reading a newspaper in front of a blazing fireplace. And there was the mother in the kitchen, and there was the little girl, about Harlan's age, at the counter doing her homework. It was the Christmas season after all, and he was tempted for a moment to knock on the door, but he had heard about the Georgia chain gangs, and knew that if they called the police he would be taken away. So he turned from the light and the warmth and walked back to the outhouse, and slept on the floor, and was gone the next morning before dawn.

Harlan was always looking in windows, and country music was the greatest window of all. Country music was the song of his life, of what it had been, of what it would be, of the pain and joy he had felt and would feel. With country music he opened that window and entered a different life.

Harlan took music with him wherever he went, if not on the radio, then in his head, in the lyrics he was always writing. He took the music with him the day he borrowed his foster parents' new Packard and wrecked it and got sent away again. He took the music with him the day he and his buddies stole a car, and when they got caught he was the child no parent came to take home, the child who got put away. Music was the one thing he had that nobody could take away.

Harlan loved those sad love songs, but he was too shy to have a girlfriend. He was shy in part because he felt so uncomfortable about his appearance. He, in fact, looked as if had been brought up with a lack of certain nutrients. He grew to be a gangly six feet, three inches tall. He had a long, raw, narrow face, a big squat nose, long slits for eyes, great tufts of brown hair, and a closed-mouth smile designed to disguise the fact that he was missing his front teeth.

Harlan had only a ninth-grade education. It was either the assembly line or volunteering for the army. Harlan chose the army. He didn't have much money, and often he and his paratrooper buddies sat around the barracks at Fort Benning, Georgia, singing country tunes, furthering Harlan's musical education.

Harlan knew that he wanted to be a country songwriter. He just couldn't figure how he was going to get there. He hadn't picked up any skills as a paratrooper. Upon leaving the army, he returned to Michigan, where he worked in a factory. There he met and married his first wife, Trudy, with whom he had a daughter, Jennifer. He still had that dream of being a songwriter. He thought about Nashville but figured that Los Angeles was a better bet since he could get a factory job there to keep his little family together. He put their belongings together in his old car, and the family headed west. They got as far as Tucson, where Harlan was struck with polio. For a while he couldn't walk. His wife stayed with him when he was dreadfully sick, but she was tired of life with Harlan Howard. When he began to recuperate, she left him for good, taking the car and the baby, and moved on to California.

Harlan spent a year in Tucson working in a lumberyard, saving his money. In 1955 when he had enough to buy another old car, twenty-eight-year-old Harlan drove on to Los Angeles. He got a job driving a forklift truck in a printing factory. When he delivered a load, he would hide back behind a wall of boxes for a half hour or so writing a song. At three when he got off work, he often drove his old car onto the freeway heading down to the publishing companies in Hollywood. The publishing executives left at four, just as this scrawny, nervous would-be songwriter showed up toting a cheap guitar. Harlan didn't even know enough to have a tape of his songs. In most of the offices he was treated as friendlily as if he had been holding a tax lien in his hands, not a bunch of country songs.

One afternoon Harlan was walking up to one of those upstairs offices when he saw two men dressed as cowboys sitting in an office with their boots up on the desk as if they had just come in from the range. Harlan knew the men from watching *Town Hall Party* on TV. One of them, Tex Ritter, a singing cowboy and former cowboy movie star, was the emcee. The other man, the singer/songwriter Johnny Bond, had been Tex's sidekick in some of those movies, and he was on the show too.

"Sit down, son," Tex said in his east Texas drawl, sensing Harlan's nervousness. "What you doin'?"

"Got me some songs I've written."

"Well, let's hear 'em, right, Johnny?"

Harlan was so nervous he could have fled down those stairs, but he strummed the chords and sang three of his songs in his best Ernest Tubb imitation.

The two men listened intently. "Now here's what you gotta do, Harlan," Tex said finally. "You gotta get yourself a tape recorder and give 'em back to us. You hear."

Harlan made the tape, and in the end Tex recorded one of his songs, and Johnny Bond recorded another. They introduced him to another country singer, Wynn Stewart, one of the great largely forgotten voices of country music, an influence on a whole generation of West Coast country singers. Wynn didn't believe that the physics of life was such that if you helped lift someone else up, it pulled you down. When Wynn learned that Harlan was living in a boardinghouse, he invited his new friend to move in with him. Harlan did for about six months. Wynn introduced him to a new generation of singers and songwriters, including Buck Owens, who when he got a record deal, recorded Harlan's song "Above and Beyond."

In April of 1957, Wynn introduced Harlan to Lula Grace Johnson at a honky-tonk. Lula looked at this undernourished drunk who appeared to her "like a puppy that had been kicked once too often." She "couldn't believe he'd brought this creep over to introduce him to me." Lula was a half-Irish, half-Cherokee, twice-divorced waitress with three kids. She carried so much baggage that any savvy young man would have fled the first time she told her sad tale. Harlan not only listened but started hanging out over at Lula's apartment. A month later the couple married in Las Vegas. Lula changed her name to Jan Howard, and Harlan began helping her with a singing career, recording a demo tape of her songs.

Harlan was still driving that fork truck, punching in that time clock every day, needing that fifty-five dollars a week. Despite that, he was a songwriter now, with a publishing company pitching his songs, and a songwriter was always working. He was sitting in George's Roundup late one night, waiting for Wynn to finish his set. The club was one of the libraries where he went to study that book of life. People came here looking for love and laughs, but Harlan saw despair and loneliness in restless eyes across the dance floor. He was half listening to good old Wynn when he saw the woman at the next table stand up and shout angry words at the man who had brought her: "Well, you can just pick me up on your way down!" The words stuck with him, and about a year later he wrote "Pick Me Up on Your Way Down."

Ray Price, one of Nashville's big new stars, got Charlie Walker to record "Pick Me Up on Your Way Down." It took forever to get royalties, and Harlan was still driving that forklift when a foreman told him he had a call. Over the roar of the printing presses, Harlan heard Ray Price's voice asking him if he had any new songs for himself.

Harlan always had new songs. One day he had been remembering how back in the army everything had been done by the numbers. Out of that came "Heartaches by the Number." Harlan was only thirty years old, but he was already a worn old prince of sadness, finding in that glorious tortured love between a man and a woman all the material he would ever need to write his own heart out and then some. Harlan mailed a demo tape to the singer, and both Price and the pop singer Guy Mitchell made hits of "Heartaches by the Number."

Up until then the biggest single check Harlan had ever received was for a whopping twenty-seven dollars that he used to buy shoes for his three adopted children. Harlan heard his songs on the radio, and knew he was due some money, but it took months before the record companies paid royalties. Harlan was still driving that forklift the day he got a letter from his publishing company with a check for $48,000. Three days later he got another check, this one for $52,000. Harlan had his first Christmas. He went out and peeled off $5,200 cash for a snazzy new white-on-white Cadillac Coupe de Ville, a car bigger than some of the apartments he had lived in. He bought himself a fancy guitar, and he put that guitar and his wife and his adopted kids in there too, and headed east to Nashville.

Harlan arrived in Nashville in June of 1960. There was a new generation of singers in town who didn't write their own songs and only a handful of songwriters to meet their needs. Harlan kept his old union card in case things didn't work out, but God knows he didn't want to go back to that. He wrote day and night, song after song after song. It was like some terrible fever. He woke up at night in a sweat and wrote down some lyrics. He would be in the car driving somewhere and suddenly it would get him, and he would write down some words on a scrap of paper.

Harlan considered the bars and clubs the universities of the heart. At night he hung out at Tootsie's and Linebaugh's, or caroused down at the Capitol Park Inn with George Jones and other music people. Harlan finally had found a few places he thought he belonged, places where he could be with his friends as long as he wanted, places where people respected him, knew his drink, and filled his glass. There were no fancy offices for songwriters then, and Harlan got many of his best ideas sitting on a barstool, half tanked, listening to a waitress tell her woeful tale, eavesdropping on a couple at the next table, or sweet-talking some little thing.

Harlan never forgot that the greenest grass grows in the darkest soil. In one of his great early songs, "Busted," he told the story of a coal miner who loses everything. Johnny Cash got him to change it to a cotton farmer, but the truth was the same. Harlan knew what it had been like. He had been there when the only friend you have is the one you haven't yet hit up for a loan.

> Me and my family got to pack up and go
> But I'll make a living, just where I don't know
> 'Cause I'm busted.

Harlan knew that life wasn't fair, and in his music he often dealt with the emotional costs of that unfairness. He was a lover of women. He loved to sit with them and hear their tales of love and woe. He wrote for women, to chronicle their dreams and despair. He saw that even their dreams were different.

In the rural and small-town America of the sixties, the young men wore jeans and T-shirts and were for the most part happy to live as their parents had lived. The young women read the movie and fashion magazines, dressed as they thought they dressed in the big cities, and dreamed of getting out. That stark difference was a recipe for broken hearts, cheating, and lives full of unhappiness.

One Saturday night at the Opry, Harlan saw a married couple. She was a looker, dressed to kill. Every man in the place was eyeing her, and she was eyeing back. Her husband was this sorry sort, with greasy nails and a tired look. Out of that in 1966 Harlan and Tompall Glaser wrote "Streets of Baltimore." The classic ballad is the tale of a farmer who sells his farm to move to the big city to make his wife happy. He gets a job in a factory, but his wife won't stay home and ends up making her living on the streets of Baltimore.

> Now I'm going back on that same train that brought me
> here before
> While my baby walks the streets of Baltimore.

Harlan knew he couldn't have written songs like "Streets of Baltimore" if he had been sitting at home watching *I Love Lucy* on television and helping his stepkids with their homework. He couldn't have written those good old cheating songs either if he hadn't walked that walk too. He lied about it when he got home, but when he looked in the mirror in the morning he saw a face he didn't like very much, and he knew that his wife knew. He knew that he had done wrong, and he poured all his guilt and emotions into a song.

Harlan knew that he shouldn't have been married, but he was the marrying kind. After he and Jan divorced, he married his third wife, Donna, a secretary on Music Row. This decade-long marriage proved even more troubled than the last. Out of it came a divorce, a son, Harlan Perry Howard Jr., and a song, "I Don't Remember Loving You."

To Harlan love was a beautiful butterfly that every time he grasped ended dead in his hands. He was a generous, passionate man to his lovers and wives, even if he was incapable of being loyal to them. He was there for them, and then one day he would be gone. He still had an orphan boy's soul, having learned so long ago that the one friend you can trust completely is yourself. He went off by himself for days on end to his little Quonset hut on Center Hill Lake, over an hour from Nashville, fishing and thinking up songs.

Harlan thought that he was writing out of his unhappiness, but in the mid-seventies he was feeling a despair beyond despair. He feared that he had written himself out, that it was over. He had once had this magical spigot that poured forth songs, and it had gone dry. It happened to practically every songwriter sooner or later, and there was no good reason that it shouldn't happen to him. Out of this long darkness came perhaps the most sentimental of all his songs, "No Charge," a number one hit for Melba Montgomery.

"No Charge" is the tale of a boy who presents his mother with a bill for the work he has done around the house. His mother turns the paper over and writes down "no charge" on her bill for everything from bearing her son to the "nights she sat up with you, doctored you, prayed for you." In the end, the little boy takes back the bill and writes "no charge."

Tough-talking truck drivers came up to Harlan and said that they were so moved by the song that they darn near wrecked their rigs the first time they heard it. Nonetheless, "No Charge" was a song that made those who hated country music cringe with embarrassment at the maudlin excess, but there was no parent who had not at some time felt that their children thought that love was a one-way street. It was a great country song, a sweet and tender lesson, passed out into the world through the radio waves, and in jukeboxes, and phonographs.

By the mid-eighties, Harlan was back writing again in full form. He didn't have the same energy he used to have, and he usually wrote with some of the top writers in Nashville. He married for the fourth time, to Sharon Rucker. They had a daughter, Clementyne, and this marriage ended too, leaving Harlan alone pushing sixty, competing against songwriters half his age, hanging out at whatever bar was happening at the moment.

Harlan showed up most days at Maude's Courtyard, a favorite writers' hangout just off Music Row. He was a loner and he was alone. He was the father of six children, three of his own and the three of Jan's he had adopted. One of Jan's sons had committed suicide and another had died in Vietnam.

Harlan was the great old man of Nashville songwriters, and people were always coming over to pay deference. "Harlan! How are you," shouted a young man, his voice charged with camaraderie.

"Drunk."

"Well, somebody's gotta do it, Harlan."

"I'm doin' it for you, so you can get out safe to your pretty little wife out in Murfreesboro."

The fellow was like most of the new ones. They kept bankers' hours. They talked about their stock in Cracker Barrel. They had firm handshakes. They looked you in the eye. Then sometimes some sniveling weasel of a human being would come up to him, give him a handshake that felt like grasping a grease gun, mutter some sort of greeting while looking at his boots, and slither away. Harlan knew who the real songwriter was, and it wasn't Mr. Colgate Smile, standing there offering him another drink. It was that weird kid who disappeared out the door. As likely as not that messed-up piece of humanity had gone back to his little room to write his sad little heart out. Of course, give Mr. Colgate Smile a divorce or two and he might be able to write himself a good country song too.

A couple of drinks were all it took to anesthetize Harlan's shyness. Then he began hitting on seemingly every attractive woman who came into the place. To some he appeared this pathetic drunken old fool standing there leering down with his big beet red nose attempting to seduce young women with honeyed words culled from four thousand songs.

But that was not Harlan Howard standing there waiting to be

rebuffed. He had lived through and by his heart. Harlan wasn't looking to score a quick romp in the hay. That was a young man's diversion. He was looking to feel and to care, and out of that to turn his emotions into songs and his songs into money.

One evening late in 1986, sixty-year-old Harlan was sitting in the bar at the Third Coast. On another stool sat twenty-seven-year-old Melanie Smith, a recent divorcée from a small town in Tennessee. Melanie had a degree in mass communications, but as a new arrival in Music City she had worked here as a waitress, though she now had a job in music publishing. Tonight she was in enough of a party mood to accept Harlan's dinner invitation. He was a meat-and-three kind of guy, but she led him to a sushi restaurant. She didn't know he was a legend, but he was a man she could talk to and laugh with like a rare old friend.

The next day when Melanie listened to her messages on the Code-a-Phone, she heard Harlan singing a song he had written to her. No man had ever done anything like that before, and she began seeing Harlan regularly. Melanie was a pretty, vivacious young woman who did not have to look to a four-time married sexagenarian for an admirer. She saw in Harlan a wonderful friend, not a future lover. They continued dating other people. After a year Harlan said he wanted to kiss her and she said that would be all right now. And soon after that in August of 1989, they married.

The way Harlan figured it there were only about five or six things to say about love. Day after day he tried to find a new way to say the same old few things, but he was discovering there were new things in this world. One of them was Harlan's love for Melanie. He called her his "child bride." The old man knew that he had something now he had never had before, and no way was it ever going to end. He'd always been the one to head for the door when they asked him to leave, but not anymore, not this time. He had written a song about it called "I Ain't Leavin', I'll Chain Myself to the Trees." That about said it.

"It took me sixty-eight years to figure out how to handle this love thing and by God I just refuse to leave," Harlan said. "I ain't gonna be mean. I just lay on the floor and let her pick me up. And when they set me up, I'll fall back down. You know what I mean.

The hell with all the getting into somebody's face, having a few bad days when she doesn't love me. Hell, leave me alone a little bit. But don't leave. And don't let those words get too harsh. I mean I've done it and I know there's a couple of wives that regretted everything. But, hell, they wanted a divorce. I took them at their word and they got one. But see the whole trail led on. So I couldn't have Melanie now if I hadn't done that. So I'm glad we got all them divorces."

It was quitting time along Music Row, and the little bar at the Sunset Grill was filling up with people ready to start their weekend. As the new arrivals pushed their way into the room, those who knew Harlan nodded a greeting, slapped him on the back, or told him the latest gossip. Behind his back some of them shook their heads and said they couldn't understand why Harlan was still hanging out here. He had a wife he loved, and had just come back from the dead. He should have appreciated God's blessing and heeded His warning, stayed home with his wife and away from the bottle.

Harlan was a man of habit, and this glass he was drinking was one of those habits he had for forty years. So were this bar and this day. A few years back Harlan had been sitting over at Maude's before that old writers' saloon had been turned into Trilogy, Naomi Judd's restaurant. On a bar napkin he wrote down the words to a song about how he wanted to die. He called the song "When I Fall Off This Barstool."

Harlan knew he had been given a special blessing and wanted to use it to write good old country songs. Harlan was a man of immense shrewdness, a measure of it being that he had learned to disguise the trait. Shrewdness, after all, is one of the most maligned of human characteristics, but without it courage fails, enterprise falters, and creativity dies.

Humans trade in life in whatever quality is cheapest to them. Some of it is money. To others it is beauty, wit or charm, or family name. For Harlan, it was his legendary status in the music community. Singers and songwriters were always coming up to Harlan wanting to write with him. He was ready with what he called "the back stroke" telling them, "Hey, pal, I'm sorry. I'm not in the mood." He was Harlan Howard, after all, and nobody got pissed at a legend. He was Harlan Howard and when he did cowrite, it was with the best. He was the motor and they were the batteries, coming in to charge old Harlan up. He spent much time helping young singers too, figuring he might get some more cuts that way.

Harlan hated what he saw out there in the new country music. Harlan despised the way Nashville treated the older acts, killing their record deals and not playing their songs on the radio. The past was Nashville's capital. It was exploited in sentimental bios on TNN and out at the tourist attraction Grand Ole Opry. But Nashville's past was like money that sat in a drawer drawing no interest, slowly and inexorably declining in value. He hated the clone factory of Music Row, trying to re-create the magic of George Strait and Garth Brooks instead of doing something new.

He hated what the industry was doing to these kids, bringing them here, running them through the machine, then sending most of them back where they came from. He hated what he saw happening to Garth Brooks. The man was selling out arenas night after night, but he had forgotten what brought him there. It was great songs, and he didn't have them on his new album. Harlan figured that unless he got back to that it was all over for him.

As Harlan sat drinking, the freeways were jammed with thousands of fans heading back home. They had had a memorable week at Fan Fair '96. Some of them had been there when Garth had arrived Tuesday morning. By standing there all those hours, Garth had sanctified the covenant between a country artist and his fans. The fans were leaving with his autograph and memories of their moment with Garth that they would tell their friends, children, and grandchildren about. Many of them had met Shania and Vince and Patty, taking home precious pictures and autographs. A few had even been there for Wynonna's auction. They had sat in their seats at the Speedway hearing LeAnn, Mindy, Mandy, James, and other new Nashville artists for the first time. Most of them had been there for the Arista show to see Alan and Kix and Ronnie, tickets that would have cost them Lord knows how much anywhere else. For the most part these fans didn't know the names of Tony Brown, Tim DuBois, and Scott Hendricks, and the other label executives. They didn't even know the names of celebrated songwriters like Harlan. They cared about the music, and some of them went away with a sense of disquiet, wondering what was happening to this music that was so precious to them, and for how long would they be able to return to spend such a splendid week with the stars of Nashville.

The fans were going away happy, but as Harlan knew, Nashville wasn't about T-shirts and autographs. It was about songs. That was Nashville's gift to the world. He still heard great songs at Douglas Corner, the Bluebird, and a score of other places where the songwriters sang, but most of these songs never got cut.

Harlan hated much of what he heard on country radio. It wasn't music for a person like him, not anymore. If he had written many of his classic songs today, they would not have been played on the radio and possibly not even recorded. "Streets of Baltimore" was about a woman becoming a prostitute, an unseemly X-rated business, hardly the fare for family-oriented country radio. "Pick Me Up on Your Way Down" was a downer, not a song to play during drive time. Country radio wasn't much into cheating and drinking songs, another staple of country honky-tonk, and of Harlan's repertoire.

Harlan hated all of this, raging at the betrayal of what his music had become. In hating it, he saw nothing but opportunity. He had been there before. He knew the worse it got, the better it was going to be.

They would come back to him and to his true colleagues, because they would come back to life. They would come back because human beings didn't change. Harlan knew that for the people he wrote for love was the great diversion and obsession of their lives. They looked for love when they were young. Often they thought they had found it, but it was usually fool's gold. More than anything, they wanted to love one person, and to have that person love them in return. It didn't happen most of the time, and when it turned out wrong or weak or untrue, people thought about what might have been, about loves passed by or spurned. That was his great theme, and he would write it until he died.

Harlan felt the pulse of life now, felt it as deep and as strong as he had ever felt it. He was full of the most passionate dreams and aspirations. He sensed the first tremors of something good happening in Nashville. He was blown away by LeAnn Rimes singing "Blue." Other young singers and songwriters were passing through who had something different that Nashville had been missing recently, something that was both old and new. Harlan wanted to be part of that.

He didn't know how much time he had left. He hoarded his time and his energy with a miser's passion. He didn't like to answer the phone. He was setting up a new office in his guest house at home so he could fall out of bed and start writing.

All Harlan wanted to do was to write some more good country songs and have a few more hits. To do that he was trying to rid himself of all the barnacles of savvy that had attached themselves to him over the years. He said to himself, "Man, I want to see if I can get me back where I was in the fifties before I got smart, before I really knew what a hit was." He was writing songs for himself now, not for radio, not for any fool kid artist in a cowboy hat, but for himself.

Sitting here at the Sunset Grill, talking to the waitresses and the barmaids, Harlan was listening to the music of life, and it was the same song it had always been. There was the same joy, the same heartache, the same dreams. As he scribbled notes on a bar napkin, he was going back to what was simple and good, going back to what had always worked. He had said it long ago when they asked him what a country song was, and he was going back to that now, to "three chords and the truth."

20

~

Epilogue

Mandy Barnett's first album met with critical success, though it sold disappointingly. In the spring of 1997, she was back in the studio recording new songs for her second album.

★

James Bonamy's song that he sang at Fan Fair '96, "I Don't Think I Will," reached number two in the *Billboard* country chart. His second album, *Roots and Wings,* came out in May 1997.

★

Garth Brooks continued his worldwide tour, keeping a nearly invisible profile in Nashville. He went back into the studio, but no one at Capitol Nashville knew what he was recording or when they might expect a new album. By the spring of 1997, Garth had sold over sixty-two million albums. Bob Doyle returned as his manager.

★

Brooks & Dunn won the coveted 1996 CMA Award as Entertainer of the Year. Their new album, *Borderline,* with its number one single, "My Maria," brought the duo back to the height of popularity, and Brooks & Dunn won a Grammy for the song. In 1997, their tour with Reba McEntire as coheadliner was the most anticipated of all country music events.

★

Tony Brown was the most successful producer of 1996 both commercially and critically. At the 1996 CMA Awards, his artist George Strait won Male Vocalist of the Year and Album of the Year for *Blue Clear Sky*. Another of his artists, Vince Gill, won Song of the Year for "Go Rest High on That Mountain."

★

BR5-49 was the only country music act named to *Rolling Stone*'s "Hot List." Their first album received enthusiastic reviews, and the group was nominated for a Grammy as Country Duo or Group for the song "Cherokee Boogie."

★

Mary Chapin Carpenter's 1996 album, *A Place in the World,* did not receive as strong reviews as her previous release, and it did not sell as well as her greatest successes. The album was nominated for a Grammy Award for Female Country Artist. She sang at the opening of the 1997 Super Bowl in New Orleans.

★

Tim DuBois continued his successful record at Arista/Nashville, with both Brooks and Dunn and Alan Jackson continuing as leading acts.

★

Gaylord Entertainment sold CMT and TNN to Westinghouse in February 1997, a harbinger of major change for country music media.

★

Vince Gill's song "Go Rest High on the Mountain" won the CMA Song of the Year Award, and Vince's duet with Dolly Parton, "I Will Always Love You," was named the Vocal Event of the Year. Vince won two Grammy Awards for Male Country Vocal, singing "Worlds Apart" and Country Song of the Year for "High Lonesome Sound." In April, Vince's wife, Janis, filed for divorce.

★

Emmylou Harris's album *Wrecking Ball* received the 1996 Grammy Award as Best Contemporary Folk Album of the Year. A documentary on the making of the album was shown widely on public television. Emmylou continued to tour both in the United States and Europe. She began writing songs for her new album.

★

Linda Hargrove decided that in order to protect her resources, she would have to divorce Charley Bartholomew, her husband. Linda continued to seek a record deal and began producing her album herself with Jack Grochmal.

★

Scott Hendricks was well on his way to turning Capitol Nashville around. Trace Adkins started having hit singles and his debut album went gold. Another new artist, Deana Carter, made a stunning debut with her double platinum album *Did I Shave My Legs For This?*

★

Harlan Howard went into the hospital in December of 1996 for a knee operation. He recovered slowly, and began writing songs again. In June, he was scheduled to be inducted into the Songwriters Hall of Fame in New York City with other new inductees, including Joni Mitchell and Phil Spector.

★

Alan Jackson's new album *Everything I Love* reached number one. By the spring of 1997, Alan had sold over twenty-three million albums.

★

Patty Loveless's beloved older sister, Dottie, died a few days after Fan Fair '96. In October, Patty was named the CMA Female Vocalist of the Year. Patty's album *The Trouble with the Truth* received many accolades. *Time* named it one of the ten best albums of the year in all genres of music. It won a Grammy nomination for Country Album of the Year.

★

Mindy McCready's album *Ten Thousand Angels* sold platinum. In 1997, she began her touring career opening for George Strait. She moved out of David Malloy's house into a newly purchased town house where she lives with her brother, T.J.

★

Reba McEntire's new album *What If It's You* did not sell as well as her major successes, but it received better reviews than her album of pop cover songs. In 1997, she went out on the road with Brooks and Dunn, sharing headliner billing with an act that once had opened for her.

★

LeAnn Rimes's phenomenal success continued. Her first album, *Blue,* sold in excess of three million copies. Her new album, *The Early Years,* debuted as number one not only on the *Billboard* country chart but on the pop chart as well. At the Grammys she won both New Artist of the Year and Female Country Vocalist.

★

Shania Twain's album sold eight million in the United States and two million in the rest of the world by the spring of 1997 and still was a top seller. Shania gave up plans to write her autobiography and went back into the studio with Mutt Lange, her husband and producer.

★

John Unger resigned from managing Wynonna.

★

Ron Wallace continued singing demos and seeking another record deal.

★

Walt Wilson resigned from his position at Capitol Nashville as executive vice president/general manager late in 1996.

★

Wynonna gave birth to a daughter, Pauline Grace, the week after Fan Fair '96. After John Unger left, her management was taken over by Larry Strickland, her mother's husband. Naomi appeared onstage several times with Wynonna, and there were persistent rumors that the Judds would soon stage a reunion tour.

Bibliography

Applebome, Peter. *Dixie Rising: How the South Is Shaping American Values, Politics, and Culture*. New York: Times Books, 1996.

Bane, Michael. *The Outlaws*. New York: Country Music Magazine/Dolphin Press, 1978.

Bart, Teddy. *Inside Music City USA*. Nashville: Aurora Publishers, 1970.

Bufwack, Mary A., and Robert K. Oermann. *Finding Her Voice: The Saga of Women in Country Music*. New York: Crown, 1993.

Cantwell, Robert. *When We Were Good: The Folk Revival*. Cambridge: Harvard University Press, 1996.

Cash, W. J. *The Mind of the South*. New York: Knopf, 1941.

Clarke, Donald. *The Rise and Fall of Popular Music*. New York: St. Martin's Press, 1995.

Clayton, Bruce. *W. J. Cash, a Life*. Baton Rouge: Louisiana State University Press, 1991.

Cook, Sylvia Jenkins. *From Tobacco Road to Route 66: The Southern Poor White in Fiction*. Chapel Hill: University of North Carolina Press, 1976.

Cooper, Daniel. *Lefty Frizzell: The Honky-Tonk Life of Country Music's Greatest Singer*. Boston: Little, Brown, 1995.

Cusic, Don. *Reba: Country Music's Queen*. New York: St. Martin's Press, 1991.

Doyle, Don H. *Nashville Since the 1920s*. Knoxville: Univesity of Tennesee Press, 1985.

Ellison, Curtis W. *Country Music Culture: From Hard Times to Heaven*. Jackson: University Press of Mississippi, 1995.

Escott, Colin, with George Merritt and William MacEwen. *Hank Williams: The Biography*. Boston: Little, Brown, 1994.

Farr, Jory. *Moguls and Madmen: The Pursuit of Power in Popular Music*. New York: Simon and Schuster, 1994.

Fong-Torres, Ben. *Hickory Wind: The Life and Times of Gram Parsons*, New York: Pocket Books, 1991.

Gubernick, Lisa Rebecca. *Get Hot or Go Home: Trisha Yearwood, The Making of a Nashville Star*. New York: William Morrow, 1993.

Guralnick, Peter. *Lost Highway: Journeys and Arrivals of American Musicians*. New York: David R. Godine, 1979.

Hemphill, Paul. *The Nashville Sound: Bright Lights and Country Music*. New York: Simon and Schuster, 1970.

Horstman, Dorothy. *Sing Your Heart Out, Country Boy*. Nashville: Country Music Foundation Press, 1985.

Howard, Jan. *Sunshine and Shadow*. New York: Richardson & Steirman, 1987.

Jones, George, with Tom Carter. *George Jones: I Lived to Tell It All*. New York: Villard, 1996.

Judd, Naomi, with Bud Schaetzle. *Love Can Build a Bridge*. New York: Villard, 1993.

Kaufman, Phil, with Colin White. *Road Mangler Deluxe*. Montrose, Ca.: White Boucke, 1993.

Kirby, Jack Temple. *Media-Made Dixie: The South in the American Imagination*. Athens, Ga.: University of Georgia Press, 1986.

Lomax, John, III. *Nashville, Music City USA*. New York: Harry M. Abrams, 1985.

Malone, Bill C. *Country Music USA, Revised*. Austin: University of Texas Press, 1985.

Malone, Bill C. *Singing Cowboys and Musical Mountaineers: Southern Culture and the Roots of Country*. Athens, Ga.: University of Georgia Press, 1993.

Malone, Bill, and Judith McCulloh. *Stars of Country Music*. Urbana: University of Illinois Press, 1975.

Marcus, Greil. *Mystery Train*. New York: Dutton, 1975.

Mason, Michael, ed. *The Country Music Book*. New York: Scribner's, 1985.

McCall, Michael. *Garth Brooks*. New York: Bantam, 1991.

McCauley, Deborah Vansau. *Appalachian Mountain Religion: A History*. Urbana: University of Illinois Press, 1995.

McCloud, Barry. *Definitive Country: The Ultimate Encyclopedia of Country Music and Its Performers*. New York: Berkley, 1995.

McEntire, Reba, with Tom Carter. *Reba: My Story*. New York: Bantam, 1994.

McNeil, W. K., ed. *Southern Folk Ballads*. Little Rock: August House, 1987.

Miles, Emma Bell. *The Spirit of the Mountains*. New York: J. Pott, 1905.

Morris, Edward. *Garth Brooks: Platinum Cowboy*. New York: St. Martin's Press, 1993.

Naipaul, V. S. *A Turn in the South*. New York: Knopf, 1989.

Nash, Alana. *Behind Closed Doors: Talking with the Legends of Country Music*. New York: Knopf, 1988.

Porterfield, Nolan. *Jimmie Rodgers: The Life and Times of America's Blue Yodeler*. Urbana: University of Illinois Press, 1979.

Roland, Tom. *The Billboard Book of Number One Country Hits*. New York: Billboard, 1991.

Squires, James D. *The Secrets of the Hopewell Box: Stolen Elections, Southern Politics, and a City's Coming of Age*. New York: Times Books, 1996.

Terrill, Tom E., and Jerrold Hirsch, eds. *Such As Us: Southern Voices of the Thirties*. Chapel Hill: University of North Carolina Press, 1978.

Tindall, George B. *The Emergence of the New South: 1913–1945*. Baton Rouge: Louisiana State University Press, 1967.

Tischi, Cecelia. *High Lonesome: The American Culture of Country Music*. Chapel Hill: University of North Carolina Press, 1994.

Tolin, Steve, ed. *The Official Country Music Directory*. Palm Springs, Ca.: Country Music Directory, 1996.

Tosches, Nick. *Country: The Biggest Music in America*. New York: Stein and Day, 1977.

Index